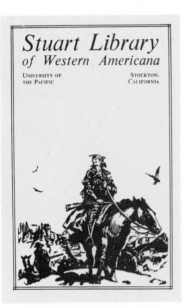

CENTURY IN THE SADDLE

CENTURY
IN THE
SADDLE

By Richard Goff and Robert H. McCaffree

Illustrated by William J. Culbertson, and with reproduction of drawings by Frederic Remington from Century Magazine.

Published by the

Colorado Cattlemen's Centennial Commission

Denver, Colorado

Printed and bound in the United States of America by the
JOHNSON PUBLISHING COMPANY
Boulder, Colorado

TABLE OF CONTENTS

Foreword	vii
Names of the Colorado Cattlemen's Association	viii
Preface	ix
Frontispiece	xi
Chapter One—The Beef Critter	1
Chapter Two—The First Herds	12
Chapter Three—Forming the Organization	22
Chapter Four—The Indian Problem	38
Chapter Five—The Big Build-up—The 1870's	48
Chapter Six—The Round-Ups	83
Chapter Seven—The Decades of Boom and Bust	103
Chapter Eight—The Cost of Free Grass	141
Chapter Nine—Running Down the Cattle Thieves	197
Chapter Ten—From Range to Ranching	213
Chapter Eleven—Furor Over Fences	240
Chapter Twelve—Between the Wars	250
Chapter Thirteen—The Outfit Today	277
Chapter Fourteen—What Price Beef	306
Apendix A—Officers and Directors—1867-1967	319
Appendix B—Cowbelles and Juniors	339
Appendix C—The Local Associations	345
Acknowledgment	353
Bibliography	355
Index	359

DEDICATION

To the late Tom Field, one of the great men of the Colorado cattle industry, CCA president for 1956-57, and the man who first asked me to write this book.   R.G.

FOREWORD

This organization has a mighty interesting history. As far as we know, this is the oldest cattlemen's association in the West. For a hundred years we have been working in this way to help ourselves and our industry.

The men who formed this organization endured many hardships to get a start in the cattle business, and many more to stay in business after they got started. Yet, during this past century, every cattle grower has had to face problems. Some of our present-day difficulties are just as tough to handle as fighting Indians or running down cattle thieves.

Our world today is changing fast. Business everywhere is getting more technical and more complicated, and the livestock industry is no exception. People in any business today must work together through an organization in order to accomplish anything. Alone we can do very little, but by working as a group toward a common goal we can get our ideas accepted. Only through an organization of this kind can we maintain the idea of greater individual opportunity through free enterprise.

In the years ahead, all agriculture may have many adjustments to make in order to keep pace with the progress in transportation, marketing and production. Adjusting to some of these future changes may cause hardships to us that are just as painful as those our pioneer stockmen suffered. Only the scars may be a little different. We may have more ulcers and fewer saddle sores, but the idea is the same.

We are at a cross-road now in beef production. Changes have to be made and soon. By looking back over the trail into the past, we may get a better idea of how far we have come and a little help on the direction we may want to take in the future. One thing, however, is certain. Every livestock producer in

America will have to do his part and pay his own way if he expects to stay in business during the next few years. More of his time and more of his money must go into a group effort to help his industry.

This story of our past can show us the way to new opportunities ahead—if we are foresighted enough to see them.

W. P. "Wad" Hinman, 1967 President
Colorado Cattlemen's Association

THE NAMES OF THE COLORADO CATTLEMEN'S ASSOCIATION

At various times during the past century, the Association has changed its name and often its by-laws to fit changes in policy and economic conditions.

In 1876, for example, the name was changed from the Colorado Stock Growers Association to the Colorado Cattle Growers Association. James M. Wilson, then president, announced that this change was made because the sheep raisers were forming their own organization, and it was becoming increasingly apparent that the two groups had "very little in common."

At other times, the words "Horse Growers" and "Feeders" were added as special concessions to these groups. Listed below are the different names and the approximate dates they were used. Wherever possible the current name has been used. While this may be a bit confusing at times, it seems to fit the situation better than a standardized name throughout.

1867-1876	Colorado Stock Growers Association
1876-1900	Colorado Cattle Growers Association
1900 (about four months)	—Western Range Stock Growers Association
1900-1904	Cattle and Horse Growers Association of Colorado
1904-1918	Colorado Cattle and Horse Growers Association
1919-1930	Colorado Stockgrowers Association
1930-1949	Colorado Stock Growers and Feeders Association
1949-	Colorado Cattlemen's Association

At times the organization was the spokesman for all livestock interests in the state, including hog producers. Then, as the various groups decided to have their own organizations, these special activities were dropped. Today, however, the cattlemen, the sheep producers, the feeders and the horse breeders are working together more closely than ever before in history.

PREFACE

This book is the culmination of a long-time interest in the cattle industry that was acquired from my father, Jesse O. Goff, who spent his entire life in the business and knew a great deal about cattle.

The specific interest in the Colorado Cattlemen's Association began with an interview with Dr. B. F. Davis in 1952. He had retired in 1949, after 26 years as Secretary-Manager of the Association. Shortly before then, he had delivered to the State Historical Society archives the early records and minutes books of the organization. Repeated inquiries failed to locate this material. After nearly three years, they were eventually found in the farthest corner of the basement vaults, mislabeled and mislaid.

Here were the original minutes of the organization, with the first faded entry dated November 30, 1867. There were other papers and records that told on their yellowing pages the terse drama of one of the most exciting periods in American history. But this material was far from complete. There were great gaps in the story, often covering whole decades.

It took years of research to fill in these missing years. The complete list of officers in this volume, for example, is the first such roster ever compiled. This information was slowly pieced together from various documents and the crumbling pages of old newspapers from every section of the state. Much of this work was done by Mrs. Alice R. Gray, a capable archivist and a trained librarian. My wife, Jane, also a librarian, spent much of her time for the past decade in verifying dates, names, people and places, plus the last few weeks in proofreading endless galleys of type.

Some of this material was first used in a series of articles for the Convention issues of Cattle Guard magazine in 1956, 1957 and 1958. A great deal of it has never appeared before.

When we became acquainted with Bob McCaffree and learned of his long-time interest in the early cow country and Indian history, we enlisted his support. His background was similar—a father who ran cattle and several years of experience in newspaper work and agricultural journalism.

We have finished this work with the conviction that no other industry in the United States has a more dedicated group of people than the cattle business. The leaders in this Association have shown consistently a broad sense of public responsibility. It is a pleasure to present this side of the story for them.

One example is their use of public lands. Over the century this has been a constant political issue, with the cattlemen frequently condemned as wanton despoilers of public domain. In fact, however, no other group has contributed more time, effort and money to improvement and development of public lands in the West than the stockmen. They have always used these lands, it is true, but they have paid in cash for the privilege ever since the federal leasing program was established in 1905.

There have been periods, too, when these lands were abused from a grazing standpoint. In most instances, however, these abuses were fostered by impractical or politically motivated land policies of the federal government.

In recent years, however, progress has been made. Enlightened efforts on all sides are producing better results for everyone. The real problems today arise no longer from misuse, but primarily from the sheer volume of traffic. Our growing population creates problems affecting all agricultural land—both public and private. Few city dwellers, for example, can realize the problems and the extra labor and expense that our annual hunting season brings to the Colorado rancher.

In this book we have tried to tell the story of this organization, and, in so doing, give some additional background on the beef cattle industry. We hope it will help others to appreciate the long and dramatic story behind our product—beef.

1 January 1967
Richard Goff

At a Meeting of the Stock Growers
association held at the planters House on
November 30th 1867 Capt A G Reed was called to the
Chair and A S Williams Elected Sactary
the Committee appointed at Last Meeting to
Report a Conatution and by Laws for the
organization of a Stock Growers association
Reported through there Chareman the parsons
as follows Which was adopted by Sactions
                    Carried
                    attest
December 7th 1867   A S Williams Sacty
          At a Meeting of the Stock Growers
association held at the Planters House in
Vernon Co 2 on the above date Meeting called
to order by A G Reed President

It was moved that the thanks of this association
Be spread on minnits of the association
for the Present from M W Atkins for the
Book for this association
                    Carried

Moved by M Maguess that We adgourn for 2 weeks
and that all Members be Requested to Bring
ther brands for Record
                    Carried
December 17th 1867
              Meeting Called to order
By Allen G Reed in the Chaire

Being no further Business the Meeting
          agorned
              attest
              Alx Davidson
                    Sacty

Jany 18th 1868 Meeting called to order by
A G Reed in the Chaire the president was
fully authorized to Employ dectives for the use
and bennifitt of the association Being no further Business
the Meeting agorned untill the Bill Passed the
Legislate and the Sacty ordered to procure the Same
and to have it at our next meeting Carried
              attest Alx Davidson Sacty

CHAPTER ONE

THE BEEF CRITTER

The cattle business is different in many ways from any other industry. It operates under some peculiar economic laws of its own, influenced by the remarkable physiology of the bovine cow, the weather, and the consumer's desire for beef.

Its history is one of the most exciting and colorful chapters in the annals of mankind. It is one of the earliest forms of food production, yet it has changed surprisingly little in the past century.

The husbandry of the beef critter has to follow a number of natural laws that allow for very little variation. Men have come and gone, wars have swept across the world, nations have fallen,

1

but the mother cow operates in the same basic manner today that she did in biblical times.

Whether the herdsman was one of the sons of Solomon, a Spanish ganadero in days of Ferdinand and Isabella, or one of the Colorado "cattle kings" of the 1880's, operating methods were surprisingly similar.

Even today, the cow-calf operator follows pretty much the same basic patterns of herd management as his forebears. But, thanks to revolutionary changes in transportation over the past century, his marketing methods are much more efficient when the animal is ready to sell.

Once slaughtered, carcass beef now goes through one of the most sophisticated distribution systems ever devised by man. Through the modern supermarket, beef is handled, prepared and distributed with an efficiency and speed that would astound the old trail drover of the 1870's.

But the raising of the cow and calf, the over-all management of breeding, and selection of the better animals to build up the herd, have not changed much. The biology of the beef cow, her genetic values, her nine-month gestation period and the operation of her four remarkable stomachs are essentially the same today as they were a hundred, or even a thousand years ago.

These immutable factors shaped the course of biblical tribes, molded the destiny of nations, and turned the Western frontier of our own country into one of the great sagas of man's endeavor.

It is interesting to look back over this past century and study the type of men that were attracted to the early cattle business. They came from a variety of backgrounds. Some failed and some prospered. But the successful ones invariably had, or quickly developed, a deep understanding of bovine nature and the peculiar economics of the industry.

In so doing, they acquired the characteristics of the cattleman.

Historically, whenever conditions are favorable for beef cattle production, man has been the one who adapted to the requirements of the cow, rather than she to his.

True, the master breeder has stamped his mark on successive generations of beef cattle. By applying his knowledge of genetics, nutrition and beef characteristics, the breeder makes slow progress along the lines he selects as a measure of quality.

But in looking back over the past century, it is surprising how small the basic changes actually are. The improvements in nutrition have probably out-weighed improvements in breeding.

Consider this cow critter carefully. To understand some of the things that happened in this industry during the past hundred years, it is important to know how she functions.

To begin with, the cow is a ruminant. Her digestive system is built around a rumen, the largest of her four stomachs. This organ utilizes bacterial action to help break down grass or roughage into more digestible compounds.

An amazing chain of chemical reactions takes place inside this remarkable animal, and in this is the real key to her cash value. This bovine "plumbing system" functions somewhat like a brewery. With it, this animal can turn grass into beef. This ability gives her a profound economic significance.

It was gold, and the dream of sudden wealth that brought people to Colorado in the 1850's. Gold was a fever. It was more than a precious yellow metal. It was instant success. It meant a sudden, glorious escape from the everyday drudgery of working for a living.

The news of those first spectacular strikes in Colorado spread like wildfire throughout the country. Men, women and children caught the gold fever. Soon a great migration headed west, to the mountains.

To get here they had to cross a thousand miles of grassland. With every mile their boots crushed the green blades of a dozen different kinds of grass. Their wagon wheels cut deep ruts into a type of pasture land that few of them had ever seen before. It was short grass country.

Their oxen and their horses could have told them it was some of the most nutritious and most palatable feed that man had ever seen. It was grama and buffalo, sand blue-stem and wheatgrass. It needed only a minimum amount of rainfall to grow. It was a mixture of grasses that could simply sit and wait during drouth. It didn't die, it just stopped growing until rain finally came again. Then it sprang into new life. It was richer in protein than any of the grasses in the East, and it had another remarkable quality. When frost came it didn't just wilt and turn brown. Because of the dry climate and the high protein content of the slender blades, it cured into a dry feed that stayed palatable and nutritious all winter long.

There were millions of acres of it, too. But few of the goldseekers saw it, for they looked only upward to the snowcapped mountains. This grassland ran a thousand miles east and west, and double that distance north and south. It ran from the Mississippi River to the foothills of the Rocky Mountains. And it ran on from there up into the fertile valleys, across the wide mountain parks and on and on to the shores of the Pacific Ocean. It was a vast, waving, fragrant meadow every spring. But as grass, it was worthless to man.

He couldn't eat grass, and couldn't make anything out of it. Its only value was to keep his saddle horse and his oxen in good condition on his way west. But for centuries it had maintained the greatest red meat supply ever concentrated in one area before or since—the vast herds of American bison. Literally millions of these great animals roamed the plains for a thousand years. They supplied the pioneers with food, just as they had the Plains Indians for countless generations. Here was the key, for the buffalo were ruminants, too.

But the pioneers came for gold, and it was a long time before they looked at the grass beneath their feet. The early explorers' reports said that this land was a desert, unfit to grow anything of value. And they were right. Alone, this dry land grass was worthless. The tonnage it produced per acre was thin and sparse. But figured in terms of digestible nutrients, this grass crop had a cash potential that was worth many times all the gold, silver, lead, zinc, iron and copper that would be taken out of the mines of Colorado during the next century.

At that time it was free and available to anyone who wanted it. Soon a few of the more observant people began to see some of its possibilities. A dozen different reports have been written into the early histories about this. They all read like this: Fall had come and some freighter turned his oxen out into the storm because he had no feed, expecting them to die of starvation during the winter. He was surprised in the spring to find them fat and in fine condition.

They had survived on the winter-cured grasses and found shelter in the willows along the creek beds. At any rate, the point was made, and some people could see that this grass had value.

Finally, they realized that this was cow country. And that is where our story begins. For in order to make money from grass, it had to be "processed" by a ruminant.

Grass is cellulose—a low-grade carbohydrate, as far as nutrition is concerned, and a cow can utlilize that low-grade feed. She is a mobile, self-powered processing plant, that needs no other raw material except water. Her rumen is a 30 to 40 gallon fermentation vat. Here the bacteria and yeast cells consume the cellulose. These one-celled plants multiply. They in turn are eaten by one-celled protozoa, which are animal life.

It is at this point—in the change from plant to animal tissue—that the conversion from carbohydrate to protein takes place. The rest of the plumbing system, including the other three stomachs, helps to change the protozoa into amino acids. These in turn are converted to muscle tissue and energy in the cow and her calf.

This is the way beef is made. It is the most profitable way to market grass and hay—most of the time. From here on you have another product to sell—beef. And beef has historically been man's most popular form of protein.

In the years immediately following the Civil War, there was a population upsurge. Beef was in great demand. The East was feeling the effects of the industrial revolution and an increase in buying power.

The War had disrupted traditional marketing channels, so that uncounted millions of Longhorn cattle had been accumulating in south Texas and along the border. They were running wild and literally breeding themselves out of feed and range land.

The end of the War released thousands of young men who had lost many of their home and business ties. They wanted freedom, opportunity and escape. So they headed west to look for gold. A few of them found it. Others spent a few months or years in hopeful digging until their supplies ran out, then began to look for some other way to make a living.

Any farm boy from Ohio or Pennsylvania could see the possibilities for profit when trail cattle were selling here for $4.00 to $6.00 that he knew would bring $25.00 or more back home. But to do anything about it, he needed intelligence, business ability, capital and hard work. Some of them had all these things, and they were the ones who started the Western cattle industry, they and the Texans who started the trail herds into Colorado.

Most of the first cattle operations started small, but they soon got bigger. The very nature of the cow critter makes the cattle business a large scale operation from necessity.

The size of the animal, the tonnage of feed required, the breeding cycle, the long-range management problems, and the complex operations of marketing cattle and beef, make it a big business proposition.

It is a high risk business, too. Bad weather, disease, thieves and falling prices—all factors beyond the control of the operator —could wipe out an outfit almost overnight. It has always been, and still is, a business that takes a lot of capital, a lot of nerve, and a fairly large number of animals to be economically sound.

The cow business has traditionally been built on low grade, low cost feed. The only land that will produce grass economically is cheap land. Here it was, in abundance. All it needed was cattle.

Give a cow 30 to 40 pounds of grass a day and 10 or 12 gallons of water, and she'll produce beef. How much, and what grade of beef depends on her breeding, the quality of the grass and water, the weather—and the kind of bull she runs with.

How profitable this beef is has always depended on the price of cattle and the cost of getting a calf to market—plus a few other factors.

In the first place, cows and people just don't mix. As the population rises, people start competing with cattle for land. Land costs go up. In order to pay off, more cattle must be raised on a given amount of land, and the more cattle are confined, the more management problems arise.

These are some of the basic factors that give the cattle business a general air of conflict. The reasons for it are primarily economic.

The classic concept of a cattle ranch is a scene of pastoral serenity. The average city person visualizes an idyllic picture of cows grazing belly deep in grass or contentedly resting under a big shade tree, but a closer look will show some of the fallacies in this idea.

Face-to-face, a beef cow is well over half a ton of stubborn, complicated and highly perishable merchandise.

Moreover, it is 2,000 miles and a complex job of finishing, marketing and processing between a beef animal on Colorado range and the three-pound roast on a dinner table in New Jersey. The retail price of those few pounds of roast beef has a long way to go before somewhat less than half of it eventually trickles back to the pocketbook of a cowman in western Colorado. A great deal of it seems to rub off along the way.

The basic process of marketing beef has changed but very little in the past hundred years. Getting beef from Western ranges to the retail stores and the dinner tables of the East goes through much the same set of hands today as it did then. Better transportation, mechanized feedlots and vastly improved refrigeration have greatly reduced waste and the time involved, but each step is fundamentally the same.

In the 1880's, a Colorado steer would normally run with the beef herd on grass until he was from three to four years of age. By this time he could weigh anywhere from 800 to 1200 pounds, depending on the quality of his breeding and the feed supply available to him.

From here he sometimes went to slaughter, but more often to some Midwestern farmer who fed him corn for a few months, then sent him to the packer. From there on the distribution pattern was much like the present. Only now beef is sold in a supermarket instead of a butcher shop, and pre-packaged cuts are wrapped in pliofilm instead of butcher's paper.

The efficiency of the beef supply line has been greatly improved, but cow herd production has not kept pace. Nature is slow to change.

The beef cow will produce at best only one calf per year. Under modern management practices in use today, the average calf crop for the state is no more than 80% of the total producing cow herd.

This means that every five cows in the state produce only four calves per year. One cow out of every five is a "free-loader" and an economic loss to her owner. It means also that a cow with an average life span of eight to ten years can produce from four to seven calves in her lifetime, if she first calves as a two-year-old heifer. Under early range conditions, her life expectancy would probably average about seven years.

From the time the bull breeds the cow and a calf is conceived, until the calf is born, grown out to breeding age and able to produce a calf of its own, there is a minimum time requirement of about three years. The gestation period of a cow is 280 to 284 days, or about nine months. It takes at least a year after the calf is born to develop to breeding age. So far no one has been able to change this.

As a result, the cow business is not something that a man can get into and out of easily. Nor is it something that is subject to short-range production controls.

They tell the story about an absentee owner in the early days who received a frantic telegram from his ranch manager. He asked for authority to hire additional help and buy extra feed for his cow herd during the spring calving season. Severe storms during calving and a shortage of help were causing heavy death losses of both calves and cows, the manager advised the owner. Back came a succinct telegram from the distant owner, based on his own experience with production line problems in the manufacturing world—"Stop calving immediately!"

Needless to say, the cow business is never that simple. Once the calf crop is started the only way to stop it is to kill the cow. At times, this was exactly what happened in one way or another.

In the range country, even today, changes in the weather cycle can cause wide fluctuations in grass and feed production over vast areas. A section of grassland that might conceivably carry a hundred head of cows during years of good rainfall, could decline in a few months of severe drouth to the point where ten head would starve to death on the same acreage.

Few of the armchair critics who have always been so quick to charge the cattleman with overgrazing his range, have any conception of this extreme variation in grassland productivity, nor of the resulting complications involved in cow herd management.

As the drouth condition developed, the cowman faced a dilemma. Two painful choices were open to him. First, he could wait and hope for rain. Sometimes, a sudden thundershower could change his position overnight.

The alternative was to trail his herd to a railhead and ship them to slaughter. There was seldom any other compromise, since trying to move to another range was often impossible and buying feed was a losing proposition, and still is today. Involved in these agonizing decisions are numerous complications that depend on the physiology of the cow herself.

First of all, if the cowman elected to stick it out and pray for rain, he faced the grave possibility that the cows would become so weakened by lack of nutrition that they would be unable to move to a shipping point. Then too, the drouth usually dried up the streams and water holes that he had to depend upon for stock water enroute. This often meant that he was helpless. He could only watch his cow herd die off one at a time while he eyed each passing cloud in a blazing sky with anxious hope.

Furthermore, if he was fortunate enough to get his cattle to a shipping point, he must then face the immutable laws of supply and demand. In a wide-spread drouth, other cattlemen faced the same condtions. A sudden influx of cattle into the market quickly glutted supply and processing facilities, and brought an immediate drop in prices. As a result he not only sacrificed his breeding herd, but did so at a catastrophic loss in value.

Anyone whose family has been connected with the cattle industry for a generation or more can recall stories of cattle shipped to market under crash conditions that actually brought less than the total amount of the freight bill. This happened as recently as the 1930's.

Then, when the dry cycle eventually ended and the rains finally came again, everyone wanted to buy cows for restocking. Without cows the new grass crop could not be harvested, so bidding for the diminished supply of cows remaining caused prices to skyrocket. Any capital the stockman had left would buy only a small fraction of the replacement females he needed. So he started over with a few head, saved as many heifers as he could to rebuild his cow herd, and began the long cycle all over again.

All agriculture is still at the mercy of the weather, but today we have many safeguards that were not available to the early-day cattle producer. Probably the greatest of these is fast, low-cost transportation, plus instant communication. But even these modern tools cannot always prevent the loss of a lifetime of work and saving.

Drouth, cloudburst, or the sudden onslought of a new disease can cause either a quick loss or the slow attrition of a man's capital. It is estimated today that cow-calf operations over a 25-year period have probably returned less than three per cent on invested capital—considerably less than the same amount of money would earn in any government insured savings account.

The present cost-price squeeze, soaring land costs and the increasing shortage of experienced help is slowly but surely ending the cow-calf business as we have known it for the past century. Perhaps new methods of management, new types of operation, and vastly different forms of financing and marketing can again revive the cattle industry in this country.

In 1865, the Colorado cattle boom started. For a hundred years it has never stopped. There were times when it stumbled badly and things slowed down to a crawl, but it never turned back.

Today—in 1966—the cattle industry of the state is worth more dollars and is producing more beef than at any time in history. Where it will go in the next century—or even in the next ten to twenty-five years is hard to say. Science and industry are developing so fast that predictions are difficult to make.

Probably never again in the history of mankind will a century see such a radical change in man's civilization. In 1867, man was still traveling much as he had for the past two thousand years. The horse was still the principal means of locomotion. Railroads were being built, but their average speed was still not too much beyond the limits of a fast horse.

Today we have reached a point where the achievements of science strain the limits of comprehension. We cannot realize the effects these great scientific and engineering advances may have upon the lives of our children and grandchildren. Only by looking back occasionally can we see where we have been, and perhaps gauge with some modest degree of accuracy how far we have come.

For this reason, the story of the Colorado Cattlemen's Association over the past century may have dual interest to the student of the beef industry. For one thing, it can tell the story of the methods of operation in a rapidly changing industry as we know it. Secondly, it may, to more perceptive and analytical minds, foreshadow some trend of the industry in the century to come.

CHAPTER TWO

THE FIRST HERDS

The cattlemen who built the Colorado range industry in the later 1860's and the 1870's were not all heroes, nor were they all villains. However, there were both heroes and villains among them.

Essentially they were pioneers, with the foresight to see a future in the cattle business here on the frontier. They were willing to take great risks, both physical and financial. They also had the energy, the intelligence, and the judgment to manage their affairs. And they had a sense of humor to help accept things gone wrong.

The majority of them also had this in common—they were

stockmen to the core. Most of them had been raised on farms or ranches and had grown up with livestock. It was natural for them to look to this field when they arrived in Colorado Territory.

But, those who attempt to force the cattlemen into a homogeneous group, even today, should remember that one of the typical traits of a cattleman is his individuality. The nature of his work, much of it performed alone, encourages the development of this trait. It is undoubtedly true, too, that the individuals of the industry differ among themselves more widely than any other economic group.

Another quality that is essentially a stockman characteristic is tenacity — his ability to endure long periods of severe weather, economic depression, and other forms of adversity.

It is this same quality that has undoubtedly helped the organization to survive through recurrent periods of depression and general decline, then seemingly spring to life again when group action was needed to solve some wide-spread threat to the industry.

These men were observant and they were practical. A great many of the earlier arrivals came from the East and the Midwest where growing conditions, rainfall and weather were vastly different from this area.

Yet, they adapted quickly. They saw the Spanish system of handling cattle, branding and of organization, and they adopted it because it worked. The Spanish-Americans who ranched along the Huerfano, the Arkansas and the Purgatoire rivers for a generation or more before most of the Anglos arrived were pioneers themselves. They had brought their herds and their families over the Sangre de Cristo Mountains from the Rio Grande Valley and the long-established Spanish settlements north of Santa Fe.

With them came their centuries-old customs of land and livestock management—customs that had been developed in Spain and Mexico to fit this same type of country. They contributed their basic ideas of rangeland law, too, that still persist today in the statutes of our state.

These laws have endured because they were practical, they

were simple and they were eminently fair. They were based on the simple assumption that those who braved the first hardships of a wilderness area were entitled to protection from the encroachment of later arrivals.

This basic idea of "first in use, first in law" is best exemplified in the priority rights of our irrigation laws. Many of our earliest ditch rights for water go back to early Spanish development work along the streams of southern Colorado.

Even our present fence laws are still based on the Spanish concept of rangeland usage. Here in Colorado the basic differences between English law and Spanish law first met head-on. On several occasions conflicts have arisen between these two legal philosophies that brought the issue either to a vote or to the courts. So far, the Spanish law has always prevailed.

To simplify the two ideas and reduce them to bare essentials, the difference is merely this: English law held that the owner of livestock was responsible for his cattle and he was expected to fence them in. Spanish law on the other hand, assumed that range land was open to all and that the owner of crop land was himself responsible for the protection of his crops. The farmer who raised a garden or grain crop was therefore expected to fence cattle off his land, if he wanted to protect it from the destruction of roving livestock. Thus, English law held that the cattle owner should fence cattle in, Spanish law compelled the land owner to fence them out.

Essentially this same philosophy is incorporated into our present day fence laws.

The Spanish contributed the fundamental ideas for our modern brand laws too. At one of the first meetings of the Association, members were urged to come and register their brands with the organization. As the direct result of this early organization, Colorado has probably the most effective brand laws in the nation today.

For nearly a century now, a registered Colorado cattle brand, burned on the hide with a hot iron, has been accepted in almost every court in the state as basic evidence of livestock ownership. It has essentially the same standing as a personal signature on a check or other legal document.

Despite the first feverish excitement of the gold rush, numerous early arrivals turned to livestock as a means of earning a living, preferring it to the uncertainties of mining. An advertisement in the Rocky Mountain News that ran in December of 1859 reads as follows:

> "Henderson's Island—This celebrated ranch is now open for the reception of all kinds of stock to winter. Being the largest ranch near the cities of Auraria and Denver, containing 320 acres, and being well-timbered and watered, and having on it a splendid picket corral, with stabling for two hundred head of horses or mules, it offers extra inducements to persons having stock to winter. Cattle, horses and mules taken by month or for winter. This season's grass still uncut and 80 tons of hay in stack.—John D. Henderson, Proprietor."

This was the first public corral or stockyard in the region. Jack Henderson was one of the early freighters to the area. He arrived in the fall of 1858 with a train of supplies from Lawrence, Kansas. Having no shelter for his ox teams that first winter, he simply turned them out on the plains to forage for themselves, as others were doing.

Early the next spring he rode out into the country east of Denver, toward Bijou Creek, to hunt buffalo. Along the way he saw some cattle grazing, rode over to investigate and saw that they carried his brand. They were in fine condition, he reported later, and had grown fat on the native grasses. He gathered up the cattle and drove them back to town, pleased with the discovery that livestock could subsist through the winter without special care.

Williams and Blake were two other freighters who brought in a train of ox wagons loaded with supplies from Iowa in 1858. They took the abandoned adobe corral at old Fort Lupton as headquarters and turned their cattle out along the South Platte river bottom. They, too, gathered their cattle the following spring in greatly improved condition. Most were fat enough for slaughter as beef—a profitable commodity in a frontier town after a hard winter. Williams later was one of the founders of the cattle Association.

Irwin and Jackson turned loose 400 head of footsore draft

oxen in the fall of 1859 on the Bijou, near the present location of Deer Trail. They had the same experience and thus a general practice was born. The foundation was laid for a new frontier industry.

Others apparently made the same discovery—an unexpected one because of previous reports from military explorers and trappers that the area was a great American desert, unfit for agriculture and generally assumed to be worthless.

Be that as it may, from here on out many of the early settlers began to look to the grasslands as the basis for their living. Although Jack Henderson probably gets credit for starting Colorado's first commercial feed yard, it is surprising how fast things developed from this small beginning.

The mushrooming city of Denver needed food for the thousands of new people who were arriving each year. New strikes in the mountains brought more gold to the frontier capital and business boomed. During the early 1860's long trains of freight and emigrant wagons pulled into the city, unloaded merchandise and eager new citizens. All of the heavy wagons were drawn by oxen, and many of the newcomers brought milk cows and some beef animals with them from the Midwest.

The valleys leading out from Denver were quickly taken up with small farms. Soon vegetables and grain from these local farming areas began to appear on the Denver market. Most of these first cattle herds in this region, however, were small and were handled more as farm herds rather than as range cattle.

It is an interesting commentary on these early Colorado settlers, to find that agricultural organization efforts in some form or another began to appear very early. Perhaps this was due to the editorial inspiration of William N. Byers, publisher of the Rocky Mountain News in those embryonic years, for he was an enthusiastic backer of group agricultural projects.

As early as July 31, 1861, a notice appeared in the News to call a meeting of those interested in forming a Colorado Agricultural Society. Among those listed as signing this first call was A. G. Reed, who was to become the first president of the Colorado Stock Growers Association six years later.

The first effort was unsuccessful in getting any sort of organization under way, but an agricultural society was finally formed on March 28, 1863. Article II of the constitution of the organization stated—"Its object will be to promote the interests of stock raising and husbandry in all its branches, and by every means and measure which will conduce to the benefit of its members."

This organization was active enough to sponsor an Agricultural show in Denver by September of 1866. A full report on the event was made to the Territorial Legislature in November, along with a request for a bond issue to cover the indebtedness incurred by the Society. Richard Sopris, president of the Society, reported that the organization owed some $8,765. This, he said, was secured by a 40-acre tract of land which had been purchased as a site for the event. He added also that stables had been built to accommodate 110 horses and that pens had been constructed for cattle, sheep and swine. An irrigation ditch ran through the property and a half-mile race track with a suitable stand for judges had been completed.

This same talent for organization in the territory was demonstrated by a unique idea developed by those who wanted to take up land for farming.

The land north of the Arkansas River at that time was still technically held by the various Indian tribes in the area. In those early years, Congress had not passed any legislation setting up a procedure for preempting land and securing a valid title.

Mining claims were generally recognized and were the only accepted means of asserting title for the use of land. However, there was as yet no established method for claiming agricultural property in this area.

The only solution was to stake out a claim and give public notice of the boundaries of the property. But these early settlers developed an ingenious method of gaining public acceptance of the title through a system of organized Claim Clubs.

A duly organized county club was formed to record all such early land claims. Title to the property was attested by all members, giving a quasi-public acceptance of the title until legal machinery under the new territorial laws could be established to handle the problem. This was then Kansas Territory.

One of these was the Arapahoe County Claim Club which met on August 8, 1859, and adopted resolutions outlining the conditions for establishing title to a land claim for farming purposes. Since Arapahoe County at that time went all the way to the Kansas line, this initial organization had far-reaching influence.

From this information it would seem that the early pioneers of Colorado had, indeed, a genius for organization. It was entirely logical therefore, that the same idea would be utilized a few years later to solve the many problems of livestock control and range management.

This answers the question of how the idea of a livestock association developed, and why it happened here.

The growth of the cattle industry and the rapid influx of the lawless element of the frontier region were far ahead of any attempts to organize a law enforcement system.

Cattle running at large on the unfenced plains were almost entirely unprotected. Although all the livestock owners in the region quickly adopted the Spanish practice of branding their animals, respect for this indicator of ownership had to be maintained by a law enforcement organization. Here, there was no law except in town. There a duly elected town marshal, backed by the cooperation of citizens, could enforce the basic statutes of law and order.

During the 1860's, however, in Denver and many of the other towns in the territory, law ended with the city limits. Outside of these towns there were marauding Indians, bandits, thieves and murderers.

Today they are known as psychotics, and put safely away in government-sponsored institutions. In Colorado Territory, however, they roamed at large over an almost untracked wilderness. The only defense against them was a ready weapon and the ability to sleep lightly. When every cent a man had was invested in a string of Longhorns, his investment was only secure as long as he had them in sight.

This kind of business property was highly mobile. It had a

tendency to drift with a storm, it was perishable, and most important of all, it was edible. This, coupled with the fact that cattle were easily marketed, either on the hoof or as beef, made the business of cattle raising for profit a precarious vocation on the frontier.

During the territorial days, both cattle numbers and thieves apparently increased in about equal proportions. And, on top of this, there were other problems.

The build-up of cattle numbers in the territory during this period came from two entirely different sources. A surprising number of cattle were being driven in from the states—"American cattle," they were called.

A great many of these were good blooded stock. Sam Hartsel, an early settler in South Park, bought out two men from Iowa who had trailed about 20 good Shorthorn cows and two or three registered bulls of the same breed to Colorado in the spring of 1861.

These animals worked out so well on his South Park ranch, that in 1864, Hartsel went east to Missouri and bought 148 Shorthorn cows and several bulls from Tom Gordon, a prominent Clay County breeder. All of these animals were top quality cattle and eligible for registration.

He headed west for Colorado along the Santa Fe Trail in company with a large caravan, trailing his valuable herd across the plains. Because of marauding Indians, however, it took him nearly two years to get them home. He wintered the herd the first year at Fort Larned, Kansas, on the Arkansas River and went on the following spring, with a large caravan under military escort, arriving at his ranch on the South Platte that fall.

This was the first group of blooded stock to arrive in any quantity, but smaller numbers were also appearing in the state.

The real problem lay with the other group of cattle that were furnishing most of the stocker cattle for the state . . . the Longhorns. These cattle coming up from the border country were tough as rawhide and practically immune to every type of disease. They were literally crawling with ticks, but through long association had built up a complete immunity to the virulent tick fever.

However, when these animals came in contact with the "American" stock, the better cattle had none of the protecting antibodies. They contracted the disease quickly—and died like flies.

No one knew the real cause of the disease at that time. They only knew that the source of the infection was Texas cattle. The term "Texas Fever," therefore covered the situation.

Replacement cattle were hard to come by and mighty expensive in this country at that time, so feeling was strong against the deadly contagion brought into the state by the trail herds.

Efforts were made as early as 1861 to stop the influx of Texas livestock. One of the first bills passed by the first Territorial Legislature in 1861 was a law prohibiting the entry of any cattle from Texas into the southern counties of the territory. There was no way to enforce the law, however, and the movement failed.

The economics of the situation were against the quarantine effort also. Longhorns weren't much for quality, but they were available and they were cheap. There was a tremendous demand for cattle of any type. The sheer weight of numbers, plus the fact that the first winter weather usually killed the southern ticks, finally helped to overcome some of the opposition. Eventually, a partial solution was found by compelling the cattle to winter at a point 300 miles south of the Colorado border, but even this was not worked out until some years later.

The first cattle trailed into southwestern Colorado were Missouri Shorthorns brought in by Fernando James and Frank Wadsworth, who attempted to stock a range in southeastern Colorado. They were denied admittance by the Ute Indians, who controlled the area from Pueblo into Utah.

James and Wadsworth then took their cattle over Raton Pass into the Santa Fe and Taos area, then on to the Farmington country. Here they persuaded Indians to allow them to enter what is now Montezuma County.

The cattle were broken up into a number of small herds which were parcelled out, each placed in care of an Indian family. The two white men furnished supplies and good horses and allowed the Indians to butcher animals for their own use. They received a share of the annual increase. The Indians learned to drive their cattle to the high mountain ranges in the country, bringing them down to the valleys in the fall. This system continued for some 15 years. The cattle, largely excellent grade Shorthorns, were the source of foundation stock for many of the better herds in western Colorado in later years.

The Planter House, 15th and Blake Sts., Denver, where the Colorado Stock Growers Association was organized November 30, 1867. —Colorado State Historical Society photo

CHAPTER THREE

"FORMING THE ORGANIZATION"

For three weeks, from November 2, 1867, until the day of the meeting, the Rocky Mountain News carried the following ing notice—

"Notice to stock men. A meeting of all persons interested in stock raising, and stock traders, will be held in the city of Denver, on Saturday Nov. 24, at the Planter House, at two o'clock, afternoon, for the purpose of effecting an organization, and to secure the passage of laws at the next legislature, for protection, &c.

Thomas B. Farmer
A. G. Reed
McLaughlin & Wilson
and Twenty Others."

It was the same approach that had helped to launch the successful Colorado Agricultural Society a few years before, culminating in the first territorial Agricultural Fair and Horse Race at Denver in 1866. This was a major success for the fledgling agricultural industry in the frontier territory. The 1867 Fair, held in October, had more than 40 head of horses and cattle on display, many of them good blooded stock.

The preliminary meeting of stockmen was called to appoint a committee to prepare a constitution and by-laws. Then on November 30, 1867, a formal meeting was held at the Planter House hotel.

The terse record of that first official meeting and the formation of the first stock grower's organization in the West, reads as follows:

"At a meeting of the Stock Growers association, held at the Planter House on November 30, 1867, Capt. A. G. Reed was called to the chair and A. J. Williams was elected Secretary. The committee appointed at last meeting to report a constitution and by-laws for the organization of a stock growers association reported through their chairman, Dr. Parsons as follows which was adopted by sections. Carried. Attest. A. J. Williams, Secty."

The minutes book contains no record of the constitution and by-laws mentioned, but the next entry reads as follows:

"December 7, 1867.
At a meeting of the Stock Growers Association held at the Planter House in Denver C. T. (Colorado Territory) on the above date. Meeting called to order by A. G. Reed President.

It was moved that the thanks of the association be spread on the minutes of the association for the present from Alex M. Atkins for the book for the association. Carried.

Moved by Mr. Magness that we adjourn for two weeks and that all members be requested to bring their brands to record. Carried.

(no signature)."

At a later meeting this recording of brands was apparently the only part of the meeting that was considered worthy of record. The minutes read simply—

"December 17th, 1867.
Meeting called to order by Allen G. Reed in the chair. Being no further business the meeting adjourned.

Attest Alex Davidson, Secty."

No explanation is offered for the change in secretaries.

Then at the bottom of the first page are the minutes of another meeting that would soon have violent repercussions.

"January 18th, 1868.
Meeting called to order by A. G. Reed in the chair. The president was fully authorized to employ detectives for the use and benefit of the association. Being no further business the meeting adjourned until the Bill passed the legislature and the secty ordered to pursue the same and to have it at our next meeting. Carried.

Attest Alex Davidson, Secty."

"February 1st, 1868.
Meeting was called to order by A. G. Reed in the chair.

The minutes of our last meeting was read and approved. It was moved that we adopt the acts of our legislature as part of our by-laws. Carried.

Moved by Mr. Steele that Articles 4 and 5 of our By-laws be construed to apply to horned cattle only.

Moved that the President, Vice President and Secretary be appointed a committee to wait on the butchers and commission merchants and acquaint them with the law and furnish bonds.

The motion was carried.

Moved by Mr. Steele that each member brand their horses, mules and asses where they please if they want the protection of the Association, but are respectfully requested to record the same on the books of said association. Carried.

Moved by Mr. Brown that a vote of thanks be tendered John W. Martin, Esq. for the free use of his room for the association for their meeting.

Carried.

Moved to adjourn.

Attest Alex Davidson, Secty."

Then, on April 25th, 1868, there was the first indication of some sort of problem within the organization. The minutes of this meeting read as follows—

"At a meeting of the Colorado Stock Growers Association at

the office of R. S. Wilson, Esq. called by A. G. Reed in the chair. Minutes of last meeting read and approved.

On motion it was ordered that there be a committee appointed to examine the books and find the amount of money on hand and also to look up certain names that were lost. The chair appointed Messrs. Parsons, Lilly and Magness said committee.

There being no further business before the meeting it was moved that we adjourn to meet on Thursday, April 30th, 1868.

(no signature)."

(Robert S. Wilson was at this time a police magistrate. Later he became a livestock dealer and auctioneer.)

In these terse entries, written in an old-fashioned hand on the faded pages of an old ledger, are the elements of a frontier drama.

It has taken more than 15 years of research and study to understand what happened and the nature of the people involved. Some of it still does not add up to a neat solution. But in looking back toward the misty days of those early times, we can piece together the events from these brief entries. The reminiscences of those involved, and the comments of later writers who knew the people concerned, have explained most of the story.

To begin with, the first Colorado cattle boom started about 1865, right after the Civil War. Trade was re-established with Texas and the trail herds were once more pointed north through the Indian Territory into Colorado. The trail blazed by John Dawson as an agent for Goodnight in 1859, and Lovell and Reed in 1860, came up through present-day Oklahoma, then known as Indian Territory, and into southeastern Colorado. Goodnight and Loving trailed up through the Llano Estacado—the Staked Plains of eastern New Mexico—and into Colorado, first over Raton Pass and later over Trinchera Pass.

By 1867, it was estimated there were some 147,000 head of cattle in the state of Colorado—and about 30,000 people. The cattle were doing fine, but some of the people were causing trouble.

Farms had been established up and down the South Platte River Valley from Denver. Farmers were active also in both Clear Creek and Bear Creek valleys, as far west as the foothills. Others were in operation up the Cherry Creek Valley and both branches of Plum Creek to the south had some early farms and livestock ranches.

Because Denver had by this time established itself as the trading center of the vast high plains region along the front of the mountain country, most of the traffic of the day eventually came this way.

With it came some of the country's outstanding crooks, thieves and more talented desperadoes. There were others, too, who simply could not face the thought of hard work. Loose cattle, protected only by the presence of an unrecorded brand on the left rib or hip, presented too much of a temptation to resist.

As a result, frontier farmers and stock raisers were at a distinct disadvantage in trying to hold their assets together.

Although cattle stealing in the earlier days was a spasmodic thing, largely confined to branding unmarked cattle, or the occasional slaughter of a stray for beef, by 1867, it had reached serious proportions. Increasing numbers of animals were being stolen, driven into Kansas and sold, or hidden in some valley in the foothills until they could be slaughtered and sold for beef at the mining camps.

Since most of the local cattle were then of the "American" type, these stolen animals were valuable—often bringing many times the market value of the tough Longhorns. Gradually, the thievery spread until it reached unbearable proportions. Outlaw gangs were operating all over the territory and into the surrounding states and territories as well.

Things finally reached a point where each man had to slap his iron on almost any calf he could find in order to stay in business at all, purely as a means of survival.

It was in desperation then that some 20 to 30 stockgrowers, principally those within a few days' ride from Denver, decided to organize an association that would stop this thievery through group action.

Several of them had been involved in the successful formation of the Colorado Agricultural Society a few years before and had sufficient experience to know how to go about putting such an organization together. The same technique was used—the announcement ad that ran for more than three weeks in the

Rocky Mountain News, calling all interested persons to a meeting of stock raisers at a meeting in Denver at the Planter House at two o'clock, Saturday afternoon, November 24th, 1867. This was for the purpose of discussing the problem of cattle thefts and working out the aims of the association.

The preliminary meeting was held and the interest displayed indicated that stock raisers everywhere were getting fed up. Apparently, the only official business that took place at this time was to appoint a committee to prepare a constitution and by-laws and set the time and place for a second meeting.

At the next meeting, on November 30, the official organization of the Colorado Stock Growers Association was effected. The brief paragraph that suffices for the minutes of this meeting, probably falls far short of doing justice to the occasion.

Since the constitution and by-laws had already been prepared under the direction of Dr. John Parsons, considerable thought must have gone into them.

Parsons was an early arrival on the frontier and was undoubtedly an educated man. He came to the territory in 1858 from Quincy, Illinois. Early in 1859 he had gone to the Tarryal region in South Park and done reasonably well in the gold mines there. Later he brought in dies, established a mint there the following year, and started the production of $2.50 and $5.00 coins which circulated rather widely in Denver and the territory for a time.

He came back to the Denver region about 1866 and started a dairy down the South Platte a short distance below the city. He was apparently running a number of beef cattle or crossbreds, also, and he, like the others, was probably suffering the frequent loss of valuable animals.

Later, in 1872, he set up an office as a practicing physician at the Springbank house, although his primary interest seemed always to have been with agriculture. This was the man who wrote the by-laws for the organization which still speaks for the cow business of the state today.

That original document was lost or destroyed sometime during these intervening years, but the basic provisions probably were similar to the by-laws of 1872, which are reproduced later.

In essence, they were banding together to solve a problem much bigger than any of them could tackle alone.

And, it was primarily the people involved that would make the idea work. At any rate, Doctor Parsons was around for some time and active in the organization for the next ten or twelve years. And, in just a few months, he would be called upon to help save the infant organization from collapse before its first real test.

Three other men in the first meeting merit some special attention also. They were key people in the small group that formed the Association and weathered its near collapse during its very first year of existence.

The first person was Capt. Allen G. Reed. This Captain Reed was another old-timer on the frontier. According to Richard Sopris, who was later mayor of Denver, Reed was one of the first men to bring a trail herd up from Texas, apparently in either 1859 or 1860. Sopris said he remained here about ten years and then returned to Lexington, Missouri.

At any rate, Reed was one of the signers of the first call to form an Agricultural Society in 1861. When the group was finally organized in 1863, he was one of the charter members. He had some standing in the community also, for he was called upon to judge the sheep exhibit at the first Agricultural Fair held in Arapahoe County in 1866 and also acted as a judge for the horse races, held at the same event. Now, a man could serve as a judge of sheep and not be too influential on the frontier but a judge of early day horse races was not selected lightly. Sheep were one thing, but horses were mighty important animals at this time in the West.

As a Missourian, Reed grew up in an area where horse racing was a major event. He must have been well respected at this time. Furthermore, a later biography of David C. Wyatt, a substantial cattleman and president of the livestock organization in later years, states that Reed was in partnership with Wyatt on a ranch on Plum Creek, about 14 miles south of Denver sometime around 1862. Wyatt served nearly ten years on the Executive Committee of the Association and was president for six years in the 1890's.

The events that followed over the next six months simply don't add up on Allen Reed. Reed's associates and his early record don't seem to offer an answer to the riddle of the "big blow-up" later.

Another key man in this early chapter of the story was A. J. Williams. Here was a solid citizen. If any one man deserves credit for saving the Association and eventually getting it on its feet, Williams is unquestionably the man to receive the acclaim.

Andrew J. Williams arrived in Denver on November 1, 1858, in company with his partner, Charles H. Blake. They arrived with four wagons, each pulled by four yoke of oxen, and they brought in the first stock of merchandise for the first store in Auraria. The following month, when the first survey of the Denver townsite was made, Williams carried the chain for General William Larimer.

Although he was only 25 years old he was no tenderfoot. In 1853, he had gone to Salt Lake City as clerk to Colonel A. W. Babbitt, Secretary of Utah Territory, along with another man, M. V. Brewer. The assignment turned out to be a tough one and Williams was the only one of the three to get out alive. Brewer was killed by Mormons, and Colonel Babbitt was killed by Indians in 1856. Williams went back to Council Bluffs, Iowa, and worked as a miller for awhile. Then, when news of the Pikes Peak gold strike reached Iowa, he and his partner, Blake, loaded their freight wagons with merchandise and miner's supplies and headed for the new settlement on Cherry Creek.

In the spring of 1859, he built the first hotel in the new town of Denver—the Denver House—and then watched it burn to the ground a year later. Thereafter, he discontinued dealing in merchandise and turned to freighting and contracting in Colorado and New Mexico.

By 1865, he had become interested in the cattle business and for several years, in the 1860's and early 70's, he bought large herds of cattle in Texas, trailing them to Colorado. At the time he was asked to serve as temporary secretary for the initial organization meeting of the Colorado Stock Growers Association, this was his business.

He seemed to have a knack for being at the right place at

the right time and was always in on the ground floor. He traded and ran cattle until 1869, when he was one of the incorporators, a director, and later president of the Exchange Bank. He died in Denver on May 30, 1895 at the age of 62.

The third man who played a major part in this scene of turmoil and strife was David J. Cook—although his name is never mentioned in the records of the Association until many years later.

At this point, David J. Cook was only 27 years old, but he was serving his second term as City Marshal of Denver. In addition, he had already chalked up a spectacular record of success as a frontier detective in Colorado for the War Department. He was a tough, shrewd and dedicated law man.

He was the man chosen when the stockmen voted to employ a detective "for the use and benefit of the Association." They picked the right man, or possibly the wrong one as events later turned out.

Dave Cook was also one of the early arrivals in the territory, entering the settlement of Auraria with his younger brother in the spring of 1859, headed for the gold diggings. The two boys had modest success for the next year or two working on a claim at Missouri Flat, between Russell Gulch and Black Hawk.

When a thief stole the small "poke" of gold they had accumulated, Cook started out to track him down. He succeeded, recovered the stolen gold, and in the process launched himself on a lifelong career of law enforcement and detective work.

This event in 1868, however, was the first meeting of Cook and the cattlemen's Association. It was a connection that lasted for nearly 30 years—and it had a major influence on both of the parties involved.

When he received this first assignment from the fledgling stock growers organization, Cook had only recently formed the Rocky Mountain Detective Association. At that time, it was little more than a general agreement between Cook and other law enforcement officers in the towns throughout the Territory of Colorado and the surrounding region. They had agreed to work together under his direction, and to exchange information about the movement and activities of thieves and

crooks in the West. From the start, it had been highly successful. Until Cook's central information exchange was set up,
thieves could steal horses or cattle in one area and take them
to another location for sale. A bill of sale or other indication of
title was easily forged and there was no way to check its valid-
ity.

The stock-growers' request was his first big private assignment, and Cook was anxious to demonstrate his ability and the
efficiency of his new organization. He at once set out to learn
everything he could about the cattle industry—the movement
of cattle, marketing, raising and management of the entire
livestock business.

When he had finished his investigation and made out his
report, he probably knew more about the cattle industry than
most of the people engaged in it. Furthermore, the amount of
misleading information that had been given to him in the
beginning aroused his resentment and increased his determination to get to the bottom of the situation.

As a result, his report went far beyond anything the officers
of the Association had ever expected or intended. In it he listed
the individual losses of each of the members, explained what
had happened to the stock, and then named the people involved. It was a surprisingly complete and detailed report, inspired largely by the apparent disregard for his ability which
the officers of the Association had displayed. As near as he
could determine, they had never expected him to turn up much
of anything.

He prepared his report with grim humor and waited until the
next meeting of the Association was in progress. Then, during
a heated discussion of the continuing losses of livestock, he
sent the document to the presiding officer with the innocent
suggestion that his information might have some bearing on
the discussion.

The chairman, without looking at it, passed the report over
to the secretary and directed that it be read at once.

"I have here," the secretary said as he arose, "the report of
D. J. Cook, superintendent of the Rocky Mountain Detective

Association, who was engaged a few months ago to investigate cattle thefts in this area."

The members leaned back comfortably in their chairs, expecting to hear the usual type of committee report. As the secretary read on, however, they soon found out this was something entirely different. They began to sit up and take notice. The reader, in typical indifference to the content of the report, read on, hardly noticing the context of his statements.

"It has been possible to run down most of the 'rustling' to its sources. Herewith are submitted proofs of the guilt of those who have been most active."

There was a quick stir in the audience and the members came to alert attention.

"The chief rustlers are—," the secretary suddenly stopped and his face blanched.

"Go on! Who are they?" came the shouted demand.

The secretary hesitated, looked at the grim audience, and then read on slowly. The list of the guilty parties included the names of three officers of the Association, plus some of the other members.

The meeting was thrown into an uproar. In the midst of the confusion there were several quick departures from the hall and a general exodus from the platform. The meeting promptly broke up and the officers later sent in their resignations.

The minutes of the Association meetings for this period are fairly complete, but none of this detailed information and description of the meeting is shown in the records.

The description of the incident is taken from a biography of Dave Cook, written in 1936. He died of a heart attack on the morning of April 29, 1907 and left a fairly complete collection of memoirs. When he passed away he was 66 years of age, but was vigorous and alert until the last few days.

This version of that eventful meeting was written by his two biographers, William Ross Collier and Edwin Victor Westrate, in their book, "Dave Cook of the Rockies." It is not mentioned in Dave Cook's own book of memoirs published in 1897. Collier, however, claimed to have known Cook well.

The basic information is also verified by Fred J. Johnson,

who was secretary of the Association in the early 1900's. Johnson was also editor at that time of the Denver Daily Record Stockman and a responsible writer. He was undoubtedly well acquainted with many of the early members of the Association, several of whom were still living at the time he held office.

The subtle presentation of the report is certainly in keeping with Cook's methods of operation, too. One thing that stamps this version as a possible "re-creation" however, is the term "rustling." The term rustling was never used, either in the records of the Association, or in reports of speeches by the officers of the organization, until 1898.

Those who stole cattle were simply cattle thieves, crooks or outlaws. The term "rustlers" was probably a journalistic invention of the dime novel era. It was undoubtedly based on the commonly used expression, "to rustle," generally applied to a person, or more often to a cow who was energetic and active. A cow was a good rustler if she could seek out good grazing areas and shift for herself under adverse conditions.

Most early cattlemen would have resented the term, since it connotes an air of tolerance for the crime involved. Cattle theft is grand larceny and a major offense. Yet, even today, there is often a feeling that stealing cattle is not quite as serious a crime as stealing a car, for example. The effect of this is seen in the frequent difficulty encountered in getting a jury to convict a man caught in the act of stealing cattle. This apparent prejudice has existed almost from territorial days.

In marked contrast is the fact that a man stealing horses was never a horse "rustler." He was, and still is, a horse thief. In the early days of the Association, a horse thief was usually hanged. But cattle thieves often went free—and still do.

There is no record of the officers of the Association being prosecuted for their offenses. However, Cook's biographers say that the accused men did make restitution for losses and that there was a general re-shuffling of the cattle population among the members.

Here is what the minutes of the organization record for this eventful period:

Denver, April 30th, 1868

At a meeting of the Stock Grower's Association held at the office of Robert S. Wilson, Esq. The President and Vice President being absent, A. J. Williams was called to the chair.

On motion of Dr. Parsons, R. S. Wilson was elected an honorary member of this association and that he be exempt from the payment of the five dollars required by the By-Laws.

The resignation of A. G. Reed, President; Andrew Slain, Vice President; and Alexander Davidson, Secretary were received and accepted.

On motion of Mr. Trumble, Dr. John Parsons was elected President; Joseph Block, Vice President; and Robert S. Wilson, Secretary.

The secretary was instructed to meet with Alex Davidson and also to write to F. Pope.

H. F. Ford and Wm. D. Ford being present signed the constitution and paid the fee.

On motion the meeting then adjourned to meet on Saturday, May 16, 1868.

Robert S. Wilson, Secretary

It was probably at the meeting of April 25 that the Cook report was read. Unfortunately, no reference to nor any copy of that report is contained in the Association minutes, nor has it been found to date. The venerable Rocky Mountain News did not carry any mention that the cattle thefts had been solved, either. The cattlemen of those days were not inclined to wash their dirty linen in public. The matter was straightened out and they went on about their business.

But David J. Cook was not forgotten. For the next 30 years his assistance was a vital part of the Association activities. However, not until 1884 is there any record of a contract with him or the Rocky Mountain Detective Association. From all indications, his early work was a carefully kept secret.

It is probably no coincidence, however, that Cook received high honors during the administration of Governors John L. Routt and Job A. Cooper, both prominent cattlemen who later served as president of the Stock Growers Association.

The prestige and the effectiveness of the organization suffered from the impact of this incident, however. Many of the newer members dropped out of the Association in disgust.

Others stayed because it was still the only central clearing house for brand registration and estray information.

The new officers worked hard to rebuild some of the earlier enthusiasm for the aims and efforts of the group, but it was an uphill struggle. They did manage to hold the organization together with the faithful support of A. J. Williams, who had built up a sizeable trail herd business, and was in the process of organizing the Exchange Bank.

The truth of the matter was, however, that the organization did not become important until 1872 when a group of the old hands got together and decided to pump new life into the Association.

In the meantime, Williams had replaced Dr. Parsons as president, but he had apparently no desire to function in that capacity. Williams, it seemed, was always the man called to preside at emergency meetings, but he invariably stepped down as soon as a new officer was elected to take over the chair.

During these intervening years, the nature of the Colorado cattle industry was undergoing a rapid era of change. Cattle were coming into the state from Texas at an ever-increasing rate. The rich grasslands and the burgeoning mining industry provided ample grazing and an expanding local market for beef.

The territory was relatively free from Indian problems for these few years, the weather was good, and things were booming. The average value of cattle increased nearly 20%—from $22.10 per head in 1867, to $26.30 in 1872. Cattle numbers in the territory increased from 147,000 in 1867 to 355,000 in 1872, by official count.

In 1869, the Kansas Pacific railroad had been completed as far as the town of Kit Carson, Colorado. It was from this terminus, later that same year, that the first trainload of cattle to be shipped east by rail from Colorado was loaded out. This was a herd owned by George Thompson of Las Animas.

The railroad reached Denver the following year, and by 1872 movements of Colorado cattle east by rail were assuming sizeable proportions. In that year, 428 cars were shipped from Denver, 85 from Deer Trail, 162 from Kit Carson and 116 from

Cheyenne Wells. In addition, Colorado cattlemen sold 35,250 head that year for delivery to North Platte on the Union Pacific to fill Utah and Montana contracts. This made the rail shipments from the state for that one year come to a total of 46,208 head that were valued at more than one million dollars. Cattle marketed eastward that year, mainly for slaughter, brought about $35.00 per head, while stocker cattle moving west or north sold for an average of $17.00 per head.

No record is available for trail herds coming into the state for this year, but the number could have been well over 250,000 head. Many of them moved on north into Wyoming and Montana, and others were slaughtered for beef to supply Army post and Indian reservation contracts.

At any rate, during this four-year period from 1868 to 1872, there was a net gain in the total cattle population of the territory that averaged better than 50,000 head per year.

The industry had reached the proportions where group action was more and more important. Up to 1870, each owner gathered his own cattle in the spring or fall, but numbers were increasing to the extent that an organized round-up was necessary.

With the increase in population, new talent had come into the territory and cattle thefts were again on the increase. After some discussion a new plan of action was decided upon.

A public tribute to the success of their efforts came thirty years later at the organization meeting of the National Stock Growers Association held in Denver on January 25-27, 1898.

The Honorable Ralph L. Talbot, attorney for the Colorado Cattle Growers Association had the following to say to more than a thousand stockmen from all over the United States:

"As introductory matter, I feel it is not out of place to state briefly the special work done in this direction by the Colorado Association, the oldest society of this character in America, and the only one which has kept up a continued activity since its members first adopted their constitution and by-laws.

"It has profited by its own mistakes and ought now to serve as a model for similar organizations throughout the Union. Its aims, objects and ambitions from the beginning have been to prevent the stealing of cattle and to propose legislation directed against frauds and swindlers, and thus to further the stock interests of the state.

"The statutory regulations now on our books governing butchers and other licensed slaughterers of livestock; the provisions regarding estrays; the protection granted by the agistor's lien law; the recovery of damages for stock killed by railway companies; the precautions taken against contagious diseases; the creation of districts, roundups, commissioners, inspection commissioners and cattle inspectors; the sale of mavericks under legal limitations; the requirements controlling the grazing of cattle by non-residents; the penalties imposed against false registration of pedigree; the establishment of the State Veterinary Sanitary Board; the creation of stockyards and the regulation of packing interests; the requirements as to brands and the markings of animals running at large, are among the many important enactments outlined by this body of men, voluntarily serving together without pay, and without receiving a just public appreciation of the labors performed and the results accomplished by them."

Wm R Culbertson
57

CHAPTER FOUR

THE INDIAN PROBLEM

Indians plagued Colorado stockmen for almost a quarter of a century after the first herds were established on the eastern plains. They stampeded trail herds, murdered solitary cowboys, killed and butchered cattle and used them for target practice, ransacked and burned isolated cow camps, and exacted blackmail, demanding free beef in return for nonaggression. On a few occasions, however, Indian depredations became so serious and general that cattlemen retreated temporarily to the settlements near the mountains.

As a result of these annoyances, Indians didn't rank among the cattleman's favorite people. However, they didn't cost him any great amount of sleep either. The average stockman was a matter-of-fact person who considered the dangers of his occupation a part of the day's work. To him, the Indian was an irritating pest who had to be dealt with on occasion. Cattlemen and cowboys were generally better armed, better mounted, and more capable of decisive action than Indians.

Typical in attitude, if somewhat extreme in method, was the Texas cowboy who looked up from branding a calf in a lonely place to discover a murder-bent Indian creeping toward him. The Indian fled when the cowboy pulled his pistol. The cowhand jumped on his horse, roped the Indian, and dragged him back to the fire, where he branded him on the rump, notched his ears with his employer's earmark, and turned him loose with a kick.

Cattlemen operated over vast areas in relatively small numbers. Their buildings were meager, but substantial, for defense. The average cattleman didn't scare easily and he didn't bluff easily. Consequently, Indians confined their forays against stockmen to attacks on solitary herders or one-man camps, and to running off stock. They found easier and more tempting targets along the wagon trails and on the outskirts of settlements.

Not all cattlemen detested Indians. Notable among the exception was John Wesley Prowers, who married Amache Ochinee, daughter of a minor chief of the Arapaho nation. She occupied a place of honor and respect in the Boggsville and Las Animas communities during her long residence there. Reportedly, John W. Iliff was friendly with Indians, too.

However, Indians didn't let friendship interfere with business. They pestered Prowers and Iliff along with the more unfriendly stockmen.

Charles Goodnight occasionally found it expedient to bargain with Indians when they confronted him during a trail drive. Goodnight, and other drovers as well, found it easier to cut a few head of trail-worn steers from a herd and give them to the Indians than to risk stampedes if the savages tried to take them by force.

Mrs. R. T. Wilson accompanied her husband when he drove nearly 1,000 head of cattle from Cedar Rapids, Iowa, to Denver in 1860. She said the cloud of dust raised by the cattle convinced the Indians at first that they were cavalry on the march. Later, they discovered their mistake and attacked the Wilson party several times.

By the time the range cattle industry began, Indian warfare on the plains was nearly over. Nearly, but not quite. The years 1864-69 were the bloodiest years on the plains, years of sporadic fighting and continuous hostility. Indian troubles, which began in the spring of 1864, reached at times into every portion of the plains. As far as Colorado's plains were concerned, it ended July 11, 1869, when the Fifth U. S. Cavalry under Colonel Eugene A. Carr, with the assistance of a battalion of Pawnee Scouts under Major Frank North, virtually wiped out Tall Bull's Cheyenne Dog Soldiers at Summit Springs in northern Washington County.

Indians raided communities in Kansas, Nebraska, Wyoming, and Colorado repeatedly during the spring and summer of 1864. In April, they ran off 175 head of cattle from the herd of Irwin and Jackson, government contractors camped in the Bijou Basin about 40 miles east of Denver. In the middle of June, Indians stampeded stock on Box Elder Creek and murdered the Hungate family.

During the next few months, hostile bands burned every stage station on the Overland Trail along the South Platte, between Cottonwood Springs near present-day North Platte, Nebraska, and Latham, near today's town of Kersey in eastern Weld County—with one notable exception. At American ranch, south of the present town of Merino in Logan County, tough old Holon Godfrey barricaded himself and his family in the sod stage station and fought off Indian attacks for three days. In recognition of his feat, what had been called Godfrey's station, became popularly known as Fort Wicked. Godfrey, 53 years old at the time of the fighting, proudly accepted the title and emblazoned it on a sign outside the station. Godfrey later became a farmer and stockman near La Salle. In 1875, he joined a party in pursuit of a raiding band of Indians.

The principal stockman victims of the war of 1864 were the operators of "road ranches" along the Overland and Smoky

Hill Trails—men who furnished hay and fuel to stage stations, operated small stores, and made a business of reconditioning worn-out oxen and trading to emigrants for more of the same.

Governor John Evans panicked in August, 1864, when Indian raids stopped the flow of supplies into Denver, and reports of Indian attacks came from many sections. "Extensive Indian depredations, with murder of family, occurred yesterday 30 miles south of Denver," Evans wrote Secretary of War Stanton. "Our lines of communications are cut and our crops. . . are all in exposed localities. . .large bodies of Indians are undoubtedly near Denver, and we are in danger of destruction both from attacks of Indians and starvation. It is impossible to exaggerate our danger." Evans asked Stanton to return to Colorado, Colonel Ford's Second Colorado Cavalry regiment, then stationed at Fort Riley and Fort Larned, Kansas. Later, Evans asked for 5,000 troops.

Two days after Evans' frantic message, two Cheyenne Indians told Indian trader Elbridge Gerry, whose wife was a Cheyenne, that Indians planned a series of simultaneous raids August 21 on Fort Lupton, Latham Junction (just west of today's Fort Morgan), the head of Cherry Creek, and Pueblo. Alerted by Gerry, Governor Evans had Colonel John Chivington dispatch all available militia and one-hundred-day volunteer recruits to these places.

On August 22, Indians raided Gerry's ranch, possibly in retaliation for his warning which had thwarted their mass attack. Somewhat calmer in the face of trouble than the Governor, Gerry sent the following message to Evans from his ranch at the mouth of Crow Creek: "A party of ten Cheyenne Indians came into my ranch yesterday evening and ran off all of my horses and also Antoine Raynal's, about 150 head. As far as I can learn the party is about 150 men, but whether this is true I cannot tell. . .If I can raise a party of ten men I will start after them in the morning."

By September 7, Governor Evans was beside himself. He wired Secretary Stanton: "Pray give positive orders for our Second Colorado Cavalry to come out. Have notice published that they will come in detachments to escort trains up the Platte on certain days. Unless escorts are sent them, we will evidently have a famine in addition to this gigantic Indian war. Flour is $45.00 a barrel, and the supply growing scarce, with none on the way."

The Second Cavalry was not returned to Colorado, but other reinforcements were already on the way when Evans wired. Three days later, troops of the Seventh Iowa Cavalry began to establish and garrison Fort Sedgwick, a mile west of Julesburg. A company of hundred-day volunteers had been federalized into a mounted unit and stationed at Fort Lupton. Chivington had other federalized militia units positioned at stage stations along the trail.

On November 27, 1864, the Third Colorado Cavalry, troops from the First Colorado Cavalry, and a detachment of New Mexico Infantry, massacred a village of peaceful Cheyennes on Sand Creek, north of Fort Lyon on the Arkansas. This incident served to intensify the ferocity of the Indians.

Julesburg was plundered and burned January 7, 1865. Thanks to the presence of nearby Fort Sedgwick, then known as Camp Rankin, the town's residents found refuge and none was killed.

Attacks on stage stations, isolated homes, and solitary cow camps continued for several years.

In 1867, a Cheyenne-Arapaho war party raided the Monument Creek Valley, killing three people, and driving off all the stock they could gather.

Gerry's ranch was the scene of a tragedy, August 24, 1868, when Indians murdered William Brush and two companions, putting up hay for winter feed on the Kersey bottoms. Brush was a brother and partner of Jared L. Brush, one of the most prominent of Colorado's early cattlemen.

There were other incidents in the fall of 1868. In August, Nicholas O'Cam was shot, stabbed and scalped by raiders who ravaged property and ran off stock on Plum Creek. Warfare broke out all along the Smoky Hill Trail from a short distance east of Denver into Kansas. A woman and a boy were killed on Kiowa Creek. Indians were sighted on Cherry Creek, 18 miles from Denver, and Governor Hunt asked for troops. When his request was denied, he called for volunteers.

In September, the Lilleys, Skeltons, Bowles, McBrooms, and other ranchers along Cherry Creek and the Platte River above Denver, came into the city for safety. Raids were reported in the Fountain Valley, near Pueblo, and along the Arkansas.

In the South Park, Samuel Hartsel had his second encounter with Indians. In 1862, a Sioux-Arapaho war party had raided his ranch while returning to the plains from a fight with the Utes at Granite. According to Hartsel, on that occasion they stole everything but a red hot cook stove and whipped his herder with ramrods from their gun barrels when he tried to stop the robbery.

In 1868, Hartsel, himself, was captured by a war party of Sioux or Cheyennes who had become lost while returning from a raid on the Utes. They forced him to guide them to the Ute trail leading to Colorado City and the plains, then released him, although he had expected to be murdered when he had served their purpose.

In January, 1869, Sioux burned and destroyed an Iliff cow camp at old Camp Sanborn on the South Platte, near the present town of Orchard. They ran off 100 head of cattle. Elbridge Gerry led a pursuit party which failed to find the Indians, but recovered most of the cattle, which had been abandoned at a river crossing.

The last two Indian battles on the Colorado plains were the Beecher Island fight on the Arickaree fork of the Republican River, south of Wray, September 17, 1868, and the battle of Summit Springs, south of Sterling, July 11, 1869.

For years, small bands of hostile Indians continued to harass stockmen and other settlers. Some were plains Indians on hunting pass or French leave from reservations. Others were Utes, who preferred to fight other Indians, but didn't overlook opportunities to plunder and rob whites if the odds favored them sufficiently.

One evening, in April, 1873, marauding Sioux attacked the Iliff ranch at the forks of Crow Creek, south of Briggsdale. They set fire to the house and threw powder down the chimney. Phil Bernard, an Iliff herder who was alone at the ranch, crawled out the door unobserved in the darkness and made his escape after a walk of many miles. Dave Wyatt, later president of the Colorado Cattle Growers Association, found Bernard on the prairie the next day, his feet filled with cactus thorns, and took him to Cheyenne for treatment.

In 1875-76, came the last great war effort of the Sioux, Cheyennes, and other northern plains tribes. It reached its peak with the Custer Massacre on the Little Big Horn in eastern Montana, June 24, 1876, then dwindled quickly as the hostile tribes were beaten into submission. During these two years, there were a number of raids which reached into northeastern Colorado.

A. R. Ross, later a Greeley resident, said Indians burned the ranges on which he was located, on the Fort Morgan flats and along the Arickaree, in 1875. Like others in the area, he gathered the stock nearest to him and moved westward to safety in the Greeley area. Ross said few people were actually killed in these raids, but there was a general exodus toward the mountains.

Raiding parties had great respect for cowboys in groups, and concentrated their attacks on those they found alone or in very small groups, he said.

"The cowboys had them pretty well trained to stay away from the camps and not come too close to the riders on the range, or else. Bullets would be dropped close enough to make them face the other way, expecting other bullets to fall much closer the next time."

Ross told about four cowboys, employed by a rancher named Tracy, who left the round-up and started for Julesburg with a bunch of beef steers. Indians killed three of them. The fourth, the foreman, escaped after a long chase because he was riding a very fast horse.

In the late 1870's, many of the Utes began to harass white people. Colorow, a White River Ute chief, led his band into many parts of Colorado, terrorizing and pillaging farms and ranches.

Things didn't go exactly as he had planned when Colorow invaded Joseph W. Bowles' Bar Eleven ranch in southern Yuma County one day in 1876.

Bowles came out of the house with a rifle across his arm and listened as Colorow delivered an ultimatum for Bowles to leave the country, speaking through an interpreter, a sub-leader named Washington. Bowles listened, then, without moving, answered: "Washington you know English words I say. Tell Colorow if he does not behave himself, I'll shoot a hole in him a dog can crawl in. Now, all of you, git!" They got, disappearing over the sandhills as Bowles and his family dug a square pit on a knoll near the house and prepared for a fight. The Indians reappeared twice, but did not venture to attack.

On the western slope, Indian troubles began later and ended later, continuing into the 1880's.

In the late 1870's, friction between the Utes and whites came to a head in numerous small encounters. Settlers in increasing numbers were encroaching on Indian lands, while the Indians themselves kept bumping into white people on their hunting trips and war expeditions against other Indians.

Barney H. "Judd" Day said that soon after his parents settled in Middle Park in 1876, Utes told them they must leave the park by a certain time. When an Indian returned to discover the men in the neighborhood moulding bullets and preparing to fight, they left and did not again molest the few settlers in that area.

The Denver Times, on July 3, 1876 stated, "The Mountaineer reports that about thirty Utes camped near South Park show a disposition to cause trouble." Two months later, another Times story reported that, "The Indians have lately burned three cabins," adding that the Southern Utes in Animas Valley" are a constant source of trouble and dread to the few settlers in their vicinity."

Troubles became more and more intense in 1877. The Denver Times quoted Judge Clements from Routt County as reporting in December 1877, that "Douglas, a Ute chief, said the Indians would be on the warpath in the spring."

General W. T. Sherman saw trouble building up early in 1878. The Indians were unwilling to permit further reduction of their limits, while the whites continued to move into the Ute territory in their quest for gold, silver, and land.

Unrest finally boiled over in the Meeker massacre late in September, 1879, at the White River agency near Meeker, Agent

N. C. Meeker's efforts to force Indians to work as a part of their civilization training triggered the attack. Meeker was assaulted by a half-breed named Johnson. He sent for assistance from Fort Steele, Wyoming. Troops under Major T. T. Thornburg were on the way when the Indians attacked the agency, killing Meeker and nine other men, carrying away three women and two children. At almost the same time, another band attacked Thornburg's column of 160 men at Milk Creek, north of the agency. Thornburg and 13 others were killed, 35 wounded and the entire detachment besieged for several days until General Merritt arrived from Fort Russell with reinforcements.

This affair led to the relocation of the Indians from Colorado to the present Ute reservations in the southwestern corner of Colorado and to Utah and New Mexico, in September, 1881. This opened up nearly all of western Colorado for settlement.

Stockmen had been coming into the area for several years, but they began to arrive with large herds about 1884. Prior to that time, the only cattle in the Meeker area were about 1,000 head owned by Dunc Blair, who had earned the privilege of running cattle on Indian lands by marrying a squaw.

Indian troubles continued for several years on a small scale. Mrs. Elizabeth Simon Hammon, who moved into Montezuma County with her parents in 1881, recalled that "The Indians were always a source of more or less uneasiness." Shortly before the Simon family arrived, Indians had killed three men, Dick May, John Thurman and Byron Smith. The three men had gone to look at horses owned by Thurman that May and Smith planned to purchase. Smith's body was never recovered. In the same year, two settlers, Willis and Melvin, were killed in the Sierra La Sal Mountains on the Colorado-Utah border.

In 1885, stockmen in the country north of Dolores, killed 11 Indians for running off and slaughtering their stock. This fight was known as the Beaver massacre. Indians later retaliated and killed several settlers in the Montezuma Valley. A number of the cattlemen banded together at Narraguinnep Spring and built a fort of large pine logs. This was used for two weeks until the Indian scare subsided. The fort was located in Narraguinnep Canyon, about 25 miles north of Dolores.

Ben Laughlin, one of the early settlers in the Yampa country, said the party which he accompanied from Elbert County to settle in Egeria Park, fought Indians all one night. The following evening, he said, there was a fight with Indians near Steamboat Springs.

These incidents were typical of the Indian problems in the cattle country. In general, the stockmen took them in stride as part of life on the frontier. After the Meeker massacre and the subsequent relocation of the Utes, the danger from molestation faded into the past. The virtual extermination of the buffalo had been a major factor in the subjugation of the plains tribes, and these events left the entire high plains region open to cattle grazing.

Frederick Remington, from Century Magazine—1887

CHAPTER FIVE

THE BIG BUILD-UP — THE 1870's

The last spike was driven at Strasburg, Colorado, to complete the Kansas Pacific railroad into Denver on August 16, 1870.

On that day Denver became a transcontinental rail terminal. From this point it began to build up rapidly an already established reputation as the business capital of the frontier. By this time, Denver and Colorado Territory had become the crossroads of the Western range cattle industry.

Colorado's position was unique among the Western range states. It was settled and developed much faster, and it went through the cowboy and Indian stage about ten years before Wyoming and Montana.

Because of this it escaped much of the publicity and flamboyant news coverage that marked the range life of Wyoming. By the time the dime novel writers found out about the exciting life of the cowboy, the Colorado cattle industry had gone through this period and had begun to settle down into a substantial business operation.

Furthermore, that "genius for organization" which the Colorado cowmen displayed, made this transition much smoother and somewhat less spectacular than the same period in Wyoming history.

In many ways, the Colorado Stock Growers Association was a more democratic organization than the Wyoming group. True, it was run largely by the bigger cattle operators, but this is understandable because they had men with more experience in management and planning. But nowhere in the minutes of the organization is there any indication that size of the operation was any factor in membership, influence or eligibility for office. In fact, most of the Association presidents were average-size operators.

From the very beginning all memberships were issued to individuals. A corporation membership was usually held by the manager. If a man had 50 head or 5,000 head of cattle, he still had one vote. When money was needed, however, the assessment was nearly always made on the number of cattle. In this way the big operators carried a major part of the financial load, but maintained the democratic spirit of the organization.

Joseph L. Bailey, proprietor of the Bull's Head Corral, outlined something of this in the notice he inserted in the Rocky Mountain News, for the first week in January, 1872. In it he called all persons interested in livestock to attend a meeting scheduled for January 6, 1872, at the American House.

The purposes of the meeting were: "To protect the interests alike of stockmen, ranchmen and farmers, and to harmonize as far as possible, whatever might be conflicting in the great interest of agriculture and stock raising."

The meeting of January 6 was a harmonious one, according to the Rocky Mountain News the following day.

"It was a large meeting and conducted with a broad and

liberal spirit that promises to lead to the happiest results," the paper reported.

That dependable bulwark of organization, A. J. Williams, was called to the chair. He was the one officer who carried over from the original group in 1867. He and Bailey had determined beforehand that the Association would have to be reorganized along more permanent lines if it was ever to accomplish its original objectives.

Bailey explained their aims at the meeting, giving all the reasons in detail. He then offered a resolution that a committee of five be appointed to prepare a new constitution and by-laws for the organization. The move was seconded by the Honorable John G. Lilley, who was then serving in the Territorial Legislature. It passed by unanimous vote.

Williams immediately appointed Joseph L. Bailey, J. P. Van Wormer, J. H. Pinkerton, W. W. Roberts and George W. Brown to this committee.

Lilley then proposed that a committee of five be appointed to prepare a bill for the protection of stock to be presented to the legislature. This met with approval and the following men were appointed to this committee: John G. Lilley, L. F. Bartels, Peter Eskins, John S. Wheeler and John Hittson.

Mr. George W. Brown then presented the resolutions adopted by the Southern Colorado Stock Growers Association. These were read and then turned over to the committee on legislation for drafting into bills. (NOTE: This is the first recorded example of a practice still followed nearly a century later. Local organizations today use this same method of resolutions to make their policies known to the state Association. The Southern Colorado Stock Growers organization is still active and one of the largest local groups in the state, incidentally.)

Brown then moved that Chairman Williams be made an ex-officio member of all committees. This passed and Williams took the opportunity to outline some of the livestock legislation that was needed. Not many new laws were required, he pointed out. Many of the old ones should be brought up to date and made more effective. He described some of the activities of the organization in the previous years and told of their work in breaking up several rings of cattle thieves. A broad organization and wider group effort would be necessary, he said, to clean them out completely.

Better laws for the registration of brands, the recent problem of stock killed by the railroads, and the increasingly difficult problems of round-ups were some of the other tasks that faced them, he declared.

Bailey agreed, and added that the present severe winter had scattered stock to a greater extent than usual and that there would be much difficulty in recovering these cattle in the spring.

Mr. R. P. Snow of Wyoming was introduced and was asked to comment on the problems of stockmen in that territory. Snow stated that Wyoming cattle growers were suffering severe losses from cattle thieves and from the devastation caused by large trail herds passing through their best hay and meadow lands.

He told of losing 64 head from his own herd. When searching for them later, he found the thieves with more than 200 head of stolen cattle.

Remarks and discussion followed, the News reported. Among those taking part in the comments were Lilley, Pinkerton, Bartels, Scherrer, Judge Wheeler and others. The paper declared that this meeting was but the first of a series that would be of great benefit to the livestock industry.

At the next meeting on January 19, 1872, held in the territorial library, the new officers for the year were elected and the new constitution adopted.

The officers named were: John G. Lilley, president; J. L. Bailey, vice president; W. Holly, secretary and A. J. Williams, treasurer. An Executive Committee was also elected of the following men: W. W. Roberts, James M. Wilson, Jared L. Brush, Alfred Butters and George W. Brown.

The Executive Committee was a significant new development in the organization. It was undoubtedly set up to prevent any re-occurrence of the 1868 fiasco, and it continued to be an important part of the organizational structure for at least half a century.

Here are the Articles of Association and By-Laws of the Colorado Stock Growers Association as adopted by that group meeting in the territorial library that cold winter evening on January 19, 1872.

ARTICLES OF ASSOCIATION AND BY-LAWS
OF THE
COLORADO STOCK GROWERS ASSOCIATION.

This Association formed for the mutual benefit and protection of all persons engaged in stock growing and stock dealing in the Territory of Colorado shall be called

"THE COLORADO STOCK GROWERS ASSOCIATION."

Any persons engaged in raising, herding or dealing in live-stock, may become members by signing these Articles of Association and paying into the Treasury the sum of five ($5.00) dollars.

The officers shall consist of a president, vice president, secretary, treasurer and an Executive Committee of five.

It shall be the duty of the president to preside at all meetings, to call special meetings at the request of the Executive Committee and to sign all orders on the treasury.

It shall be the duty of the vice president to act in the absence of the president.

It shall be the duty of the secretary to keep minutes of all meetings, inscribe them on the Records of the Association. He shall keep a book in which shall be entered the brands of all members of the Association, with the usual range of the stock bearing such brand; he shall keep a book in which shall be entered all reports of stray stock furnished by members of the Association, which report shall immediately be transmitted to the owners of said stock. He shall conduct all correspondence of the Association and discharge such other duties as may be necessary for the benefit of the Association.

It shall be the duty of the treasurer to receive all moneys due for membership or otherwise and pay the same on the order of the president.

It shall be the duty of the Executive Committee to audit all accounts of the Association; to have the general superintendence of the Association and to make calls for special meetings through the presidency.

All officers of the Association shall be elected by ballot and shall hold office for one year.

It shall be the duty of each member of the Association to report to the secretary any estrays which he may see, find, or be informed of.

The Annual meetings of the Association shall be held in the

City of Denver on the Saturday succeeding the first Monday of January in each year.

The Regular meetings of the Association shall be held on the Saturdays succeeding the first Monday in January, April, July and October.

Special meetings of the Association may be held on the call of the president and secretary, at the request of the Executive Committee, at any time where the interests of the Association require action.

Any member desiring to alter or amend these Articles of Association and By-Laws, shall give thirty days notice of his intention to present such alteration or amendment.

JANUARY 19, 1872

This document is interesting in its directness and its simplicity. It specifically details the duty of the secretary to keep a book in which all brands used by the members of the organization will be entered; it obligates each member to report estray animals and through the Executive Committee, sets up a system of checks and balances on the officers for the benefit of the organization as a whole.

The most important thing about it is the fact that it worked. From here on the organization was on solid footing. Then, too, the cattle industry had by this time reached a more stable condition. It was getting to be a substantial business.

At this point it had entered the heyday of the open range era. Cattle were being trailed into and through the state in ever-increasing numbers. Railroad shipments were building up with surprising speed.

This was the time when the big individual cattlemen were made. The next decade, the 1880's saw the rise of the big cattle companies, but the 1870's was the decade of the cowman, the so-called "cattle baron" or "cattle king," whichever term best suited the personal style of the more enthusiastic journalists of the day.

Many stories of fabulous gains are told about some of these early cattlemen. Many started out with a pittance and built huge operations. They were the Horatio Algers of the frontier and the open range.

Typical of the journalistic tribute to such individuals is the writing of A. A. Hayes, Jr., an early journalist who traveled through Colorado as a writer for Harper's Magazine. Listed as a Fellow of the American Geographical Society and the Royal Geographical Society of London, he visited southern Colorado in the 1870's to write a series of articles for his publication.

In a volume published in 1880, entitled "New Colorado and the Santa Fe Trail," Hayes gives a glowing description of his visit to Pueblo and a stay at the ranch of "Uncle Pete" Dotson, which he located about 35 miles southwest of Pueblo, near the Wet Mountain Range, and close to Greenhorn Mountain.

He relates the story of a "Mr. Ayliffe" (Iliff) who, he was told, started out 15 years before with a total capital of $100 and had an estate of $1,500,000 when he died in 1878. His range extended between Denver and Julesburg, the writer explains. But the most interesting paragraph in his chapter on the ranches of Colorado is the explanation he was given for Iliff's success. Another cattleman and a friend of Iliff's told him the secret of this Colorado success story.

"Some people try to attend to several things, or to do more than one kind of business, but he only thought of one thing for those 15 years, and that one thing was cattle.

"And attending only to that, and thinking about it all the time he came to understand it wonderfully well, and then have perfect judgment about making the most of stock."

This was a pretty good summary of the situation. Anyone who did business with Iliff came to have a high regard for his knowledge of cattle and the nature of the cattle business. His early death, however, cut short a truly fabulous career. Several of his close friends in the Association said that his death was due to overwork and exposure, the direct result of this same intense devotion to his business.

But Iliff was not the only one who built fame and fortune in the cattle business during these early days. Nearly every officer and member of the Colorado Stock Growers organization in the 1870's had a similar tale to tell.

In fact a number of them started with even less than Iliff, who, more reliable witnesses testify, had an initial gift of $500 from his father when he left home to seek his fortune in the West.

John G. Lilley arrived in Boston as an immigrant youth from England; A. J. Williams, James M. Wilson, Joseph P. Farmer, all one-time presidents of the Association, started from scratch and built up with the industry. Many others came into Colorado as $15-a-month trail hands, their sole net worth invested in a saddle and a pair of boots.

Some had modest success in gold mining, but pulled out and invested their savings in cattle to get a start. It is possible, too, that others used the much maligned method of a fast rope and a hot cinch ring to get their foundation herd started, then later became respectable as their credit standing improved.

Among the former trail hands who built sizeable empires in Denver and Colorado were W. H. H. Cranmer, F. P. Ernest, the Wyatt Brothers, John Hittson and many others.

Each year the build-up continued and the Association grew with it. At the next annual meeting of the organization, held in Denver in January, 1873, the Rocky Mountain News gave detailed coverage of the event.

William Holly turned out to be a devoted worker and a thoroughly able secretary. In planning the annual meeting in 1873, he had arranged for a number of papers to be presented by leading stockmen from various parts of the state. This was a first move to make the organization a state-wide clearing house for livestock information, marketing reports and range condition reports that would be of great value to all members.

In his report, Holly said that the organization had, through its committees, made a number of suggestions to the Territorial Legislature for livestock laws, and that many of these had been passed in the session.

He said severe storms had caused considerable death loss among Colorado cattle on the range, possibly as much as ten per cent he estimated, with an additional five per cent depreciation in loss of flesh.

The first fears of catastrophic losses during the winter were largely allayed, he added, by the effect of an early spring and a remarkable growth of grass on the plains for the past season.

This was, he pointed out, the result of a wide-spread covering of snow from those same storms. The early spring feed thus helped to recover some of the losses of the previous winter.

He reported to the members also that a paper, prepared for the group by Dr. Henry Latham of Wyoming, had been widely quoted by Eastern papers, and had brought the organization much attention throughout the nation.

The wide reputation of the author, he said, had done much to restore confidence in Colorado as a livestock producing country, and to offset earlier reports of exaggerated storm damage. (Dr. Latham was then ranching in the Laramie plains country, but had previously become widely known as an agricultural writer for the Union Pacific railroad.)

He reported also that the results of the round-ups were not generally satisfactory to those engaged in them, and he hoped that further experience would enable the organization to work out some of these difficulties.

He declared that losses from thieves were still considerable, and that many unauthorized persons had taken to skinning dead animals killed by storms. This practice prevented the identification of carcasses by those in search of estrays, and was thus doubly damaging in its effects.

He added, however, that this practice had been almost entirely stopped by notices published in leading newspapers which warned the parties engaged in this activity that they would be prosecuted by the Association and convicted for hide thefts.

Other cattle had been stolen by irresponsible men in charge of trail herds that were passing through Colorado ranges. These persons, he explained, had been in the habit of appropriating any strays that came their way. To stop this practice he advocated an Association inspector be hired with authority to examine all herds passing through the state.

He had been requested also, he added, to recommend the appointment of various committees, who would be instructed to report during the present session, and to act as standing committees for the ensuing year.

The committees to be named were to handle such problems as Round-ups, Transportation, Claims and Damages, Printing and Publications, Protection and Maintenance of Ranges, "Blooded Stock," Territorial Register of Brands, and Pedigrees and Owners.

(This, too, was a milestone, for the same practice is still followed, and the present-day organization has similar standing committees, including modern committees on Brand and Theft, Range Improvement, Transportation, Cattle Improvement and Public Relations.)

Holly also advocated the appointment in each county of a member of the Association to act as correspondent for the organization and assist in collecting statistics on the industry. Such facts were then very difficult to obtain.

Holly then reported some general statistics on the growth of the livestock industry in the territory for the past year. Well-informed men declare the industry is still in its infancy, he said but his figures would show that it was bound to become one of the principal sources of wealth in the territory.

The abstract of returns in the territorial auditor's office, which were not yet published or final, showed that in 1871 there were assessed 142,178 head of cattle, compared to 242,372 in 1872, an increase of 100,224 head. Horses increased from 15,580 in 1871, to 20,371 in 1872, an increase of 4,791. Sheep went from 184,577 in 1871 to 266,015, an increase of 81,438. Mules in 1871 totaled 2,365, compared to 2,390 in 1872, an increase of 25.

He pointed out that the assessments undoubtedly gave an incomplete figure, but they did indicate a steady increase in numbers. He said, too, that a great many pedigreed animals had been imported into the area, including 87 purebred Shorthorns, Jersey, Devon and Galloway bulls; 21 stallions and 456 Merino, Southdown and Leicester rams.

In addition there were some 200 grade bulls of various breeds, 132 carloads of horses, averaging 18 head each, principally mares, and about 300 Cashmere goats. Three purebred breeding farms had been established in the past year and several more were projected.

In closing, he extended the sincere thanks of the Association to the newspapers of the region that had given the organization such excellent editorial coverage.

This support, he concluded, did much to attract the attention of capital and experience that was invaluable to the industry.

At the subsequent election of officers, the group named Joseph L. Bailey, president; W. W. Roberts, vice president; W. Holly, secretary and A. J. Williams, treasurer.

In addition, J. L. Bush, James M. Wilson, Alfred Butters, W. H. H. Cranmer and William J. Wilson were elected to the Executive Committee.

Captain Joseph S. Maynard was named director from Colorado to the American Association of Shorthorn Breeders, and the following general committees were appointed.

Completing organization: W. W. Webster, J. L. Brush, J. M. Wilson, E. S. Randle and Dr. John Parsons, who was president in 1868 and 1869.

Resolutions: Alfred Butters, A. J. Williams, Rev. Winfield Scott, Jacob Scherrer and J. H. Pinkerton.

The secretary then read a lengthy letter from Mr. Atwood White of Green City, Colorado, on sheep-breeding in the southern part of the state.

The Honorable W. F. Stone of Pueblo presented a paper on "Southern Colorado as a Stock Country." In it he estimated that the Arkansas Basin area would carry as many as a million and a quarter head of cattle, with no more than a hundred and fifty thousand head in the region at that time.

He said that trail herds from Texas had declined somewhat in the past year or so, with more of the Texas cattle being diverted to Abilene and other points for shipment to Eastern markets. Local cattle growers had taken advantage of this decrease to import more purebred breeding stock and had made great strides in breeding up their native stock. The result, he said had been a great improvement in the stock throughout the entire valley.

A spirited discussion of round-up problems followed. Brush said that he felt there were too many individual round-ups in Arapahoe, Douglas and Weld counties, and that better organization was needed so that one series of round-ups could be planned.

Cranmer suggested that the operators in various areas of the country should form themselves into a company during the round-ups so that guard duty could be assigned at night when it was required.

Dr. Parsons was opposed to the whole idea. Last year, he declared, the stockmen had held a thousand round-ups in the state and it was impossible for the small operator to attend them all. In the round-ups, he went on, cattle were often taken farther from home than they were to begin with. On one occasion last year, his cattle had been driven 20 miles in the wrong direction. The present system also gave wide-spread opportunity for thieves to run off large groups of cattle.

Furthermore, he continued, many abandoned calves were found "lying around on the prairie," after one of the big round-ups last summer. In general, he said, it cost more money than they were worth to get the cattle back from the round-ups.

Brush supported Dr. Parsons in many points. He agreed that many cattle were taken dishonestly during the previous year and that there were too many round-ups. He felt that each county round-up foreman should have a complete record of owner's brands, so that he could prevent any false claims for cattle. He believed, however, that the round-ups, if well organized, would be the most efficient way to gather cattle.

Parsons replied that it was impossible to check brands during the round-up with so many cattle gathered together. The whole system was unsound, and a small farmer with only 20 or 30 head of cattle could not take part in these drives.

James Wilson suggested that the committee to be appointed should meet with the various people represented in the Association and try to develop a round-up plan that would solve many of these problems. He, personally, would rather see everybody gathering cattle together than have small groups out looking for individual herds. When there was an organized group of many men out, he felt that it would be much more difficult to steal cattle. Without round-ups, he could not see how stockmen would get their cattle.

Lilley said he had not attended any of the large round-ups

and suggested that the committee be composed of men who had experience with them.

Dr. Latham of Wyoming said they had had reasonable success with their round-ups in that territory, although there was no basic law to govern such operations there as in Colorado. He volunteered the observation that without the round-ups the thieves could probably get the cattle much more easily than the owners. In the Laramie Valley, he reported there were now about 20,000 head of cattle and they held two round-ups each year.

Brush then suggested that one person should be designated by law to attend the round-ups and to take charge of any unbranded cattle. A county brand could then be put on these animals until they were claimed by a valid owner, and when the proper ownership had been established they could be rebranded.

Edward F. Bishop, who was attending the meeting to represent John W. Iliff, said he was satisfied that properly conducted round-ups would stop most of the stealing that was going on. The system as a whole, was the best method that had been invented for cattlemen, both large and small.

J. H. Pinkerton of Evans, said that one difficulty last year had been the fact that the round-up had been put off too long for the dairymen. He suggested the small owners of stock and dairymen have a round-up before the general round-up. This would get the small herds off the range before the main round-up started. He pointed out, too, that most of the small operators were located west of Box Elder Creek, while most of the larger stockmen were below this point where few of the smaller herds were ranged.

At this point, Lilley adjourned the group until the evening session. When the gathering convened after dinner, president-elect Joseph Bailey called the group to order.

"Gentlemen of the Colorado Stock Growers Association," he began.

"You have this afternoon done me the honor of electing me to the responsible and honorable position of president of your organization for the year 1873.

"I can only say that I shall endeavor to discharge the duties of this office to the best of my ability. Your secretary's report shows the main features of the work being done by your Association during the past year. The adoption of the suggestions made respecting committes to whom shall be referred the various matters claiming the attention of this body, renders it my duty to make these apointments.

"I shall therefore appoint the committees as follows: On Round-ups—James M. Wilson, J. L. Brush and William J. Wilson.

On Blooded Stock—J. S. Maynard, Winfield Scott and I. W. Chatfield.

On Transportation, Claims and Damages—W. W. Roberts, Jacob Scherrer and W. Holly.

On Printing and Publications—W. Holly, C. S. Rothschild, and J. H. Pinkerton.

On Improving and Maintaining the Range—Joseph P. Farmer, H. M. Falls and Andrew D. Wilson.

On Register of Brands—A. J. Williams, John G. Lilley and Alfred Butters.

"These committees have important duties to fulfill in preparing the work to be acted upon by the Association and in shaping in a great degree its future policies," he declared.

"Perhaps the most important of these are the round-ups. This is a matter that has engaged the attention of the best men in the business but which, from the peculiar formation of the grazing grounds of Colorado, is still almost as much a puzzle as when the legislature first attempted to frame a law to govern and control them. Since I have appointed gentlemen entirely competent to report a plan for your consideration, I shall offer no further suggestions on the subject.

"The annually recurring losses by stock owners from irresponsible individuals in charge of herds on their way through the territory, who gather up and drive off single cattle or small herds are, in the aggregate, very serious. No one individual can protect his herds, nor can he follow and regain stolen cattle. Protection and reparation can only be secured by concert of action.

"Without a compact organization, having means at command to detect and punish wrong and to protect ourselves against these cases of imposition, we would be in the position of the horseman who locks his doors after the steed was stolen.

"The old adage of 'an ounce of prevention is worth a pound of cure' can be applied with peculiar force to all the stockmen of Colorado.

"The improvement and maintenance of the range requires earnest and immediate attention. We have in Colorado millions of acres of fine grazing lands, capable of subsisting more than ten times the number of cattle now upon them. Artificial means for furnishing stock water for much of this area are urgently needed.

"Steps should also be taken to stock the barren portions with artificial grasses, such as the Alfalfa which is doing so well in California," he said.

"And last, but not least, arrangements must be made with the railroads running through our stock ranges for the annual plowing of a strip of land on either side of the road to prevent the spread of fire, kindled by sparks from the passing locomotives.

"To answer the numerous inquiries that come to us from all parts of the country respecting the soil, climate, water and other advantages for a stock country, a publication of some kind, prepared with special reference to the stock interests of Colorado, should be issued as soon after the adjournment of this meeting as possible.

"I hope I may be pardoned if I speak briefly of the future of the stock-growing interests of Colorado, which are so closely identified with all its great industries that every person here is more or less affected by its success or failure.

"There are many millions of acres within our borders that for many years can only be made available for pasturage. These acres produce natural grasses of such quality that animals are fattened without a kernel of grain, even in the dead of winter.

"So long as the only expense from one year's end to another is only that of herding, stock-growing must continue to be profitable. But I anticipate more than this. In every part of Colorado there is interest in the improvement of stock by the use of thoroughbred males. It is the experience of all who have handled both common and improved stock that the cost of the latter is but slightly in advance of the former, while the profit is in many cases a thousand per cent more."

With these cogent remarks, Bailey concluded his address.

Next he introduced Mr. William E. Pabor, secretary of the Fort Collins Agricultural Society, who delivered a lengthy paper on "The Ranchman and the Colonist." The editor of the Rocky Mountain News regretted that space did not permit its publication.

Dr. H. Latham of Wyoming was then introduced and read a paper on the subject, "Have we Stock Growers Enough?".

He gave a brilliant analysis of the possible trends for the future of the Colorado livestock industry. He painted in glowing terms the rosy outlook for the livestock industry in the territory. He outlined the rapid increase in population since the War, the results of increasing industrialization on the income of the producing classes. All this, he said, indicated an expanding demand for beef, for wool and for horses.

The writer painted a picture of ever-increasing prosperity for the frontier grasslands. He warned only that the stockmen must not expand their production so fast that they would produce more than the market could consume.

He also outlined a plan for increasing the available grazing areas which utilized the high mountain parks on a seasonal basis in the manner now used in grazing leases on the federal lands.

The population growth, the rising trend of immigration, and the increasing practice of corn feeding in the Midwest, he predicted, would all help to expand the demand for Colorado-grown feeders and beef cattle.

There was also a great future in wool production in the West, he said, and quoted figures to show the increasing demand for this fiber. Horses, too, he pointed out, were a type of livestock that the West could raise very profitably. There was a booming demand for horsepower, he stated, to work the new farms being developed in the Midwest areas of Kansas and Nebraska, and the Dakota country.

Dairying, too, presented a bright future, Latham predicted.

He compared the mountain valleys of Colorado with those of Switzerland and New York, and predicted the territory could eventually surpass those areas in the production of butter and cheese.

He urged the stockmen to expand in every field of livestock production, and to expect an ever-increasing demand for their animals and produce.

The final speaker on the program was Judge H. P. Bennett, whose humorous comments on the livestock industry brought much merriment and applause from the audience, the News reported.

It was a typical meeting of stockmen, and it set a pattern that has been followed with surprising similarity for the past nine decades.

By the time this meeting in 1873 had adjourned and the various newspapers of the territory had copied excerpts from the full coverage of the Rocky Mountain News, the Association had begun to attract some attention. It was gradually becoming the spokesman for the livestock industry over a wide area of the Rocky Mountain cattle country.

During the previous year, William Holly and president John Lilley had launched the revitalized group on a substantial basis. Then, when Bailey became president, he and Holly carried on the expansion of the organization.

It was under Bailey and his successor James M. Wilson, that the local county and regional associations began to develop and to work with the Colorado Stock Growers Association. By this time it was obvious that officers of the group considered this organization a territory-wide operation. They immediately cooperated with the new county and district organizations that were being formed, encouraged these efforts and saw from the beginning how these groups could add to the scope and effectiveness of their work.

Holly attended several meetings of the Bent County Stockgrowers and the Southern Colorado organization also, and discussed with them ways that the various groups could work together.

An example of one of the joint projects Holly had in mind is outlined in the following notice which the Association published in the Las Animas Leader on May 23, 1873. Undoubtedly this notice also appeared in other publications in the territory at this time.

Col. Stock-Growers' Assn.
Denver, March 10, 1873.

One of the principal objects of this association being the collection of accurate, reliable statistics, relative to the livestock industry, you are requested to furnish full and complete statistics relating to the following points: The stock brand of each member; present condition of the stock and beef cattle; number of beef cattle for sale; number of stock cattle for sale; number of thoroughbred bulls, and of what breed; number of grade bulls; number of cows kept for dairy purposes; number of thoroughbred stallions without pedigree, but having claims for speed, action, or draft purposes; number of mares kept for breeding purposes; number of sheep; number and breed of pure blood rams; number of grade rams; number of breeding stock farms; number of dairy farms.

Until there shall be established associations looking to the development of bee culture and fish culture in Colorado, it will be appropriate for this association to secure reports and information, and encourage the development of these industries; it is to be hoped that all persons engaged in these branches will furnish their names and statements of what they are accomplishing. It is very essential that a full report of pedigrees of all thoroughbred males and females should be obtained for registration. Owners of breeders will serve their own interest by reporting their births, with names claimed. The information thus obtained will be placed in appropriate books, and will be furnished to such newspapers as desire to publish it. Such statistics as relate to the number of beef and stock cattle held for sale, should be furnished at once, to be of benefit the present season.

It is very necessary that prompt responses should be made either directly to this office or through the office of the county secretaries. By furnishing such information, its circulation both in the territory and at the east can be secured, bringing the advantages of Colorado prominently before the public.

A plan for the publication of a weekly live stock report is being considered. To make this useful and reliable, stock-growers should report sales whenever made, giving number, age, and condition of cattle, and price per pound or per head.

To make the Stock-Growers' association serviceable the active and prompt action of all stockmen is required.

J. L. Bailey, Pres't
W. Holly, Sec'y.

A financial crisis swept the nation in 1873 that started a long decline in cattle prices, but the expanding frontier was not too badly affected.

The Fifth Annual Report of the Denver Board of Trade for the year ending December 31, 1873, had this to say:

"For a territory of 125,000 inhabitants our trade is enormous. Our production is doubtless greater per capita than any other territory!"

The same publication contains the following quotations on livestock prices for the area: Texas cattle (per head), yearlings, $8.00 to 10.00; two-year-olds, 12.00 to 13.00; cows and three-year-olds, 16.00 to 18.00; beef steers, 20.00 to 25.00 per head. American cattle, yearlings, 12.00 to 15.00; two-year-olds, 18.00 to 20.00; three-year-olds and cows, 30.00 to 40.00; extra good milch cows, 50.00 to 70.00; beeves, 35.00 to 40.00 per head. Work oxen, 80.00 to 100.00.

The horse market quoted "Pony or bronco horses, good under saddle and many of them work well, $40.00 to 100.00, American horses, suitable for road or farm work, 125.00 to 200.00 per head; carriage horses at fancy prices."

The next annual convention of the Stock Growers Association, was held on January 20, 1874 in the Exchange rooms of the American House. At this meeting the Rocky Mountain News stated that the official members of the convention consisted of delegates from the various county stock growers associations. The publication failed to list the associations represented, however, and the minutes of the Association do not record this information.

Apparently the various delegates attending did vote as representatives of an area or a group, however, for the meeting had just convened when M. P. P. Wilcox of Douglas County moved that a committee on credentials be appointed. President Joseph L. Bailey, who was presiding, then appointed J. L. Brush of Weld County; J. M. Wilson, Arapahoe County; J. Hutchinson of

Lake County; J. G. Evans, Arapahoe County and P. P. Wilcox to this committee.

The committee retired and after consultation reported back with a resolution that all members of the territorial association and all delegates of county associations be admitted as members of the convention, and be entitled to take part in the proceedings. When this resolution was adopted, a gentleman who said he was not a member of any organization, rose to ask the chair if he would be considered an intruder. The group then passed a qualifying resolution which opened the meeting to all people interested in stock growing, but specifying that only accredited members would be allowed to vote.

This policy has also generally prevailed throughout the balance of the century, for nowhere since that time in the records of the organization has a closed meeting of the members been found.

At this point, the treasurer, A. J. Williams, made his report and stated that the organization had received 29 paid memberships during the previous year at five dollars each, making a total of $145.50 income. Disbursements were $105.10, leaving a total balance in the treasury of $40.40. The extra 50 cents in the fund was not explained, but was possibly a carry-over from the previous year.

President Bailey summarized the general condition of the industry in his report by saying—

"During the past year a panic occurred in the financial world. The effect has been to depreciate the value of all commodities, and has affected the livestock interests most seriously.

"Our cattle and sheep were never in better condition for shipment than during the fall of 1873. The withdrawal of money from use and the shrinkage of values has knocked the bottom out of the market. This has forced owners to sell at a sacrifice or hold over to another year the stock which was ready for market.

"The prospects are that this condition of affairs will speedily change for the better and give stockmen an opportunity to retrieve their losses," he added optimistically.

(Events later proved him wrong and cattle values continued

to slump for the next five or six years, although numbers increased and the industry continued to expand.)

Following the president's optimistic address, J. H. Pinkerton suggested that it might be advisable at this time to discuss some of the livestock measures before the legislature, since a majority of the members of the council and the Territorial Legislature were present at the meeting.

The members concurred and decided to postpone the regular order of business in order to take advantage of the opportunity. Whether a majority of the legislators were present because they were interested in the cattle industry, or there in deference to the political influence of the organization was not explained, but the incident gives an indication of the interest which the Association had aroused among the lawmakers of the period.

The secretary read several bills which had been passed at the recent session of the Wyoming Territorial Legislature in regard to the herding, branding and care of livestock.

A bill introduced by Mr. Hutchinson in the Colorado Legislature was then read and discussed by Brush, Pinkerton and Wilcox. Pinkerton felt that when a stockman left the territory he should vacate his brands.

John Hittson was called on for comment. He declared that he was in favor of sound laws on branding, and that every cattleman should know the brands used by his neighbors and respect their property. He believed that a rigid brand inspection system should be maintained. His vent (or cancellation) brand, he explained, was the letter "S" just above his holding brand, which was placed on every animal that was sold.

Captain Baron, of Hugo, observed that it was very easy to make laws and set up offices, but it was extremely difficult to get men who were capable of filling the positions created. If all men were as capable of filling the job of superintendent of round-ups as Mr. W. H. H. Cranmer there would be no trouble. He knew his business and was a man of judgment and ability. Not all men in such a position of authority were always disposed to be fair and square, he added.

Mr. Bonnifield of Douglas County said that many of the people in his area were opposed to the round-ups last year. Many thieves followed the round-up party and stole stock that had been gathered up, claiming estrays and unbranded stock.

In his opinion, such crooks should be treated summarily on the spot without judge or jury. He urged the setting up of legal provisions which would permit stock owners to control their brand in any county in the territory.

J. G. Evans of Cherry Creek explained that in his neighborhood the stockmen recorded their brands in a local brand book and they also maintained a record of brands of livestock owners in the association. This system worked well for them, but he could not say that it would be successful on a larger scale.

(Editor's Note: Whether Evans referred to a local Arapahoe or Douglas County association is not clear, but the implication would be that he was speaking of an existing local organization, probably Douglas County. These groups were often rather loosely organized at this time and maintained primarily through a local round-up committee, but did get together and send a delegate to the territorial meeting each year. Usually the smaller groups took their name from the local area, such as the Cherry Creek Valley, etc. Over the years these small informal units generally worked with the county or regional organization and these in turn with the territorial or state group. This general pattern of operation was convenient and practical and has continued through the century to the present time. Since very few of these local groups were ever incorporated and were largely dependent on the energy and interest of one or two local leaders, they became active for a number of years, then when the "spark plug" of the organization died or retired they were simply dropped and forgotten. In general, they served a very definite purpose and were an effective channel of communication from the central territorial or state organization down to the local level. They worked equally well from the local level up, also. At the present time many of these small units over the state are still active and cooperate closely with the state Association.)

Judge Sherwood of Larimer County was called on by J. L. Brush to give an account of his experience in conducting round-ups in that county. The judge told his experiences in "graphic style," according to the Rocky Mountain News.

The judge explained that there were some estrays left after all the branded cattle had been sorted out, and that he did not know how these were disposed of. Where two men claimed the same animal he improvised a court and settled the case then and there. But he urged the organization to develop a systematic plan for controlling the round-ups.

Mr. J. A. Kountz of Douglas County stated that he was against round-ups in general, but would not oppose the will of the majority. He inquired about a proposal to finance the round-ups by a property assessment.

Captain Baron said that he was emphatically in favor of continuing the present system and supported the idea of a property assessment to cover the round-up expense. He suggested to Mr. Kountz that the proposition was similar to school matters. Bachelors had to pay a school tax whether they enjoyed the benefits of the schools or not. (This brought a round of laughter).

Mr. Andy Wilson then called on a Mr. Craig to explain the California stock laws. This gentleman was apparently familiar with this matter and spoke at some length.

At this point the familiar figure of Dr. John Parsons rose to make a lengthy statement against the round-up law and the practice of those who had been connected with its operation over the past two years.

Jared Brush then spoke in support of the current law and explained that with experience they were developing modifications to the present system and that it was progressively being made more effective.

Judge Sherwood commented that many of the objections were not with the law itself, but with the abuses practiced by the unprincipled parties who attended these meetings.

John W. Prowers of Bent County rose to tell of the round-up program in his county. He said that people in his section of the territory generally approved the present law with the exception of the estray clause.

The report of the committee on round-ups, headed by J. L. Brush, was read and approved.

While there were opinions for and against the issues discussed, the tone of the meeting was entirely democratic and impartial, with the majority vote of the organization deciding the policies to be carried out.

The final business for the day's meeting was the election of officers. Those named were: J. L. Bailey, president; James M. Wilson, vice president; William Holly, secretary and A. J. Williams, treasurer.

The Rocky Mountain News also listed the following members being elected to the Executive Committee: J. L. Brush, P. P. Wilcox, James M. Wilson, Alfred Butters, J. H. Pinkerton.

However, on the following day the president announced a new Executive Committee along with a number of other committees.

These committees were: Executive Committee: Alfred Butters, A. D. Wilson, J. P. Farmer, J. L. Brush and W. W. Roberts.

Committee on Round-ups: Weld County, J. H. Pinkerton, David Wyatt, L. H. Cole; Arapahoe County, J. P. Farmer, J. M. Wilson, C. C. Gird; Douglas County, A. D. Wilson, W. Bonnifeld, W. H. H. Cranmer.

Committee on Premiums (for Agricultural Show): J. M. Wilson, C. C. Gird, Alfred Butters.

Committee on Range: A. D. Wilson, J. P. Farmer.

Committee on Finance: A. D. Wilson, J. P. Farmer, J. W. Barnes.

During the afternoon session, considerable time was spent discussing the current stock law and the group adjourned about four o'clock.

From the minutes of this meeting it is apparent that the organization was beginning to assume some rather extensive management duties for the entire industry. Its influence in the Territorial Legislature was becoming impressive.

During the next decade it would shape the legal status of the livestock grower and assume an even greater responsibility for the over-all management problems of the industry.

The fact that Credential committees were appointed at each annual meeting of the Association in the early 1870's to qualify the delegates from these local groups indicates a growing number of these organizations. In addition, committee appointments were often listed with each man accredited to certain counties.

It should be mentioned too that these early counties were large areas. Weld County, for example, included the entire northeastern corner of the state all the way from the mountains to the Nebraska line. Bent included the entire southwestern corner of the state, and Arapahoe County included all of its present area, plus the present Jefferson and Adams and extended all the way to the Kansas line. It incorporated most of the present-day Washington and Yuma counties. Douglas County also extended from the foothills all the way to the Kansas line and included much of our present Elbert, Lincoln and Kit Carson counties. In fact most of these early counties were considerably larger than most Eastern states, incorporating many millions of acres.

It was during this period that the land was largely taken up for ranching. Ranch headquarters were being established along the streams throughout eastern Colorado and some of the mountain park areas that were not actually located in the Ute Indian territory.

The individual operations that had been started in a small way in the early part of the decade, had by the latter part of the seventies, begun to assume more impressive size. With increasing size, of course, the unit cost of running cattle declined, and the cattle growers were able to take the decline of prices pretty much in stride.

In fact, President Bailey declared in his address to the membership at the annual meeting in 1875 that the livestock industry was in good shape, no severe losses having occurred during the previous year from either storms or Indians.

Despite a general decline in livestock values during this period, costs were low and beef cattle stayed relatively profitable. It was the era of cow herd build-up for the individual operators that later made their fortunes. However, it was a long, uphill struggle against a great many natural and man-made problems.

In the ten-year period from 1870 to 1880, cattle numbers in the state increased from 291,000 to 809,000 head. Dairy cattle increased from 5,000 head in 1870 to 25,000 head in 1880. Furthermore, at nearly every meeting of the Association during this period, the president included in his annual report a discussion of the dairy industry and its importance to the development of the territory.

The decade of the seventies was also the time of railroad building, and with the railroads came other problems.

At the annual meeting in 1874, the committee on stock laws was directed to insert in the amendments to the stock law a provision for the protection of the range from fire.

Mr. Farmer said that the railroads should be compelled to plow a sufficient stretch of land on each side of their right-of-way for the protection of grass. He said that all stockmen should be interested in securing this protection since, he pointed out, cattle would drift into other ranges when the grass was burned off of the ranges bordering the railroads.

At the same meeting, President Bailey in his opening address to the members said—

"The great loss to the stock interests of the territory annually by the burning of grass in the fall and winter along the railway lines that are started by cinders and sparks from locomotives, should be provided against by a series of furrows parallel to each road. These should be plowed late enough in the season that grass and weeds would not spring up."

He went on from this point to outline another source of trouble from the railroads.

"In the case of stock killed by railroads, the officers of the roads should be required to make a return of the brands of such stock."

This, too, was a growing problem and the Association brought considerable pressure on the legislature to enact a law concerning both of these issues.

As early as February 9, 1872, the Territorial Legislature had enacted a law to provide for payment of stock killed by the railroads. The law specifically made all railroads in the territory liable for such damage and listed the following price schedules for the animals killed.

Texas cattle were set up under the following values per head

—yearlings, $7.00; two-year-olds, 12.00; three-year-olds and cows, 16.00. American cattle had these values defined by law— yearlings, 12.00; two-year-olds, 22.00; three-year-olds and cows, 30.00. American work cattle were listed at 37.50, American sheep at 2.50 and Mexican sheep at 1.50. Half-blood Texas and American stock were to be counted as Texas cattle and three-quarter blood American and Texas cattle were to be counted as American cattle. Thoroughbred cattle, sheep and horses were to be paid for at two-thirds of their actual value.

At the meeting in 1875, Bailey said that many of the railroads had taken some steps to establish fire guards along their rights-of-way, but that the measures taken were still inadequate.

He urged the organization to appoint a special committee to work on this important matter, since the loss of range grass from this cause was a serious concern to all stock growers.

Another significant resolution passed at the close of the 1875 convention was to set up a committee to draft a memorial to the General Land Office urging that the surveyed lands of Colorado, which had been open for pre-emption for three years, be offered for sale. Presumably these were lands which had not been filed on for homestead, or were possibly less desirable lands which had been filed on and not proved up under the provisions of the Pre-Emption Act.

This, of course, was part of the continuing effort to acquire land in order to establish the cattle operations on a more secure basis. It would indicate that efforts were made to buy government land in many cases, and that not all of the stockmen were trying to take over the vacant public lands without due process of law.

New people were coming into the territory and more and more cattle moved up the trail from Texas. Expansion and development of the industry were proceding at a rapid rate.

When the annual convention convened at the City Hall in Denver on January 5, 1876, the president, James M. Wilson, called the meeting to order and looked back with approval on the Association accomplishments for the year.

"I am gratified to know," he said in his opening remarks, "that this body has grown in public estimation at home and abroad, and that its influence and labors have been so beneficial that there has been a universal demand to have the organization continued.

"I feel sure that in the future, as in the past, cattlemen will look upon this Association and its work with pride and satisfaction.

"The past year has been one of great prosperity to the stock interests. An abundance of rain has fallen to make plenty of feed for fattening our beeves and leaving the ranges in good condition for the present winter.

"The class of cattle being grown in Colorado is constantly improving as large numbers of thoroughbred bulls have been brought here. The old Texas stock, from which many of our herds are bred, are being rapidly disposed of. Their places are being taken by the young, improved half-breeds which make an excellent class of beef, both for the home market and for shipping purposes."

Wilson went on to say that the number and value of cattle sold and shipped to the states during the past season had been far in advance of any previous year.

He estimated that at least 60,000 head had been shipped to Eastern markets at an average price of $30.00 each. He said too that the slaughter houses of LeFevre & Powers, and Goodnight & Company, both engaged in butchering and shipping dressed beef, intended to kill and ship 30,000 head of cattle during the coming winter.

He declared that the valuation of Colorado cattle sold in Kansas City during one week reached a total sum of $100,000, as reported in the Kansas City Price Current. How many more were sold in Chicago and other markets, he had no information about, but pointed out that many of the territory's largest shippers sent cattle in that area.

He said one important piece of legislation was greatly needed for the benefit of livestock. This was a law to make an owner's registered brand the prima facie evidence of title, with a provision to compel owners to vent their brand when they sell. This law was of special importance, he declared, since there were very few owners who could identify and swear to their stock except by their brand. This fact made conviction for stealing extremely difficult at the present time.

He called attention to the fact that the condition of the range upon which all their stock must subsist and fatten, was a matter of the greatest importance to all.

"The belief seems to prevail with those who have not watched its steady decline, that our range is unlimited. Now the range of Colorado is large and the feed good, but the idea that it is unlimited and cannot be overstocked is simply nonsense," he declared.

"The sooner we realize this truth the better for ourselves and the country."

"Already large portions of our territory, where cattle used to range and fatten, have become eaten out. No one in these areas can turn their stock out in the fall with any assurance that they will go through the winter with safety, unless they are fed during severe weather."

"Many of the herds from these districts have been moved for this reason. Some have gone east to the Republican and some north to Wyoming. These are facts which cattlemen know to be true. It is well for us to ponder over them and to regulate our business accordingly," he warned.

Wilson continued to say that during the previous two years serious difficulties had arisen between the sheep and cattle interests in various parts of the territory.

Grazing as they both did on the public lands, they were both trespassers on the public domain, he said, and no one could claim any right over the other, unless it be priority of settlement.

Now, he explained, they were both competing in some areas for the same range. These two interests were both of great importance to the country, but they had not one thing in common, save that they were grazing on the same grass. How to get these two groups to work harmoniously with each other, was a question the Territorial Legislature had thrown out because they did not have jurisdiction over the public lands.

It is a question, he declared, that all good, candid, right meaning cattlemen and sheepmen were asking but none could answer.

"When sheep are brought into ranges where cattle have been accustomed to run, the cattle will no longer feed there and will seek other pastures. Hence the cattleman's business is ruined, his property scattered and bad blood the consequence," he said.

"I do not believe that it is right for any cattleman to drive any sheepman away from his home, neither do I believe it is right for any sheepman to drive any cattleman away from his home, no matter what the means used to do the driving. But there are others who talk different and say that the cattlemen must give way and move back somewhere in the wilderness," he continued.

Because of this difference in the two groups, plus the fact that the major portion of the Association's business activities had always been devoted to the problems of the cattle industry, Wilson recommended that the name of the organization be changed to the Colorado Cattle Growers Association.

He explained also that the sheep growers and horse growers had each recently formed an organization of their own. For this reason he felt that the Association should concentrate on its major interest and restrict its membership to those directly concerned with dairy and beef cattle.

He urged cooperation with all groups within the livestock industry and asked the help of each member of the Association in attempting to work out any method for harmonizing the discordant elements.

The secretary, William Holly, then reported on the growing activities of the organization, and described the new offices which were located in the rooms of The Colorado Farmer, a general agricultural publication which Holly published.

During the year, he said, several thousand cattlemen from Colorado, Wyoming, New Mexico and Texas had been made welcome. Scarcely a day passed without a visit from some Eastern cattlemen, buyers or prospective settlers inquiring for facts, figures and statements to guide them in their future plans.

Accurate statistics and general facts about the growing cattle industry within the territory were almost impossible to procure, he said, but there was a great need for this type of information.

A committee, consisting of Holly, Williams and Farmer, then

presented a new set of articles and by-laws for the Association, as recommended by the president.

Article One defined the purpose of the organization—"for the mutual benefit and protection of persons engaged in raising or dealing in cattle and the development and encouragement of breeding, raising and marketing cattle," and specified that the Association be called the Colorado Cattle Growers Association.

Article Two limited membership to any person engaged in raising and dealing in cattle.

Dues were reduced to one dollar per year, but each member was to sign the Articles of Association and pledge himself to answer any and all calls for support and assistance by any member of the Association, when needed.

During this early decade the basic tenets of the organization were developed, many of which are maintained today. In essence, the principle of open membership to anyone engaged in any phase of the cattle business, open meetings, the accredited member delegate who speaks for his local association, and the standing committee principle of handling special phases or projects, are all standard practice in this century, much as they were established then.

So active was the organization during this period that the celebrated Joseph G. McCoy, early historian of the cattle industry, made specific reference to the Colorado Association in his book, "Historic Sketches of the Cattle Trade," which was published in 1874. McCoy had this comment after a visit to Denver in the fall of 1873.

"Perhaps in no state or territory in the Union are the stockmen so wide awake to their interests, or so completely organized, as in Colorado, where there now exists the leading state or territorial organization of stock-growers, the president of which Association is Joseph L. Bailey of Denver. The secretary, by whose exertions more than that of any other man, the Association was formed and is kept alive in effective beneficial working order, is William Holly of Denver, a man of fine energy and abilities, and one who takes special delight in performing all the duties and kind offices which his position or opportunities place within his power. He has rendered great service to the livestock men and their interests in Colorado, and deserves well at their hand."

By 1879 the legal status of the Association was firmly established, too, as the official representative of the industry. Over the years, the organization and management of the round-ups had gradually been improved. Through the efforts of the Association, a state round-up law was passed which divided the state into specified round-up districts. Special provisions were made also for handling money collected from railroads for the killing of unbranded cattle or mavericks, whose ownership had not been established.

This 1879 statute makes an interesting provision for this money. It specifies that damages for the killing of cattle by railroads whose ownership was not definitely established were to be paid to the treasurer of the district cattle growers association.

The same statute also disposed of all mavericks and unbranded cattle which were unclaimed at the round-ups in a similar manner. If the ownership of the cattle was established within six months, the animals could be returned to the owner. If not, then the cattle could be sold and the money went to the general fund of the district cattle growers association. From this it would seem that the establishment of county and district round-ups had progressed rapidly from their first beginnings in 1872 and 1874.

This was the era of the so-called "cattle king," if there were men who deserved the title. The newspapers of the period were fond of the term and often applied it to John W. Iliff. Others mentioned frequently as "range kings" or cattle kings were John Hittson, Finis P. Ernest, J. L. Brush, John W. Prowers and from time to time, the term was used in connection with Hiram S. Holly, James C. Jones or any person the journalist using the term wanted to flatter.

At any rate, the cowmen of this period were remarkable individuals. Most of the men prominent in the organization at this time had started early, some as far back as the early 1860's, and built their operations from practically nothing.

They had gone into a frontier that was only wilderness, they had located a ranch, built their headquarters and working corrals, bought a few foundation cattle and slowly built up their herds.

Hardship, high risk and often great personal danger had been their lot. Indians, severe storms, drouth and cattle thieves had made the fight a long and sometimes bloody one. But, it was the story of their success that caught the imagination and the admiration of the world. The extent of this public captivation with the story of the cow business is apparently undiminished today—nearly a century later.

This decade was theirs—the 1880's belonged to the big cattle companies. But it was the glamour of the 1870's that made the day of the big cattle companies possible. It made every man yearn to be a part of this exciting business, and Eastern stock promoters took full advantage of it.

Colorado cattle company stocks sold like the proverbial hot cakes in London and Edinburgh as well as Boston and New York. It was during this easy money period of the early 1880's that many of the self-made cowmen cashed in. The agents and the promoters came to Colorado looking for land, cattle and colorful "front men" for their paper empires.

In 1877, a new secretary was elected to replace the capable William Holly. The new man was Capt. Samuel E. Wetzel, a native of Pennsylvania and a former Union officer in the 29th Indiana Volunteers.

Wetzel left the Army on December 15, 1865 and began investing in cattle. When he came to Colorado in 1873 he already had property here and began ranching as a full time occupation upon arrival in the state.

Wetzel was an organizer in contrast to Holly whose talents lay in promotion. The rapid expansion of the cattle business in the state had multiplied the problem of controlling and inspecting cattle brands.

When he joined the Association, this was becoming a major concern of the organization. The task of issuing and maintaining records on brands and who was officially credited with the right to use each was getting critical.

The early brand laws in the state followed the practice in Texas of recording brands with the county clerk. This meant that the same brand could be issued to another man in the next county. Since cattle were not respecters of county lines, or state lines either, there were frequent mix-ups, disputes and occasionally shootings over the matter.

Wetzel was in an ideal spot to direct and organize this effort and he began to compile an authentic record of cattle brands in the state with the name and address of each owner. His first list was a handwritten book containing some 165 pages of brands, notes and owner's addresses. This document is still preserved in the archives of the State Brand Board, and was the basis for the first state brand book published in 1885.

Shortly after assuming the position of secretary of the Colorado Cattle Growers Association, Wetzel was also designated the first State Brand Commissioner. In this capacity he started the first move to organize and classify the cattle brand recording system of the state of Colorado.

This was a major contribution to the livestock industry of the state. It laid the foundation for the present State Board of Brand Commissioners and a state brand recording system that is considered the most efficient in the nation today.

This was just one of the many accomplishments of the organization in this eventful decade. By the time the 1880's arrived, the cattle industry had passed from a frontier operation to a major industry. In ten years the number of cattle in the state had increased from 291,000 in 1870 to 809,000 in 1880.

The state was growing too, and the population went from a mere 39,864 in 1870 to 194,327 in 1880—an increase of nearly 500%.

It was a time of self-made men, and the president elected in 1877, Joseph P. Farmer, was a typical example. Farmer was born in Ireland and came to Colorado as a young man in 1860. Like many of the other early settlers, he tried mining with very little success. He first started a ranch on the Cache la Poudre, relocated a couple of times and then built up a good ranch on Bijou Creek near the town of Byers.

His operation here consisted of 800 acres which controlled the creek for nearly five miles. In 1877 he moved to another ranch near Kit Carson where he ran nearly 5,000 head of cattle.

The ranch at Byers was changed to a sheep ranch and he ran some 7,000 head of sheep on this outfit.

Farmer served one term as president of the Association in 1877. He died on December 31, 1878, at the age of 36. At the Association meeting a few weeks later, the group passed a memorial lamenting the loss of a capable and much loved member of the industry.

The next president, Alfred Butters, was a former schoolteacher who also came to Colorado in 1860. He settled on Cherry Creek in Douglas County, about 20 miles from Denver, and for eight years worked at farming, barely able to eke out a living. He turned to cattle raising and eventually built up a large herd. His range lay between Cherry Creek and Box Elder Creek, and for many years he was in partnership with C. C. Gird, a long-time member of the Stockgrowers Executive Committee. He moved to Denver in 1871 and was an active member of the Association. He served one term in the Territorial Legislature, was speaker of the House and president pro tem of the first Colorado Legislature, then was elected to four terms as State Senator.

It is interesting to note that Farmer was an active Democrat and a leader in that party, owning a controlling interest in the Denver Daily Democrat at the time of his death.

Butters on the other hand was a dedicated Republican and equally active in that party. It was largely through Butters' support that the legislation was passed which established the State Board of Brand Commissioners and the state round-up laws.

These were the men who directed the course of the Colorado Cattle Growers Association through the seventies—the founding years when many of the basic principles of the group were established. It was a time of vast growth within the cattle industry, and a decade of rapid maturity for the organization.

CHAPTER SIX

THE ROUND-UPS

Gathering cattle and branding were two of the biggest jobs involved in running livestock from 1870 to 1900, during the period that the open range lasted.

If seized with wanderlust, a range cow could take off in a straight line and go for miles across the grasslands of eastern Colorado during those early years of the cattle business. To find her, and her calf, often led a rider over a lot of country, riding a "wide circle" as the round-up boss directed.

Fortunately, most cattle have always been practical animals and as long as they had grass, water, and some shelter in one particular place, they generally stayed put. Storms, drouth, or the movement of a big trail herd were about the only things that caused a particular bunch of animals to stray from a general location. Aside from cattle thieves, that is.

In the 1860's, when herds were few and far between, each man generally was able to gather his own animals about twice a year—in the spring, for branding and putting cattle back on their own ranges, and in the fall, for sorting off the beef end of the herd that would go to market.

As more and more of the better meadows and bottom lands were taken up and additional ranch headquarters established, cattle numbers increased and there was a greater tendency for cattle from one herd to mix with another.

This made the job of cutting out the strays from each herd a bigger problem every year. The logical solution was for the ranchers in a general area to get together and stage a cooperative round-up, starting at a previously agreed upon time and place.

The round-up basically was as simple as that. However, as more ranches were established and the cattle business expanded, more men were involved. Management of these increasingly bigger round-ups became a problem and incurred legal considerations and more executive ability.

Discussions about the most effective way to handle and direct the round-ups became one of the major topics at the early Association meetings, particularly in the 1870's.

It was logical, therefore, that the Association should become the instrument for planning, directing, and managing these major group activities within the industry.

There were many problems encountered in getting a round-up organized and a lot more came up when it was under way. In the first place, there was a great deal of money involved.

A man's right to claim ownership of a particular animal was based almost entirely on the legibility of a brand burned on the rib or hip. When a brand is not put on properly it is difficult to read. If not burned deep enough, or when the iron was too cold, very little scar tissue was formed on the skin. Later, this brand would "hair over" during cold weather or gradually fade out with age and be difficult to read.

If the iron was too hot, or held on too long, the resulting brand might "blotch" and become an illegible mark that is easy to see but difficult to decipher.

Sometimes, two brands that were somewhat similar could look very much alike under these conditions. Quite frequently, therefore, there could be two owners claiming the same animal when the collected herd was being "cut" and the cattle for the various ranch herds were being sorted off.

At this time, the round-up captain for that district was the chief arbiter. His decision was final. Sometimes he made the decision himself, sometimes he might appoint a small group of cattlemen to act as jurors and conduct a horseback court.

By the late 1870's, the Association-sponsored round-up law had established the legal procedure for this state-wide round-up. This law set up a system of 16 round-up districts with specified boundaries. The governor was directed to appoint three commisisoners for each district, on or before the first of March of each year. It was the duty of these commisisoners to arrange the program for the annual spring round-up in their district by the first of April, to fix the date for starting the round-up, and to hire the round-up foremen or remove them for incompetency, neglect of duty, or any other reason deemed sufficient.

The law specified that the foremen were to receive three dollars per day for their services.

The lack of organization, and the absence of any legal backing for the district captains and the foremen of the round-ups, during the early territorial days, were probably the two principal reasons for the dissatisfaction with round-ups in general during that time.

As each stockman grew more familiar with the general plan of the yearly round-ups, the operation became more efficient. By the late seventies, it was generally agreed that they were the only practical way to gather cattle in large numbers over wide-spread areas of range land.

The round-up regulations of the 1870's show a progressive development from the first law passed in 1872, into the law that was finaly amended and reached workable form in the session of 1881.

In 1872, the legal power for the round-up call had been delegated to the county commissioners. The statutes passed that year specified that these officials had the power to order cattle to be gathered together and rounded up at such a time and place that was convenient and desirable to the stock owners of the county.

The commisisoners were also authorized to set up such rules and regulations for the round-ups, appoint persons to take care of all unclaimed and unbranded stock, and pay these persons from the sale of estray animals. Public notice for 30 days prior to the round-up was specified.

By 1876, the law had been amended to specify that the commissioners could call such round-ups "on request," generally by the state or district stock-growers associations. It was about this time, too, that these district organizations were designated to receive the money from the sale of the estrays and also the money for damages paid by the railroads for killing of unbranded or unclaimed cattle. Such designation by law established the legal standing of the district organizations as well as the state cattlemen's Association at this time. By the early eighties, the state Association had also been designated the custodian of the estray fund, inasmuch as they were doing the brand inspection work for the state and maintaining a central record of the brands held by the members of the organization.

Because of the broad expanse of open range, and the sparsely settled nature of the territory, the administration of the round-ups and the problem of cattle stealing were the two main issues at nearly every meeting of the Association during the middle seventies.

It was during the early development period that many debates occurred at Association meetings on the value of the round-ups. The faction opposing round-ups were the small operators along the foothills and near the larger towns. Those along the Platte and fairly close to Denver, ran numbers of dairy cattle and "American" stock. These people had very little trouble gathering their cattle, which were more domesticated and inclined to stay close to home, where feed was available.

The spokesman for this group at the Association meetings

was Dr. John Parsons. Parsons, at this time, was operating a dairy farm on the South Plattle River, somewhere between the present location of the Denver Union Stockyards and the town of Brighton.

Parsons was against round-ups in general, and his objections were understandable. His dry cows and yearlings probably tended to range a little farther than his milk cows and calves. They may have mixed with beef herds as they were running on the prairie, and were gathered up and taken along to the sorting areas when the round-ups were conducted, usually in the late spring and fall.

His comment that his cattle ended up 20 miles farther away from home after the round-up than they were before, was undoubtedly true.

On the other hand, the stockmen running large herds out on the eastern plains had no other method of gathering their cattle. If a cow got an urge to see what was over the horizon, there was nothing to stop her travels, except lack of feed and water.

Furthermore, there was comparatively little shelter in the plains country of eastern Colorado. When a storm blew in, many of the cattle would simply drift with the storm until something in their way stopped them. In many cases, this meant they went all the way to the Arkansas River before they hit a barrier of any kind.

For this reason the older and larger operators were all for the general round-up practice. Since cattle numbers were increasing rapidly during this time an organized program of round-ups soon became a necessity.

The Association took on the task of getting the huge program under way, and Jud Brush, as chairman of the Round-up Committee, was the ramrod for this effort.

The Round-up Law of 1881 was, in effect, the culmination of a long series of efforts on the part of the Association and its members to get a sound legal basis for operating the round-ups and providing for a system of brand inspections, at the same time.

It directed the Governor to appoint, on or before the first of May of each year, five commissioners, each from a different section of the state, to be known as the Board of Inspection Commissioners. Each was to be an actual owner of cattle running upon the public range.

It was the duty of this board to employ competent cattle inspectors, not exceeding eight in number at any one time, and to distribute them at various points in the state to prevent the illegal slaughtering or shipping of cattle.

They were to furnish each inspector with a list of brands owned by residents of the state, for the purpose of identifying the various owners of cattle involved in the round-ups. The inspectors were to be subject to such rules and requirements as the board directed, and were to be paid not more than $100 per month.

Another clause in the statute, directed that a levy be made on all taxable property in the state amounting to 1/15th of one mill on each dollar of assessed valuation, and that this money was to be kept in a special inspection fund and be used to pay the expenses and salaries of the inspectors.

Although a later Board of Stock Inspection Commissioners was set up for the purpose of maintaining brand inspectors around the state, this appears to have been the predecessor for the present board. However, the bill made no provisions for setting up a permanent body for this purpose and a new board was appointed each year, usually from a list of candidates suggested by the cattle growers Association.

It was not until 1885, that the first official state brand book was published. In the meantime, the Association published its own brand book, but this was confined to brands owned by members of the organization. At this time, also, the Association was paying its own brand inspectors and range detectives for the apprehension of cattle thieves.

As a result of the continuing efforts of the Association, however, the round-ups gradually became a relatively smooth-working operation. During the early 1880's, they undoubtedly reached their peak, for after 1886, they began to decline and, as more and more homesteads were taken up and more fences installed, the state-wide round-ups became less practical.

In their heyday, the round-ups were impressive affairs, and

the few eyewitness accounts that survive that period paint a fascinating picture of a long-forgotten phase of the industry.

Some of the largest round-ups in the state were run in District Seven in the southeastern part of the state, along the Arkansas River. Another big round-up in Districts Ten, Eleven and Nine, usually started at Julesburg and worked up both sides of the South Platte River to Greeley. Parts of both of these groups then worked up the Sand and Bijou creeks, into the Bijou Basin and Kiowa country as far as Cherry Creek.

The District Seven area lay north of the Arkansas River from the state line west to about the present position of Hugo, then up the Big Sandy to River Bend and Simla, south on the present El Paso and Pueblo County lines to the Arkansas River and down the river to the state line.

This was a big area that carried a lot of cattle and the round-up in this district was one of the largest in the entire West. For management purposes it was generally divided into four sections, with a foreman for each area.

In the spring of 1886, Governor Benjamin A. Eaton, a stock-grower and an active member of the Association, appointed Hiram S. Holly, Myron W. Jones, and W. S. Pugsley as Round-up Commisisoners for the district. The foremen they appointed to ramrod the round-up in the four sections of the district were: Charles Reynolds (who had previously been foreman of the Double S ranch owned by Holly until he sold out in 1882 to a British syndicate), I. Dedman, W. A. Wagoner, and Jack Lyons.

When the wagons gathered near the old Holly ranch headquarters, near the site of the present-day town of Holly, there were between 25 and 30 wagons pulled into the camp area, along the river bottom.

Each wagon had a cook and usually a helper to chop wood, run errands, and do other chores. The cook furnished grub at all hours for 10 to 20 cowpunchers. The number of riders varied somewhat with the distance the round-up was working from the home range of each outfit, with the number of cattle being worked, and with the size of the territory to be covered.

A chuckwagon that wasn't feeding too big a crew usually took in a few "reps" from other outfits that were a long way from home, expecting the return of the favor when the round-ups moved into other districts where they had only one or two "reps" to represent them.

Each rider also had a string of horses, normally from six to ten mounts. This meant that each wagon had a "cavy-yard" (a corruption of the Spanish caballado) of horses that could run from 60 to 100 or more animals.

A couple of young boys usually went along to wrangle the horse string. They saw that they were grazed during the day, watered, and readily available when the riders needed fresh horses, day or night.

The ranch foreman of the outfit furnishing the wagon, was generally the ramrod for that particular wagon. He, in turn, took his orders from the round-up foreman in that area, then directed his men in the country they were assigned to cover.

The yearly campaign was thoroughly planned ahead of time by the three commissioners, and each stockman in the district would be notified of the over-all program, including the number of men he would be expected to supply in each area. As a result, nearly every man had a pretty good working knowledge of the round-up plan well in advance.

Camp was generally moved from six to ten miles per day, always to a pre-determined spot. The cattle gathered in the day's drive would be headed toward the camp area and there "cut" into herds by brands. If a large number of cattle was gathered in one day, an extra day might be taken at one camp area while the main herd was worked and the cattle belonging to the local outfits on that range were cut out. Many of the round-up captains preferred to gather cattle in the morning and cut in the afternoon.

The older and more experienced hands did most of the cutting, since reading a brand quickly and accurately was a job that took a lot of experience. The men who did this work for each outfit usually had two or three special cutting horses in their string, trained for this type of work. Both the horses and the men became highly skilled at this cutting job and developed an uncanny ability to spot their own cattle among a milling herd of several thousand head.

Not only were top cutters expert at reading brands—both their own and their neighbors — but they developed a remarkable ability to spot their employer's cattle by conformation, markings, and other characteristics, such as head shape, the twist of the horns, and even behavior. This was possible because a stockman generally tried to buy bulls that were all of the same breeding. As a result, the calves in his herd were stamped with the same "family" characteristics. A good cowman familiar with a herd can spot these features quite easily, even today.

Visit a large, modern commercial cattle outfit and the owner can often point out most of the 20 to 25 calves from a particular bull, even though they may be running in a herd of several hundred head of cows and calves.

In the early days of crossbreeding with Durham or Shorthorn bulls on Longhorn cows, the same characteristics would usually be distinguishable to the men who were working the cattle all the time. Naturally, these men were proud of their skill and the training of their horses. (The ability and the teamwork of a trained cutting horse and rider can be seen today in the cutting contests held at most stock shows and rodeos. These surviving features of those old-time round-up operations still persist in the cow-country of the West.)

The spring round-ups ordinarily did not move as fast as the fall round-ups because of the young calves and the need to brand as the herd was gathered. In some of the round-ups, the bigger ranches sent a separate wagon and branding crew along that took over the ranch herd as it was gathered, branded and tallied the calves, steered the bull calves, and then trailed cows and calves back to the home range.

The Iliff outfit was one of the first ones to adopt this practice when the round-up moved through their range—an area that covered a large part of the land north of the South Platte River from Julesburg to Greeley and up to the Wyoming line. Jud Brush had a big outfit later in this country with his headquarters place about ten miles west of the present town of Sterling, Colorado. He, too, followed the same practice.

With all this activity going on, the round-ups were some-

times an enormous project. Moving camp would involve thousands of cattle, hundreds of horses, plus numerous wagons, each
carrying bedrolls and "warbags" holding extra clothes and personal gear for the men in their outfit, plus enough food and
supplies to run for several weeks. One report said more than
50 wagons met for the start of the round-ups in eastern Colorado during the early eighties.

Sometimes, a half-broke team hitched to a chuck wagon
would spook and run away with the outfit, scattering bedrolls,
equipment, and supplies all along the trail. If the wagon was
broken in the excitement, the riders had to "rustle" grub from
some other friendly outfit until the repairs were made, or a replacement wagon could be obtained.

One young rider, arriving at his first round-up camp down
on the Arkansas, said there were more than 30 campfires going
at dusk, with men riding in from all directions. In the area
surrounding camp for several miles, half-a-dozen separate herds
were being held until they could be started back to their home
range.

In general, the night herders stood a two-hour watch starting about ten o'clock in the evening, after the herd had pretty
well settled down for the night. This probably varied with the
personal preferences of the individual foreman, however, and
the plans of the round-up captain in that particular area.

Oftentimes, too, the round-up would be split into two or more
groups to work different areas, and then meet at some pre-
arranged location farther up the river. It seems to have been
a general practice in eastern Colorado, to work up-stream in
most of the valleys. This was because the cattle tended to
drift down the various river and creek valleys, and follow the
line of least resistance as they grazed.

During the decade of the big round-ups in the state, from
about 1875 to 1886, it was usually the custom to start a big
round-up from Holly, and work the entire outfit west along the
Arkansas River and north to the Chivington Battleground on
the Big Sandy and the Sheridan Lake area. Here the round-up
would split, with one-half going up the Big Sandy and working
as far north as the divide between the South Fork of the Re-

publican River and the Big Sandy. The other group would work up Rush Creek to the present location of Calhan and Simla, and then turn north to meet the first group at River Bend, then a major shipping point on the Kansas Pacific railroad.

As it was then managed, the personnel of the round-up was changing constantly. Each outfit furnished a chuck or "mess" wagon as it was frequently called in this state. This was probably due to the influence of the U. S. Cavalry, who were quite active in the area. A great many of the cowhands in Colorado were former horse soldiers who persisted in using military slang.

While the chuck wagon for a particular ranch was with the round-up, from 10 to 20 men from that outfit would be working. Then, as the round-up moved out of their territory, the wagon and some of the men would head back to the ranch headquarters, taking with them the cattle bearing their brand that had been cut out of the main herd as they were gathered each day.

The way this worked, the round-up captain would assign each foreman a general area. He and his men would head out at daylight to "ride a big circle" in that area so that his men were strung out in fan shape, and then work back toward the round-up camp, gathering all the cattle in that territory with them as they came.

Sometimes, this big circle might involve a large area covering a good many square miles. Then, one or two wagons would be assigned to go along, if the swing would take several days before the men and cattle would again meet the main round-up at a future camping place.

It was hot, hard riding from dawn to dusk, with frequent night herd duty thrown in. During good weather, things could be interesting and pleasant. During storms and cold weather, however, it could be tough going that was hard on men, horses, equipment, and cattle. Some men, working as "reps", would be out on round-ups for months at a time.

During drouth years, when cattle were in poor condition, death losses could be substantial if the animals were not handled with considerable care. On at least two occasions, the big round-ups were cancelled because of poor range conditions when severe drouth hit the country.

The dry years of 1880 and 1885, were two instances when the round-ups were discontinued in certain areas. The next year, when conditions improved and cattle could again be gathered, cattle were found scattered all over the country.

The Iliff Cattle Company (an organization formed by Mrs. Iliff after John Iliff's death in 1878) reported that some of their cattle were recovered as far south as Texas and the Oklahoma Territory in 1881, after the 1880 round-up had been cancelled the year before.

Irresponsible cowboys were sometimes hard on stock too. A special warning was put out by the round-up commisisoners prior to the round-up in 1886, concerning the effects of the rough handling of stock during the dry year of 1885. It was estimated that the death loss in some areas, during that year, had run as high as five per cent because of rough handling or "chousing" of the cattle that were in poor condition due to the lack of feed.

Another round-up was called off because of an epidemic of Texas Fever near Hugo, Colorado, in the fall of 1884. At that time, it was not known that ticks were carrying the disease, nor that when the cattle were crowded together the ticks were rubbed off from one animal to another, thus spreading the infection.

The cattlemen's associations frequently made arrangements to gather cattle during the round-ups for widows or small farmers who could not attend the round-up in person. Generally, a charge of two dollars was made for this assistance, the money going into the estray fund or being used to defray the expenses of the round-up operation.

When John W. Iliff died in the fall of 1878, the Association voted to gather Mrs. Iliff's cattle for her in tribute to her husband's support of the Association in years past. This happened on numerous other occasions, when men were ill or in bad straits, or in the case of widows of stockmen in the region.

Because of the size of the round-ups, and the action around the herd when it was being worked while cattle carrying various brands were being cut out, the scene attracted a great many sightseers, drifters and loafers. It finally became a general practice in certain areas, particularly in the Southern Colorado Cattlemen's Association area, to charge fifty cents a day for grub provided to anyone who was not an authorized "rep" or a working member of an outfit running a chuck wagon.

Unless special provisions could be made for these "tourists", they were pretty generally discouraged. However, in 1875, the end of the round-up at the Wilson ranch, near the present location of Agate, was the scene of a special celebration, planned by the Colorado Cattle Growers Association for the townspeople of Denver.

The following excerpts, from the reporter's stories that ran in The Daily Tribune that week, tell the story pretty well:

"June 18, 1875
The Round Up at Wilson's Ranch.
A Rare Old Time.
The Work of the Herdsmen.
The Round Up on Wednesday.
"The round-up of cattle on the range about Wilson's ranch, commenced on Tuesday. About 3,000 cattle were rounded up on Wednesday. Over 150 men and some 300 horses were employed in doing this. A few days ago about 3,500 head were rounded up at Holdt's ranch. The work commenced on the 20th of May, and will continue until the 12th of July, by which time all of the thousands of cattle roaming the vast plains of the Territory, will have been gathered together. There have been already over 105,000 head rounded up since the commencement of the season's work.

"A Round Up
"To the readers of the Tribune it is hardly necessary to describe a round up, for most of them have witnessed the proceeding, and those who have not should avail themselves of the first opportunity that affords for so doing. But to those who have not the privilege of observing for themselves, we may remark that at certain stated periods all stockmen assemble for the purpose of gathering the cattle that graze upon the ranges and thereby enabling each stockman to collect those animals that are designated as belonging to him by the brand they bear. The process is something like this: At an early hour after breakfast a detail of men is sent by the foreman, who, by the way, is an

experienced herdsman, employed to superintend the whole enterprise, toward the head of some running stream, where the cattle are sure to congregate, for the purpose of driving them to a certain given point, where herds from other points are also congregated, for men are sent by all directions to gather up and drive the grazing cattle to a general locality. This is called round-up. When this has been done each stockman rides into the herd, and aided by his followers, selects such cattle as bear his brand, and takes them to a given point until all bearing his brand are gathered together in one bunch. This is called

CUTTING OUT,

and it is just at this point that the fun of the whole thing comes in, for it is not the easiest thing in the world to drive a stubborn steer out from among his followers and to the particular point selected for him to occupy until the whole herd can be selected. If any one thinks so just let him try for himself, or go over to Londoner Bros., corner of Blake and Fifteenth Streets, and ask Wolfe to tell them his experience."

(Editor's Note: This editorial aside refers to the fact that Wolfe Londoner, the sociable Mayor of Denver, took with him to the party, a generous supply of staples including 17 gallons of his best brandy, two barrels of whiskey, besides cigars, pipes, pickles and miscellaneous items. Another prominent supply house in Denver, the firm of Schaffer & Hibschle, also contributed a half-dozen kegs of lager beer for the benefit of the excursionists.)

"Evening's Entertainment

"After the day's work had been ended, the ladies and gentlemen who had been driven out in wagons to witness the round up, returned to the ranch of their host and were soon joined by the herdsmen themselves. A sumptious supper was provided by the Messrs. Wilsons, of which all partook freely. Afterward, when night fell, and the stars shone low and bright, campfires were lighted and those from the different camps gathered about the ranch. A couple of kegs of beer were opened, and then a number of gentlemen from abroad were called upon to "say their say." In response, short speeches were made by Messrs. Smith, Miller, Bacon, Holly, Col. Howell, of the Tribune and others.

"Music and the Dance

"Then a fine string band struck up, and all joined in the dance, and under the starlight and the moonlight danced away the small hours, while others spread their blankets and buffalo robes underneath the cottonwood trees, and were sent into the arms of morpheus, enjoying the sweet sleep of the weary and the just.

"Wm. Holly's Part

"The excursion which afforded so many novices, such genuine pleasure, was planned and organized by Mr. Wm. Holly, of the Farmer, and Secretary of the Colorado Stock Growers' Association, to whom the thanks of the excursionists are due and were graciously rendered. The wants of the party were anticipated in every direction and in every particular.

"Grasshoppers Leaving the Plains

"A noticeable feature of the ride over the plains, was the conspicuous absence of grasshoppers. We were told that the varmints had been gradually disappearing for some days, and were now almost entirely gone. Perhaps they thought they might be rounded up with the other inhabitants of the plains, and that speedy departure was necessary to their future salvation. But here, seriously, let us remark that while the agricultural interests of the Territory have suffered so greviously by the ravages of the grasshopper plague, the cattle interest has proved correspondingly prosperous. The loss of one interest is counterbalanced by the gain of the other, and thus the prosperity of the territory continues accordingly.

"Condition of the Cattle

"It was generally remarked by the stockmen with whom we conversed that never before have cattle at this season of the year been found in such excellent condition. Some of the cattle were literally as fat as butter."

On Saturday, this final wrap-up of the series appeared as the exhausted reporter penned his last note of the event:

"We promised yesterday, to truthfully record our experience in 'cutting out' at the recent 'round up', at Wilson's ranch. Our intentions were perfectly honorable; if any one doubts it let them ask Wolfe Londoner. But Londoner, even, doesn't know how tired we are. Frankly, we have not slept for forty-eight hours—(Londoner's brandy will keep any man awake for forty-eight hours!)

"And then what's the use of telling people how they took us for a man who couldn't ride a bronco, and how we did ride, and lassoed the bull, and afterward went into the herd and 'cut out' the heifer. No, no, life is too short. We did our duty like a man, and we are not to be blamed if we did not meet the expectations of those other 'fellows'. Farewell!"

Similar excursions were set up in later years, during the spring round-up season, one being held with the Burlington &

Missouri Railroad at Brush, Colorado, in June of 1884. These were the first "good-will" and promotion efforts of the cattle growers' Association. They were organized to show the press and the citizens of Denver some of the activities of the cattle industry.

Not all of them were on the scale of the big 1875 party, but from all indications, most of the special excursion trains were well filled.

Although information is scarce on the handling of "horse round-ups," the Association meeting of January, 1885, discussed this matter at length, and prepared a bill to submit to the state legislature on the sale of unbranded horses found at large on the range.

The bill provided that all horse stock found running at large in the state without a mother, and upon which there was neither a mark nor a brand, should be taken in charge by the captain or foreman of a "legal horse round-up." These animals were then to be sold, at such time and place, and in such manner, as determined by the executive committee of the district association of cattle growers in the district where the horses were taken up.

The money for such sales was to be paid into the treasury of the Association. If the stock was claimed and identified within six months, the approved owner was to receive the money paid for his animals. If not, then the money was to go into the general fund of the district cattle growers' organization.

At the same meeting, it was also directed that three horse growers be added to the Executive Committee to assure representation of this branch of the livestock industry.

An amendment to the constitution of the Association was passed which empowered the Executive Committee to levy an assessment of up to one cent per head on horses and cattle to defray the expense of the various Association activities.

At the same time, a list of names was approved for submission to the Governor for appointment as inspectors. They were: J. L. Brush, Greeley; F. P. Ernest, Deer Trail; R. W. Moore, West Las Animas; Oli Haley, Bear River; George H. Adams,

San Luis; George W. Thompson, Trinidad; and L. R. Tucker, Denver. (Although the newspaper account lists these men nominated as "inspectors," they may have been named by the Governor as Inspection Commissioners after the new Brand Law was passed in the session of the legislature which followed.)

Later that year, 1885, the first state brand book was published. It was a large, leather-bound volume containing a number of advertisements to help pay the expense of the effort, and it marks the first official recognition of all the brands then recorded in the state.

Earlier in this same meeting, the members of the Association had outlined the provisions of the bill. It passed later and established the state brand recording system under the office of the Secretary of State.

It required all owners of cattle and horses to record their brands with the county recorder for a fee of 25c, and also with the Secretary of State for an additional fee of 50¢. It provided, however, that the county recording was temporary and could not be used by the applicant until the brand was approved by the state official. This was to prevent duplication and the subsequent problems of having one brand used by several people.

The 1885 and 1886 brand books do show many duplicate brands, due to the fact that recordings were made by county clerks who were unable to check duplications in other parts of the state. Gradually, however, most of these conflicts were eliminated and a system developed to prevent the inadvertent issue of duplicate brands.

All of these actions facilitated the identification of brands by the round-up captains, and gave better control over the disposition of branded animals during the progress of the round-up work.

The previous brand books used by the round-up captains had been issued by the cattle growers' Association, which listed only the members of the organization. Some of the local associations also published brand books, at about this time, but these too, only displayed the brands used by their members.

By supporting the bill for the establishment of a state brand board and the publication of a state-wide recording system, the Association made a major contribution to all owners of livestock in the state.

The first brand book issued by the Secretary of State was a formidable volume containing more than 50,000 individual brands. The large number of duplications revealed immediately the weakness in the previous practice of having each county clerk issue brands for his county. Some of the simpler brands were being legally used in nearly every county in the state. Since cattle were no respecter of county lines, the results were obvious.

In time, many of the duplicate brands were eliminated, and an improved filing system developed which made it easier to check for identical brands before another was issued. By the turn of the century, the Colorado system of brand registration and inspection was generally recognized as one of the most effective in the West.

Even after the State of Colorado had taken over most of the brand inspection work and the handling of brand registration, the Association continued to supplement the efforts of the state inspectors.

The close relationship between the Association and the State Board of Inspection Commissioners, is brought out in the minutes of the Executive Committee for June 4, 1884.

These interesting resolutions were unanimously adopted:

"That the State Board of Inspection Commissioners be requested to instruct the State Inspectors that inspect the cattle killed on the railroads to extend their inspection outside of the state on the railroads far enough to protect the members of this Assn. at the expense of this Assn. That is, the time they are outside of the state be paid by this Assn. pro rata also.

"That they are also authorized to pay certain inspectors employed by them if they see fit in their opinion to pay more than the $100.00 per month as authorized by the State that this Assn. will pay the excess.

"That they be authorized to instruct the State Inspectors in cases where the shipper refuses to deliver up any animal belonging to a member of this Assn. to the Inspectors, to take said animal by due process of law and this Assn. will pay all expenses so incurred."

This decision indicated that the Association had sufficient standing and influence to direct the State Inspectors to perform special services for its members in the recovery of stolen animals, and to make inspection of animals owned by members that were killed by the railroads outside of the state boundaries.

From this, it would indicate that the transition from Association inspection of cattle and brands may have been somewhat of a gradual affair. There was, obviously, a close working arrangement between the cattle growers' organization and the state department which had taken over the duties previously handled by the Association.

At the July 30, 1886 meeting of the Executive Committee, it was voted to employ C. Edgar Wetzel as the assistant secretary of the Colorado Cattle Growers Association and also as assistant secretary of the Board of Inspection Commissioners at a salary of $100 per month for the ensuing year. Ten days' notice of leaving was to be given each side!

From the standpoint of the cattlemen, it was a perfectly logical arrangement. The Association committees had developed the entire procedure for the round-up of cattle, the system of brand registration, and the methods of inspection.

The group had written the laws for the state legislature and helped to get them passed for the benefit of all the cattle growers in the state, large or small. In fact, during the earlier years, it had paid for the prosecution of thieves caught stealing cattle anywhere in the state, even though many of the owners of the stolen cattle were not members of the Association.

After the severe winters of 1886 and 1887, herds were so decimated that the big round-ups were temporarily discontinued. Then, as hordes of homesteaders flocked into the high plains country, fences and plowed fields ended the need for the big "cow hunts" for all time.

In the remaining big ranches, however, round-ups continued

on a gradually diminishing scale until World War I, with some outfits and cattle pools running a chuck wagon or two in the mountain country until the middle 1930's.

After the turn of the century, however, the big round-ups became history. The chuck wagons were parked back of the horse barns and slowly rotted away as time and weather took their toll.

Although most of the homesteaders gave up and left after a few short years of battling the dry lands, the scars they left on the plains and their rusting fences marked the end of the open range—and the round-up was no longer needed.

Townspeople and ranch women drive out to watch the roundup excitement near Westcliffe in the Wet Mountain Valley, probably about 1890.   *Photo from George Vickerman*

CHAPTER SEVEN

THE DECADES OF BOOM AND BUST—1880-1900

Although cattle prices continued to decline from 1873, following the panic that year, until they hit a low point of $14.30 per head in 1879 and 1880, the slump did not appear to cause undue hardships.

For one thing, costs were low and cattle could be run with very little expense. Herds were increasing in size, but the increase in numbers had not yet been excessive, and there was still not too much competition for land.

The "shoestring" outfits, which included nearly everybody in the late sixties and early seventies, were coming into their own,

The long hard years of fighting the frontier were beginning to pay off for most of the cattlemen in the territory.

The organized efforts of the Association against the gangs of cattle thieves in the area had proved effective, and losses from theft had been reduced over the years. There were always new recruits to the ranks of the lawless, but the big gangs of organized bandits were pretty well cleaned out by the beginning of the eighties.

In general, conditions had been good for the past few years and feed was plentiful on the range. Despite low prices, the cattle industry was booming.

At about this same time, the new state of Colorado was beginning to receive an increasing amount of attention in the press. The first major publication to tell of the opportunities here for profit in the livestock industry, was a book entitled "Historic Sketches of the Cattle Trade of the West and Southwest," written by Joseph G. McCoy.

Although this volume was primarily a general survey of the newly developing cattle industry in Kansas and the Texas trails, it contained many references to the fertile grasslands of eastern Colorado. It told of the many young men who had started out with little more than a saddle horse, good health and optimism and built themselves a fortune in the cattle business.

Harper's Magazine, a leading publication of the country, had also carried a series of articles about Colorado and life on the ranches of the territory. In 1880, this series was published in book form entitled "New Colorado and the Santa Fe Trail," under the by-line of the original author, A. A. Hayes, Jr.

Then in 1880, another volume appeared that painted a glowing account of the profits to be made by raising cattle in the West. This exciting book was entitled "The Beef Bonanza; or, How to Get Rich on the Plains." It was written by General James S. Brisbin, U.S. Army, a frontier cavalry officer who had been stationed in the West following service in the Union Army during the Civil War.

Brisbin became smitten with the excitement and opportunity of the entire West, from Montana to Texas. He believed that stock-raising on the plains was a sure way to rapid riches.

His book appeared at the turn of the decade, just at the time the country was recovering from the long after-effects of the money panic of 1873. In it, Brisbin related "success" stories, and letters from people who had come West and made a fortune in livestock in a short time.

Land, water and feed were free and readily available to anyone, Brisbin declared. All that was needed was a modest amount of capital to buy foundation stock, and the natural increase of the herd would more than repay this original investment, along with an average annual profit of some 20 to 25 per cent.

Few historians consider this volume as a factor in starting the rush to the grasslands of the West, but there is a significant appendix in this book headed "Cattle Raising in Colorado."

In this, Brisbin quotes a lengthy letter from Judge David W. Sherwood of Connecticut, to the Editor of the magazine, "Spirit of the Times."

Judge Sherwood commented on a previous article by Brisbin in the magazine in which the enthusiastic Army officer said:

"I have often thought if some enterprising person would form a joint-stock company for the purpose of breeding, buying and selling horses, cattle or sheep, it would prove enormously profitable. I have no doubt such a company, properly managed, would declare an annual divdend of at least 25 per cent. Such a company, organized with a president, secretary, treasurer, and a board of directors, and conducted on strictly business principles, would realize a far greater profit on the money invested than if put into any other form of business. Nothing, I believe, would beat associated capital in the cattle trade. The ranches or ranges should be located with a view of ultimately buying the land or securing control of it for a long term of years."

Judge Sherwood then went on to say that he, for some time, had been of the same opinion. He was part owner of the Huerfano Cattle Company, located on the Huerfano and Apache rivers in Huerfano and Pueblo counties in southern Colorado, about 30 miles south of Pueblo City.

The ranch extended along the sides of both rivers for about 11 miles and controlled the adjoining government lands as a grazing range. The cattle herd now numbered between 5,000 and 6,000 head and was mostly American cattle, improved from Texas cows by the use of good Kentucky bulls.

The Judge explained that he had come east with a view to forming such a stock company with the help of Eastern capital, and had arranged for the other owners of the ranch to turn the whole business over to the company on a low cash basis, and take stock in the new company for their interest.

He had entered into a contract with Col. William Craig, who owned an extensive ranch adjoining the property to the east, on the Huerfano and Cucharas rivers, extending along both sides of these rivers for some 17 miles.

The two properties together comprised about 80,000 acres, secured by United States government patent with a river frontage of approximately 28 miles. In addition, this deeded land controlled a grazing range of nearly 500,000 acres, well known as one of the best grass districts in Colorado. Four thousand acres were bottom lands, under cultivation and irrigated by ten miles of ditch. More than $150,000 worth of improvements had been put on the two ranches.

He proposed to sell 5,000 shares of $100 each to develop the land, buy more stock and operate the company. This range would, he estimated, carry at least 20,000 head of cattle, and the business would, if properly managed on so large a scale, pay dividends of as high as 50 per cent per annum.

The profits of cattle raising in Colorado were enormous, he declared. There is no business like it anywhere in the world, and the whole secret of it is, it costs nothing to feed the cattle.

"They grow," he promised enthusiastically, "without eating your money, and literally raise themselves."

The Judge continued with facts and figures about the great future of the beef industry. He quoted Governor McCook on the benefits of cattle growing in Colorado as follows:

"The natural grasses of our hills and valleys are equal in nutritious qualities to the Hungarian or other cultivated grasses of the East, and their abundance is such that the herds of a dozen states would have fine pasturage; and the winters are so mild that shelter or hay is unnecessary. The natural increase of cattle is 80 per cent per annum."

He quoted the late John W. Iliff and Jared L. Brush, prominent Colorado cattle "kings", as expert witnesses for the assurance of unlimited profits.

Brush, he declared, says the average profit on capital invested in cattle in Colorado will not fall short of 40 per cent per annum, over and above all expenses. Stockmen in Colorado often pay interest rates of 18 to 24 per cent per annum for money to invest in the cattle business and have then made large profits, he added.

This enthusiastic treatise may been the spark that ignited the bonfire, for within the next decade some 226 cattle companies were formed in the state of Colorado, with an authorized capitalization of nearly 100 million dollars in proposed stock.

The book's timing was almost perfect for the cattle boom that immediately followed. It seems significant, too, that the companies formed in such numbers were so similar to the proposal outlined by Judge Sherwood. The relative accuracy of the book probably mattered little as far as its initial effect was concerned. Basically, the story was true. Certainly never before or since was there such an unusual opportunity to make money on cattle as in the period from 1867 to 1885. The last five years, from 1880 through 1885, saw the biggest cattle boom in history.

When the annual meeting of the Colorado Cattle Growers Association convened in January of 1880, the organization had on its rolls nearly 70 prominent stockmen, some of whom had figured extensively in the history of the state.

Besides the members present were such visitors as Frank P. Sheafor of the Commercial Indicator, a business publication in Kansas City, and "a number of Boston capitalists." These latter were not identified, but were presumably visiting the area to look over prospects for investment capital in the region.

Present at this meeting, too, was D. B. Berry, secretary of the Southern Colorado Cattle Growers Association with headquarters in Pueblo. Berry said their organization was flourishing, their cattle were doing first rate and had not scattered too badly. Most men were well satisfied with the inspection system

which the organization had set up, but were a little dissatisfied
with the round-up system. He said, too, that the butchers in
that part of the state were not complying with the new inspection requirements for slaughter cattle and thought the matter
should receive some attention.

The Inspection Committee reported that 73,799 head of cattle had been inspected during the previous year at the following
points:

Omaha and Council Bluffs	16,107
Kansas City	38,139
Driven out of the state	9,829
Home consumption (local slaughter)	9,724
	73,799

Cattle saved to Colorado stockmen by inspection 192
Cattle saved to stock of adjoining states and territories 400

Other matters discussed included the report of a special
committee previously appointed to look into the matter of
horses stolen by the Cheyenne Indians during their raid through
Colorado in 1878. The committee announced that efforts to
recover the stolen horses had proved fruitless. As for relying on
military aid, they added, this was beyond expectation.

The secretary read the following resolution from a group
of stock-growers from Kansas City, who had visited the Association the past year.

"Resolved that we hereby express our admiration for the
earnestness and unanimity of purpose exhibited by the members
of the Colorado Cattle Grower's Association in advancing the
stock interests of their state and urge the stockmen of the West
to follow their excellent example in encouraging such organization. We feel the lack of words in attempting to return thanks
for the kindly reception given us by the members of this
organization while in their city, but beg of them to accept our
deepest gratitude, which we most heartily tender."

The summer of 1880 was a busy one with more cattle coming
into the state, more ranches being developed, and more fences
under construction.

That fall and winter brought a severe strain to cattle herds on the plains. An early blizzard in October, followed by a cold winter, was made still more difficult by a spring storm in March.

Cattle drifted south and gathered along the South Platte and the Arkansas rivers. Although travelers returning to the East on the Burlington and Missouri and the Santa Fe carried back tales of a regional disaster, the spring round-up gave the stockmen a chance to tally losses, and they were not too bad. Later, H. H. Metcalf estimated losses at a maximum of 10 to 15 per cent, with most herds around five per cent.

Assistant Secretary Wetzel said that losses had averaged no more than 10 to 20 per cent of the plains cattle, but that the resulting moisture from the storms had produced an excellent grass crop. Improved feed conditions in the summer of 1881 helped to offset the losses of the previous winter.

By the spring of 1882, the Colorado cattle boom was in full swing. Promoters and potential investors were crowding Denver hotels and visiting ranches all over the state. Cattle syndicates were being formed left and right.

The organization in 1881 of the spectacular Prairie Cattle Company had electrified the entire West. Starting with the purchase of the JJ outfit from the Jones Bros., in Bent County, Colorado, this British firm acquired the Cross L ranch in New Mexico, and later, the LIT ranch in Texas.

The Prairie Cattle Company was a promotion of Underwood, Clark & Company of Kansas City, Missouri. It was organized under the laws of Great Britain, and most of the money for the grandiose project came from Edinburgh and London.

The Colorado operation alone controlled some 2,240,000 acres —of range land—about 3,500 square miles—and ran nearly 54,000 head of cattle. The Cross L ranch was somewhat larger, controlling about 2,580,000 acres and 57,000 head of cattle. The LIT ranch was the smallest division with 256,000 acres of land and about 30,000 head of cattle.

It made a tremendous impression upon the financial world on both sides of the Atlantic, and upon the livestock industry as well, when the company paid a dividend of 20½ per cent to the shareholders in 1883.

The news made Denver the financial cow capital of the West, and brought new responsibilities to the Colorado Cattle Growers Association. The organization was flooded with inquiries about new investment opportunities, about the reliability of various investment propositions, the reputation of individual promoters, and even an occasional inquiry from anxious parents whose son had gone West to become a cowboy and had not been heard from.

The years of 1882, 1883 and 1884 were extremely favorable for the cattle business in Colorado. The weather was good, prices were up, and there was apparently no end to the amount of money available from the financial centers of New York, Boston, London and Edinburgh.

The records of the Colorado Secretary of State reflect this increasingly bright outlook in a very tangible way. Here is the list of cattle corporations organized during the period from 1873 to 1900, with the total authorized capital stock issued for each year.

Colorado Cattle and Livestock Companies
Organized 1870 to 1900

Year	No. Comp.	Total Capitalization
1873	1	$ 200,000
1876	1	$ 300,000
1877	1	75,000
1878	1	150,000
1879	1	180,000
1870's Totals:	5	$ 905,000
1880	3	$ 175,000
1881	4	1,362,000
1882	23	4,840,000
1883	29	7,974,000
1884	58	25,295,000
1885	44	32,297,000
1886	25	2,855,000
1887	17	1,925,000
1888	9	435,500
1889	13	1,225,000
1880's Totals:	225	$ 78,383,500

1890	11	$ 15,892,500
1891	8	890,000
1892	7	686,000
1893	11	815,000
1894	4	405,000
1895	13	1,145,000
1896	9	318,000
1897	8	390,000
1898	8	240,000
1899	3	350,000
1890's Totals:	82	$ 21,521,500
1900	11	$ 499,000
Total Capitalization from 1873 thru 1900:		$101,309,000

According to the records, a large percentage of these companies were fully subscribed at the time the articles of incorporation were filed. In fact, it is quite common to find amended articles filed within the first year, which record an increase in the capital stock of many of the companies.

Very little of this phase of the cattle story has been told in the annuals of Western history, but this second "Gold Rush" was, in many ways, far more remarkable than the '59 era.

Many of the bigger ranches changed hands at this point, and the records of the Association show the addition of some formidable new names within the industry.

Nearly every officer and member of the organization was involved, in some way, in one or more of these deals. A typical example was the sale of the SS Ranch, established by Hiram S. Holly in the early 1870's on the Arkansas River. The ranch headquarters were located near the present site of the town of Holly.

Hiram S. Holly came to Colorado from Stamford, Connecticut, about 1870, as a young man. He started punching cows, and went on several trail drives bringing cattle up from Texas. Then, beginning with a small outfit, he eventually built up a large ranch—one of the biggest spreads in the southeastern part of the state. It was a typical success story.

Holly was in partnership on the ranch with Dennis Sullivan, Denver financier and banker, and was one of the first of the big cattle operators to fence in his range as well as his deeded land.

The fence was thought to enclose the total of 640,000 acres of land, but later events revealed it to be short of this amount. It also included about 30 miles of river frontage on the Arkansas River.

The actual deeded land transferred in the sale contract to the British syndicate was only 14,147 acres. The balance of the property was "unclaimed" government land, which the deeded land controlled by ownership of available surface water and the surrounding fence.

During the early stages of the negotiation, Joseph A. Thatcher was brought into the deal through the simple fact that he owned a block of patented land within the fence and also bordering the Arkansas River. His land amounted to "about 2,400 acres of land lying on the north and south sides of the Arkansas River and comprising a portion of the land included within the bounds of what is known as the 'Holly Ranch' and used as a cattle range."

For this portion of the deal Thatcher was cut in on a full one-third of the sale price, plus a five per cent commission as agent. This, and the other part of the deeded land, was owned by transfer of U.S. Patents on the property. Another block of 880 acres inside the fence was owned by Ginkle, Thomas and Jones. The three partners had to acquire this additional property, plus some 18 forty-acre tracts lying along Wild Horse Creek.

In addition to the land, the new company—known as the Arkansas Valley Land & Cattle Company of London, England— was to receive 17,000 head of cattle at $20.00 per head, all brands in use by the ranch, plus all machinery, horses, equipment, buildings and tools.

The original price agreed upon was $875,000, although this appears to have been modified through a later adjustment in the amount of government land and the number of cattle delivered to the buyers.

The deed for the principal part of this ranch is an interesting document. In it Dennis Sullivan and Hiram S. Holly conveyed to James Duff, as Trustee for the British Syndicate, their rights to "about seven hundred thousand acres of land *belonging to the government of the United States,* lying on the north and south sides of the Arkansas River and being a portion of the land enclosed by said first parties by a wire fence and used by them as a cattle range." This deed is dated 11 July 1882.

Then, on December 29, 1882, the following letter was written to James Duff, Agent for the Arkansas Valley Land & Cattle Company:

"29th Decr. (1882)

"To James Duff, Agent
Arkansas Valley Land and Cattle Co.
"Dear Sir; -

"It has been called to our attention that the amount of government land included within the fence of the Holly Sullivan Ranch is less than six hundred and forty thousand acres which by our London agreement we agreed to convey to your company—the shortage being about two hundred thousand acres,—we propose, if it meets with your approval, to bind ourselves to cover the deficiency as follows: We will either extend the fence, making the present north line the south line of the proposed extension, taking in the said 200,000 acres of government land additional to that which you now have, meaning that the said fence when completed shall, together with the land already enclosed, include the full six hundred and forty thousand acres of government land; the said fences to be built in the same manner and to be in every particular as strong and durable as the present fence in its completed parts.

"Or we will pay such a sum of money as may be necessary to construct a fence sufficient to take in the additional amount of government land required by our contract, together with all the expenses connected therewith.

"Or we will make such other or different arrangements as may be by you deemed just and equitable in carrying out our contract.

(signed) Holly & Sullivan
by Dennis Sullivan
J. W. Thatcher"

This proposition was apparently accepted, for the final payment on the deal was received by Holly, Sullivan and Thatcher on March 1, 1883.

The settlement credited the company with receiving less than the full 17,000 head of cattle, specifying that the final tally was short some 8,301 stock cows, 16 bulls at $70.00 each, and

18 old cows at $10.00 each, which had been killed since the date of the agreement.

With this deduction of $167,320, the three partners received a total of $707,680 for the ranch, cattle and equipment. It was a spectacular deal, but it was also typical of dozens of others that were made during that period.

From these and other similar sales much of the financial foundation of the state was established. Downtown Denver and the surrounding area still shows the results of this money and the way it was used. The Cooper Building at 17th and Curtis Streets, the Clifford Block, the old Ernest & Cranmer Building, which was recently torn down to provide a drive-in banking facility for the Colorado National Bank, the Adams Hotel (built by George H. Adams, owner of the Baca Grant ranch) and numerous other present-day Denver business institutions owe their initial backing to these early cattlemen.

A quick check of nearly any Colorado bank in existence at that time will show an impressive array of members of the Colorado Cattle Growers on their roster of officers and directors.

Cattle money was a major factor in the banks of Trinidad, Pueblo, Lamar, Colorado Springs, Denver, Greeley and Sterling, many of which were financed with these corporate deals of the 1880's and 1890's.

Most of these cattlemen were solid business men who invested their money in land, real estate developments, office buildings, packing plants, stock yard companies, and banks. The interesting thing is that much of it is still intact today.

Many of the mining fortunes, on the other hand, were often lost before the men who struck it rich passed away. The Tabor family is a notable example.

Of course, not all of the cattle companies made money, and not all of the cattlemen held on to what they made during the boom days. In fact, many of the big syndicates which bought into the industry at the peak of the market, show a pretty sorry return over the years.

Many of the most astute cattlemen were also caught up in the fever of the times and formed other large cattle companies, wholly financed by their own funds.

Holly, Sullivan and Thatcher, for example, turned right around and formed the Columbia Land & Cattle Company on March 26, 1884. The incorporators listed were: Dennis Sullivan, Henry M. Porter, Joseph A. Thatcher, Hiram S. Holly, and John L. Mitch.

Capital stock of $300,000 was authorized, consisting of 3,000 shares at $100 each. The office of the company was Denver, Colorado, and the operations of the company were intended for Pueblo and Elbert counties.

There were literally hundreds more, plus many individual operations that were not incorporated. Cattle and money poured into the state. The membership of the Association grew from 71 members at annual dues of one dollar in 1880, to several times that number within the next five years.

At the meeting of January 7, 1885, the assistant secretary, C. E. Wetzel, announced that the membership had grown to 238 members and that 62 applications for membership were awaiting approval. In addition, the annual dues had been raised to $10.00, and the Executive Committee was authorized to assess members up to one cent per head of cattle owned whenever additional funds were needed.

By the next year the membership had increased to 532 members and the activities of the organization had grown in proportion. It was the peak of the cattle industry and a high point in the political and economic influence of the Association.

From this point on a series of events occurred which shook the cattle industry and the Association to its very foundations. These were the effects of a number of conditions that practically ended the range cattle industry for all time, and it changed the entire outlook of the cattle grower's organization, and the cattle business as well.

The booming condition of the industry, meanwhile, had attracted every promoter in the country. A growing number of fake cattle companies was the major concern of the organization at the meeting on January 26, 1886.

A Mr. Ferguson pointed out to the organization that they had an obligation to the thousands of misguided people in the East who were buying Colorado cattle company stocks.

Eastern swindlers were trading on the good name of Colorado as a range cattle state to fleece innocent investors, he said.

"I am called East several times each year, and on almost every trip I run across some new bogus cattle company, almost invariably located in Colorado.

"The prospectuses and 'maps of their range' that these fellows publish and scatter broadcast is simply astonishing. Their victims have neither the time nor the opportunity to visit Colorado and investigate conditions themselves," he declared.

He demanded that the Association appoint an investigation committee, composed of two members from each district, who could report to the secretary, the true nature or condition of any "wild cat" company that advertised itself as owning large tracts of land and of conducting large cattle operations in the state.

This would help to protect uninformed investors, and, at the same time, help legitimate stockmen to form companies that would materially expand their business.

In some cases the swindlers, who "can lie faster than a horse can trot," have even represented themselves as members of the Colorado Cattle Growers Association, Ferguson said. He urged all members of the organization to keep the secretary informed about new outfits moving into their districts.

In the meantime, the boom continued to gather speed. In the two years, 1884 and 1885, more than 100 cattle companies were set up in the state with a total authorized capitalization of more than $57 million.

The Association activities grew in proportion. At a meeting of the Executive Committee on April 29, 1885, the following matters were acted upon, which will give an idea of the influence and the scope of the organization at this period. These are verbatim excerpts from the minutes of that meeting:

> "A man was employed on the Detective force in conjunction with the Wyoming Assn. at $20 per month to be stationed at Ft. Collins on request of J. L. Brush.
>
> "It was ordered that all outside complaints be referred to the Attorney and, if on investigation, any Detective service is re-

quired the Att'y shall refer it to the Ex. Committee for action, or in case of their absence to J. A. Cooper, Prest. for action.

"The Ex. Com. hereby recommend to the Veterinary Sanitary Board (of the state) that all Missouri cattle be refused Bills of Health (for entry into Colorado) until all infections and contagious diseases are thoroughly eradicated in that state.

"It was ordered that the Assn. loan the State Vet. San. Board the money required to meet their actual expenses inasmuch as the State Legislature neglected to appropriate the sum allowed by Law for that purpose.

"The following resolution was passed.

"Resolved, That the thanks of this Assn. are hereby tendered to the Hon. N. J. Colman (U.S.) Commissioner of Agriculture for the appointment of H. M. Taylor of New Mexico as Agent of the Bureau of Animal Industry, thus recognizing the Range Cattle Industry in the appointment of one of the most energetic and capable of Cow Men and one fully conversant with our views and wants.

"Comm. then adjourned.

H. H. Metcalf, Secy"

At the same meeting, the bills paid included the sum of $534.40 to D. J. Cook, head of the Rocky Mountain Detective Association for his work in running down thieves.

The Association had an attorney by the name of L. R. Rhodes engaged nearly full time working closely with Cook in directing the prosecution of cattle thieves throughout the state.

The group was still maintaining a number of special inspectors, under the direction of C. E. Wetzel, on a part time or split salary deal with the State and with other state cattle associations, principally the Wyoming organization.

Nearly all of the officers and members seemed to be connected in some way with one or more of the new cattle companies. Henry H. Metcalf, secretary of the Association, was also president of the Elbert County Live Stock Company, a corporation that was formed on May 19, 1882. By October 24 of that same year, an amendment to the articles of this company was filed with the Secretary of State which increased the authorized capitalization from $300,000 to a new maximum of $600,000.

Jared Brush and former Governor John L. Routt and his wife,

Eliza F. Routt, had formed the Brush Land and Cattle Company, with $600,000 in paid up stock.

The Arapahoe Cattle & Land Company was headed by Alex Scherrer, and included such prominent stockholders as J. Jay Joslin, the department store magnate, George F. Eitel, and two physicians, Drs. F. Whitman and J. F. Ward.

The Western Land & Cattle Company listed former Governor John Evans, Chas. W. Hayden and William Gassoway as incorporators.

The largest of the cattle companies filed in the state was the Rio Grande Land & Cattle Company with an authorized capitalization of $10,000,000. Next in line was the $5,000,000 Antonio Land & Cattle Company.

In general, however, the bulk of the capital structures were from $25,000 to $500,000. Even the huge Prairie Cattle Company began operations with no more than $1,500,000 in cash on hand, an ample amount in those days.

One significant organization formed on June 1, 1881, was the Denver Union Stock Yard. The incorporators were John A. Clough, F. P. Ernest, James M. Wilson, S. E. Wetzel, Jacob Scherrer, J.A. Cooper and William B. Mills. The trustees or directors named in the initial filing were: Joseph L. Bailey, David C. Dodge, A. A. Egbert, John A. Clough, James M. Wilson, F. P. Ernest and S. E. Wetzel for the first year. Nearly all of these individuals were officers of the Association or men who had been holding office in the past few years.

A few years later, on March 25, 1886, this earlier firm was apparently taken over by a second company known as the Denver Union Stock Yard Company. The incorporators were Charles F. Morse, Simeon B. Armour and Watson J. Ferry, all of Kansas City, plus two of the organizers of the original company, James M. Wilson and Stephen H. Standart, both of Denver.

The directors listed for this company were: Charles F. Morse, Simeon B. Armour, Watson J. Ferry, C. W. Bangs, E. E. Richardson, S. H. Standart, Henry Gebhardt, F. P. Ernest, and James M. Wilson.

This marked the beginning of the first major livestock terminal here, which was built at the same location of the present-day Denver Union Stock Yards. The same group, with the addition of Henry Gebhard of Denver, another prominent member of the Association, also organized a separate company known as the Denver Stock Yard and Abbattoir Company. This was primarily a construction company to build the facilities at the yards, including "the construction, maintenance and operation of stock yards and . . . such buildings as hotels, railways and switches that may be necessary."

But, like every boom, its own momentum brought on its own downfall.

Easy money brought on excesses, and the excesses brought on a wave of jealousy against the prosperous, free-spending cattlemen. The fact that most of them had put in years of back-breaking work to reach this position was forgotten. New settlers and homesteaders surged into the state, lured by the publicity and the promise of instant success. But the contrast between their position, and the men who had spent 15 to 20 years getting established, was too much to bear.

Resentment against the "Cattle Barons" flared into active opposition. Now that a semblance of law and order had been established, the newcomers could appeal to the courts and to Congress for help. They looked for the chinks in the armor—and they were easy to find.

Nearly every pioneer cattleman had taken proprietary control over large areas of range land that were deserted and unclaimed when he arrived. He established a ranch headquarters along some creek or river, and reasoned that grazing rights were much like water rights. He assumed that the right of prior use would protect him, as long as he maintained and protected his priority.

Even those far-sighted few who advocated the purchase of range land were unable to do so. There was simply no legal machinery set up to convey title to much of the range when payment was offered.

Efforts to get a "desert homestead" or a "range land homestead" bill through Congress were hopeless. So, reasoning that possession was the first requisite, nearly every range man in the state went about improving and managing "his" land.

As soon as barbed wire came on the market, this opened up the first avenue to positive control of his acreage. Literally hundreds of thousands of dollars were spent on carload after carload of bright new barbed wire.

John W. Prowers shipped the first carload of wire into the state in 1878, according to the minutes of the Bent-Prowers Stock Association. With it, he fenced in 100,000 acres of unpatented government land on the north side of the Arkansas River to be used as a holding pasture for steers until they could be shipped to market in the fall.

The Holly enclosure, as previously described, was approximately 640,000 acres. Henry H. Metcalf had 200,000 acres under fence along the Bijou in Elbert County. These are just a few representative cases. It was a common and accepted practice, but it could not be justified by law. It had been a big factor in bringing law and order to the range, and the instrument by which control and proper management of range land grazing was possible, but this was no defense.

Cows could not vote, and when angry homesteaders began bombarding members of Congress with letters and telegrams demanding access to this "free" land, there was no doubt of the outcome. The fences had to come down.

When they did, there was another scramble for free grass. Every homesteader soon discovered that he had been sold a pipe dream by the government with his pitiful 160 acres of "desert estate." Used as range it might carry five or ten head of cattle in a good year. As farm land, it had to be broken and tilled in an entirely different manner from the rich eastern acreages.

The techniques of dryland farming on a big scale were unknown and undeveloped. Nine out of ten of the homesteaders were licked before they even started. Within a few years their deserted sod houses and tar-paper shacks bore mute testimony to the folly of the federal land policy. Families who had staked their life savings on a 160-acre "ranch" on the high plains, soon found that they were the victims of a cruel political hoax, fostered by a group of lawmakers who had no conception of this region or the semi-desert lands it contained.

No one knows how many dry cows or fat steers were given to starving homesteader families by the sympathetic cattlemen. Every family history in the region bears frequent reference to the help that ranch families gave to these pitiful groups, who staked their "land claims" in the most unlikely and inhospitable places.

But, despite their sympathy, the cattlemen could not help but be bitter and angry at such stupid farming efforts and complete lack of knowledge of the land and the climate. Farmers who had been growing crops in an area of 30 to 40 inches of annual rainfall, came out here and broke up the native grasses. Then they tried to plant the same crops and use the same farming techniques in this arid soil where 8 to 12 inches of rainfall were all that could be expected for an "average" year. It was a frustrating and heart-breaking trend—and it not only broke most of the homesteaders, but it ruined the grassland, too.

Once the grass was plowed up, it took almost another generation for the native grama and buffalo grass to re-seed itself. In dry years, the hot winds picked up the fine soil and sent it rolling across the plains in great billowing black clouds.

Many of the homesteaders, who had a little capital left, soon saw the hopelessness of farming, and bought cattle to run on the newly opened range that was exposed when the big cattle companies took down their fences under court orders.

The scramble to get the grass first, before someone else's cattle got to it, brought on a vast surge of overgrazing. Then came the reckoning.

It started with the weather.

On January 6, 1886, a blizzard swept down across Wyoming and onto the plains of Colorado. Temperatures dropped to 20 below zero with high winds and snow causing severe hardship to cattle.

Herds in the southeastern part of the state were especially hard hit because of seriously depleted range feed and an unusual condition of overcrowding with livestock.

Hordes of cattle had come into the state the previous fall from the Cheyenne-Arapaho reservation in the Indian territory, in what is now western Oklahoma. A proclamation by

President Cleveland on August 23, 1885, had ordered stockmen to move all cattle off of these lands immediately. Several hundred thousand head had to find new grazing lands, and since much of Kansas was closed to them by quarantine, Colorado was the only accessible range country available.

Despite the efforts of the Bent County association to keep these animals out, some 200,000 head were estimated to have been driven into western Kansas and southeastern Colorado grasslands. These cattle had been run on the reservation for years, under a long-standing agreement with the Indians. When the Federal government ordered them off the Indian lands, the pressure on the surrounding range lands was serious.

When the 1886 storm hit, these cattle were in poor condition to withstand much stress. The first storm took a heavy toll of the weaker animals, then a second cold spell of sub-zero temperatures lasted four days, from January 16 through 20, and the losses were again serious. The weather then warmed up, with temperatures up to 62 degrees in Denver on January 24, but with this sudden change came high winds that never dropped below 25 miles per hour for seven days. These warm dry winds swept across the plains, literally scouring the grassland.

On February 1, another storm hit the plains and heavy winds continued fom February 8 to 25. The wind, cold, and sudden changes of temperatures brought more suffering to livestock. More snow fell, started to melt, then froze again into a thick crust of ice that covered up nearly all of the remaining range feed. Cattle were unable to break through the ice to reach the grass, and they died by the thousands.

Herds, drifting with the storms, piled up along the north banks of both the South Platte and the Arkansas rivers. One observer claimed it was possible to walk from Greeley to Julesburg on the north bank of the Platte and never set foot on the ground, simply by stepping from one animal carcass to another. A similar statement was made about the Arkansas.

The losses were staggering, although it was not until the spring round-up that any real tally of dead cattle could be made. In the meantime, the Executive Committee of the Association met on January 30, to discuss reports of illegal skinning of dead cattle.

A report of B. F. Kidwell of Nepesta, had warned the group that hide scavengers were at work on the dead animals. Hide Inspector Ramsey was directed to investigate the situation and procure evidence against the thieves.

As a solution to the problem, the secretary of the Association was directed to "make a contract with H. Haltchuson of Colorado Springs, authorizing him to skin all dead cattle belonging to members of the C. C. G. A., to have all hides inspected by the Association hide inspectors, and to sell the same at commission of five per cent or buy them at market price at the option of the C. C. G. A., provided the expense of skinning and marketing said hides did not exceed the proceeds of same."

Another contract was made with J. L. Brown of Denver, on February 19, concerning hides taken from dead cattle.

On April 5, 1886, the committee met again to handle the business of the Association. S. H. Standart, the former secretary having resigned, H. H. Metcalf was elected secretary for the balance of the year. A new assistant secretary, M. J. Fitzgerald, was also employed to replace C. E. Wetzel, who had resigned the previous month.

Then it was ordered that the following parties be paid money due them from the hide account. This amount represented the net proceeds from the sale of hides taken from dead cattle following the winter storms. It was based on a gross of 25 cents per head for each hide. Of this amout, the Association took 10 cents for handling the hide contracts, and 15 cents was paid to the owner of the dead animals, identified by the brand on the hide.

Payments were as follows:

Arapahoe Land & Cattle Company	$ 50.00
American Cattle Company	60.00
Arkansas Valley Land & Cattle Company	40.00
Columbia Cattle Company	1,200.00
N. Dowling	175.00
Eastern Cattle Company	80.00
F. P. Ernest	200.00

Gentry & Reynolds (H. S. Holly)	175.00
H. B. Ketchum	75.00
H. H. Metcalf	50.00
Mill Iron Cattle Company	175.00
W. S. Pugsley	600.00
C. A. Pugsley	300.00
Republican Cattle Company	40.00
	$3,220.00

Heaviest losses were among outfits running in the southeastern part of the state, with the Holly interests (Columbia Cattle Company and Gentry & Reynolds) taking very severe punishment. It should be noted here that this list was probably far from complete and cannot be considered as an indication of total losses. The Bent County Cattlemen's Association also had a skinning contract, and there are indications that many of the large cattle outfits, such as the Arkansas Valley Land & Cattle Company, also employed skinners on their own range. These hide sales would not be included in the Association accounts, of course. However, on the basis above, this series of payments would represent more than 20,000 hides salvaged in approximately six weeks. Reports in livestock papers indicated that some outfits suffered losses ranging from 25 per cent to as high as 90 per cent of their herds, but individual reports varied widely. Others in more sheltered locations, and where feed conditions were more favorable, reported much lighter losses, generally from five to ten per cent. One livestock report estimated total losses on the Colorado plains as high as 40 per cent of the cattle population. However, on the basis of the annual cattle numbers reported for these years, this would appear to be much higher than the actual death loss, although 25 per cent might be a conservative estimate. As H. H. Metcalf remarked, at one time, one of the biggest problems of the Association was to get reliable statistics on the cattle industry of the state.

In the meantime, the cattle business continued. A new calf crop was born as spring returned to the range. More cattle came up the trail from Texas, despite continuing opposition from the Bent County Association.

The summer of 1886 was another dry season. Feed was again short. Although cattle numbers were somewhat reduced in the spring because of the heavy losses during the preceeding winter, by fall the total numbers were again nearly equal to the year before, as a result of the influx of trail cattle.

In the spring of this year, however, both Colorado and Montana passed a quarantine law against Texas cattle. Inspectors were stationed at the Colorado line near the Cimarron River to intercept trail herds from the south coming into the state. Only cattle that had been held for 90 days below the quarantine line and north of the 36th parallel of latitude, were permitted to come into the state. It was assumed that cattle held this far north and for this long had lost their infection, and were thus safe to bring into the area. Dr. George E. Glover was the inspector on a joint deal with both states. In 1886, he alone inspected 242,000 head, most of them headed for Montana and the Dakotas.

These cattle were following what was designated as the National Trail, a strip of land along the eastern boundary of the state. Efforts were made to have Congress establish this as a national preserve, set aside for the sole use of trail herds headed north.

Although railroads were hauling an ever-increasing number of southern cattle into the northern range areas, the trail herds continued into the 1890's. The peak years on the trail were probably about 1875 to 1885, as far as Colorado arrivals were concerned. The Colorado State Veterinarian reported that 182,052 head passed through Trail City, Colorado, in 1885, and at least that number passed this check point in 1886. A report from the "trail cutter," Inspector C. H. Marselus, said that 57 herds, totalling 126,951 head, crossed the Arkansas River near Trail City between June 9 and June 20, 1886. This would mean an extremely crowded trail with as many as four herds per day passing the check point. In such a congested movement of cattle, it would be difficult to keep the herds apart, especially in the event of a severe storm or a stampede. Most drovers liked to keep at least five miles, or about half a day's drive, between herds to prevent this likelihood. These dates, therefore, are suspect.

It was in 1885 that one of the most notorious trail towns in the entire West was established directly on the Colorado-Kansas line between Coolidge, Kansas, and Holly, Colorado. The townsite was on Cheyenne Creek, about a mile north of the Arkansas River, not far from the Santa Fe Railroad.

It was laid out expressly to provide "extra-legal" advantages to a specialized clientele—the trail drovers and cowboys who were bringing Texas cattle into Colorado and the northern states. The builder, one Martin Culver, laid the townsite out exactly on the Colorado-Kansas line, so that his transient customers could quickly step from one state into another, in the event lawmen began to ask embarrassing questions.

Culver had a large saddle and supply store in Trail City, and there were several saloons and a hotel. Because of its convenient location, it soon developed a reputation as the wickedest town on the trail. Lurid tales have been told of the "recreational activities" that occurred there when the unwashed and untamed trail hands hit town.

Aside from this, however, it was for about five years, an important cattle buying and trading center. Colorado and Wyoming cattlemen frequently met the trail herds here coming up from Texas, and bought cattle for stocking their own range. Bovina, in east-central Colorado, was also a well-known buying point.

Toward the beginning of the 1890's the trail herds had begun to decline, and many stockmen preferred the faster method of shipping cattle in from Texas by rail, despite the higher cost. Both Hiram S. Holly and Finis P. Ernest expressed preference for rail shipments in bringing in stocker cattle from Texas, and both men were bringing in large numbers each year.

A National Cattle Association Urged

During the middle 1880's there was increasing talk about the advisability of forming a national cattle growers organization, to help unite the efforts of the various state and regional groups. One such conference was held in St. Louis, Missouri, on November 14, 1884, and a second meeting was held on November 25, 1885. During the latter month a similar "national" cattlemen's group was holding its annual session in Chicago. Delegates from the Colorado Stock Growers organization attended both meetings, but it was generally felt here that the Chicago group was dominated by the market and packing interests in the Midwest. Previously the Colorado association had sent out warnings to all stockmen to avoid dealing with the Swift Bros. there. The packing firm had bought steers from W. J. Wilson, a prominent member of the association, given a $3,000 draft on the contract, then refused payment on the draft when the market dropped, and the cattle arrived in Chicago on a down market.

This, and other similar incidents, had made Western cattle growers suspicious of the packing, market and railroad interests, particularly in Chicago. Consequently, the Colorado cattlemen were skeptical of the Eastern meeting, despite the fact that former Governor John L. Routt was named acting chairman of the St. Louis convention.

The Midwestern and Eastern people had no understanding of the needs and problems of the Western range man, they said. It was understandable, then, that the organization went all out to support the proposed International Range Association, when that organization was launched, particularly since the headquarters were to be in Denver.

The International Range Association was the idea of Richard G. Head, former General Manager of the Prairie Cattle Company, and a member of the C. C. G. A. Executive Committee in 1885. It was first presented and endorsed by the New Mexico Stock Growers at their annual meeting, then brought to Denver. Head, a resident of Trinidad, was considered one of the top management men in the range cattle industry. Born in Mississippi, he had drifted to Texas at an early age and learned the cattle business as a cowboy. For a time he was driving cattle up the trail to Colorado, then went into business for himself, buying and selling as an independent trader. His knowledge of cattle, his honesty, and his business ability earned him a top reputation. He was named manager of the huge Prairie Cattle Company in 1885, replacing W. R. Green.

Head was reportedly paid the staggering salary, for that time, of $20,000 a year. He was the "miracle man" picked by Underwood, Clark & Company to get the huge company on its feet. When the company directors went on an economy crusade in December of 1885, they proposed to cut his salary to $15,000, a figure that would have still left him one of the highest paid executives in the entire West. Dick Head, however, resigned. He could, he said, make that much or more by dealing in cattle on his own. He was described by John Clay as being vain, and having aspirations of becoming the Napoleon of the western cattle business. It is possible that he and Clay clashed because they were two of a kind, since John Clay was never accused of being overly modest, himself.

At any rate, Head was certainly the originator and the ramrod of the International Range Association. It was a grandiose idea, aimed at incorporating the entire range cattle industry of the West, including Canada and Mexico into one great organization.

The organization was incorporated under the laws of Colorado on February 3, 1886, with the following objects and purposes:

> "To advance, foster, preserve and protect the interests of all its members in and to their range neat cattle and horses; to guard and protect their said livestock from all contagious and infectious disease; to prevent the same from being stolen, driven away without authority, or wrongfully converted, and to discover and bring to justice all such person or persons as may or shall steal, wrongfully drive away, or convert the same; to guard and protect the owners of such property in their possessory rights on and to the public domain, to the extent that the same may foster, encourage and maintain a kindly feeling, honest dealing and the interchange of views by and between all persons interested in said property, either directly or indirectly, and generally to do each and every needful and lawful thing that may, from time to time, be found necessary and requisite in and about the furtherance and enforcement of the objects and purposes aforesaid, and each thereof."

Among the 20 original directors were, besides Head, such names as Moreton Frewen, Esq., of the British Possessions, H. M. Mundy of the Republic of Mexico, J. M. Carey of Wyoming, W. P. Herring of the Indian Territory, J. J. Gaspar of Arizona, Chester G. Cutter of California, William Thompson of Kansas, John A. McShane of Nebraska, Peter French of Oregon, George Russell of Nevada, S. McIntire of Utah, John Sparks of Washington, E. S. Newman of Montana, Henry G. Weare of Dakota Territory, and others. Later C. C. Slaughter of Texas was also named to the Board of Control.

At the meeting in Denver the next year in February, 1887, Head was re-elected President. First Vice Pesident was Jared L. Brush, Treasurer was Job A. Cooper, and J. C. Leary, Secretary.

A third annual meeting in March, 1888, again in Denver, saw the organization expanding and giving every indication of becoming an influential power. The attitude of the group then was expressed by Colonel H. M. Taylor of New Mexico.

"In the conduct of range matters there are numerous questions of common interest to all stockmen of the plains in which our Eastern brothers have and take no interest. By the union of range men in a stock working organization they will be prepared to give crystalized views to the representatives of the Consolidated Cattle Growers Association to meet in Chicago next fall, thus giving it aid and strength it could not otherwise have."

He continued to express another basic policy of the Westerns: "Paramount to everything else is the necessity of such concert of action on the part of all associations in the range country as will absolutely protect us from all possible danger from contagious animal diseases. It is a matter of history that the introduction of one infected animal upon the ranges of Australia caused a loss of over forty millions of dollars, and practically wiped out the range cattle industry on that continent."

Henry H. Metcalf, Secretary of the Colorado Cattle Growers Association, read a memorial passed by that association at its annual meeting, held the day before the International Range Association convened.

It, too, dealt with the need for national animal health control and urged the passage of needed legislation by Congress to protect against importation of animals from countries infected with contagious diseases. It asked more rigid protection laws to prevent the spread of contagious diseases into the unfenced grazing lands of the West, where it was impossible to maintain adequate quarantine of range cattle.

Metcalf reported that the Colorado Association memorial had also been telegraphed to the President of the United States and to both houses of Congress.

The Rocky Mountain News for March 28, 1888, gave considerable coverage to this meeting, quoting various stockmen at length on major issues. The News also printed a letter from Fort Worth businessmen which suggested that a cattle growers' "Live Stock Exchange" be established at some designated place in the West, such as Denver or Fort Worth. It was to be operated and controlled by stockmen "for the purpose of furthering the interest of the cattle raisers of the United States."

The letter declared that the writers believed that the livestock business was then controlled by a few individuals who, through their organizations and concentration of capital, were able to manipulate and deal in their livestock to the detriment of the producer.

The paper also pointed out that a startling proposal to solve this situation had been presented at the annual meeting of the year before. Under the head "M'Gillen's Bomb," the paper had this to say:

"The special sensation of the last convention was the scheme of Mr. McGillen to form an association to include all of the cattle interests of the country, for the purpose of dealing directly with the consumers and controlling the beef markets. The project was so stupendous that it took the breath away of the convention. When men had sufficiently recovered to think it over, the more thoughtful members of the body admitted that Mr. McGillen's plan contained the pith of the only method of protection against combinations to prevent free and fair markets. This impossibility of securing such a counter-combination was recognized, but the main idea was not lost, and it is worthy of careful consideration by cattlemen."

This group, and the organization known as the Consolidated Cattle and Horse Growers Association, were the first major efforts to form a national federation of cattle growers. It is especially interesting to note that the International Range Association memberships were open only to "Associations that are now or may be hereafter organized for this purpose . . . the members of which shall be directly interested in the growing and breeding of neat cattle and horses on the range, and no one shall be an officer of this company who shall not be engaged in that calling."

The continuing decline in cattle prices, the after-effects of the severe winters of 1886 and 1887, and the rapid influx of homesteaders who filed claims, plowed up the range, and built fences around their property, soon took a heavy toll of the range cattle operations. With the rapid disappearance of the open range, the main impetus back of the International Range Association was destroyed. The organization faded away with the foundation upon which it had been built.

Not until more than ten years later was the effort made successfully to launch another national livestock producers organization. It, too, was headquartered in Denver, and backed by the enthusiastic support of the Colorado Stock Growers Association.

As the 1880's declined, along with the price of cattle, the high plains began to shake out the less stalwart of the homesteaders, and the brutal weather cycle effectively turned the less productive dry farms back to grass. The dry land wheat that had replaced the grama, the prickly pear and the spiked yucca, sure signs of virgin grasslands, was in turn replaced by Kochia and tumbleweed, trademarks of abandoned farm lands.

Prices improved somewhat between 1890 and 1892, and some of the old-time cattlemen who had stayed with the business were able to recoup part of their losses. But the panic of 1893 sent prices into a spiral again, and values in 1894 hit bottom for an all-time record low. The January, 1895, price report for the preceding year, listed the average value per head at only $14—the lowest point of the century, and 30 cents per head under the previous low in 1879 and 1880.

Still more of the big stock companies folded up. With their range lands wiped out and cattle prices at rock bottom, there was little left to operate on. The trusting investors, from the titled families of England and Scotland to the frugal widows of Boston and Philadelphia, received bitter instruction in the capricious economics of the cow business. Only the most astute and well-financed stockmen were still on sound footing. The money panic hit the farmers and the homesteaders as well. All agriculture looked bleak. Still more of the soddies and shacks out on the plains were deserted.

The winters of 1892 and 1893 were severe ones, the worst since the bad years of '86 and '87. In fact, one bad blizzard of the year hit on May 31, 1892, and caught a number of early trail herds on the divide north of Hugo.

Two of these herds belonged to the Reynolds Brothers, from Albany, Texas. Heading north to the Dakotas, they had 4,400 head of cattle, split into two separate herds. The first was located about 25 miles north of Hugo, the second, some 40 or 50 miles to the south. In between were four herds belonging to the XIT outfit, strung out about ten miles apart. Altogether there were about 10,000 head of XIT cattle on the trail between the two Reynolds herds.

The storm hit at night, and by noon the next day there was as much as 18 inches of snow on the level. The drovers were unable to control the cattle in the blizzard, and the animals drifted southward until they hit the right-of-way fence along the Kansas Pacific railroad.

By the time the weather cleared, all six herds were mixed up along the track—and 14,400 head had to be cut and re-sorted before the drive could be resumed. The Reynolds crews reported the additional loss of 28 head of horses because of the storm, and the resulting overwork of trying to hold the cattle in the snow.

This severe weather, and the following decline of prices brought serious repercussions to Colorado agriculture. During the middle of the 1890's, the Colorado Chamber of Commerce and the state legislature became gravely concerned about the mass exodus of emigrants from the state, returning to more hospitable climates. Nevertheless, incoming arrivals more than offset the disillusioned who were leaving and in time, the mercurial Western weather improved.

All through the decade of the "gray" nineties, the Association continued its activities, although at a greatly diminished level. David Wyatt became president, taking over the position from J. L. Brush, just as the 1893 panic hit the industry and sent it reeling.

In August of 1893, the Wyatt Brothers sold 500 cows for $8 per head with a few late calves thrown in, from their ranch near Eaton. It was a time of retrenchment, and every stockman had his hands full just to hold his herd together and stay in business. For the next six years Dave Wyatt and his loyal officers, Joseph W. Bowles, Henry H. Metcalf, and J. G. Benkleman, kept the organization running. All four stayed in office for six years. Not until the end of the decade when cattle prices started upward again in 1898, did things begin to revive. In the meantime they had fought a series of tough political battles in the state legislature, as the power of the livestock and agricultural interests declined.

On one occasion, dissident political groups attempted to smear the organization by a lawsuit against Secretary Henry Metcalf, charging misappropriation of state funds in the organization's handling of the Estray Fund—money received from the sale of unbranded cattle picked up by the brand inspectors. After a direct appeal to the Governor, Metcalf was vindicated, and the Association's long-standing right to administer the fund was upheld.

The imminence of war with Spain and the subsequent build-up of the nation's military forces brought an increasing demand for more beef, and prices improved during the last half of the decade. By 1898, an air of guarded optimism returned to the cattle industry and the Association began to revive.

It was apparent, however, that the old days of range cattle operations would never return. The power of the agricultural interests declined appreciably in both the state and the national political scene. It was evident that livestock interests all over the country would have to fight for political consideration with growing industrial and labor groups. The more foresighted cattlemen began to talk again of a national livestock organization to represent the industry.

A committee of the Colorado Cattle Growers Association met with the Live Stock Committee of the Denver Chamber of Commerce and Board of Trade in the fall of 1897. The result was a general appeal for a national organization of livestock producers from all over the United States.

During the previous two years the livestock industry had experienced a general revival, but business and political conditions were not the same. In order to meet the demands of the new era, the group decided on a national appeal for unity.

A joint committee was formed, chairmanned by George L. Goulding. Secretary of the group was Arthur Williams, who was also secretary of the Denver Chamber of Commerce, with Dennis Sheedy, Treasurer. Others included J. M. Kuykendall, Chairman of the Finance Committee, Governor Alva Adams, Chairman of the Reception Committee, Peter McCourt, Chairman of the Entertainment Committee, and Charles F. Martin, Press Secretary.

Martin was then chief of the Associated Press bureau in the city, and a key man in the highly successful effort to get the national organization under way.

The Committee of Arrangements who set up the project included David C. Wyatt, Henry H. Metcalf, George W. Ballantine, J. K. Mullen, John W. Springer, Chas. E. Stubbs, A. E. de Ricqles, S. K. Hooper, George W. Vallery, E. Monash, George L. Goulding and F. A. Keener.

On November 16, 1897, a call for a National Stock Grower's Convention to be held in Denver was sent to every state and territorial governor, every state and local livestock organization, every agricultural college, every stock yards organization, every cabinet member, every state sanitary board, every chamber of commerce and to every livestock journal in the nation. Transportation companies and livestock commission men were also invited. A system of delegates based on the number of livestock represented was outlined, and an invitation extended to present papers on a list of suggested topics pertaining to the industry.

January 25, 26 and 27, 1898, were the dates named for the meeting and despite a siege of severe cold weather with snow, more than a thousand delegates turned up at the Denver Coliseum for the convention.

Governor Alva Adams, himself a prominent Colorado stockman, called the meeting to order until the assembly could elect a temporary president. In his opening remarks, the Governor commented on the poor condition of the livestock industry over the preceding ten years, but called attention to recent indications that prosperity seemed to be returning.

The old days had passed, he said, when haphazard ways could be tolerated. Now to succeed in the stock business required the closest management and the finest business wisdom. No longer could a herd be built up with no capital but hope, energy and a branding iron. General laughter greeted this reference to the easy-going days of the past.

"Rustling is no longer popular and has become very dangerous, fortunately," he pointed out with a chuckle, in which the audience joined.

"But there is no change as great in this industry as that which has been brought about by the invasion of the agriculturist into the domain of the range man.

"This great march is continuous and it is irresistible," he declared. "We must adjust ourselves to this new condition, for the man with the plow and the hoe is forcing the range man to retreat."

The Governor did not view this as a catastrophe, however. It was simply part of the march of progress and a trend that would result in greater protection for livestock. The time had come when no man could afford to keep more animals than he could shelter and feed when winter storms hit the range.

In closing Governor Adams recalled some of the colorful days of the cowboy era, noting that many in the meeting were veterans of that period who had now matured into stockmen, running sound business operations.

George Goulding, chairman, called for nominations for temporary president of the convention, and Governor W. A. Richards of Wyoming rose to propose the name of John W. Springer of Denver.

Immediately, Lt. Governor Jared L. Brush of Colorado and A. P. Bush of Texas seconded the nomination.

Springer was nominated by acclamation and came forward to take over the meeting. Although he had not been active in the state Association, he had developed a wide acquaintance among stockmen throughout the area. He had a ranch in Texas, another in Colorado and a horse ranch in Montana. In addition, he was active in packing plants in Denver and was vice president of the Continental Trust Company here.

Springer was a graduate of DePauw University Law School and an accomplished orator. His acceptance address demonstrated his forensic ability as well as his knowledge of the livestock business. Under his direction the organization of a national association got under way.

Despite repeated efforts from other Chamber of Commerce groups to have the newly formed organization permanently located elsewhere, the talents of John Springer and Charles F. Martin were undoubtedly the main reason for its continued location in Denver. Springer was reelected president for the next six years, serving until the National Live Stock Association merged with the American Cattle Growers Association in 1904.

Martin later became General Secretary of the national organization, serving until his death in 1902, a victim of tuberculosis. At the organization meeting in 1898, however, Martin was instrumental in drawing the large attendance, for a continuous stream of bulletins on the proposed convention had gone out all over the United States on the Associated Press wire.

In the ensuing meetings, the assembly heard some of the great national figures in the livestock business. Comments and papers delivered at the conference highlighted the basic problems of the industry.

Col. J. G. McCoy of Kansas, the man who had launched the first trail terminal at Abilene more than 30 years before, told the stockmen that they must organize or perish.

Ralph Talbot, attorney for the Colorado Cattle Growers Association, spoke on the protection of livestock property rights and explained the system of brand registration developed by the Colorado organization. The Colorado system had been developed by the cattle growers into one of the most effective in the West.

Governor Richards of Wyoming, gave a comprehensive outline of the public lands outlook and the need for a national land policy to make the settlement of these areas practical and reasonable. He urged a program of ceding these lands to the state or territory, so that local jurisdiction could administer them more efficiently.

A. P. Bush of Texas, presented a paper on the special problems of the Western livestock interests and pointed to the urgent need for a national organization to represent the industry.

In all, more than 24 papers were read on varied aspects of the livestock industry, and nearly every speaker mentioned the need for organization.

When the convention completed its deliberations at the end of the three-day session, there was generally unity on all proposed resolutions, except the one of cessation of public lands to the individual states. This also involved the question of leasing the grazing rights from the federal government. After considerable discussion the resolution came to the floor as the last piece of business before the meeting adjourned. C. H. Harris of Glenwood Springs made a final plea against the resolution, stating that such a move would eventually lead to a leasing program which would seriously damage the operations of the small cattleman. Put to a vote, the resolution was defeated. But the issue was not buried. The leasing question later caused a serious rift in the Colorado Association, and remained a major issue for many years throughout the West.

In the final business session, John W. Springer of Denver was elected the first President of the National Live Stock Association; John M. Holt of Montana was named Vice President; C. W. Baker of Illinois, Treasurer; Arthur Williams of Denver, Secretary; and Charles F. Martin, also of Denver, Recording Secretary.

This marked the organization of the first permanent national group to represent the livestock industry. The support of the Colorado stockmen, attending more than 400 strong, was a prime factor in launching the new organization. Equally enthusiastic backing came from the Texas delegation, who had sent more than 350 delegates to Denver for the event. It was truly an industry-wide movement, but the major interest was definitely from the range areas of the nation. Here distances and the larger average operations pointed up the need for united action much more than the farming areas of the Midwest and East.

By now the war with Spain was fast approaching. A few months later, on May 1, Admiral George Dewey sailed into Manila Bay and captured the Spanish fleet. The war brought still more demand for beef, and prices climbed until the panic of 1903 collapsed the market and brought more economic stress to the industry.

The dawn of the 20th century saw the old range era vanish into history. The decade of the 1890's saw the last of the National Trail. Only a few old die-hards attempted to trail cattle for any distance after 1900, and these drives were viciously resisted by the new settlers along the way. Even the Longhorn had been largely replaced by better quality animals. A new age of beef production began to take shape. The old Durham Shorthorn had begun to lose ground to another breed, the whitefaced Hereford. These cattle proved themselves highly adaptable to the new methods of herd management. Although Angus bulls had been imported into the state from the early 1870's, the horned Herefords soon began to surpass them in numbers, and Colorado quickly gained a national reputation for its herds of whitefaced breeding stock.

Undoubtedly much of the credit for this interest in improved breeding stock was inspired by the efforts of the Association to encourage the use of pedigreed bulls in the range country. As early as 1880, the Association had obtained a law requiring the use of purebred bulls on the open range in the state. Shortly after the turn of the century a new law specified only registered bulls be used, a practice that still stands for herds running on the public domain.

GEO. W. ALLEN.

P. O. Address, Longmont, Col.

Range, North side of South Platte, Cedar and Crow Creeks.

Brand, same as cut.

Earmark,

Other Brands, I0 on left side and hip. I0 hip. I0 stifle. 20

200  left side. Horse Brand, IX left hip.

D. J. COOK.

P. O. Address, Denver, Colo.

Range,

Brand, same as cut.

Earmark

ILLINOIS LAND AND CATTLE CO.

P. O. Address, Greeley, Col.

Range, Crow Creek, Narrows on the Platte to Chalk Bluff, Colorado and Wyoming.

Brand, same as cut.

Earmark,

Other Brands, 70 HD ⁊ ∧ V

Horse Brand, 70 left hip.

Page from the Association Brand Book of 1884 showing brand recorded by David J. Cook.

CATTLE AND HORSE GRAZING PERMIT.

No. _93_

ACT OF JUNE 4, 1897.

Department of the Interior,

GENERAL LAND OFFICE,

Washington, D. C., _May 13_, 190_3_.

Under Department regulations, as amended December 23, 1901,

M_ss. & C. F. Albertson_, of _Burns_ _Colorado_ is hereby authorized to pasture _Two hundred & thirty (230)_ head of cattle and _Twenty (20)_ head of horses within the _White River Plateau (No. 6)_ Forest Reserve from _April 15th_, 1903, to _November 15th_, 1903: _Provided_, That the animals shall not intrude upon (to which this permit does not extend) any place of public resort or reservoir supply, nor upon any of the areas, localities, and tracts described as follows, to wit:

Brand X U. V-E.
send me the name of your Herder
Veatch
Supr

This permit is issued on the conditions that the said _Mss & C. F. Albertson_ _have by their_ has, by his application No. _93_, dated _Jany 16_, 190_3_, agreed to fully comply with all and singular the requirements of any law of Congress now or hereafter enacted relating to the grazing of live stock in the forest reserves, and with all and singular the requirements of any rules or regulations now or hereafter adopted in pursuance of any such law of Congress, and that he _their_ his employees engaged in caring for the animals while on the reserve, will extinguish all fires started by himself or _themselves_ by any of said employees before leaving the vicinity thereof, and to cooperate generally, so far as possible, with the forest officers and rangers in protecting the reserve from fires and depredations, and that as soon as the said animals shall enter the reserve, and thereafter, to notify the Forest Supervisor in charge of their specific location, giving a description of the range occupied: _Provided_, That this privilege is extended with no obligation or agreement to maintain an exclusive possession upon any part of said reserve to any one person or firm, nor as to adjustment of any conflict as to possession.

For a violation of any of the terms hereof, or of any of the terms of the application on which it is based, or wherever an injury is being done the reserve by reason of the presence of the animals therein, this permit will be canceled, and the animals will be removed from the reserve.

APPROVED: _May 13_, 190_3_

J. H. Fimple
Acting Commissioner.

Thos. Ryan
Acting Secretary of the Interior.

A "Cattlemen's Special" coach on the Harp Stage Line is ready to leave Rifle for a Cattlemen's Association meeting at Meeker, about 1900. The leasing policy question on public lands caused much debate—and record attendance at Cattleman's meetings during this decade.

Photo courtesy Russell Harp, Meeker

CHAPTER EIGHT

THE COST OF "FREE" GRASS

The use and management of public lands has been a major concern of the cattlemen's Association throughout the century. One of the first projects after its organization in 1867, was an effort to have the Territorial Legislature restrict grazing on Colorado lands to livestock owned by inhabitants of the state. A statute enacted, but never enforced, specifically prohibited the importation of Texas cattle for grazing purposes.

From that time on, although its attitude toward Texas cattle was soon reversed, the Association was deeply involved in the long series of conflicts over public lands.

Colorado's total land area comprises 66,510,000 acres, of

141

which 53 per cent—35,471,000 acres—is still used exclusively for grazing land and for the production of livestock feed and forage.

The land has little potential for other uses. At one time, particularly in the late 1880's and 1890's, the landscape of every Colorado range was dotted with the sod houses and tar-paper shacks of homesteaders. Millions of acres were plowed up, only to revert to grass as nature, cruelly but efficiently, separated those lands economically suited to cultivation from those adapted only to grazing. Two great drouths—in the 1890's and in the 1930's—were the principal instruments of this selective process. In recent years, new pump irrigation techniques have made it profitable to convert some grazing land to cropland, but the percentage is very small.

Of the total lands used for grazing and feed production, 28,088,735 acres is privately-owned land which yields tax revenues for all levels of government. The remaining acreage produces income for school districts and state and federal governments in the form of lease payments and grazing fees.

The public domain comprises 41 per cent of Colorado's total land area. The federal government owns 36 per cent of the lands in the state—24,101,065 acres—the state owns 3,098,438 acres and local government units 293,439 acres.

Much of the public land is used entirely or to a large extent for grazing. Because of this and the fact that public and private grazing lands are interdependent economically, the administration of public lands has been a matter of great importance to cattlemen and their state organization.

When Colorado became a state, the federal government presented lands to the new commonwealth for educational purposes, public buildings, and internal improvements. Sections 16 and 36 of each township in the state were designated school lands. In many cases, these specific sections were already in the hands of private individuals or inside the boundaries of Indian reservations. For this reason, Governor Routt's land commission was able to exchange these sections for other federal lands, usually on the eastern slope, in the South Park and the San Luis Valley. Later, when the national forests were established, the state exchanged the school sections within the forest boundaries for other federal lands in a similar fashion. As a result, a majority of Colorado's state lands lie in the eastern and southern parts of the state, whereas the bulk of federal lands is in the mountains and on the western slope.

The state lands, including school lands, are administered by the State Board of Land Commissioners. They include both farming and grazing property. State lands are handled on a lease basis, the lease price and conditions depending upon the location and value of the specific tract. A person wishing to obtain a state lease can do so by placing a bid when the lease on a particular unit expires. However, the person holding the lease, may retain it, if he meets the highest competitive bid.

The cattle business of the open range days was established on a foundation of free land, cheap cattle, and low operating costs. As these factors changed, the industry had to adjust to survive. The fact that the production, fattening, processing, and marketing of beef today is a dynamic, prosperous enterprise, demonstrates the ability of the industry to adapt to changing conditions.

But the adjustment was often a painful process.

In the 1860's the land was free, available to the man who had the courage to risk his neck and a very small amount of capital. By gaining possession of the water holes and streams in an area, he controlled land as far back from water as a steer could graze and return in a day's time.

There was plenty of land for all, at first. If a man found someone ahead of him on a particular range, he moved on until he found unoccupied territory. By tacit agreement, the principle of "first in time, first in right" applied to the range as it does in irrigation law of the mountain states. Few people contested the right of the first comer to the land which he grazed. A man felt justified in using whatever means were necessary to protect his grazing rights. They were rights which he had established by possessing and putting to use a wasteland. There was no law which said the range belonged to him—but, on the other hand, there was no law which said it didn't. People who trespassed on a man's range were considered range pirates.

During the very early years, the open range cattle business

operated within definite guidelines of range courtesy, custom, and principles, aided and abetted by some state laws enacted to establish order in the absence of any semblance of federal regulation.

A man's range was well defined, if not by metes and bounds, by agreement with his neighbors. Twice a year, stockmen gathered their cattle in the big round-ups, sorted them out, and each man trailed his own stock back to his own range. The state Association, cooperating with local stockmen's organizations where these existed, acted as general business agent and coordinator for the industry. It maintained a brand book, assisted in the organization of round-ups, and even hired detectives to apprehend cattle thieves. Later, all these functions were turned over to state government.

The early homesteader usually found the cattleman a good neighbor. After all, there was still plenty of land. As long as the settler didn't fence in the water or interfere with the free movement of cattle, he was welcome—in small numbers. Homesteaders, the early ones, often helped out as cowboys and ranch hands as they needed the work. The 160-acre homestead was designed in the East for a more fertile and more humid region. A quarter section of good land in Colorado might conceivably support five or six head of cattle, but it couldn't keep a family fed and clothed. It was a grimly, humorous statement in the early West that the government was willing to bet 160 acres that a man couldn't live on it for five years.

At first, there was peace on the range. Then came the day when homesteaders poured into the country, first by hundreds and later by thousands. They filed claims to the best lands and tied up the water where the stockmen hadn't taken precautions to gain legal ownership.

There really wasn't anything the stockman could do to dam the flood of settlers, however fervently he might damn it. All he could do was adjust. The "free" land, after all, was open to anyone willing to pay the price in blood, sweat, and tears.

At about the same time, came the big die-ups of 1885-1886 and 1886-1887, coupled with a severe summer drouth on the central and northern plains in both 1885 and 1886. These terrible blizzards, with continued snow and bitter cold which kept the grass buried under sheets of ice, killed hundreds of thousands of cattle. This, and the coming of fences, virtually wrecked the open range business.

A majority of the investment syndicates which operated the larger cattle outfits at that time, had bought in when prices were high. A great number of them had purchased cattle on a "book count" which later proved to be far less than the actual number. Very few of them operated as efficiently as the ranches of the 1870's, when the owner usually was a dyed-in-the-cowhide stockman and the active manager of his outfit. Only a handful of the syndicates survived. The range cattle business fell apart.

The open range days were over. No longer would the combination of free land, cheap cattle, and low operating costs prevail. From now on, a stockman was going to have to feed his cattle during the winter, practice range conservation, and build fences.

The open range days were over, but millions of acres in Colorado remained the property of the federal government—unsettled, unfenced (legally, that is), and unmanaged. Beset by homesteaders, sheep men, and migrant cattlemen, many ranchers fenced huge tracts of what they considered their own ranges under the "first in time, first in right" principle. This was done not only to secure the range for their own use, but for other reasons as well.

The fence builders were quick to point out that their actions kept out the worst of all range pirates—migratory sheep and cattle outfits which drifted into the state, paid no taxes, used up range, and moved on. Also, by fencing his cattle, a stockman was able to fence out inferior bulls and to upgrade his Longhorn herds by using purebred Shorthorn and Hereford bulls. By installing windmills, he could bring stock water to previously dry land, making it unnecessary for animals to travel great distances to water. A man could fence off grass for winter use and provide better care of his stock in the winter. He could put on more beef per animal with less grass.

Fencing the public lands brought on a storm of protests and an epidemic of fence cutting, some of it done openly, some at night. The matter finally came to the attention of Congress. In 1884, a congressional delegation investigated illegal fencing in Colorado. At that time, the committee reported, the Prairie and Arkansas Valley cattle companies each had more than a million acres of public land fenced, and the Carlisle company had fenced an unspecified, but very large, quantity of government land.

The following year, there were 193 cases of illegal fencing reported to the General Land Office, two-thirds of them occurring in eight Colorado counties—Bent, Las Animas, La Plata, Pueblo, Fremont, El Paso, Park, and Weld.

In 1885, Congress authorized the President to remove illegal fences. President Cleveland issued a mandate August 7, 1885, ordering all fences on public lands removed. At that time, it was estimated there were 2,640,450 acres of federal land in Colorado illegally enclosed. The President's action was very badly timed. Two weeks earlier, he had ordered all livestock removed from the Cheyenne-Arapaho Reservation in the Indian Territory. The two tribes occupied the present Oklahoma strip and the northern two-thirds of the western third of the remainder of the state. This area cornered Colorado. Between 200,000 and 300,000 of these cattle were driven into eastern Colorado right at a time when the fences had to come down and during a drouth season when the grass was short. The results were disastrous. Resentment against the federal government smouldered for years. Later acts of government land administration fanned the flames.

The removal of illegal fences ushered in an era of severe land abuse. The range was already becoming overstocked as the available acres shrank and competition increased. In the 1870's, the range sheep industry had come into being, largely as a result of removal of flocks eastward from California and Oregon during drouth years. These competed with cattle and homesteaders for the public lands on the western slope. Southwestern Colorado cattlemen complained bitterly at the intrusion of nomad stockmen from Arizona, New Mexico, and Texas. Egged on by real estate promoters, settlers broke up millions of acres of grazing land that were completely unsuited to cultivation.

No one felt responsible for the public domain. Each of the conflicting interests—cattleman, sheepman, and homesteader—mined the land to the greatest extent.

Through the years, United States government land policies had been haphazard. They never were adjusted to the conditions which existed in the sub-humid West. Originally, the government offered its lands for sale, establishing low-price purchase programs to encourage settlement, which, in turn, would develop tax revenue for the government. This system later gave way to various other methods of disposing of the public lands, all geared to stimulate settlement and development. They included grants to railroads, to educational institutions, to men who had served in the military forces. They also included homestead programs and combination homestead-purchase plans. The objective was to get the lands into the hands of taxpayers. Unfortunately, people who knew and understood the lands to be disposed of, and the conditions which prevailed in the unsettled areas, were seldom consulted and their advice was even less frequently heeded.

The government made tragic errors in applying its land policies to the arid and semi-arid areas of the West. Among the more ridiculous programs was the Timber Culture Act, which offered a quarter of a section of land to any person who would plant and cultivate a certain number of acres of land to trees. Whether or not the trees grew—and they seldom did—was immaterial. Such programs invited fraud and increased the stockmen's contempt for government policies.

The people of the Middle West and the East, unfamiliar with arid regions, thought the efforts of Westerners to have the size of homestead units increased to permit economic operation was a land grab attempt for the big operators.

Edward T. Peters, in an article which appeared in the February 1883 issue of Century Magazine, summarized a common Eastern viewpoint toward the public lands, the West, and its settlers: "Western competition, in one form or another, is the thing most commonly complained of as a cause of diminished prosperity . . . the Western farmer or stock-raiser, in practically receiving his land for nothing (is) being placed at a great ad-

vantage over his Eastern competitor, whose land usually repre-
sents a large investment of capital . . . apart from abuses and
violations of law, our public land laws are themselves far too
liberal to the settler . . ."

As early as 1879, a delegation of Colorado Cattle Growers
Association representatives testified in Washington on suitable
land policies for the West. These included J. L. Brush, Bruce
Johnson, George H. West, James C. Jones, Albert W. Archibold,
H. N. Arms, James B. Belford, Doctor M. Beshoar, Silas Bent,
and Richard L. Wootton. Using their recommendations as a
basis, the Public Lands Commission recommended that a "pastoral homestead" unit should be not less than 2,560 acres. Congress couldn't see it that way, however.

Through the years, the Association continued to urge larger
homesteads in the grazing areas. The Act of February 19, 1909,
increased the homestead size from 160 to 320 acres, which greatly improved the settlement success of the dry-land farmer, but it
did little to assist the homestead rancher. In 1916, Congress
passed the Homestead Grazing Act. Its intention was excellent
—to provide a unit large enough for a family to make a satisfactory living for ranching. However, instead of 100 head, which
cattlemen figured the minimum for a profitable ranching operation, Congress settled on 50 head as an economic unit, then determined that 640 acres was sufficient to maintain 50 head of
cattle the year around.

By 1916, the land that was left for settlement had been picked
over and passed up, much of it turned back after failures of
earlier homesteads. In spite of the odds against them, settlers
flocked to file on the 640-acre homesteads, so many that within
a few years 30,000,000 acres in the 11 Western states had been
removed from the public domain. The inadequacy of the 640-
acre grazing homestead unit led to flagrant abuse of the land,
and encouraged more overstocking of the remaining public
lands.

By 1890, Congress was finally becoming aware that the land
was no longer free, and that the supply was fast dwindling. The
remaining public lands were, to a large extent, picked over. It
was badly abused—overgrazed and oversettled.

After years of neglecting the public domain, the federal government took its first action toward conservation of its most precious natural resource—land. Congress, on March 3, 1891, authorized the withdrawal of lands from the public domain for forest reserves, but made no provision for their administration. In the same year, President Harrison set aside the first forest reserves. Presidents Cleveland, McKinley, and Theodore Roosevelt added to them. By 1900, there were some 40 million acres of land set aside for this purpose.

For a decade, these lands were locked up, their use forbidden. A resolution issued April 18, 1894, specifically prohibited pasturing livestock on the forest reserves. Coming as it did when competition among cattlemen, sheepmen, and homesteaders was at its height, the regulations against grazing the reserves precipitated troubles which boiled over into violence and continued to simmer for the next 40 years.

In Colorado, much of the mountain forest lands on the western slope had been sheep range. Nomad or migratory sheepmen, who moved their flocks from public range to public range and from state to state with the season, would move into Colorado from Utah and Wyoming for late spring, summer, and fall grazing, depending on the area and the type of range. They pastured the high mountain grasslands during the summer, the sagebrush flats later in the season, then moved on when the grass was gone.

Banned from the forest reserves, these outfits in desperation, invaded the territory of the cattlemen, who were already harrassed by the incursions of homesteaders and local sheepmen and the fact that the nomad bands traveled through their ranges on the way to and from mountain pastures. Range war broke out in several areas of western and southern Colorado, as it did throughout other regions of the mountain West. Cattlemen posted deadlines beyond which they would not permit sheep to pass. They bludgeoned sheep to death, killed sheepherders and their dogs, and drove sheep outfits from their areas under threat of death.

Near Craig in June 1896, a masked band killed two of three Mexican sheepherders and clubbed 300 sheep to death. They warned the owner, Jack Edwards, to leave the country. Edwards, a doughty Welshman transplanted to Wyoming, talked them into permitting him to keep 800 ewes on the Colorado range until October. Ten days later, however, Edwards still had 30,000 sheep in Moffat County. Armed riders caught up with Edwards, put a noose around his neck and hoisted him into the air two or three times before he agreed to leave the country. Despite this attack and his promises, Edwards continued to run sheep into Moffat County for several years.

In southeastern Colorado, nomad cattlemen from Texas, New Mexico, and Arizona invaded the ranges. On August 18, 1893, the Bent County Cattle Growers Association moved to "use all lawful means and take whatever steps necessary to protect our business and our range rights." Terming the invaders "range pirates," the association's resolution stated, "We will not gather their cattle, brand their calves, or allow their employees to board with our outfits." The resolution charged that these invaders, bringing in cows without bulls and monopolizing range and water to which they had no right, had reduced the calf crops of association members to the point where their future existence was jeopardized.

The Prairie Cattle Company, east of Pueblo, was invaded by New Mexico sheep. These were driven out by armed cowboys. Whether or not this was an act sanctioned by the Prairie company was never established in the law suits which followed.

On the western slope in the early 1900's, range pirates from Oklahoma and Texas shipped hundreds of cattle into Delta and Montrose by train, trailed them across the public domain, up valleys into the Uncompaghre Forest where they grazed them without permits through the summer. There were no law enforcement agencies to handle this situation, and the invaders were too many and too well-armed for local ranchers to resist. About all a local rancher could do, was to watch for his chance to slip out the local cattle which had been gathered up with these herds on their drives to and from the mountain ranges.

This was not an age of reason. Embattled and bitter over the senselessness of government land policies, the futility of permitting homesteaders to tear up millions of acres of grazing land which could not produce crops in dry years, and now, when the migratory livestock crowded into the reduced acreages of what he considered his rightful range, the average stockman was goaded beyond reason. He was unable to review the situation dispassionately, to realize that he was no longer master of the range, that there was no longer, in fact, an open range as he had known it.

In vain, cooler heads among the cattlemen argued against violence. These men, and they included the most successful and, consequently, the bigger operators, pointed out that the old days would never return. The solution was to work for legislation which would open forest ranges to grazing and bring order out of chaos on other public lands. Work for a leasing program which would give preference to those living nearest the public lands, those most dependent upon them, and those who had historically used it, they urged. Some of them recommended a program under which the remaining public domain would be turned over to the states.

"The only way to stay in the cattle business permanently is to have a lease law and lease as much government land as you can," counseled Frank Benton, colorful rancher, humorist, and philosopher. "Run your cattle under fence, sell four-fifths of your saddle horses and buy registered bulls with the money. Have your cowboys raising hay instead of raising hell."

Benton made these and other pointed, pungent remarks at the annual meeting of the American Cattle Growers Association in Denver, March 5, 1902. He was then living on his 70 Ranch at Hardin, east of Greeley. Later, he operated extensive ranching enterprises in Burns Hole in Eagle and Routt counties. Benton, author of the humorous book, "Cowboy Life on the Sidetrack," was known as The Philosophical Cowman, from his newspaper column of that name, which was published in the Denver Record-Stockman for several years.

Benton classed the anti-leasing people into three groups. "The first and most numerous are men that run their cattle on the open range and have succeeded so far in keeping a reasonable amount of range for their cattle by drawing deadlines, making threats, writing anonymous letters to sheepmen signed with a skull and crossbones, wearing black masks when a crowd of them visit a harmless Mexican to warn him to move his sheep, and once in awhile. . .to enforce obedience. . .they have been obliged to shoot a few sheepherders and club a few thousand harmless sheep to death with wagon spokes taken from the wheels of the sheep wagon."

Benton added that this class of men had only a temporary hold on their range as a result of these tactics. "You many break the laws of the land for a while, ladies and gentlemen, but finally you have got to come to the feed rack of law and order, whether there is any fodder in it or not."

The second class opposed to leasing, Benton said, were "the men who have fenced in large areas of government land and so far have been able to keep other people's livestock out of their pastures and violate the government law against fencing up the public domain and are not paying any lease. This class of cattlemen are continually hollering, 'Let us alone!' "

The third class, according to Benton, "do not own a water gap or a round-up wagon. They won't even ride on circle at the round-up, but come to the herd after it is rounded up and get some good-natured man to brand their calves and ship their beef. . .They sit by the fire at the village grocery in the winter while their cattle are starving and breaking into some man's hay stacks. . .They say, 'There ain't any money in the cattle business now, and we don't see how we ever could make anything and pay lease on government land.' "

Despite the efforts of Benton and other cattle industry leaders to make them see the need for a leasing law, the answer of the rank and file cattlemen was a loud, violent, and profane "No!" The only immediate result was a split in the ranks of the cattlemen which threatened to wreck the cattlemen's Association. The big cattlemen were conspiring to gain control of public ranges by leasing, it was charged. The newly formed National Live Stock Association was assailed for its stand in favor of leasing.

The leasing controversy came to a head on February 24, 1900, when stockmen from Garfield, Eagle, Delta, Mesa, Gunnison, Rio Blanco, and Routt counties met at Glenwood Springs and organized the Western Range Stock Growers Association to fight leasing. Loud and bitter in their denunciation of migratory sheepmen and other range pirates, these men feared leasing even more.

George Yule, of Divide Creek, who had brought the first cattle into Garfield County many years before, said leasing would make the range cattle business impossible. C. P. Larson, of Garfield Creek, told the group, "If we have to lease the range, we will have to go out of business."

W. Lloyd Grubb, of Carbondale, was elected president of the new organization.

Grubb's brother and former partner, Eugene Grubb, of Carbondale, was the only person present to speak out in favor of leasing. "I can sympathize with you fellows," he told the group, "but you want to remember, there are 8,000,000 head of sheep in adjoining lands waiting to come in, and they have just as much right as cattle to free range." Why not, Eugene Grubb urged, work for a leasing bill which would give residents of the area a one-year option on leases? His voice was lost in a storm of boos and catcalls.

A similar meeting held at Rifle, March 23, 1900, engendered additional enthusiasm against leasing and more feeling against big cattlemen. Inspired by the early success, the group scheduled a meeting at Denver, April 9, 1900, to unite all anti-leasing groups throughout the state into one organization.

There were 592 men in attendance at the Denver meeting, which was shifted to the Tabor Opera House when the Chamber of Commerce quarters proved too small. It was a wildly enthusiastic, easily stampeded crowd, dedicated blindly to the policy of a free range for cattlemen alone.

The result was the organization of the Western Range Stock Growers Association on a state wide basis, with W. Lloyd Grubb as president; H. D. Williamson, of Eagle County, secretary; A. A. McIntyre, of Lincoln County, treasurer; and R. A. Palmer, of Douglas County, corresponding secretary.

In its resolutions, the new organization attacked leasing on many grounds: The presence of free land enhanced the value of nearby agricultural lands; leasing was impossible for the small cattleman, who couldn't afford to fence his alloted portion to himself; the crowding out of small herds would lead to the swallowing up of small farms and ranches by powerful corporations; "It will concentrate the wealth occasioned by free grazing of stock into a few hands," then moving in an oblique direction, "It will close up all avenues by which all stock owners have climbed from a few head to large herds."

According to the resolutions, leasing "would cause endless litigation or manifest injustice between stock owners whose herds commingle," and "the use of the public domain for grazing under the present system is most satisfactory," a rather surprising conclusion in view of the violence of recent years. The association also felt that leasing would put too much power in the hands of the Secretary of the Interior as the administrative official.

Charged with evangelistic fervor, leaders of the new organization carried their cause into all parts of the state. They were instrumental in having an anti-leasing plank inserted in the platform of each of the four major political parties in Colorado, in 1900. They gathered recruits and financial strength. The Colorado Cattle Growers Association awoke to find many of its active members in the new camp. Its very existence was threatened.

Alarmed at the manner in which the anti-leasing movement was gaining momentum, the older, cooler heads of the state Association quietly laid the groundwork for a return to sanity. At about the same time, Grubb, and other leaders of the Western Range Association, began to consider the range dilemma in a more objective manner. Gradually, they began to realize the futility of trying to stop the hands of the clock. At chance meetings, whenever they met any of the leaders of the Western Range Association, men like Samuel Harstel, E. M. Ammons, H. H. Robinson, and Dr. Charles Gresswell casually discussed the situation with them.

Meanwhile, the Western Range Stock Growers Association continued to gain members at the expense of the state organization. The rallying cry, "protect the little cattleman from the

big man" had proven effective. By fall, the state Association was
the smaller organization.

When the Colorado Cattle Growers Association convened
for its annual meeting, at the Albany Hotel, in Denver, December 13, 1900, there were 132 delegates in attendance, many of
them members of the Western Range group. E. M. Ammons,
of Douglas County, who was later governor of the state, presided. Soon after the convention opened, he appointed Samuel
Hartsel, M. H. Murray, and F. P. Johnson to meet with W. L.
Grubb, H. D. Williamson, and other officers of the Western
Range Association to discuss uniting the two groups.

In a hotel room, they hammered out a merger agreement
which enabled the Western Range Stock Growers Association
to retire from its anti-leasing stand with dignity, to satisfy its
members that it had not retreated, and to maintain an effective,
unopposed state organization. The Western Range Association
was to become the state stock-growers association, with the
understanding that it would change its name at the annual
meeting in April. The leasing issue was to be passed up to the
National Livestock Assocation for settlement, the state organization withdrawing from the leasing controversy on the grounds
that this had now become a strictly national issue.

Grubb, in later appearances, explained that the anti-leasing
movement in Colorado had served its purpose by securing
pledges from the state's political candidates to fight leasing in
Congress.

The fight within the organization was over. Colorado's cattlemen closed ranks and began drawing plans to secure the best
terms possible under a leasing program. However, many cattlemen continued to resist, protesting the impossibility of paying
for the right to graze on public lands.

Meanwhile, the government's ponderous machinery had
clanked into action. Congress finally recognized the need to do
something about the forest reserves. The Act of June 4, 1897,
outlined the principles under which the reserves would be administered. On June 30, 1897, Secretary of the Interior Hitch-
cock, ruled that grazing of public lands on forest reserves would
not be prevented "as long as it appeared no injury was being

done to forest growth, and the rights of others were not jeopardized." This act, however, specifically forbade the grazing of sheep on forest reserves except in the humid states of Oregon and Washington, reflecting a belief that sheep were injurious to ranges in arid areas. The sheep ban was rescinded in 1902.

A forestry bureau was established in 1901, as a branch of the Department of the Interior. In 1905, administration of the forests was transferred to the Department of Agriculture, and the forest service came into being. This marked the beginning of federal grazing administration. The transfer to the Department of Agriculture recognized the importance of using forest service land for meat production.

Administration of the forest reserves began with the issuance of temporary grazing permits, effective until a permanent system could be developed. No fees were charged for cattle under the first temporary permits.

In the summer of 1904, when it became apparent that the Department of Agriculture would become the administrative agency, Secretary of Agriculture Wilson, called a conference of Western livestock growers to assist in developing the principles for a grazing program. These principles include:

1. Those persons who were already using the ranges should have priority in the award of grazing privileges.

2. Any changes in numbers or methods of handling stock would be made gradually after due notice had been given.

3. Small owners should have preference in the allotment of permits and would be exempted from reductions in numbers of stock.

4. Every effort would be made to carry on forest improvement programs without excluding areas to livestock grazing.

5. Maximum use would be made of forage on the forest reserves consistent with good forest management.

6. Stockmen would have a voice in making the rules for management of their stock on the range.

Provisions were made for forest service advisory boards, made up of members of national, state, and local livestock associations who held grazing permits.

Trouble hadn't ended on the national forest ranges, but the

situation had entered a new phase. The advisability of government control and systematic grazing had been established. Henceforth, the battles would be fought over administrative problems.

There was a lot of right and a lot of wrong on both sides in the ensuing bitter conflicts, in which the forest service, the small cattlemen, the big cattlemen, local sheepmen, and migratory sheepmen were allied and/or opposed in ever-changing combinations.

The forest service, at its outset, was staffed by Eastern and European-trained forest rangers and other officials whose sole knowledge and concern was timber, and with untrained Westerners who understood the West and the livestock business, but knew nothing about forestry.

The stockmen were independent, hard-headed, often belligerent pragmatists. A great many of them had been forced to go along with the new order, but their attitudes had changed very little, and they had no intention of being pushed around by government employees.

The idea of conservation and range management was new. There were no range technicians and no yardstick to work with. The program had to be developed by trial and error.

The stockmen had a tendency to forget that the national forests had other purposes than that of supplying seasonal pasturage, that frequently parts of the forest must be closed to protect young trees, that erosion control was necessary, and that the forest ranges must be administered so that their grazing capacity could be sustained through the years. In addition, their ranks included men who abused grazing allotments, slipping many more than the allotted numbers onto the forest ranges.

On the other hand, rangers often overlooked the problems of the stockmen. Some failed to comprehend that forest ranges served only a part of the season and must fit in with a stockman's year-round program. Frequently, their knowledge was theoretical and impractical, or applied to Eastern and European forests without practical value in the West. Another cause of irritation, was the arbitrary attitude of certain forest service officials imbued with an exalted sense of their own importance and the authority of a government office.

That things ran as smoothly and efficiently as they did, is a tribute to the dedication and good sense of a great many forest service people who were actually on the ground working with the stockmen, and to the guiding influence of local advisory boards, whose members supplied practical knowledge, pertinent local information, and helped keep the more bellicose stockmen in check.

While rates and values have changed, the fee system for the forest ranges has remained virtually the same through the years. Charges are based on three factors—the number of animals authorized by a permit, the number of days in the grazing season, and the monthly rate. Grazing reductions or increases can be effected in two ways, either by changing the number of animals, or by changing the length of the grazing season.

The carrying capacity of ranges is figured in terms of animal unit months—the number of acres required to feed one animal for one month.

To the casual observer, the grazing fees for use of public ranges may seem low in comparison to the prevailing charges for use of privately-owned pastures on the plains. It must be remembered, however, that public range is interdependent with commensurate property. Experience has shown that a substantial increase in grazing fees causes a decline in the value of commensurate property unless the increase is part of a general economic upswing. Also, Colorado State University studies show that production costs are consistently higher for cattle enterprises using public range than for those confined entirely to privately-owned land. Maintaining cattle on mountain lands is expensive, requiring much more labor. The cost of user-financed improvements to the public ranges is a major additional expense. It is justified in economic terms only by the fact that it enables a stockman to put more animals on an allotment—at an extra charge—and by the fact that it prevents injury to the land.

The major obstacle, once stockmen had been convinced they must pay grazing fees, was that of reducing grazing numbers.

The ranges had been overstocked in the free-for-all competition before the controls were established. Rangers and local advisory boards decided their best policy was to disturb the existing pattern as little as possible until a permanent program had been developed, then work gradually into the necessary reductions. This probably prevented a major upheaval at the start, but it caused an ulcerous irritation which continued for years as the forest service worked to bring grazing down to conservation levels.

In later years, the inconsistency of government policy and a tendency to go beyond conservation to "preservation" levels, were added causes of conflicts. In the earlier years, the local advisory boards assumed much of the responsibility for determining grazing levels and establishing a balance between sheep and cattle, which undoubtedly kept the death rate of forest service personnel at the lowest possible rate.

Permittees were divided into three priority groups—first, the local, family-size operator who had first preference and was protected from reductions in his grazing allotment; second, the larger sheep and cattle ranchers with permanent locations and private or other public areas; and third, the migratory or tramp outfits, which were last in line for permits.

The early years were rough and rugged for the forest range program.

At Rifle, on February 11, 1907, 54 cattlemen signed this agreement: "We, the undersigned, each and all of us hereby agree not to pay a fee for grazing upon the forest reserves, and if any of us have applied for a permit, we shall refuse to accept the same; and we further agree that any expense incurred by reason of the arrest or prosecution of any signer of this agreement, for the defense of the same, shall be born (sic) by all of us, pro rata according to number of stock owned, to be collected by the secretary of association in whose locality the signer may reside or run his cattle."

The first man to sign the agreement was Fred Light, of Snowmass, president of the Garfield County-Grand River Stock Growers Association and a prominent member of the Colorado Stock Growers Association. Light was the first of the signers to be prosecuted by the forest service for trespassing. Light had homesteaded in the 1880's, on Roaring Fork, near what later became the Holy Cross National Forest. His ranching enterprise was dependent on the forest reserves for grazing. He had opened much of the land to grazing 20 years earlier.

Light maintained that he was right in refusing to pay for grazing land which he had used for years, and which was a part of his homestead ranching enterprise. He and the other old-timers who had homesteaded in the 1880's and 1890's, stoutly insisted that the free use of open range land was one of the reasons why they had settled in that area. They had been promised this privilege as a part of their homestead agreement with the government, they declared. Light, Joseph Yule, John Gant, and others who told of this promise, were solid, substantial citizens, men whose good character was known. There is every reason to believe that they had been assured by government officials that they would have the right to free use of public range as long they continued to live on their homesteads.

Fred Light maintained that it was not his fault if his cattle strayed onto forest lands while grazing other ranges of the adjacent public domain. The Colorado Stock Growers Association, supported by the American National Livestock Association, joined Light in defending the suit. They contended that the forest service was subject to the provisions of the Colorado fence law, which provided that livestock were not trespassing unless they broke into adequately-fenced lands.

Light lost his case in successive courts. The United States Supreme Court finally found him guilty of trespass in a decision of May 1, 1911, a decision which he accepted philosophically and without bitterness.

Through the next few years, relations between the forest service and the stockmen improved. The government officials were quick to credit the advisory boards and the stockmen's associations for their efforts to promote harmony, and their assistance in developing and securing acceptance of regulations.

Soon after World War I began in August, 1914, cattle prices zoomed to unprecedented heights. Spurred by prosperity and an abundance of credit, stockmen expanded their holdings to the limit. The number of cattle and sheep on the range increased rapidly.

Immediately after the war, prices leveled off, but livestock numbers did not. A wide-spread drouth in the West, in the summer of 1919, was the first event in a chain which soon led to serious troubles for the cattle business. The drouth was followed by a long, cold winter—still remembered by old-timers as the winter of the big snows. Then came the crusher. Livestock prices suddenly collapsed under the pressure of excessive numbers and the post-war economic slump. Range empires crashed. Worried bankers, crowded by Eastern financial underwriters, called in loans and the source of livestock credit dried up. Losses were tremendous.

The sheep industry recovered rapidly, thanks to a favorable year in 1922, but cattlemen remained in trouble. At the instigation of the Federal Reserve Bank, metropolitan banks throughout the nation formed a $50,000,000 emergency credit pool for cattle loans. This gave cattlemen an opportunity to tread water while they groped for permanent solutions. John Clay, writing in the mid-1920's, when the cattle business was still deep in depression, pointed out that large-scale liquidation was the only permanent solution.

There were too many cattle, a slack demand for beef, and prices failed to improve sufficiently for stockmen to break even. No one wanted to loan money on range cattle.

The small operator tightened his belt, and a great percentage of this group managed in some way to ride the trouble through. "God knows, the ranchman of the West is living mostly on what he can't sell," Clay wrote. By the time an increased demand and higher prices brought relief, many of the larger operators had liquidated.

The big sheep and cattle outfits had been major users of the forest ranges up to this point. Their mass liquidation depopulated the forests. Grazing receipts dropped sharply. For the forest service, reductions in personnel and slashed operating budgets were imminent. In 1927, came orders from Washington, "Build the grazing numbers back up to their former levels."

While not recognized as such, at the time, this order was the first shot fired in the forest service-stockman war which raged through the 1930's and 1940's, and into the 1950's.

The Monitor Livestock Association members in Delta County found themselves in a typical predicament when they received instructions to increase the number of cattle on their allotment or lose their permits. The association was comprised of a group of small ranchers, who shared a grazing allotment on three mesas on the Uncompaghre National Forest, an allotment later reduced to two mesas.

Hard-pressed after years of livestock troubles, and able to survive through the early 1920's only because they were small enough to "live on what they couldn't sell," the Monitor members laughed grimly, a few years later, when writers in metropolitan newspapers assailed them as "cattle barons" and "overlords of the range" who were allegedly despoiling the national forests.

The association was ordered to double the number of animals on the allotment. To do this, involved not only purchasing more cattle, but also buying or leasing additional land for wintering the extra cattle.

The laws of economics (as well as forest service regulations) required "commensurate property"—late fall, winter, and spring pasture and feed, to sustain their livestock when they were not on the forest lands, which were generally used for summer and early fall grazing.

"We did what we could," Floyd Beach, president of the group, recalled. "Those of us who had the money or the credit put more cattle on the forest. I lost a large part of my range because I couldn't raise enough money to buy the additional cattle. They cancelled the 'right-of-non-use' which had been a help during tough periods, in the past. When they threatened to give part of our allotment to 'other classes of livestock'—which meant sheep—we got neighbors and other ranchers to put stock on those mesas. We even agreed to care for their cattle free of charge if they would help us protect the allotment."

Generally, the forest service personnel in direct contact with the stockmen, were sympathetic. They understood the situation more than their superiors in Denver and Washington, but had little opportunity to express themselves. They simply carried out the orders.

To meet the forest service ultimatum, cattlemen invested in more land and in cattle, as heavily as they could under the tight credit policies for range cattle which existed at that time. They went into the 1930's in poor financial condition for the ordeal of economic depression and range land drouths which followed. The average cattleman's equity in land and cattle was virtually wiped out as prices sank to the lowest levels in the century. He could only hang on and hope that an upturn would enable him to work his way out.

Finally, the Western range cattle business hit bottom. The worst drouth in the historic West dried up the grass in 1934. It dried up the water holes and streams on the public domain at lower elevations, causing cattle to drift up into the forests in search of water and feed. This complicated an already serious situation with an influx of trespass animals.

As the effects of the drouth became apparent, the forest service people in Washington panicked. Suddenly, there came orders for large scale reductions in grazing permits, without regard for the consequences. A 67 per cent reduction was ordered for the Uncompaghre National Forest.

Cattlemen throughout the West were stunned at the pronouncement. If carried through, it meant the liquidation of every cattle enterprise dependent on forest range—at a time when cattle were worth only a fraction of their purchase price or production cost. It was unbelievable.

Donald Stubbs, then a young Montrose lawyer, and later a prominent Denver attorney, who fought his earliest legal battles for the cattlemen, summarized the situation: "The cattlemen were suddenly faced with going out of business. That's what it meant. These men had geared their entire operations to a dependency on the forest for summer range. They had invested hard-earned money for commensurate property. Economic conditions were terrible. They owed heavily at the banks. Their equity had disappeared. You couldn't liquidate and come out, yet the decree of the forest service meant liquidation. There was no other way. It meant complete ruin for every cattle operation on the national forests. The cattlemen were fighting for their very existence. We found we couldn't tolerate what the forest service proposed."

Worst of all, from a strictly legal standpoint, the forest service was right. Its officials ignored the orders of only a few years before to build up the numbers on the allotments. They reminded them that they were "permittees," without any legal right to use the public lands except at the discretion of the forest service. There was no redress, nothing to fall back on. The plight of the stockmen was desperate. "We were faced with an administrative agency that had all the autocratic power in the world," said Stubbs.

The impact seemed to be more drastic in the Uncompaghre than in other Colorado forests. "The forest service claimed that this was a general order, but when we checked with cattlemen from other areas, it appeared that their reductions were much smaller. We decided that the strategy was to use this situation as a means of getting all cattle off the national forests, one forest at a time, starting with the Uncompaghre."

Utter failure greeted the first efforts of the Monitor association and other users of the Uncompaghre land to secure a modification of the order. Meeting after meeting ended in frustration, hard words, and hard feelings. On the one side was "Jimmy" Beals, a dedicated and dogmatic but undiplomatic civil servant who had strict instructions to see that the reduction order was carried out. To Beals, an order was an order. If he was charged with its enforcement, his duty was to enforce it, and he intended to do just that, without modification or delay.

On the other side were Roy Case, Kelso Musser, Art Starr, Wiley Freeman, Floyd Beach, and other leaders of the Uncompaghre Valley Cattle and Horse Growers Association which led the cattlemen's fight. These were "a bunch of guys that don't get shoved around real easily," as Stubbs put it.

"We never got to first base," said Stubbs. "I actually was afraid that this would develop into something we'd all be sorry about, because, after all, these fellows were fighting for their existence." Stubbs didn't call those sessions "meetings." He called them "confrontations."

At the same time, the enraged cattlemen were fighting the battle on other fronts. Through their local associations, the Colorado Stock Growers and Feeders Association, the American National Livestock Association, local business groups in the livestock area, and through their senators and representatives, they bombarded Washington with petitions and demands.

"It got to where the boys in Washington realized that we could never talk with Jimmy Beals," said Stubbs. E. A. Snow replaced Beals. Snow turned out to be a diplomat, a man who understood the cattlemen's plight and didn't mind bending a few regulations to fit practical situations. The cattlemen re-established communication with the forest service.

"Ed Snow realized that it was not proper for the United States government to close down entirely the cattle business in western Colorado, and that was exactly what they were trying to do," Stubbs said. "The Uncompaghre was their test case. Somewhere along the line, though, Ed Snow must have been able to persuade his superiors in the forest service that the rule of reason would have to prevail. He couldn't have done all that he did without some backing from the higher-ups."

Snow and the forest service permittees executed a Memorandum of Understanding, to be effective on a trial basis for three years. This document, drawn up in Stubbs' office, was the forerunner of agreements executed some 15 years later which turned the forest service and another group of fighting-mad cattlemen into a working partnership for conservation.

Under the memorandum's provisions, the permittees agreed to eliminate trespass animals. This included policing their own ranks to stop the practice of slipping extra animals into the forests under an allotment, measures to prevent the entrance of trespass animals owned by others, and the elimination of the large number of wild horses and wild burros that ran in the forest. The cattlemen removed as many of these animals as they could capture, and shot the others.

The memorandum also bound the stockmen to respect a "range readiness" standard developed by the forest service and themselves. This device provided a yardstick to determine when the range was ready for use in the summer, and bound the cattlemen and sheepmen to keep animals off until that time. They further agreed to erect fences, where necessary, to control animals and keep out trespass animals.

The forest service, as represented by Snow, agreed it would order no reduction in allotments during the three-year period and would cooperate in programs to improve carrying capacity.

The arrangement was a success. By tacit agreement, the memorandum was continued in force as long as Snow was the forest supervisor. There were some reductions in allotments, voluntarily accepted by the stockmen as necessary to protect the grass.

The Monitor association faithfully executed its responsibilities under the memorandum. Its permittees built drift fences, developed watering places, built ditches to carry water out of canyons and spread it over larger areas for irrigation, built stock ponds and reseeded grazed-down areas. Its members spent an average of one dollar per head, per season, in actual money on range improvement work, in addition to countless hours of their own labor. At one time, when an operator could be employed, the association owned its own bulldozer. The forest service furnished part of the materials for the work, also.

Although Snow cooperated willingly in the work, there were certain restrictions on his authority. On one occasion, the Monitor members needed a bulldozer to run spreader ditches. The forest service had in the vicinity, just the machine which they needed. Snow informed the ranchers, regretfully, that government regulations would not permit using the machine for their work. Almost immediately, however, Snow had to leave on business. By some chance, the bulldozer was left in the open, the key in the switch, the gas tank full, and several extra cans of gasoline strapped on the side.

While another rancher operated the tractor, Floyd Beach walked ahead of it, holding a carpenter's hand level, and marked the line of the ditches. Snow apparently never noticed that the bulldozer had been used, but he and other forest service officials declared no ditches could hold when built to such an unorthodox survey. A quarter of a century later, they're still in use.

Not all of the permittees cooperated in the range improvement program, however. Many of them refused to spend more money improving forest ranges when they expected to be removed at any time, and when they received no credit for the work on their grazing fees.

On the other hand, a great many forest service officials didn't see eye-to-eye with Ed Snow on his lenient treatment of a group of trouble-making cattlemen. Very few cattle remained on the Pike National Forest. Numbers had been reduced drastically all along the Front Range of the mountains. The Western Slope Livestock Protective Association had reached an agreement with the forest service under which the association members agreed to accept a 25 per cent reduction, with the understanding that there would be no more cuts. Now, they were informed that they must undergo another 25 per cent slash.

The June 21, 1948 issue of USDA, a publication for employees of the Department of Agriculture, contained the following news item:

"The following employees have been awarded pay increases for superior accomplishment:

"DANIEL E. GIBSON, District Forest Ranger, for exercising unusual foresight and initiative in the re-analysis of range survey data which led to the adoption of a plan to remove 19,700 sheep from the Hans (Hahn's) Peak Ranger District by the season of 1949."

At about the same time, city conservation writers were publishing numerous feature stories purporting to show how stockmen had destroyed the ranges in the national forests and how vital to the future it was to eliminate the curse of "range barons" from the forest lands.

In rebuttal, two editors of Farm Journal magazine, Ray Anderson and Paul Friggens (who is well-known today as a roving editor for Readers Digest magazine), charged the forest service with attempting to climb on the bandwagon of the popular conservation movement by ridding the ranges of livestock, and of aiding and abetting misleading articles which discredited the stockmen of the West.

Anderson and Friggens toured the 11 Western states, and published numerous documentary pictures of excellent ranges which had been closed by the forest service. They said C. M. Granger, assistant chief of the forest service, termed the so-called conservation articles, "a damned good thing."

The real issue, the two writers concluded, wasn't conservation but a government bureau's move to eradicate all opposition to its absolute dictatorship.

When C. K. Collins succeeded Snow as supervisor of the Uncompaghre National Forest, and Roy Williams became supervisor of the Grand Mesa National Forest, these two areas became the focal point for the last bitter campaign in the stockmen's fight against the forest service. The Memorandum of Agreement was abruptly wiped out. The 67 per cent reduction was again ordered into effect.

Hell broke loose on the Uncompaghre.

Montrose county commissioners issued a fiery resolution, charging both the forest service and the Bureau of Land Management with unjustified and arbitrary reductions of grazing rights on public lands in Montrose County, the number of head being cut from 70,000 to 55,000 in five years. This, they charged, despite the fact that "independent examinations of the range land in Montrose County indicate that this land is in better condition than it has been for a number of years, and in far better condition than stated by reports of the forest service and the Bureau of Land Management."

Collins retaliated angrily, denying flatly that there had been any cuts. In a sizzling letter to the Montrose commissioners, he said, "A range survey was made of some of the cattle allotments on the forests, in 1937. The survey was made by a competent crew. One of the commonly accepted methods of taking range surveys was used. The survey indicated many cases of severe overstocking, based on usable forage.

"The cattlemen protested the survey and the forest service foolishly yielded to the pressure exerted by the livestock organizations. In checking the record you can observe that there has been a virtual moratorium on reductions during that time.

"Our inspections over the past few years, including this year, indicate that the majority of these ranges are over-utilized."

A week later, on December 17, 1948, at the annual meeting

of the Uncompaghre Valley Cattle and Horse Growers Association, Floyd Beach appealed for a united front to curb the autocratic power of the forest service. "We do not want the present system of the forest service being the judge, jury, and prosecuting attorney continued." Beach reported that the Colorado Stock Growers and Feeders Association was trying to raise $5,000 for a public relations program to tell the stockmen's side of the story to the general public.

At this meeting, a resolution prepared by the Association's range inspection committee, charged that the findings of C. K. Collins, forest supervisor, and Kenneth Cross, range staffman, were "not substantiated by the facts of long period study." Association members who participated with forest service officials on a range ride of the allotments, in the fall of 1948, said their own observations showed the ranges to be in excellent condition.

Early in 1949, the American National Livestock Association and cattlemen's organizations of several states, protested current forest service policies in resolutions and at meetings with forest service officials.

At a Montrose Lions Club meeting, in March, 1949, Collins charged that because of the need to protect "key areas" of the forests, "further reductions" in the number of cattle were necessary, and perhaps it might be necessary to withdraw cattle from the forest altogether. He did not explain how there could be "further reductions" when just three months earlier he had maintained there had been no cuts at all.

On May 14, 1949, ten Delta area cattlemen, among them fire-eater Floyd Beach, were arrested by the forest service and charged with trespassing. E. D. Sandvig, assistant regional forest service supervisor, conducted a hearing at Delta. Collins had charged that the men had kept "something like 125 head" on the forest between November 1 and November 10, 1948, the period when cattle were being removed for the season. It developed only 23 head had been found on the forest. All ten of the men paid fines under protest. John W. Spencer, regional forester, admitted that this was far from an isolated case. "We know there is a lot of trespassing on all the forests, but these stockmen on the Uncompaghre are a defiant bunch, and we had to call their bluff."

The annual meeting of the Colorado Stock Growers and Feeders Association at Grand Junction, in July, 1949, was a virtual protest session against the forest service.

The Gunnison County Stockgrowers Association, however, refused to join in efforts to combat the forest regulations and administrative practices. Under the supervision of Ed Wright, rangers on the Gunnison National Forest had worked in close cooperation with the stockmen.

Sam Little, president of the Gunnison association, especially commended Ranger Donald Shaw, for his successful relations with 32 cattlemen and 14 sheepmen. "As soon as a permittee, or Shaw, notices the possibility of overgrazing, they get together and take necessary action," Little said. "If it is found the range is not in bad shape, a brief cutting down of stock is usually decided upon and in no time at all, the range is back to normal."

In November, 1949, regional forester John W. Spencer, added fuel to the flames when he notified users of the Grand Mesa National Forest, that the use of the mesa top would be discontinued the following year, but that grazing would be permitted for another year on the Roosevelt National Forest.

David G. Rice, Jr., former Delta County agent who had been named executive secretary of the Colorado Cattlemen's Association two months earlier, addressed the Montrose Rotary Club, November 30, 1949. Reported the Montrose Press, "The new secretary didn't advocate the removal from office of top forest officials as a solution, but he argued strongly for giving the stockman a real voice and hand in the management of the ranges."

The same newspaper reported that the annual meeting of the Uncompaghre Valley Cattle and Horse Growers Association, December 18, 1949, "was noticeable by the absence of the usual liberal sprinkling of forest green uniformed men. There was not a United States forest official or ranger in attendance."

The newspaper explained that the association had extended a limited invitation to the forest service personnel "to attend the meeting after 3:30 o'clock. The stockmen said they had adopted the rather unconventional method of designating a time when forest service officials would be welcome to avert a repetition of stormy scenes that have marred association meetings in recent years." One of the association officers put it this way. "We do not like to have our meetings monopolized by a forest service supervisor who appears bent for argument." Commented the Press, "The inference was taken as applying to C. K. Collins."

The next episode in the accelerating series of events was the retirement of Spencer. In December, 1949, Secretary of Agriculture Charles Brannan, announced in Washington, that "age was the only reason for the retirement of John W. Spencer as Rocky Mountain regional forester." Spencer was succeeded by Ed Cliff, of Ogden, Utah, who is the present chief forester of the United States Forest Service.

At Denver, January 20, 1950, cattlemen presented their case before the National Forest Board of Review. This was a board established by Secretary of Agriculture Clinton P. Anderson, May 10, 1948, shortly before his resignation. Its members were Dr. Jonathan Forman, of Columbus, Ohio; Professor Gilmour MacDonald, head of the Department of Forestry at Iowa State College; and Dr. Roland Renne, president of Montana State College.

Spokesman for the cattlemen was Kelso Musser, of Delta, chairman of the Joint Cattle and Sheep Forest Advisory Board for Colorado. Seated very close to him, in an advisory capacity, was Don Stubbs. By this time, Stubbs was occupied with corporation law in Denver, but he managed to squeeze in a "vacation period" during the board of review hearing.

"Two things apparently became obvious to the forest service as a result of this hearing," said Stubbs. "One was that under the recently-enacted governmental procedural act, provisions had been made for redress by citizens against the actions of government employees. No longer would one tight little group in a government agency control all matters of policy and decision. Henceforth, the forest service would be answerable to other branches of government, even to the courts.

"The second thing, which the forest service seemed to realize now for the first time, was that they were not dealing with small, isolated groups of stockmen. They were dealing with a large, organized group, with a state association, and a national association."

Secretary of Agriculture Brannan announced in Washington, February 7, 1950, that he had created an independent appeal board composed of Department of Agriculture officials outside the forest service to study and act on controversial problems "in line with requests made by stockmen to the board of review on January 20, at Denver."

The tide had turned.

The effects of Ed Cliff's appointment did not immediately become apparent. Cliff moved slowly, carefully and quietly, made few promises, and no positive statements. Early in January, he attended a meeting of the Joint Cattle and Sheep Forest Advisory Board. Cliff told the group he wanted to work out problems with forest users, that he realized some conflicts would arise, and that there were differences of opinion. He said he believed in the scientific approach to range management, but that it should be applied with good judgment and common sense.

That was about all Cliff had to say at present. There were occasional transfers from the region, effected quietly and without much attention. Collins went to Arizona, Williams to Wyoming. Later, Sandvig went to South America.

W. K. Somerville, who had run cattle on the Grand Mesa, fired a parting shot at Williams. In a letter to Williams, dated September 25, 1950, Somerville thanked the former Grand Mesa forest supervisor for a virtual gift of $10.00. "At the time of your transfer, a bet was placed that within a very short time after you assumed your duties in Wyoming, a similar situation would occur there. In the Rocky Mountain News, for September 9, 1950, I read this headline from Sheridan, 'Stockmen, Forest Service Clash Over Grazing Order."

Congress passed the Granger Act on April 24, 1950, but not in the form that its forest service authors had submitted it. The act related to administrative procedure and powers of the forest service. Hearings on the act afforded stockmen from all over the West an opportunity to make their differences with the forest service known to members of Congress. It was a triumph for the newly-formed Public Lands Committee of the American National Livestock Association, which presented one cattleman from each of the Western states as a witness. Floyd Beach represented Colorado.

Beach testified that the forest service was attempting to force livestock from the forest ranges by charging that the ranges were overgrazed. One of the devices used, he said, was the "hoop method" of range evaluation. This consisted of throwing a metal hoop to the ground, then counting the number of un-grazed plants within the hoop. "They'd deliberately pick out bare spots and throw the hoop there," Beach said. "I told them the horse turd method was much better, and it was, but they wouldn't listen." This latter method consisted of selecting a dried horse dropping, closing the eyes, and throwing it as far as possible. "When you opened your eyes, if you could see it, the range was overgrazed. If you couldn't, there was enough grass left for carry-over."

At this hearing, chief forester Lyle Watts blandly testified that one of the purposes of the Granger Act was to enable the forest service to take more rigid disciplinary action against permittees. His comment that "the cattlemen on the Uncompaghre Forest need a spanking,' gave Colorado Senators Ed Johnson and Eugene Milliken all the ammunition they needed. When they had finished, the Senate had amended the Granger Act to the point where it afforded protection, rather than punishment, for forest service grazing permit holders. Among other things, the bill as finally passed, made the forest service advisory boards, official agencies of the grazing program. It also eliminated "transfer cuts"—the practice of arbitrarily reducing the size of allotments whenever the ownership of commensurate property changed.

Back in Colorado, about this time, two astute connivers for the public good began to plot for peace. If Dave Rice and Ed Cliff had come on the scene at different times, the ranchers and rangers might still be battling. Quietly, almost secretly, they began drinking coffee together and exchanging views—the new secretary of the cattlemen's Association and the new regional supervisor for the forest service.

The Rice-Cliff entente was preceded by a 'til-death-or-decision conference in the summer of 1949 at the Manitou Experimental Forest, 25 miles west of Colorado Springs. After a discussion with forest service officials, Rice carefully selected some of the most experienced leaders in the stockmen's fight against the forest service—Paul Hummel of Boulder, Frank Fehling of Nathrop, Clarence Curry of Livermore and Floyd Beach of Delta. The government agency was represented by three range management specialists—E. D. Sandvig and Herb Swan of the forest service headquarters at Denver and Russell Ford of Colorado State University.

These seven men were told to work out a program of range improvement on the national forests with which both the forest service and permit holders could live, and not to quit until the program was completed. The conference was acrimonious, but eventually successful.

The battle of science versus experience raged for two-and-one-half days, a portion of which time the opposing groups were not speaking to each other. From it, however, came a program which brought peace on the range and far-reaching effects. After 16 years, it is still gaining momentum.

The unsung hero of the armistice conference was Russell Ford, the Colorado State University range specialist, also a former district grazier under the Taylor Grazing Act. Soft-spoken and tactful, Ford retained a neutral position which made it possible for both sides to confide in him. In the non-speaking stages, he carried messages from one camp to the other. His careful rephrasing of suggestions and good-humored treatment of differences brought and held the group together. Ford was elected a life member of the Colorado Cattlemen's Association in 1955 for his service and advice to the Association and the beef industry in the field of range and forest lands. (Don Stubbs received a life membership the following year for his many years of service to the Association.)

The basic agreement followed the same general lines of a plan which had been used on previous occasions between ranchers and forest supervisors of the calibre of Ed Snow and Ed Wright. The cattlemen agreed, on behalf of the permittees, that they would observe strictly the dates for putting livestock on the forest and taking them off, that under no circumstances would the number of animals exceed the permitted number, and that they would use their personal influence to prevent violations. The forest service agreed to temper the policy of arbitrary reductions with judgment, making cuts only when they believed it absolutely necessary. They agreed to police their own ranks, too.

It was mutually agreed, also, that reductions could be prevented and the stocking rate even increased by a program of cost-share range improvements which would utilize the scientific know-how, technical services, and equipment of the forest service, and the experience and ability, equipment, and time of the cattlemen. Thus, the war between science and experience ended in a working partnership between the two.

In recognition of his personal expense and efforts to improve the range, the permittee would be assured of tenure on the range.

The new way of life on the forest began with a pilot project, classified as experimental so that Cliff could use forest service research funds without having to explain too much to his superiors until the program had proved its worth. Leavitt Booth's portion of the Apex allotment, on the Arapahoe National Forest near Central City, was selected for this purpose. Booth had been active in Association work for forest service permittees for a number of years. He later became president of the Association. His cattle on the forests were running on ranges which his grandfather, August Brumm, had pastured in the 1880's.

At the same time, the committee began a series of experiments comparing the weight of cattle with the condition of range. These were made on forest land used by three members of the committee—Frank Fehling, on the San Isabel Forest near Buena Vista; Paul Hummel, on the Roosevelt Forest near Boulder; and Clarence Curry, on the Roosevelt Forest near Livermore.

Fred Kennedy, who succeeded Sandvig as range supervisor shortly after Cliff arrived on the scene, was instrumental in establishing the Apex demonstration and three weight-watchers experiments.

The Apex allotment was in serious condition at the time. The permittees were faced with severe cuts. The first action on this range was to build drift fences dividing the areas for conservation purposes and for grazing control. Cattle grazing habits were changed by the simple expedient of placing their salt blocks on ridges and other strategic points. This forced them away from the grazed-down bottom land to the side hills and other places where there was plenty of grass, but cattle had failed to visit. Through practices of rest-rotation—moving cattle from pasture to pasture to give the grass a rest during the season —and other simple management practices, what had been a run-down range began to produce heavier calves. After the first year, the scheduled reductions were cancelled. It was agreed that the number of cattle in the allotment actually could be increased.

Members of the committee checked several times during the year to observe the progress of the projects on both allotments.

Work on the pilot projects continued for several years with marked success. During this time, the forest service and the cattlemen sold each other on their methods of range management, which, after all, didn't conflict as much as they complemented each other. The cattlemen learned the value of technical knowledge and research. On the other hand, the ranchers were able to convince the forest service people that true conservation—the wise use of natural resoures—could actually be more beneficial than preservation—the complete non-use of natural resources. One member of the committee pointed out, "We had to show them that the seed that went through the cow was the seed that growed, because it was trampled into the ground, while the rodents and the birds ate a whole lot of the rest."

Armed with the results of the tests, the Association began to sell its members on the new program of range improvement and teamwork. In 1957, President Robert Schafer appointed the Association's first permanent range improvement committee. It included Leonard Horn, of Wolcott; Dick Jones, of Yampa;

Floyd Beach, of Delta; the late Russell Rose, of Pueblo; the late Tom Field, of Gunnison; Hal Hall, of Lyons; and Lyman Linger, of Loveland. Field died before he could serve. He was succeeded by Ernest Means, of Sargents.

Basil Crane, a Cliff-type official who became assistant regional forester, worked in close cooperation with the Association in the establishment of this committee. He was supervisor of range management at that time.

A little known, unwritten agreement existed between this committee and Cliff. He agreed on his part to investigate thoroughly and personally any complaint against forest service personnel which was channeled to him through the committee. The committee agreed to back him in his decisions. As a result of the pact, a number of forest service personnel were disciplined or transferred. On the other hand, occasionally, the committee found itself in the unpopular position of defending the forest service against irate permittees when Cliff said his investigation showed that the forest service people were not at fault.

In 1959, the Association and the forest service launched their first full-scale range improvement demonstration project—on the Mule Park allotment, in the Gunnison National Forest, where Dewey Norrell and Sons, were running 225 cattle on a 3,365-acre allotment. The improvement program started with a conference with the Colorado Game and Fish Commission to assure that enough cover and browse would be left for wildlife. A major problem was to change cattle grazing habits, moving them from the bottoms to side hills and ridges. After the allotment had been sprayed to reduce sage brush, the salting routine was changed as on the Booth allotment. The allotment was fenced into four pastures for rotation use. The Norrells, assisted by the forest service, built 14 miles of fence, 24 stock ponds, and two cattle-guard gates. In 1960, the permit was increased from 291 to 340 head. This was raised to 344 in 1961, to 440 in 1962, to 490 in 1963.

Grazing on the Monchego Park allotment, in the Gunnison Forest, was increased from 180 to 270 cattle in four years. The Newlin allotment, on the San Isabel, was converted from a closed range to one carrying 37 head under a demonstration program.

Along with the increased carrying capacity for cattle, the demonstration allotments provided increased forage for wildlife.

In 1960, the Colorado Cattlemen's Association range improvement committee joined hands with the Bureau of Land Managemen for similar programs on BLM lands of the state.

Today, the idea born in Colorado, out of desperation and the plotting of two kindred spirits, Rice and Cliff, has spread into Wyoming, Utah, New Mexico, and South Dakota, and cattlemen of other states have expressed their interest.

The idea of cooperative range improvement ended a bitter struggle of many years' standing and embarked the Colorado Cattlemen's Association on a new public relations career. As one not altogether reconstructed cattleman growled good-humoredly, "We've got a new policy for handling the forest service. Now we love the sons o' bitches to death."

Not all the users of the national forests had come to love the forest service, however, and not all the forest service people had become as tactful and persuasive as Ed Cliff. In the San Juan National Forest, rangers conceived the idea of spraying permit cattle with brilliant red dye as they entered the forest to identify them from trespass animals. Outraged at this implication of general dishonesty among the permittees, and what she considered the police state methods of the forest service, Mary Wallace, a Mancos rancher, snatched the spraying outfit from the hands of a ranger, sprayed two rangers and their pick-up truck with red dye, broke the spraying nozzle over her knee, and went home.

However, the idea of cooperation among the forest service and the users of the forests was growing. Through the influence of Congress, the passage of the Governmental Procedural Act, and the force of public opinion, forest service officials, as a whole, were beginning to realize they must give users of the forest a voice in matters, and that these people possessed business abilities and experience which could be used to improve forest administration.

At the same time, the "multiple-use" concept of conservation was growing more and more in favor with people who lived close to the natural resources. Perhaps more than any other group in America, stockmen realized the need for conservation programs which would enable the people and industries dependent on the resources to continue to exist, and today's people to enjoy outdoor recreation. They, too, wanted the forests, the water, the minerals, and the grass preserved for future generations. Also, they knew from lifetimes of experience on these lands, that wise use of these resources is better than non-use. Nature herself is a waster, perhaps the greatest waster of all. Erosion is a part of the geologic development process. The law of nature is still survival of the fittest, and the balance of nature is maintained by savage and destructive forces. Far better than non-use is a careful management of resources and protection for them, so that they may not only continue, but increase.

These people had not taken many organized steps toward conservation of the public lands, it is true. At first, like everyone else in America, they didn't realize that natural resources were limited. Forced to compete with each other for the use of the open range, they felt no sense of responsibility. Later, when the government took over management of the public lands, they had no opportunity or incentive. Yet, under the stimulus of years of observation, many stockmen were using conservation practices on their own privately-owned lands far in advance of those used by the forest service. This was particularly true after the establishment of the Soil Conservation Service to help in this effort.

Congress passed Public Law 86-517, on June 12, 1960. This measure outlines a policy for management of the public forests based on "multiple-use" and sustained yields of products and services. The act names watershed, timber, range, outdoor recreation, and fish and wildlife, as basic renewable resources for which the national forests were established, and assures them equal priority under the law.

To assure representation for all resources, including mining, which does not renew itself, and to tap the reservoir of experience, ability, and ideas contained in the industries, regional and forest advisory boards have been established to work with the forest service in planning and in handling administrative problems. Every use is represented on these boards.

Originally launched in 1902, a permanent program for regulated grazing on the national forests developed gradually, but other public lands remained uncontrolled for many years. Competition for the use of these lands increased. Sheep and cattle conflicts continued through the years, also, at times erupting into violence.

Feeling was particularly bitter in the northwestern corner of the state, where there was more available range, and where bands of sheep from Utah and Wyoming occasionally invaded cattle ranges, only to be turned back by the cattlemen.

In December, 1911, more than 100 sheep were killed on the Woolley ranch, southeast of Craig, in a night attack by five men, apparently to intimidate George Woolley, who planned to expand his sheep wintering program.

By 1915, bills were being introduced in Congress to regulate grazing of the remainder of the public domain, but it was another 20 years before an act was passed.

In 1920, a band of 350 sheep brought in from Utah, was clubbed to death in northwestern Rio Blanco County by seven masked men.

Cattlemen's associations and serious-thinking individual ranchers worked to restrain the more impetuous men and to find legal means for solving the difficulties. Claude Rees, long-time state senator, Garfield County rancher, and a banker at Rifle and Glenwood Springs, rode all one night through rough mountain country, to locate a group of enraged cattlemen and talk them out of their plan to destroy a band of sheep and kill the Mexican herders.

In the legislature, Rees was one of the leaders of efforts to solve the conflict over the public lands. To offset the federal government's hands-off attitude, the State of Colorado, over the years, had passed numerous acts to protect and assist the livestock industry—the round-up laws, bills pertaining to brand registration, mavericks and estrays, and fence laws.

As early as the 1870's, Colorado laws made it illegal to run inferior bulls on the range. In 1923, for example, the Colorado General Assembly adopted the Callen-Warren bill, which made it unlawful to permit an inferior stallion or bull to run at large in the state, classifying as inferior any animal not registered or eligible for registry. In addition, the owner of a herd of cows was required to furnish at least one purebred beef bull for every 25 cows. No one was permitted to allow dairy bulls to run at large. In a sense, this bill may have been designed in part to protect the owners of inferior or dairy bulls from a sudden depreciation of assets, for when a man did turn one of these animals loose on the range, it frequently returned home a steer.

From the early 1900's on, administration of the public domain became a paramount issue at meetings of the Colorado Cattle Growers Association, local organizations, and most other livestock groups throughout the West.

At its annual meeting in Glenwood Springs, June 16, 1923, for example, the Western Slope Stockgrowers Protective Association stated in a resolution: "We recognize changed conditions of grazing upon the Public Domain outside of the National Forests; we believe that the conflicts of interests are such that new methods of administration of grazing privileges on the Public Domain outside the National Forests have become necessary, and we feel that the time has come when a Bill designed to give those who now use the Public Domain for grazing purposes a preference right to the range now used by such individual or individuals, upon a fair and reasonable rate to be paid to the United States government, under regulations which will insure not only preference right by reason of priority of use, but also give preference to stockgrowers actually owning land in the immediate vicinity of the ranges and producing on that land winter feed for the animals that graze on the Public Domain, should be considered seriously; it is our opinion that this question of grazing on the Public Domain might well be administered by the Secy of the Interior on a system similar to the administration of the National Forests."

At the close of the mid-summer convention at Gunnison, July 15, 1925, the Colorado Stock Growers Association, by resolution, pledged its cooperation and support of a pending investigation of all matters pertaining to national forests and public lands by a congressional sub-committee. The following report by the committee on public domain prefaced the convention's resolutions:

"We favor a system of grazing livestock on the public domain that will provide for the following:

"1. Assurance of the permanent use of the range by the established and property owning stockmen now running thereon, with a preference given to established stock ranch owners.

"2. Statement in the law authorizing such regulations of the method of determining the amount of charges to be collected for grazing.

"3. Classification of the lands of the public domain and granting of permanent grazing rights on lands not suitable for agriculture.

"4. That the regulation of livestock grazing on all government lands should be administered by a single department of government.

"5. All revenue collected for grazing livestock in excess of reasonable amounts expended for improvements used in connection with grazing should go to the state."

Early in 1928, Representative Don Colton, of Utah, introduced the forerunner of the Taylor Grazing Act. Colton was from a state where the predominance of the Mormon religion had fostered the idea of cooperative range endeavors. The Mormons had long used the grazing district system under the administration of church officials, and Utah had espoused the cause of federal grazing districts for years. Colton was a member of the House Committee on Public Lands. Now, with Colorado and many other states also clamoring for federal control of the public domain, he introduced a bill which would have authorized the Secretary of the Interior to issue permits for grazing upon public lands chiefly valuable for the production of livestock for periods of not more than ten years and at fees to be determined by the secretary, but fixed on the lowest level consistent with the benefit derived. Preference was to be given to homesteaders and other actual residents in the vicinity, and to existing occupants who owned improved ranches or who had provided water for livestock. The holders of a permit would be entitled to preference in the reawarding of permits. A grazing board was to be established in each district, appointed by the secretary from qualified residents, to cooperate with the secretary in the administration of the act.

Colton's bill failed to pass, but it planted the seed from which later grew the Taylor Grazing Act.

When Congress failed to act, the Colorado General Assembly took measures to stop the strife on the range. The Rees-Oldland Act, fathered by State Senator Claude Rees of Rifle and Representative Reuben Oldland of Meeker provided for adjudicating the entire public range in Colorado between sheep and cattle grazing interests. District courts were directed to determine who should have prior rights to graze on specific ranges and to apportion contested ground into separate sheep and cattle grazing areas. Priorities were based on use, with the year 1928 as the base year. A court was to be guided in its determinations by a board of three referees; one a cattleman and one a sheepman, "if discreet persons engaged in such businesses are available," and a third referee to be chosen by the other two. Other provisions allocated grass and vegetation for the use of wildlife, provided for conservation of the range, and for court action, if necessary, to prevent overstocking.

Passed March 19, 1929, this measure was later upheld by the Colorado Supreme Court, but before it could be tested in the United States Supreme Court, it was voided by the federal government, which, at long last, stepped in and asserted itself as the rightful owner and proper administrator of the public domain. This was in 1934, in the early days of the New Deal.

Several factors combined to set the stage for favorable consideration of the Taylor Grazing bill. Throughout the Western range states, overstocking and conflicts between those competing for use of the public domain had brought most livestock people to a realization that control was needed. Nationwide depression and the century's worst drouth in the West made everyone receptive to change. The Democratic landslide of 1932 catapulted Representative Edward T. Taylor, from Colorado's western slope, into the second most powerful office in the United States House of Representatives.

Taylor was a wheelhorse of Colorado politics. A Glenwood Springs attorney, he had represented stock-growers organizations over the years, served as district judge, and for many years was a member of the state Senate. In 1909, Taylor was elected to Congress. He was 52 years old at that time. After nearly a quarter of a century in the House, he found the Roosevelt administration in power and himself in a position to demand almost any job he desired. He chose the chairmanship of the House General Appropriations Committee. Next to the Speaker of the House, Taylor was that body's most powerful member.

As the new administration set up housekeeping and began history's most sweeping reorganization of the executive department, the new Secretary of the Interior, Harold L. Ickes, looked about for new worlds to conquer. He cast longing looks at the forest service, which had control over millions of acres as a sub-unit of the Department of Agriculture, then his eyes lighted and glowed with anticipation as he perceived the possibilities for a similar establishment in the Department of Interior. Under the nominal control of the General Land Office, an agency of the Interior Department, were millions of acres of public domain, some 171,000,000 acres, as a matter of fact. Apparently, it never before had occurred to any ranking federal official that these wasted acres, the residue of 150 years of settlement, comprised a tremendous opportunity and challenge for government activity.

Ickes had been impressed by the Colton bill, which would have brought most of these lands into a single category for federal administration as grazing districts. He was also familiar with the success of the Mizpah-Pumpkin grazing district in eastern Montana, where several classes of land, both private and publicly-owned, had been brought together to improve grazing efficiency.

Ickes instructed Assistant Solicitor Rufus G. Poole, to draft legislation, using the Colton bill as a guide, also incorporating principles proven successful by the Mizpah-Pumpkin project.

Meanwhile back on the range, cattlemen struggled for existence against drouth and depression. Some of them decided to look to the federal government for assistance. George H. Watson, president of the Western Slope Stockgrowers Protective Association, asked Farrington R. Carpenter of Hayden to address a meeting at Rifle and explain the pending Agricultural Adjustment Act of 1934.

Watson was one of the great cattlemen of the western slope. At one time, he had been a foreman for the American Livestock Company, which had ranged cattle from Mexico to Canada. Later, he was manager of the Pierce-Reef cattle outfit. He knew that Carpenter was more than an unusually capable attorney with years of experience in range litigation. He was also a homesteader, a cattleman, a driving, forceful executive, and, despite his Republican affiliation, a close friend of powerful Representative Ed Taylor. On one occasion, when Taylor was running for Congress, and Carpenter was a candidate for district attorney, they had traveled and campaigned together.

At the Rifle meeting, Carpenter explained the provisions of the proposed farm act, which would subsidize certain basic agricultural commodities. At the close of the meeting, members of the Western Slope Protective Association raised $300, and asked Carpenter to lobby in Washington for the inclusion of beef as a basic commodity. Carpenter went to Washington and began testifying before congressional committees, buttonholing congressmen and government officials.

One day, Ed Taylor stopped Carpenter. "Have you read the bill being considered for grazing districts?" Carpenter had.

"What do you think of it?" Taylor asked.

"Well, Ed, it has possibilities. It won't work the way it is, but if a stockman could get hold of it, he could twist the thing around and make it work."

Taylor had been selected by the Department of the Interior as the proper person to sponsor the grazing act, for a number of reasons. He strongly favored it. The act was one whose principles he understood and believed. His name on the bill lent prestige to it, and was calculated to instill confidence in the people of the livestock industry. As chairman of the appropriations committee, he wielded an influence over many others in Congress who didn't give a damn about livestock or the West, but were willing to horse-trade in the interests of their own projects. Also, sponsorship of a bill so important to the interests of the West was a tribute to an old workhorse of Congress and the Democratic party. Taylor, Colton, and Representative French of Idaho spearheaded the drive in Congress for the Taylor bill.

At Taylor's urging, Carpenter appeared before the House Committee on Public Lands and testified in behalf of the bill. In order to qualify himself as a competent witness, he disclosed that he was a homesteader, familiar with the trials, tribulations, and limitations of homesteading; a rancher and former cowboy, who ran cattle on the public domain; that he and his partner operated the seventh largest purebred Hereford enterprise in the United States; and that he was an attorney who had spent a great portion of his many years of practice in range litigation. He then testified that he thought the proposed grazing law could be made to work, and that it was needed to bring order out of chaos on the ranges, and prevent irreparable damage to the remaining public lands.

The Taylor Act was passed June 28, 1934. It was strongly and universally supported by local, state, and national stockmen's associations. This act was many years late, but it finally stopped the active warfare, and solved the major public lands problems which remained after the establishment of the national forests and the homesteading era.

Teamed with the Taylor Grazing Act was an executive order issued by the President, November 26, 1934, which withdrew all remaining public lands from homestead entry under existing homestead laws. The Taylor Act itself, however, provides that the Secretary of the Interior may classify lands, both outside and inside grazing districts, for possible entry under the homestead laws. No restrictions were placed on the location and entry of mining claims under existing mining laws.

The original act placed a maximum of 80,000,000 acres under the jurisdiction of the administrative agency. An amendment passed June 26, 1936, raised the ceiling to 142,000,00 acres. The

Taylor Grazing Act authorized the Secretary of the Interior to establish grazing districts in the 11 Western states and to supervise them. It provided for establishing an organization to formulate regulations and administer the provisions of the act and its supporting regulations; for establishing priorities and issuing grazing permits; for making improvements; for the sale and lease to users of isolated tracts outside the boundaries of grazing districts; and for the organization of an advisory board for each of the grazing districts.

The first step in implementing the Taylor Grazing Act was the selection of an administrator. Apparently, some persons listening in when Carpenter appeared before the committee on public lands had been as much impressed by his credentials as by his testimony in support of the grazing act, among them a former Colorado resident in the Department of the Interior.

After passage of the act, Carpenter received a letter from Oscar Chapman, who had left Denver to become Assistant Secretary of the Interior under Ickes. The letter advised Carpenter that he was considered a possible choice for administrator. Would he meet with Chapman at Salt Lake City?

After the Salt Lake City conference, Carpenter went to Washington for an interview with Ickes, coming out of the meeting with the appointment, provided sheep interests would agree that cattleman Carpenter would administer the act without showing partiality. It was a cold-headed, cold-blooded conference between two men who began to dislike each other early in their acquaintance.

"I told him the conditions under which I would accept. He was just as cold and hard as I was, but he agreed to my stipulations," Carpenter said.

"First, I told him I would not change my politics. He growled, 'That's all right. Just keep your mouth shut about politics when you're on the road.'

"Second, I told him I was not interested in building up a great new federal bureaucracy. This didn't conform to his plans, but he didn't object.

"Third, I told him that I had been active in sheep and cattle legal battles in Colorado, and that Frank Delaney, of Glenwood

Springs, and I, were considered Public Enemies Number One
and Two by the sheep people. Ickes called Wilson McCarthy,
an attorney who was later president of the Rio Grande railroad.
Wilson had represented sheepmen in court battles over the
Rees-Oldland Act. McCarthy told him my appointment would
never please the sheep people, but he would confer with them.
Later, he called back and told Ickes the sheep interests could
think of at least six people more acceptable to them than me.
Finally, after Ickes snapped at him, 'I didn't ask that. I want
to know if you think Carpenter would be impartial?' He said,
'Damn it, yes.' That settled matters."

Congress had passed the bill, but without any appropriation
to finance its administration during the first year. The administrator was paid from the secretary's contingent fund; other
workers were detached on loan from Interior Department agencies. Carpenter borrowed 15 men from the Geological Survey
and one from the General Land Office, for his staff. There were
only 28 employees in all, including clerks and stenographers.

Without Ickes being aware of it, Carpenter met with Secretary
of Agriculture Wallace and obtained from him, permission to
use two forest service officials for as long as he needed them;
men who cattlemen and sheepmen alike had advised Carpenter
were absolutely fair and understood stockmen's viewpoints and
problems. They were Ernest Winkler, forest service grazing
supervisor in Utah and Ed Kavanaugh, the supervisor in Oregon. Carpenter termed them, "two of the grandest men I ever
met in my life."

One of the first actions was to eliminate the State of Washington from the act's jurisdiction. Acreages of the public grazing
land in that state were too small, and too scattered to justify
forming a district. This left ten states—Oregon, California,
Nevada, Idaho, Montana, Utah, Arizona, New Mexico, Colorado,
and Wyoming.

When the new administrator discovered there weren't even
any maps in Washington showing the existing public domain,
he did what he had probably planned to do all along. He used
this as a device to go to the men on the land—the sheepmen and
the cattlemen—and from them obtain the information necessary

for drawing maps. Accompanied by Kavanaugh and Winkler, he conducted a series of meetings throughout the West to explain the provisions of the act and to obtain necessary information from stockmen to draw maps, form districts, and devise the Federal Range Code, which implements the act.

The meetings began with a session at Grand Junction, Colorado, September 17, 1934, concluding with a general meeting at Denver, February 15, 1935.

The Grand Junction session set the pattern for the other assemblies. It was held at Lincoln Park Auditorium with a huge crowd in attendance. Some outfits rolled in with chuck wagons and camping gear. They divided into two large camps, the cattlemen in one, and the sheepmen in the other.

Carpenter asked the sheepmen to name six representatives and the cattlemen to name six to an advisory board. That afternoon men marked out the natural boundaries for the grazing districts in Colorado, "and they remain practically the same today."

The toughest problem which confronted the new grazing administration was to answer the question, "How near is near?" Upon the answer hinged the determination of preferences in granting grazing permits. The Taylor Act stipulates: "Preference shall be given in the issuance of grazing permits to those within or near a district. . .as may be necessary to permit the proper use of the land or water owned, occupied, or leased by them."

The wording of this section is plain in expressing the purpose of the act—to enable stockmen to combine the public grazing lands with other land, water, and feed into an economic, year-round enterprise, but this very statement of principle added to the confusion of "How near is near?" Sheepmen had been making beneficial use of the public ranges for years, yet the private lands which they used in connection with the public domain, might be as much as 350 miles away. They insisted that the word "near" should be interpreted as wherever their sheep moved in the course of a year's operations. Cattlemen, whose holdings were normally much closer to the public domain, held out for a geographical definition of "near."

Carpenter transferred the meeting to the federal courtroom in Grand Junction, and there formed a jury of prominent businessmen and government officials to hear attorneys for the various interests debate the definition of "near." They argued all day. The jury was unable to agree on the proper meaning of the word. Upon Winkler's advice, Carpenter deferred his decision on this point.

Subsequent meetings merely added to the confusion over "how near is near." A Nevada cattleman insisted that anything south of the Canadian border and north of the Mexican border was near. At Bakersfield, California, Basque sheepmen testified that they moved their sheep in a 1,000-mile circle in the course of a year's grazing—that anything within that circle was "near."

Finally, at the hearing in Boise, Idaho, an attorney launched the chain of reasoning which provided the key. "Some land is near, other land is nearer, and still other land is nearest," he pointed out. Carpenter conferred with Kavanaugh and Winkler and came up with this decision: "All private lands used beneficially in conjunction with the public domain are near; lands lying close to the public domain and used in conjunction with it are nearer; lands within the public domain and used in conjunction with it are nearest." On this basis, preferences were established and proved acceptable to stockmen.

Because there were far more applications than there was land, the principle of "first in time, first in right," was also invoked. Those persons to be considered in issuing permits, it was decided, would be those who had used the public lands during two consecutive years, or in three non-consecutive years, in the period from June 26, 1929, to June 26, 1934.

In this manner, the range code was fashioned. Decisions were made after the matters had been discussed with the stockmen. Carpenter said the stockmen actually wrote most of the range code themselves. He credited Frank Delaney, Glenwood Springs attorney, and Ralph Pitchforth, a Routt County stockman, with writing more provisions of the code than anyone else.

When the maps of the public domain were finally completed, it was found that 95 per cent of all the remaining public lands were within the zone which receives less than 15 inches of rainfall annually. Much of it is desert land.

The Taylor Act divided the range into two major zones, whose boundary is the snow line running east and west through southern Colorado, Utah, and Nevada. North of this line—in Oregon, Idaho, Montana, Wyoming, Colorado, northern California, northern Nevada, and northern Utah—there is enough moisture on the ground in winter to make it usable for livestock. It also provides natural stock water during the rest of the year. Land in this zone is interdependent with private lands which supply grazing or feed for a balanced year-round operation. South of the line—in Arizona and New Mexico—there is no seasonal snow for stock. The use of these desert lands depends on developed watering places—wells, tanks, reservoirs, and taps. These lands must be combined with privately-held water supplies for beneficial use. In southern Nevada, southern Utah, and southern California, both land and water enter into consideration.

The commensurate, or base property, which an applicant must possess for beneficial use with public lands, is grazing land or feed supplies in the northern zone, water supplies in the southern zone, while all three—feed, land. and water are considered in the mid-zone.

"When it came to the question whether or not a permittee could sell his permit with the sale of his land, the forest service and I parted company," Carpenter said. (One of the forest service practices most unpopular with stockmen in the late 1930's and 1940's, was that of automatically reducing the size of a grazing allotment whenever the commensurate property changed hands.)

"I believed the sovereign grazing rights under the Taylor Act were like water rights—something you could pick up and put somewhere else, and something that couldn't be withdrawn if the land was foreclosed." This decision to allow grazing rights to adhere to the land stabilized the entire Western stock industry by enabling a stockman to prove an equity in grazing rights for loan purposes.

This was probably the most significant contribution to public land use which Carpenter made.

Much of Carpenter's effort to build the grazing program on a foundation of local participation and local control was achieved only by out-maneuvering Ickes. Ickes had envisioned an extensive organization of federal employees, with a tight control at the top. Instead, Carpenter built a small grazing administration, which necessarily worked in cooperation with unpaid local advisory boards where most of the decisions were initiated.

There was an urgent need to put the Taylor Act into operation, and no time for "the usual bureaucratic method of sending out fieldmen to find out what was going on and report back to Washington," as Carpenter put it.

"Something had to be done at once or there would be nothing left to do. The example of the Selective Service Act of 1917, when local draft boards performed practically all of the work of raising an army, and the federal officials acted only in a coordinating and directing capacity, seemed appropriate. No one knew much about the range except the local users and inhabitants, and they knew more about their own parts of it than any official could learn in years."

The Taylor Act stated that the secretary "should issue or cause to be issued" grazing permits. An order authorizing regional offices to issue permits, subject to the approval of the local advisory boards, was prepared by the assistant solicitor in the Interior Department, and adroitly routed to the secretary's desk, where he signed it before he realized it was a Carpenter maneuver.

"We made it a locally administered outfit." This proved a wise policy, he added, in dealing with the individual stockman. Each applicant for a permit was asked to file a statement, listing his commensurate property, how much stock he had been running on the public domain, and similiar pertinent information.

"They claimed they had been running twice as many head as they had, that they owned twice as much property, had twice as much feed, and so on. We used the same tactics as they did with the draft in 1917. We told every man to appear personally before his local advisory board and justify his statements.

They'd lie cheerfully to the government, but they wouldn't face local boards made up of their neighbors."

The act directed that one-half of the grazing fees be returned to the states. At Carpenter's instigation, the legislatures in each of the ten states voted to turn these funds over to the grazing districts for use in improving the lands.

There were 33 districts set up in the ten states. A great deal of the administration of these districts was subject to the approval of the advisory boards, whose members were representatives of the industry, chosen at formal elections presided over by federal officials.

The act was passed June 28, 1934; explained at meetings in the ten states between August 17, 1934, and February 15, 1935. Grazing districts, encompassing some 40,000,000 acres, had been created by proclamation and established by June 1, 1935. All applications were processed and the entire range adjudicated by September, 1935. Licenses had been issued to 14,221 operators for more than a half-million cattle and six million sheep, 14 months after passage of the act.

While in the beginning the local advisory boards had no final authority, their advice was followed in 98.3 per cent of the cases, Carpenter said.

Surprisingly little litigation attended the launching of the project. This was primarily because the participants had ample opportunity to present their views, because the decisions were made at local levels where the rights of two conflicting interests—sheep and cattle—had to be considered in every instance, and because, as Carpenter pointed out, all actions were based on established principles of law. "The method and machinery used were more unusual than the legal principles of interpretation of the act."

Carpenter served as the administrator of the grazing service for four years, during which time, his never-friendly relations with Secretary Ickes continued to deteriorate. In November, 1938, he finally left the service and returned to Colorado.

The following year, July 14, 1939, Congress amended the Taylor Act to give the local advisory boards official status. They were made a part of the administrative machinery, their actions not subject to departmental veto. This legislation was generated by the American National Livestock Association. Even today, with more and more of the administration handled by government officials, a grazing supervisor can adjourn an advisory board meeting if he deems its actions against the public interest, but he cannot alter its decisions.

The Bureau of Land Management was formed July 16, 1946, combining the functions of the General Land Office and the grazing service. Like the forest service, the Bureau of Land Management has developed a staff of range technicians. Unlike the forest service, the BLM has a history of generally harmonious relations with its permittees.

The Bureau of Land Management carries on cooperative range improvement programs with stockmen.

Today in Colorado, there are 7, 490,345 acres of public lands within grazing districts, and 599,882 acres outside the grazing districts. These latter lands, located principally in northeastern Colorado and the southern part of the state, are for the most part, leased to owners of contiguous private lands.

The state has eight grazing districts. The districts, listing the counties in which they lie, and the total number of acres in each district are:

Meeker District No. 1 (Garfield, Moffat, Rio Blanco), 1,711,720 acres; Summit District No. 2 (Eagle, Garfield, Grand, Jackson, Summit), 513,012 acres; Ouray District No. 3 (Delta, Gunnison, Hinsdale, Mesa, Montrose, Ouray, Saguache, San Juan), 1,122,884 acres; Dolores District No. 4 (Archuleta, Dolores, La Plata, Mesa, Montezuma, Montrose, San Miguel), 1,045,609 acres; Royal Gorge District No. 5 (Chaffee, Custer, Fremont, Park, Teller), 426,103 acres; Yampa District No. 6 (Moffat), 886,108 acres; Rifle District No. 7 (Garfield, Eagle, Mesa, Pitkin), 1,267,604 acres; San Luis District No. 8 (Alamosa, Conejos, Rio Grande, Saguache), 517,305 acres.

An early roundup crew and camp outfit on a roundup near Kaufman Park in Chaffee County about 1890. This is typical of the equipment used in the mountain country when gathering cattle in the Fall.

Photo courtesy Wendell F. Hutchinson

Territory of Colorado
County of Elbert
August 26th 1874 before
John Mather Coronor of said
County, upon the Dead bodies of
Jasper Marion, Tipton Marion,
Jerome Wilson, and Richard Thompson
Lying there dead we the Jurors
whose names are hereto Subscribed.
the said Jurors upon their Oath
do say Some time between one and
seven oclock this morning by some unknown
persons by being hung by the neck to the
limbs of a pine tree that death was
caused to the aforesaid persons.
In testimony whereof the said Jurors
have hereunto set their hands the day
and year aforesaid
        Signed by   E. P. Clark
                                          H. Fisher
                                          Robert McDaniels
                                          John P. Bennett
                                          Wood
                                          _____ M. Hooker
                                          Jurors

Direct methods were sometimes used to curb thieves in Territorial days, as this Elbert
County Coroner's Jury report indicates.   *Courtesy Earl Brown, State Brand Commissioner*

CHAPTER NINE

RUNNING DOWN THE CATTLE THIEVES

Cattle thieving on a grand scale provided the initial impetus for organization of the Colorado Stock Growers Association in the fall of 1867. The same problem has plagued the organization since that time.

When David J. Cook was hired as the Association detective to clear up the early problem of missing cattle, he began one of the most interesting and productive activities of the Association. Despite the fact that his first findings proved extremely embarrassing to the officers of the organization in 1868, his services were retained for more than 25 years.

It was not until 1884, however, that Association records

mentioned a definite contract between the Colorado Cattle Growers and the Rocky Mountain Detective Association. Prior to that time a great deal of secrecy was attached to this phase of the cattlemen's activities.

When first hired, Dave Cook was also serving as Arapahoe County Sheriff, a position he was prevented by law from holding for more than two consecutive terms. Later he served as Deputy Sheriff, Denver Chief of Police, Major General of the State Militia, and at various times held a number of other law enforcement offices.

He was Deputy U.S. Marshal in Denver from 1881 to 1891 and later was assigned to special cases in the Detective Department of the Denver Police Force. He died April 30, 1907 of a heart attack at his home in Denver.

The Rocky Mountain Detective Association was formed by Dave Cook during his service as a detective for the War Department from 1863 to 1866. Shortly after enlisting in the First Colorado Cavalry on December 3, 1863, Cook was ordered to special duty as a military detective. Because of his distinguished exploits in this capacity, he was made Chief Detective of the Colorado Military District in January, 1864. During this period he formed the detective association to assist in apprehending thieves who were stealing military supplies.

When the military district was discontinued in 1866, Cook was appointed Denver City Marshal and continued in that capacity until he was elected Arapahoe County Sheriff, an office he held for a total of four terms.

Originally, the detective association was a loosely connected federation of about 25 peace officers in Denver and Colorado Territory. Later, the membership was increased to as many as 75 members and included officers in the surrounding states and territories. Through this organization, Cook was able to coordinate information about the gangs of thieves operating in the Rocky Mountain region. When stolen supplies or livestock were taken to another state or territory for sale, his agents were notified and they advised him in return.

When the Colorado Stock Growers asked him to take over the task of apprehending the men who were stealing cattle and horses in the region, he had a ready-made organization to handle the job. For the first 10 or 15 years, the agreement with the stockmen must have been on an oral or a secret basis, for no mention is made of the deal in ,the early minutes of the Association meetings.

In 1884, however, a simple contract written with a pencil on cheap newsprint in Dave Cook's own hand, was added to the minutes of the Executive Committee for January 25, 1884. In it Cook agreed to do all of the detective work for the Cattle Growers Association for a fee of $100 per month, plus expenses. In the event a reward was collected, the reward money was to be deducted from the monthly retainer.

The result of the detective work in apprehending thieves was highly successful, although continued efforts were never able to stop cattle thefts altogther. Apparently there was a continual influx of new outlaws coming into the state each year. As fast as thieves were caught and either sent to the state penitentiary or strung up on a nearby tree limb, new recruits took their places.

Cattle were particularly tempting to thieves because they are run in remote areas with little or no continuous supervision. At first, no public mention was made of the work of the Association in this field, but by the middle of the 1870's, the annual report made to the members which appeared in the Rocky Mountain News, carried frequent references to men who were apprehended.

At the annual meeting in 1875, President Joseph Bailey reported that progress was being made in controlling the loss of cattle from thieves. The Executive Committee had met in March of the preceding year and authorized the president to hire one or more detectives to help in this effort. As a result of the plans devised—and undoubtedly with Dave Cook's assistance—several arrests were made and a number of cattle were reclaimed for their original owners.

Bailey added that the men who had served so well as detectives deserved commendation, but he did not feel it expedient at this time to reveal their names. This remained the general policy of the Association for some time, and it was not until

*I will take the position
and hold the association
harmless- for $100 a month
and furnish a man to go
when and where ever wanted
at the rate of $100 a month
and expenses - in the mean time
will be on the lookout for
any depredations that may come
up - or be committed and
will go personally + look after
things when ever necessary
without any extra Charge
and will notify my agents
by circular all over the state
if any reward is offered or paid
said sum to be deducted*

D. J. Cook,
Supt R.M.D. P. A.

This contract in Dave Cook's own handwriting is dated January 24, 1884.
From Executive Committee Minutes Book

the Rocky Mountain News carried a story on February 6, 1880, that the connection with Dave Cook was publicly announced. In this story the News said:

> "The State Cattle Growers Association has armed itself for a determined fight against the thieves and depredators of herds. Heretofore they have taken an interest in the affairs of owners of stolen stock who were not members of the association. The first instance that came under their observation was the case against John Hatfield. They secured the services of General Dave Cook and his corps of detectives. The case was traced to Hatfield and the Williams boys, and they were accordingly arrested. For some reason the people failed to take the interest in the matter that the exigencies of the case seemed to demand, in the eyes of the association. The result of the trials was that neither Hatfield nor the Williamses were convicted.
>
> "As the parties who lost the stock are not members of the state organization, and did not contribute to the cost of the proceedings or assist in a remarkable degree in the prosecution of the alleged thieves, the association concluded that hereafter no attention will be paid to depredations of stock owned by parties not members of the association. And further, will not rely on the ability of a district attorney to prosecute and convict, or not convict.
>
> "In pursuance of that theory the state association yesterday secured the services of Hon. L. R. Rhodes, and that gentleman will henceforth attend to all the legal business of the association, and it is safe to say that he, in company with Gen. Cook, will make matters extremely sultry for those who pilfer from the herds of members of the state association."

Later events indicated that Hatfield and Williams continued to help themselves to cattle, for their names were listed among the persons convicted and sent to the state penitentiary a few years later.

On August 17, 1884, the News carried in full the report of the Rocky Mountain Detective Association which had been made to members of the Cattle Growers Association at their annual meeting on the previous day.

REPORT OF THE DETECTIVE ASSOCIATION

The Rocky Mountain Detective association herewith submit to your association the following report of operations from January 26 to August 1, 1884. This association has during that time secured the conviction and sentence for the larceny of cattle the following parties, who are now imprisoned within the state penitentiary at Canon City:

"JEFFERSON COUNTY

John Hatfield, three years; William Williams, two and one-half years.

"BENT COUNTY

Charles Jones, three years; Carlos Briggs, three years, Richard Ward, five years; R. W. Eldridge, eight years; George Shoemaker, eight years; Robert Eldridge, ten years; W. Henry, three years; William Thomas, five years. And in addition the following parties are now under bonds to appear before grand juries of their representative counties to answer to any indictments for the larceny of cattle that may be found against them, and said association can in regard to the said parties state that it is the belief of said association that the evidence is fully sufficient to secure a conviction in each of said cases now under bonds as aforesaid:

"JEFFERSON COUNTY

J. Dewey, amount of bond $800; Chauncey Olmstead, $800; Henry Tingley, in jail.

"WELD COUNTY

George M. Ginness, in jail; David Duhum, in jail; Michael Shean, in jail; Love Wilburn, under bond, $800; Tom Sanders, $300; Tom Titus, $500; S. H. Cole, $800.

"BOULDER COUNTY

C. Corbin, in jail; Calvin Daugherty, in jail.

The association would further submit that in its efforts in your behalf it has become convinced that the following named parties, at large, have been implicated in the larceny of cattle and changing of brands but as yet the evidence has not justified an arrest and examination before a justice of the peace:

"JEFFERSON COUNTY

Peter Horn, J. Wheeler, Charles Rhyborn, H. Beady, David Springer, H. E. Matthews, James Thompson, James Hartzell, Al Hatfield, David Williams.

"WELD COUNTY
J. W. Wilber, Dave Wilber, Tom Brownlow, Tom Frire.

"BOULDER COUNTY
George Williams, John Orvis, Reuben Ripley, Hiram Ripley.

"DOUGLAS COUNTY
J. Bennet, Barker brothers, Charles Norton, A. Adams, G. Newland, William Rowley, George Montgomery.

"ELBERT COUNTY
W. D. Dyer, Paul Strong.

And in addition thereto there are certain others which this association does not desire to make public mention of.

D. J. Cook, Superintendent."

Aside from the rather startling practice of announcing those persons under suspicion of stealing cattle, this report would no doubt be comparable to others made at the annual meeting over the previous years.

By this time the organized efforts against cattle thieves were obviously working smoothly. Although the mechanics of this part of the Association activities were kept under wraps, there is some indication of the complete cooperation of the members in this task.

The agents of the Rocky Mountain Detective Association were not always identified to all the members, but whenever one of the operatives turned up he was given every cooperation. They were authorized to commandeer fresh horses from any member's ranch, in the event of the hot pursuit of a fleeing outlaw, and apparently were also supplied with railroad passes for the same purpose.

Cook directed this detective association for nearly 30 years—from 1865 to 1893, when it was finally dissolved. It was the first concept of a police "network" and one of its major activities was the apprehension of cattle and horse thieves for the stock growers Association.

The expense of maintaining this effort was for many years

the largest single expenditure of the cattlemen's Association. Occasionally, a special assessment of one cent per head on the cattle owned by the membership was levied to keep up the effort.

In addition to the expense of catching the thieves, the organization also maintained an attorney, L. R. Rhodes, whose primary purpose was to prosecute the captured outlaws and see that they were convicted for their crimes.

At the August 17, 1884 meeting, John L. Routt announced that he was voluntarily going to double the assessment on his herd in view of the excellent work that the Association was doing for cattle interests of the state.

From time to time, special agents were employed to work on individual cases or on individual ranches. These agents were apparently paid through the Rocky Mountain Detective Association and only the man's initials were used in the records for identification.

The contract with Dave Cook was also terminated from time to time, then renewed again as cases came up, according to the Executive Committee minutes. In some ten years, from 1882 to 1892, the Association paid to the Rocky Mountain Detective Association or to D. J. Cook, the amount of $5,422.36 for services and expenses over this period. No records are now available for the years prior to that time, but there are almost continuous references to the long-standing connection between the two organizations.

The first volume of the Colorado Livestock Record, dated February 1, 1884, had to say about his work:

> "General Dave Cook has recently made several important arrests of cattle thieves, who have been plying their nefarious traffic in the mountains west of Golden. In this connection it is appropriate to say that General Cook has been connected with the livestock interest almost continuously since the organization."

In 1885, the same paper reported President Jacob Scherrer as commending General D. J. Cook for his work in running down thieves during the year. Many had been captured and thieves were becoming scarce. During the year a total of 22 cattle and horse thieves had been sent to the penitentiary, Scherrer declared.

The Association inspectors also played a large part in apprehending cattle thieves. Thomas Cahill, an inspector for the Colorado Cattle Growers Association in the Sterling area, was largely responsible for a number of arrests and convictions in that region during the early 1890's. Among these were the notorious Mort G. Mortonson and Denny C. Swigert. They were arrested for stealing and killing three cattle owned by the Brown & Iliff Cattle Company on June 29, 1891. They were convicted of cattle theft by a Logan County jury on July 24.

"The wholesale killing of cattle in Logan County has about come to an end," commented the Holyoke State-Herald. "Mort Mortonson of the firm of Mortonson and Swigert, general thieves and rustlers, was yesterday finally convicted of killing range cattle. It is estimated that this firm, during the past year, has stolen not less than 2,000 head of cattle, supplying the markets of Sterling, Cheyenne, Holyoke and Nebraska points with beef at less price than farmers could afford to do. Every honest man in Logan County will rejoice when this gang of thieves land in the penitentiary."

In the same year, Edward E. Jones was convicted for stealing and butchering a steer owned by the Pawnee Cattle Company. A. H. "Bert" Tetsell of Sterling, a long-time member of the Colorado Board of Livestock Inspection Commissioners, recalled that has brother was called to testify against Jones concerning the theft of a peculiarly marked blue steer. William Tetsell owned the animal, whose hide was later found on Jones' property. Because of the peculiar markings, young Tetsell was able to make positive identification of the head and hide.

Logan County's first local association of stockmen made no bones about the purpose of its organization. It was the Sedgwick Thief Detection Association, formed at Sedgwick, November 6, 1888. Later, the name was changed to the Logan County Thief Detection Association. At that time, Logan County included the present areas of Sedgwick and Phillips counties.

The war against thieves was waged on a local as well as on a state and regional basis. Many local cattlemen's organizations employed detectives and brand inspectors. These men usually worked independently of the state Association's operatives, but also cooperated with them on complex or large-scale cases.

At the first reorganization meeting of the Bent County Stock Association at West Las Animas in February, 1874, some of the larger operators present suggested forming a vigilance committee. After meeting for several evenings, the organization decided against "extraordinary methods" in favor of trying to punish offenders by legal means.

In 1879, the Bent County association employed a brand expert who inspected all cattle shipped from stations in the county, and the hides of animals killed by trains or slaughtered by butchers.

The organization managed to reduce the incidence of thefts, but did not obtain an actual court conviction until 1884. At the annual meeting in 1884, the Bent County association in a resolution introduced by R. G. "Dick" Head of the Prairie Cattle Company, pledged "our lives, our property and our sacred honor to the proper maintenance of the law, and to that end call upon all good citizens to aid us in the suppression of crime by aiding the officers of the country in the execution of the laws, and especially the jurors to do their duty as the grand guardians and conservators of the public welfare."

The average Westerner's casual attitude toward cattle theft resulted in frequent acquittals by juries despite conclusive evidence. Even cattlemen themselves hesitated to declare a man guilty of an offense which they themselves had committed. The Denver Western historian, Forbes Parkhill, cites a Yuma County pioneer, John C. Abbot, as authority for an incident in which a jury in a cattle stealing case polled itself and found that every man on the panel had himself eaten stolen beef at one time or another. The defendant was acquitted.

Thanks to the services of Dave Cook, Attorney L. R. Rhodes, and the efforts of the Bent County association to stiffen the spines of jurymen in such cases, eight cattle thieves were sentenced to the state penitentiary from Bent County in 1884. This almost cleared the county of thieves for a period of a few years.

The Colorado Cattle Growers Association also maintained a

black list as one means of controlling thefts. By-Laws published in 1884 contained the following provisions:

> "Sec. 30. All members of this Association do hereby agree that if any of their employees are found "mavericking" or violating any of the rules and regulations of this Association, that they will discharge them at once and report the same to the Secretary, who shall keep a record of the same, and they will not employ anyone that has been discharged for such conduct."

Attached as one of the Articles of the Association, was this resolution:

> "Resolved, that when a name has been reported to the Secretary under Sec. 30, it shall be held for ten days pending action, during which time the accused shall have the privilege and opportunity of appearing before the Executive Committee for the purpose, if possible, of vindicating himself. When an accused party fails to so appear, or if on appearing, fails to secure a vindication, his name shall then be placed upon a list by the Secretary and this list forwarded by him to each member of this Association every thirty days. No member of this Association shall, thereafter, employ any men whose names are so listed. Adopted.
> "Resolved, that the Secretary of the Association be authorized to exchange the black list with the association of adjoining States and Territories."

Ernest W. Fletcher, recounting his youthful experiences as a "mavericker," in the book, "The Wayward Horseman," told how he and a friend were caught blotting brands and were "blackballed" by the Colorado Cattle Growers Association, "which made it hard for me to get a job in that state."

The State of Colorado in 1885, assumed responsibilities for maintaining the brand registration system. The State Board of Stock Inspection Commissioners became the official agency for enforcement of brand regulations and prosecution of thieves. With this innovation and the enlargement and improvement of local and county law offices, the role of the Colorado Cattlemen's Association gradually shifted. Since then, the Association has concentrated its efforts on securing good legislation and brand regulations, obtaining capable state brand officials and assisting them in their work. The Association's brand and theft committee carries on a constant program of education and information for its members, helps coordinate the activities of the various law agencies, and assists in the prosecution of thieves. Mob action broke up a cattle theft ring in Chaffee County in 1883. A rancher, Loren Edwin Watkins, had been selling beef in mining camps, to construction gangs and sawmill crews. He was suspected of stealing cattle and covering up brands with carefully selected brands of his own. Two young cowboys sent to Watkins' ranch in the guise of saddle tramps, returned to the South Park Round-up, then at Gribble Park, and reported they had seen brands changed and cattle of other owners slaughtered. Watkins was arrested, but while he was enroute with the sheriff to jail at Canon City, a mob stopped the train and hanged Watkins to a bridge. A partner, Ernest Christensen, was sentenced to prison. Another partner, Frank Reed, shot it out with Sheriff Baxter Stingley, wounded the officer and escaped. Other members of the gang disappeared.

In the same year, the United Rocky Mountain Cattlemen's Association was organized at Poncha Springs, with thief detection as a major objective. This organization offered a reward of $15,000 for the conviction of anyone for killing, stealing, butchering or illegal branding of stock in Saguache, Park, Chaffee, Gunnison, Fremont and Delta counties. Each member was charged to act on his own as a range detective.

In 1904, it cost the Gunnison County Stockgrowers Association nearly $300 to catch and convict two men who had stolen horses in the Doyleville area. Twelve of the organization's members signed a note at the bank to cover the expenses.

In 1930, Dr. B. F. Davis, executive secretary of the Colorado Stock Growers and Feeders Association, conducted a survey among local associations and county sheriffs. From this he learned that the following local associations, at that time, offered rewards for the arrest and conviction of persons stealing livestock: Routt and Moffat County Wool Growers Association, Montrose County Livestock Association, Park County Wool Growers Association, Saguache County Cattle and Horse Growers Association, Boulder County Stock Growers Association, Grand County Livestock Association, Middle Park Stock

Growers Association, Mancos Cattlemen's Association, Rio Blanco Stockgrowers Association, Gilpin-Jefferson Livestock Association, North Park Stock Growers Association.

The largest rewards were for $1,000, offered by the Saguache County and the Middle Park associations. During the preceding year there had been four cattle or horse theft convictions from Saguache County, one from Grand County. Other convictions during the preceding 12 months: Adams-3, Teller-2, Lincoln-1, Routt-3, Huerfano-5, Kit Carson-4, Las Animas-4.

During the early 1930's, a surge in stealing caused local associations to increase their efforts.

The Gilpin-Jefferson Livestock Association and the Boulder County Stock Growers Association agreed to offer a joint reward of $1,000. This amount was reduced to $500 in 1932. Later, it was discontinued. The Gilpin-Jefferson Association in 1935, authorized the payment of a $50 reward to Paul White and a like amount to Kenneth Green for their efforts in securing the conviction of cattle thieves.

This local association in 1933 took offense at remarks by a Denver commission man, which they interpreted as being an effort to prevent the conviction of a cattle thief. In a resolution, the association pointed out that it was "engaged in an active campaign against cattle stealing and butchering on the range and is making a determined effort to put an end to such practices." Stating that the commission man had "interested himself in the outcome of a cattle theft case," it added, "be it further resolved that this association request the Denver Live Stock Exchange to request its members to cooperate in every way possible in bringing guilty parties to justice."

A project of the Colorado Cattlemen's Association theft committee resulted in the appointment of a roving brand inspector by the State of Colorado in 1962. This man concentrates on trouble spots in the state, working in close cooperation with local inspectors and law officers. Not long after the system was inaugurated, he was sent to the Montrose area to investigate the stealing of cattle from Ute Indians. He planted an undercover man on a ranch where he was reasonably certain a theft was planned.

The undercover man watched a truckload of stolen cattle leave the ranch, then signalled waiting authorities from the roof of a barn with a flashlight. Officers set up road blocks and closed in as the truck was climbing Blue Mesa Pass. When he realized what was happening, the truck driver deliberately rolled the truck down a long slope. The cattle rolled out and headed for home. When arresting officers arrived, he maintained that his truck had been empty. However, officers found a calf pinned under the overturned machine. This was sufficient evidence for a conviction.

Pick-up trucks, particularly those with camper bodies, have complicated theft detection. These vehicles are fast and quiet. Many of them are four-wheel drive machines which can operate in very rough terrain, in mud and snow off the highways. There are so many campers in the range areas these days that it isn't feasible to stop each one and see if it carries stolen beef, yet campers are used regularly for this purpose.

One rancher thought nothing of it recently, when he observed that someone was camping on his meadow. The party had pitched a tent, and apparently was hunting in the area. The next morning, after the camper had left, the rancher was chagrined to find that one of his heifers had been butchered inside the tent, perhaps while he was driving by. The thieves drove off with the beef in their pick-up truck, leaving the hide, head and entrails behind.

As cattle thieves have modernized their techniques, law enforcement agencies have had to streamline their procedures. This resulted in a change of regulations which enables the Federal Bureau of Investigation to enter a case as soon at it is discovered. Formerly, the FBI was required to wait until it had been determined that stolen cattle or beef had crossed state boundaries before it could act.

Cooperation of law agencies saved M. "Mackie" McAlpine from a major loss. McAlpine, a prominent Redwing rancher and former officer and control board member of the Colorado Cattlemen's Association, sold a herd of cattle at El Paso, Texas to a Kansas man. The animals filled eight semi-trailer trucks. After the trucks had left El Paso, McAlpine became suspicious.

He telephoned the bank, and discovered that the check was worthless. The trucks had vanished. Officers could find no trace of eight huge trucks traveling in caravan and surmised rightfully that the trucks had dispersed soon after leaving the loading chutes.

Inquiry disclosed that truck drivers had mentioned a number of states and destinations in conversation with hangers-on and McAlpine employees. It was discovered that the owner of the trucks had leased grassland in Colorado's South Park under a different name. The cattle were located there through a combined operation which included the cattlemen's Association, the Colorado Highway Patrol, several Sheriff's offices and the State Brand Inspection office.

The problem still continues to be a source of constant loss to cattle growers throughout the state today. As recently as January, 1967, Earl Brown, Colorado State Brand Inspection Commissioner, estimated that as many as 500 head of cattle were stolen within the state during the past year. Many of the losses are attributed to predators or natural deaths in the more remote mountain areas, others are not discovered until too late to pursue the thief. With livestock production costs mounting yearly, however, the loss of only a few head can be a serious financial blow to the owner.

The Colorado Cattlemen's Association and the local associations continue their program to discourage cattle stealing, concentrating on efforts to secure convictions once officers have made arrests. Law enforcement agencies and State Brand Inspectors keep pace with the times, matching improved stealing with improved detection, but one and all agree that the timeless pursuit of the cattle thief will continue until human nature itself changes.

After the turn of the century, the trend to ranching and away from the range days intensified. It became the practice to winter no more cattle than a man had feed for, but despite this precaution, the cow business was still a gamble, as this old photo by Charles J. Belden suggests.

Photo from the Belden collection of the Franklin Serum Co.

Roundup crew on Piceance Creek with the horse herd in a rope corral while the riders select their mounts for the morning. Note the teepee sleeping tents. These were typical of the Colorado cowboy from 1880 to about 1910.
Photo courtesy Helen Love, Rio Blanco

CHAPTER TEN

FROM RANGE TO RANCHING

Stockmen's organizations, like mortgage foreclosures, and the development of character, flourish in adversity. The growth years of the Colorado Cattlemen's Association have been those times when the industry encountered its greatest problems, whenever cattlemen faced a challenge which required a united front, and whenever there was plenty of work for the Association to do.

During the latter part of the 1890's, the cattlemen were sorely pressed, but their problems, at that time, were not ones peculiar to the cattle business. They resulted from prolonged drouth and nationwide depression. There was even a temporary easing of pressure for the land as hundreds and thousands of disillusioned homesteaders left the range areas, victims of several years of crop failures.

Membership in the Colorado Cattle Growers Association dwindled as the century neared its close. While the organization continued its efforts to secure favorable legislation for the industry, it was not particularly active in other respects. There was little participation by the smaller operators. The organization had lost touch with the local associations.

A resurgence of interest came in 1898, with the organization of the National Livestock Association at Denver, followed the next year by a spirited, successful campaign to secure the national organization's headquarters for Denver. The Denver Daily Stockman reported that the annual meeting of the Colorado Cattle Growers Association, January 24, 1898, at the Ernest and Cranmer Building, 1647 Curtis Street, Denver, drew the largest attendance in years.

The final annual meeting of the 19th century was held January 23, 1899, at the same location. The members present reelected the officers who had served for several years: David C. Wyatt, president; J. W. Bowles, vice president; J. G. Benkelman, treasurer; H. H. Metcalf, secretary. The president appointed as the executive board: Conrad Schaefer, A. Beuck, H. H. Robinson, J. E. Painter, J. W. Bowles, H. H. Metcalf, and David C. Wyatt.

"A committee of five was appointed to attend the funeral of ex-Governor Job Cooper," the Denver Daily Stockman reported. "Governor Cooper was a member of the Cattle Growers' Association, and at one time had heavy stock interests in the state." (The newspaper's account omitted the fact that Job Cooper had also been president of the Association in 1885 and 1886.)

The turn of the century found the cattle industry of the western slope and the mountain areas in a turmoil over the question of leases for grazing rights on the national forests. This issue, which is fully explained in another chapter, almost submerged the Colorado Cattle Growers Association, but in the long run it proved the impetus for one of the greatest surges of activity in the Association's history. As a result of the leasing fight and the dexterity which the organization's wheel horses turned an impending catastrophe into a golden opportunity, the Association, under the new name of the Colorado Cattle and Horse Growers Association, became again strong, influential, and truly representative of the cattle industry of the entire state.

For some time, stockmen of the mountain areas had been incensed by the possibility that they might in the future have to pay grazing fees for running stock on the national forests, a right which they felt should be theirs without cost as early settlers and historic users of the public lands. They were particularly outraged by the National Livestock Association's stand in favor of a leasing program. Further, they feared that the larger operators would crowd out the smaller ones on the forest lands. (The story of the organization of the Western Range Stockgrowers Association to fight leasing, its campaign against the bigger stockmen, and the eventual merger with the Colorado Cattle Growers Association, are related in the chapter on the cost of "Free" Grass.)

The anti-leasing group, by stirring up the feeling of small cattlemen against the bigger outfits, and pointing out that leasing of the forests might lead also to leasing of the rest of the public domain, gathered support throughout the state.

The meteoric rise of the Western Range Stockgrowers Association to a large state organization had a drastic effect on the Colorado Cattle Growers Association. The annual meeting in 1900 was held April 26, in the meeting room of the Denver Chamber of Commerce, with a very small attendance. This was three weeks after the Western Range organization had assembled nearly 600 cattlemen in Denver's Tabor Opera House for an anti-leasing convention and the formation of a state association.

The Denver Times reported that the cattle growers' Association decided to "go on with the work of forming a strong central association if possible. It was decided to send out notices to all the old members of the Association, calling their attention to the necessity for reorganization in order to be in a position to fight when bills important to cattlemen come up in the next state legislature."

The Western Range Stockgrowers Association was never intended to be a regular stockmen's association, but was formed for the single purpose of combating the leasing of national forests. However, its rapid growth, and the attacks which it made on the larger, more successful stockmen who realized that leasing was inevitable, caused the ranks of a not-too-active state association to melt.

It was evident at the 1900 annual meeting, that something must be done to breathe new life into the organization and to close the rift which had developed between the smaller and the larger operators as a result of the leasing controversy. Just who devised the strategy which enabled the Association to end the strife over leasing and win over the entire membership of the Western Range Association is not certain. The fine hand of one of the grand old men of Colorado's cattle industry—Samuel Hartsel—was evident. Hartsel, at that time, had been a Colorado stockman for almost 40 years. He had faced Indians, homesteaders, sheepmen, range pirates, and legislature. He knew the value of a strong state organization, and how to remain calm when the other fellow was aroused. When he talked to the anti-leasing leaders, they listened.

Another was H. H. Robinson, a very prominent Denver stockman with strong political connections in the state. Robinson was a serious-minded, but personable and popular man, who had always supported changes which would benefit the industry.

Dr. Charles Gresswell, former state veterinarian, had managed to obtain his friendships throughout the state during several years in a controversial job. His wide-spread acquaintanceship and diplomatic ability helped the cause along.

To their lasting credit, the leaders of the Western Range Association made an about-face when they realized that leasing was inevitable, and that the only damage their campaign could do, would be to the state Association. (How they came to terms with the Association leaders without antagonizing their own membership is told in the chapter on "Free" Grass.)

The merger was virtually signed, sealed, and delivered when the Colorado Cattle Growers Association met at the Denver Chamber of Commerce Building, December 13, 14, and 15, 1900, for the 33rd annual meeting.

Elias M. Ammons, of Douglas County, later a governor of Colorado, presided. As a result of a very special effort by both the state organization and the Western Range group, there were 132 official delegates in attendance, as well as many others.

These were the official representatives of the stockmen's groups:

At large (appointed by Governor Charles S. Thomas)—Dr. Charles Gresswell, J. W. Bowles, H. H. Robinson.

Arapahoe County Cattle and Horse Protective Association—Conrad Schaefer, J. E. Painter, Asa Sterling, H. A. Smith, L. K. Watkins, C. W. Bowles, E. H. Dubois, Lee Kayser.

Boulder County Stock Growers Association—M. P. Fox, Thomas Miller, Mike Rosenbaum, Lon Spicer, Frank D. Baker, J. M. Platt, W. E. Hodgson, Thomas Kneale, M. E. Platt, R. L. Euler.

Bent County Cattle and Horse Growers Association—A. N. Parish, G. S. McClurg, M. J. McMillin, Luke Cahill, M. H. Murray, J. K. Mullen, J. Scott Robertson, T. D. Barroll, Charles Maxwell, Henry Keon, James Malloy, J. W. A. Towers.

Chaffee County Stock Growers Association—C. S. Ogden, Charles Nachtrieb, H. S. Tompkins.

Douglas County Stock Growers Association—E. M. Ammons, Hugh Taylor, Robert E. Palm, Charles Woodhouse.

Eastern Colorado Stockmen's Protective Association—M. C. Humberg, George Tuttle, John W. Loftus.

Elbert County Cattle and Horse Growers Association—B.C. Killin.

Eagle County—J. N. Pierce.

El Paso County—J. S. Reyonlds.

Fremont County Cattle Growers' Protective Association—John C. Heyssong, D. M. Walker, Don C. Crampton.

Grand County—Middle Park Stock Growers Association—Edmund Becker, Morton Alexander, C. J. S. Hoover, Charles Pearson.

Gunnison County Stock Growers Association—A. Hartmann, W. L. Bennett, J.J. Carpenter, W. A. Gillaspey, H. C. Bartlett, T. W. Gray.

Garfield County-Grand River Stock Growers Association—George Yule, Joseph Yule, W. R. Lee.

Roaring Fork and Eagle River Stock Association— W. L. Grubb, A. B. Foster.

Jefferson County—George Hutchinson, J. Higginson, E. E. Culver, D. P. Wilmot, K. S. Rhea.

Logan County Cattle and Horse Protective Association—W. C. Harris.

Larimer County Sheep Feeders Association—I. W. Bennett, P. Anderson, H. T. Miller, C. Blunck, R. M. Hubbell, Tom Johnson, W. A. Drake, A. Keoper, F. C. Springer, B. Preston, C. Evans, D. W. Amos, F. Kibler, I. C. Riddell, F. R. Baker, H. Strachan, D. C. Brooks, Lewis Kern, J. V. Munson, A. A. Knott.

Larimer County Stock Growers Association—T. A. Gage, N. C. Alford, F. G. Bartlett.

Otero Stock Association—J. N. Beaty, William McCaskill, C. A. Reynolds, Eugene Rourke, H. W. Potter, A. D. Best, P. H. King, M. A. Lee, J. A. Lockhart, W. G. McAtee, R. S. Watson, J. B. Manby.

Park County Cattle Growers Association—Samuel Hartsel, J. E. Herrington.

Rio Blanco County Stockgrowers Association—I. W. Chatfield.

Southern Colorado Stock Growers Association— G. F. Patrick, Garrett Lankford, George Sears, Emmett Nuckolls, E. S. Hall, William Burdett.

Weld County Livestock Association—John E. Law, R. M. Haythorn, J. A. Staylon, J. S. Gale, W. B. Starr, David Kelley,

A. A. Howard, J. S. McClair, Theodore Lucas, D. E. Severance, W. R. Jones.

Yuma and Eastern Arapahoe Cattle and Horse Protective Association—J. M. Boyd, Henry Wells, Crawford Moore, Carl Giddings.

The Saguache Stock Growers Association was not represented by delegates, but its officers telegraphed notice of their interest in a strong state organization, along with a suggested resolution urging amendments to the law requiring railroads to pay for stock killed by trains.

After secretary L. K. Watkins had read the convention call, Ammons appointed M. P. Fox, of Boulder; W. A. Gillaspey, of Gunnison; and Samuel Hartsel, of Park County, members of the Credentials committee. He named H. H. Robinson, of Denver; J. E. Reynolds, of El Paso County; J. M. Platt, of Boulder County; Robert E. Palm, of Douglas County; and J. Higginson, of Jefferson County, the committee on permanent organization and order of business.

Secretary Watkins then read the mintues of the last annual meeting and resigned. As Fred P. Johnson, editor of the Denver Daily Stockman, described it, "Watkins made a grand sneak on his job. He wanted to have his hand in the proceedings on the floor and did not propose to get tied up with the routine part of the work if he could find a substitute. A good-natured cow editor relieved him."

Whatever part Watkins played in convention horse trading, his action in drafting "a good-natured cow editor" was far more significant. The cow editor was Fred P. Johnson. This marked the beginning of Johnson's many years of service to the Colorado Association, first as assistant secretary and later as secretary. Not only did he perform all the clerical work of the secretary's office, but through the columns of the Daily Stockman, which became the Record-Stockman only two weeks after the 1900 convention, he promoted the activities of the Association and the industry. He performed similar services for local and national associations. His newspaper became known as the voice of the Colorado cattle business. Johnson was also assistant secretary of the new American Cattle Growers Association, and an ardent supporter of this group as well as the National Livestock Association.

In an editorial published during the convention, Johnson expressed his views and those of many stockmen on the decline of the state Association and the need for its regeneration:

"The stockmen in convention here are discovering that they had more kicks coming than they had thought when the convention was called. They are also candid in acknowledging that they themselves are to blame for the conditions that prevail. They have the power to rectify all the wrong they suffer from if they but work together . . . Individually, the stockmen of Colorado are an easy mark for the lawmaker, the railroad man, the stock yards syndicate and the confidence man. United, they are invincible. The remedy is so obvious that the only wonder is that any stockman can be found who would oppose a state organization in which all of the vast power possessed by the local organizations, which is now almost wasted, could be utilized for the benefit of all."

Early in the convention, Ammons appointed Sam Hartsel, M. H. Murray of Bent County, and Fred P. Johnson to meet with the Western Range Stockgrowers Association officers and work out a merger agreement.

There were a number of subjects of special interest on the convention agenda, but the hottest topic was the administration of the Veterinary Sanitary Inspection Law. Cattlemen generally were dissatisfied and disgusted with the work of the Veterinary Sanitary Board, which was not made up of stockmen. "The majority of the delegates were plainly in favor of radical action," Johnson reported.

Other topics receiving special attention included the administration of the Brand Inspection Board, the liability of railroads for livestock killed or injured by trains, and the uses of the brand fees and estray funds.

All subjects were referred to special committees for discussion and preparation of resolutions, each day's session being adjourned early to permit committees to function. Committee reports occupied most of the final two days.

There was a general laugh when Ammons announced the members of the Veterinary Sanitary Inspection committee. He named state Senator James C. Evans, of Fort Collins, chairman, and Dr. Charles Gresswell, of Denver, secretary. A few years before, Evans, as a legislator representing the lamb feeding areas, and Gresswell, as State Veterinarian, had fought heated battles over the same law. Ammons also named J. E. Law, of Greeley; J. V. Munson, of Fort Collins; and George F. Patrick, of Pueblo to this committee.

Reporting back to the convention, these five men recommended that the veterinary sanitary law be completely rewritten, eliminating all state inspections where they would duplicate federal inspections, and combining the functions of the Veterinary Sanitary Board and the Livestock Inspection Board into one board. They also recommended that the office of State Veterinarian be eliminated.

Patrick, the first member of the committee to report, charged that the Veterinary Sanitary Board was made up of men whose greatest interest was not in the livestock business, and that the state brand commission was controlled by politics to the extent that "political faith is the only qualification necessary to get a job as a brand inspector." Patrick said the chairman of the Kiowa County board of commissioners had reported an outbreak of cattle disease, and had asked the state veterinary surgeon to investigate. The answer they received, Patrick said, was that the State Veterinarian would make the investigation, but expected to be paid $20.00 per day for his work. "And yet, the taxpayers of this state are paying this veterinary $1,500 per year, and for what?" demanded Patrick.

Senator Evans charged that lamb feeders of Colorado were paying one cent per head inspection fees on sheep that no inspector ever saw, yet the state board completely ignored a federal bill of health on lambs.

After some discussion, Patrick was delegated to draft a new bill incorporating the committee's and the convention's recommendations. This was then to be referred to a special association committee which would present it to the legislature.

Other committees were named to discuss special problems and draft resolutions:

Committee on amendments to the bounty law, seeking to return to the bounty fund all returns from the special brand tax which had been used for administrative purposes—Thomas Kneale, Boulder; D. C. Crampton, Canon City; Edmund Becker, Grand County.

Committee on efforts to eliminate politics in the appointment of brand inspectors—J. Higginson, Jefferson County; Sam Hartsel, Park County; Emmett Nuckolls, Pueblo.

Committee on amendment to brand inspection law— H. H. Robinson, Denver; W. A. Gillaspey, Gunnison; C. S. Ogden, Chaffee County.

Committee on amendment to law concerning the brand clerk—J. N. Pierce, Eagle County; George Yule, Garfield County; Crawford Moore, Yuma County.

Committee on resolution protesting against the passage of unnecessary and burdensome laws—M. Mathews, Larimer County; W. R. Lee, Garfield County; A. B. Foster, Emma.

Committee to find out the amount of money from brand taxes remaining in the state treasury—Lute A. Wilcox, Denver; Judge Hugh Taylor, Douglas County; D. P. Wilmot, Jefferson County.

At the closing session on the third day of the convention, the delegates approved the merger plan—to form one state association which would be known as the Western Range Stockgrowers Association until the scheduled annual meeting of that organization in March, when a name more representative of a state-wide organization would be adopted.

The following officers were selected to serve during the interim period: W. Lloyd Grubb, Carbondale, president; H. H. Robinson, Denver, vice president; H. D. Williamson, Carbondale, secretary; Fred P. Johnson, Denver, assistant secretary; A. A. McIntyre, Glenwood Springs, treasurer. Executive Committee: C. W. Bowles, Littleton; C. Meade Hammon, Delta; E. M. Ammons, Douglas County; M. P. Fox, Boulder.

Convention time was a double triumph for Lloyd Grubb. While the tall, dignified Garfield County rancher was helping to put the state Association back on its feet, with himself as its president, his cattle were doing all right, too. He sold a consignment of fat cows for $4.05 per hundredweight, at Denver, the day before the convention opened. This was the highest price which had ever been paid, at Denver, for range cows. They averaged 1,299 pounds.

One of the less controversial resolutions at the convention was one which commended Grubb's brother, E. W. Grubb, of the Mount Sopris ranch near Carbondale, and other Colorado stockmen for winning championship honors at the International Livestock Exposition in Chicago.

There was some wonderment at the National Livestock Association's annual convention in Salt Lake City, in January, 1901, when the Colorado Cattle Growers Association failed to put in an appearance and the Western Range Stockgrowers Association contributed $500 to the national organization. While this was soon cleared up by the Colorado stockmen in attendance, the incident has confused historians ever since.

At the annual meeting of the Western Range Stockgrowers Association, in the Tabor Opera House at Denver, March 9, 1901, the name was changed to the Colorado Cattle and Horse Growers Association.

The following officers were elected: W. Lloyd Grubb, Carbondale, president; Conrad Schaefer, Duel, vice president; Charles W. Bowles, Littleton, secretary; Fred P. Johnson, Denver, assistant secretary; T. S. Harper, River Bend, treasurer. Executive Committee: W. Lloyd Grubb, chairman; C. W. Bowles; T. S. Harper; W. A. Gillaspey, Gunnison; A. B. Foster, Emma; Arnold Powell, Yampa; Don C. Crampton, Canon City; I. W. Bennett, Fort Collins; J. A. Lockhart, Colorado Springs.

Its membership, at that time, comprised some 2,000 stockmen from 28 local associations, representing every section of the state. The member associations:

Axial Basin Stock Grower's Association
Bent County Cattle and Horse Growers Association
Boulder County Stock Growers Association
Cattle and Horse Growers Association of Round-Up
    District No. 9 (Northern Arapahoe, Adams, Weld, western
    Morgan counties)
Chaffee County Stock Growers Association
Douglas County Stock Growers Association
Eagle Stock Growers Association
Edwards Stock Growers Association
Egeria Park Stock Growers Association
Elk River Stock Growers Association
Fremont County Stock Growers Association
Grand River Stock Growers Association
Gunnison County Stock Growers Association
Kit Carson County Live Stock Association
Larimer County Sheep Feeders Association
Lincoln County Cattle Growers Association
Middle Park Stock Growers Association
Montezuma County Stock Growers Association
Montrose Cattle and Horse Growers Association
North Park Stock Growers Association
Otero County Stock Association
Park County Cattle Growers Association
Roaring Fork and Eagle River Stock Growers Association
Routt County Range Protective Association
San Luis Valley Cattle and Horse Growers Association
Southern Colorado Cattle Growers Association
Steamboat Springs Cattle Growers Association
Yuma and Eastern Arapahoe County Cattle and Horse Growers
    Protective Association

Several other local organizations came into the fold in the
months that followed.

The by-laws opened the organization's membership to
"any organized association of cattle and horse growers in Colorado" with the following additional provision; "Provided, however, that we do accept as members of this association the Fort
Collins and Weld County which are strictly engaged in feeding
sheep or lambs for market and are not engaged in running sheep
on the public range."

The Denver Record-Stockman was named the official newspaper.

Before the convention adjourned, President Grubb appointed Fred P. Johnson, J. T. Monson, T. C. Munson, Dr. Charles Gresswell, and H. H. Robinson as a committee to follow the progress of livestock bills through the legislature. The Association also resolved:

"That the legislative committee of the Colorado Cattle and Horse Growers Association be and are hereby instructed to keep a close watch upon the work now being done in the legislature, and upon the adjournment of that body to prepare a report to be sent to all members of this association, showing in detail the record on each bill which this association has been interested in, to the end that we may be able to know who our friends are that we may be loyal to them in the future."

Thus, the Colorado Association—revived, reorganized, and truly representative of the industry throughout the state—began one of the most active periods in its career. As the organization's great champion, Fred P. Johnson, pointed out, the Association was: "made up of representatives of the small cattle growers of this state, the men who are building up the industry and are in the business for a livelihood. Out of the 2,000 stockmen represented by this association, probably not over twenty or thirty could muster 1,000 head of cattle . . . Probably a fair average would be about 250 head. All of these members are self-made men. They have hustled wisely for what they have. They are all taxpayers and not one ever dodges the responsibilities of citizenship."

There was need for a strong state-wide association. The cattlemen of the western slope and the mountains were confronted with invasions of nomad sheepmen and tramp cattlemen. They were also faced with the transition from free range to leasing the national forests.

On the plains of eastern Colorado, the traditional stronghold of the truly big outfits, a new type of cattleman was coming to the front. He was a hybrid, developed by crossing the most progressive strains of the old open-range cattleman with the hardiest survivors of the lowly homesteader. The dominant parent of this cross was the homesteader.

By 1900, the sod-buster was painfully aware that he could never make a living from crops on a quarter-section or even a half-section of land on the Colorado plains in the dry years. He was discovering, however, that a combination of crops and cattle would work. By running a herd of cattle on state or federal lands, in the summer and fall, and wintering them on hay, or other feed produced on his own land, he took much of the gamble out of homesteading and built a sound economic enterprise. The homesteader was fast becoming a rancher.

The editor of the Holyoke State Herald, in February, 1900, reported that although northeastern Colorado had been emptied of settlers in the 1890's, now many people were coming back and starting small cattle ranches instead of trying to exist entirely on crops. Said a State Herald editorial:

"Finally the people and the Herald saw an opening to make money in the cattle business and, although it was somewhat humiliating to admit to the once-hated cattle baron that our knowledge of the adaptation of the rainbelt for successful business had been limited, yet, forgetting all but the advantages to our county of a profitable business, there was a grand rush into the cattle business and from that time the Herald could safely refer to the owner of cattle as cattle man instead of a cattle baron . . . our population is not what it was in the boom days of '88 and '89, but the settlers who did remain are now being amply repaid for so doing. They are getting nicely started in the stock business, and that, with their dairy business and farming, gives them a prospect for the future that is certainly encouraging."

The transition from crop starving to livestock farming was happening throughout the eastern plains of Colorado.

Meanwhile, many stockmen in and near the feed-producing irrigated areas of northeastern Colorado, were going one step farther in the beef business. With the advent of alfalfa as an important crop in Colorado, cattle fattening by farmers and ranchers was started in the Greeley-Fort Collins area, as far back as 1870. With the advent of the sugar beet industry, offering sugar beet tops and pulp as excellent cheap feeds and demanding, in exchange, manure for plant food, livestock feeding spread up and down the South Platte Valley, east of Denver. At Sterling, W. C. Harris began early in 1902, to build feed lots, the first of a chain which, at one time, extended from Grand Island, Nebraska, to Twin Falls, Idaho. Rancher O. A. Sholes, of Phillips County, began fattening cattle for market, in 1903.

The Colorado cattle industry was opening new frontiers, but it was also faced with new problems, and with new versions of old ones.

The Colorado Cattle and Horse Growers Association met with little success in its 1901 legislative efforts. The General Assembly enacted only three livestock bills. One, introduced by Senator E. M. Ammons, transferred funds from the stock brand fund to the fund for payment of bounties on lions, wolves, and coyotes, thus achieving one of the Association's minor goals. Another bill re-defined the procedure for disposition of mavericks. A third bill established the North Park area as Round-Up District No. 28.

The Southern Colorado Stock Growers Association, at a special meeting, condemned the action, or rather inaction, of members of the 13th General Assembly who opposed legislation asked for by stockmen of Colorado. They requested an immediate call of the state Association. Their dissatisfaction centered around a law which, according to the association, the sanitary board had been collecting illegal fees. They urged the state Association to contest every law under which the State Veterinary had been operating, "to bring suit for the recovery of fees that have been wrongfully collected." They asked every local association in the state to campaign actively against Senators Adams, Barela, and Garcia.

John W. Springer, of Denver, at that time, president of the National Live Stock Association and later president of the Colorado Association, excoriated the legislature in an address to the Lincoln County Cattle Growers Association, at Hugo, January 8, 1902. "The stockmen do not propse that another legislature like the last one shall go down to Denver again. The members of that legislature promised us they would pass the bills we desired. We went our way believing they would fulfill their solemn promise. Deliberately, they flatly turned down our every request . . . We need a change in the personnel of the men sent down there. I cannot tell you who will be in the next legislature, but I can name a lot of men who will not."

On January 18, 1902, Governor James B. Orman issued a call for a special session of the General Assembly, principally for revenue purposes, but with the gate left open for the introduction of a great variety of bills.

The legislature was still in session March 2, 1902, when the Colorado Cattle and Horse Growers Association held its annual meeting with delegates in an angry mood regarding legislation. In a resolution, the organization pledged itself to disregard all party politics in the selection of members of the legislature and "in the future to support for such public office only those who are known to be of unapproachable integrity, absolute honesty and men who can be depended upon to support the interests of the livestock grower regardless of party affiliation . . ."

The defeat of Senator Ammons' bill to require railroads to fence their rights-of-way or become liable for all stock killed by trains, during the regular session, and the apparent doom of the same measure, which Ammons had reintroduced in the current special session, were a particular cause of anger and accusations.

Two days later, at the invitation of a legislative committee, a large number of Association members met with members of the General Assembly in an evening session in the House chamber, ostensibly to discuss the Ammons bill. According to the Hugo Range Ledger, this gathering turned into a bitter, name-calling set-to. The Hugo newspaper said several of the legislators attempted to offset and contradict statements made by John Springer in an address to the convention. Others said they objected to being blacklisted for failure to support the Ammons bill because they had done so at the wishes of their constituents.

Charges and countercharges flew back and forth between the two groups until finally "discussion became largely personal" and the cattleman walked out of the meeting.

However, in the days that remained of the special session the Ammons bill was passed.

This concession apparently failed to mollify the cattlemen. It may have been purely a coincidence, but only eight of the 65 members of the House of Representatives were reelected in the fall of 1902. After the 1902 and 1904 elections, when all of the 35 seats in the Senate had been on the ballot, there remained in office only eight senators who had sat in the 13th General Assembly.

The climate for cattle bills was much more favorable in the 1903 regular session of the General Assembly. The legislature reorganized completely the state brand recording system along lines recommended by the Colorado Cattle and Horse Growers Association. It also consolidated the old State Board of Livestock Inspection Commissioners and the Veterinary Sanitary Board into a new State Board of Inspection Commissioners, who were to be selected from the ranks of "actual and practical" men of the livestock industry, five cattlemen, three sheepmen and one horseman. The governor appointed the board. The board appointed the brand and sanitary inspectors.

The estray act was also revised.

In November, 1903, the Association's president, W. Lloyd Grubb, sold most of his Colorado property and moved to California. In a letter of resignation and farewell, he pointed out to members, "You have rewritten and had passed by belligerent legislatures nearly every law affecting sanitary and police inspection of our stock and railroad laws. You have reorganized our brand laws, besides creating a nearly sufficient fund to pay the expenses of the same. You have become a factor in the management and practical operation of the laws which you have created, even to the extent of inspiring a decent respect for our people and their rights, in the minds of politicans that usually occupy the state capitol . . . At all of the meetings of the National Live Stock Conventions, Colorado stockmen have been acknowledged to be better organized than those of any other state."

These successes didn't end the stockmen's troubles with the

legislature or the railroads, but they demonstrated the effectiveness of the state organization and helped it keep the large membership it needed to obtain its objectives.

The railroad fencing act was declared unconstitutional. A very similar measure was enacted May 30, 1911, to replace it.

A common cause of grievances was poor service by the railroads. This was almost a chronic condition. Through local and state organizations, stockmen maintained a constant barrage of complaints of various kinds. However, whenever service improved in one respect, it seemed to deteriorate in others.

One of the greatest and most continuous inconveniences was the shortage of railroad cars during the shipping season. Cattlemen and their local newspapers complained that whenever the price was up, there weren't any cars available; whenever prices were down, there were plenty of cars. In his report to the Bent and Prowers County Cattle Growers Association, February 15, 1904, Secretary M. J. McMillin commented on the slump in cattle prices, then continued, "Neither can I congratulate you on the treatment you have and are now receiving from railroad companies. The delay in furnishing railroad cars has resulted in serious loss and inconvenience to you, frequently having to turn herds loose after they were gathered because cars were not furnished, shipper in some cases waiting 30 days or longer for cars."

On November 25, 1905, Field and Farm reported, "many cattle intended for shipment this season will be carried over for lack of railroad cars."

Not all Association activity was directed at the evils of the industry. At the 1903 annual meeting, members voted to make the Association's fat stock and feeder show a permanent institution.

The idea for a livestock show sprang from the success of a showing of western range stock which featured the second annual meeting of the National Live Stock Association in Denver, January 24-26, 1899. This event was billed as the National Exhibition of Range Cattle. A small show was held in November, 1902, by the Colorado Cattle and Horse Growers Association.

Following this, the executive committee recommended that the president appoint a five-man committee to meet with a similar committee from the Denver Union Stock Yards and lay plans for an annual livestock show. The result was the National Western Stock Show, first held at Denver, in December, 1905.

The first president of the National Western was E. M. Ammons, who held this position until his death, in 1925. The secretary was Fred P. Johnson. Harry Petrie was the first manager of the show, with W. S. Guilford as assistant manager.

The success of the Association's own stock show and the interest which it aroused triggered another activity for 1903, the development of a full-fledged animal husbandry department at Colorado Agricultural College.

In his annual report for 1904, Secretary Fred Johnson said, "The exhibition of fed cattle at this show brought out quite a number of important propositions in relation to feeding range cattle, and the problems discovered in connection with this work led to the suggestion that if the attention of our State Agricultural College was called to these matters it might be of great assistance to the stockmen of the state in the way of educating the people in methods and manner of feeding.

"With this idea in view, some of our members investigated conditions at the Agricultural College, and much to our surprise discovered that the state institution was an agricultural college principally in name only, at that time was hardly in shape to undertake the line of experiments and investigations desired by us." The college had opened in September, 1879, with 19 students, three professors and one building. Despite Secretary Johnson's disparaging remarks, the college had made steady progress in those fields of education and experimentation pertaining to crops, but little attention was being paid to livestock. Animal husbandry was a minor subject.

Association officials prevailed upon Governor James H. Peabody to appoint a practical stock farmer to the state board of agriculture, which served as the college's board of regents. Peabody named Eugene H. Grubb of the noted Mount Sopris ranch near Carbondale. Grubb was a brother of the president of the state Association, and a well-known exhibitor of Shorthorn cattle. Backed by the urgent pleas of the Association, Grubb was able to talk the board into employing W. L. Carlyle, professor of animal industry at Wisconsin Agricultural College. He joined the Colorado school, in charge of the department of agriculture. Carlyle turned over the agronomy section of the department to an assistant, concentrating his efforts on animal husbandry. "Prof. Carlyle was selected as being the leading man in this line of work in the United States," Johnson told the 1903 state convention.

Carlyle and Grubb, with an assist from the Association, were able to obtain federal assistance in Washington. This enabled the college to launch a series of experiments on livestock feeding on western ranges and ranches.

Animal husbandry became a separate department of the college in 1908.

The period from 1901 to 1917 was a time of peace for the United States, but not for the Colorado Association. It battled the legislature, the railroads, the forest service, the packers and the stockyards, and, when a proposed herd law reared its ugly head, The Denver Post. It fought a series of less spectacular but continuing engagements with predators—human, animal, vegetable, and microbe.

Disease had become a major problem in the industry by the turn of the century. Well aware of the need for strong preventive measures, including the education and indoctrination of the cattlemen themselves, the Association emphasized the importance of animal health. It prepared and sponsored many acts to strengthen and up-date the state's veterinary and sanitary regulations.

In 1903, the entire brand and sanitary inspection system of the state was reorganized, with actual stockmen comprising the administrative board.

In 1905, this board was empowered to compel the dipping, spraying or other sanitary treatment of livestock exposed to mange, scabies and other infectious diseases.

In 1911, the legislature authorized the State Board of Stock

Inspection Commissioners to establish quarantines and take drastic action to control disease. The same legislature made it illegal to import bulls or female breeding stock into the state unless accompanied by a health certificate showing them free from contagious or infectious diseases, and tuberculin test charts.

In 1915, the legislature took further measures to strengthen the powers of the livestock inspection commissioners and the State Veterinarian in handling contagious diseases. These included provision of funds for programs of "investigation, extermination and eradication by destruction of livestock or other infected property" and for deputy state veterinarians to increase staffs when epidemics broke out. Veterinarians were authorized to kill animals for diagnostic purposes.

In addition to its legislative efforts, the state Association directed its own inspectors to investigate, report, and take corrective actions against disease.

At state and local association meetings, federal and state veterinarians explained current problems, control programs and preventive measures. The resolutions normally included at least one measure endorsing disease control efforts and urging all members to participate.

By 1897, according to the federal bureau of animal industry, blackleg disease was prevalent in at least 63 percent of Colorado's counties. The federal bureau launched an intensive campaign for universal vaccination. In its first year of participation, Colorado vaccinated 41,000 head. Stockmen's associations supported the program wholeheartedly. One of the state organization's activities was to distribute bulletins to all members. Within a few years, blackleg vaccination had become a universal practice, and the disease has since been kept in check by this means.

Early in the 1900's, mange, more commonly known in recent years as scab, ran like wildfire through herds in all parts of the state. It took many years to bring this disease under control to the point where it was no longer considered a serious menace. It was a skin disease which many ranchers refused to consider worthy of note. Stockmen's associations and the more progressive operators worked with government veterinarians in educational programs.

An example of the difficulty was the plight of the Bent and Prowers County Association, which launched a program against mange early in 1902. Their efforts included appearances at meetings by veterinarians, distribution of circulars, open discussions on dipping vats and the methods of dipping cattle. A large scale dipping program resulted, but the common use of the open range nearly nullified the effort. At the organization's annual meeting in 1904, that wonderful chronicler of cattle events in southeastern Colorado, Secretary M. J. McMillin reported, "I regret that I cannot report that the mange has been entirely stamped out from our herds and ranges, but the failure of some to dip their cattle, seriously threatens to infect the herds of all those who are compelled to turn their cattle on the range again this season."

At the insistence of the Colorado Cattle and Horse Growers Association, the legislature in 1905 authorized the State Board of Stock Inspection Commissioners to compel dipping, spraying or other treatment for animals exposed to mange, scabies or other infectious or contagious diseases.

In 1908, a federal mange inspector, Dr. Shumaker, reported at least half of the cattle in Baca County still infected. By 1914, another government inspector, Dr. Snyder, was able to report that mange was almost eliminated. Another outbreak occurred in 1926, however.

Poison weeds took a heavy toll of livestock in the early days of the twentieth century. Cattlemen had battled loco weed for a quarter of a century, with the assistance of the state government and the state Association. In 1881, the legislature offered a bounty, with a top price of one and one-half cents a pound for the dried loco weed, provided it had been grubbed out in the months of May, June, and July.

Because the average citizen and the average official could not distinguish the poisonous from the harmless varieties of some 140 species of Astragalus, or loco weed, in the state, and the opportunity which the bounty offered unethical persons to reap easy if undeserved profits, the law was repealed in 1885. During the first month the law was in operation, the clerk of Costilla County received 25 tons of loco weed, representing a total bounty of $832.46. On one Sunday in 1884, there was 149,911 pounds of loco weed delivered to authorities at Colorado Springs. Farmers were finding it more profitable to raise loco weed than potatoes.

The battle against loco continued, the most effective known method being to grub it from the ground, but progress was slow.

Cattlemen reported their losses from the plant totalled $1,000,000 in 1902, $1,200,000 in 1903, $2,000,000 in 1904. Local and state livestock associations went into action. The legislature appropriated specific sums for the use of the agricultural college's experiment station in poisonous weed investigations.

Colorado Agricultural College established an experimental sub-station at Hugo, with 24 head of experimental cattle, to study the loco problem.

In 1908, the federal government announced that locoed cattle could be cured with a course of strychnine treatments. However, heavy losses continued until cattlemen learned methods of preventing animals from eating loco. These included maintaining grass in good condition, because cattle prefer grass to loco weed; fencing off heavily infested areas; eradication through grubbing, spraying, burning and cultivation, and, herding cattle away from poisonous plant areas.

Similar control methods finally reduced the extensive damage which resulted from cattle eating larkspur. Larkspur was particularly harmful in the mountain areas. However, the plant had certain virtues, of a negative sort. Although poisonous to cattle, it would not injure sheep, and normally it was harmless after August first.

When cattle were moved to the high mountain ranges in southwestern Colorado in the early days of this century, it was often necessary to "ride poison." Several cowboys would be detailed to herd the cattle back from patches of larkspur when it was in bloom. Each outfit running cattle was required to furnish saddlehorses for the cowboys who were "riding poison." Once the plants had bloomed and the flowers withered, the poison assignment ended.

Many areas were reserved for sheep because of the prevalence of larkspur.

Animal enemies of the cattle industry ranged from the lordly lion to the lowly prairie dog. The most destructive was the latter. In 1903, Frank Benton estimated that prairie dogs east of the mountains were eating as much forage as 384,000 cattle. J. E. Payne of Colorado Agricultural College reported that a square mile of ordinary range land provided enough feed for 20 head of cattle, while the same area in a prairie dog town would support only five head, 256 dogs eating as much forage as one cow.

Control measures for prairie dogs developed slowly. The 1903 legislature authorized the commissioners of each county to spend up to $1,000 annually for prairie dog poison. The legislature at the same time asked the federal government to cooperate in control programs.

Colorado's pest control acts of 1911 and 1915 provided the machinery for establishing pest control districts under the supervision of the state entomologist, assisted by county pest inspectors who were appointed by the county commissioners. These acts, however, were designed prinicipally for orchard and farming areas, and made no provision for control on public lands.

In 1919, the legislature appropriated up to $50,000 to be used in matching federal funds for a cooperative predatory animal control program. This project was the joint responsibility of the federal Bureau of Biological Survey and the State Game and Fish Commission.

In 1927, a rodent pest control fund was established, funds coming from levies on range cattle, sheep and goats.

Mountain lions and bears commanded state and livestock association bounties for a number of years.

The Territory of Colorado began paying bounties for the killing of wolves as early as 1869, and the practice was continued for many years. To further encourage the wolf hunters, most of the local associations offered bounties, payable in addition to amounts collected from the state.

The North Park Cattle Growers Association, which had been formed March 15, 1899 to represent its members in the leasing of state lands, found other work early in its existence. During the winter of 1900-1901, wolf packs overran the North Park area, killing a total of three horses and 48 cattle.

At the organization's annual meeting, January 2, 1900, the North Park Association and the North Park Cattle Company announced they would pay a bounty of $30 on wolves and 50 cents on coyotes. The association paid $25 on wolf bounties, 37½ cents on coyotes, the cattle company picking up the tab for the remaining $5 and 12½ cents.

For a time, the bounties had to be discontinued for lack of funds—the association's lack, that is. The North Park Cattle Company or Two Bar was owned by Swift and Company. Very soon, the association decided on a pro rata assessment of two cents per head on cattle which provided bounty money.

The first person to collect a bounty was a man named Casteel, who sent the remains of a large grey wolf to Walden by stage from Big Creek Park in the northwest corner of the park. The wolf invasion wasn't without certain bits of humor. The North Park Union in January, 1900, reported: "The grey wolves killed a calf for the Donelson Bros. last Friday night. W. F. put out some traps and caught Frank Kellam's dog."

In 1909 and 1910, the wolf packs returned to North Park. This time the association voted to pay a bounty of $75 per head. Cattle were more valuable, and wolves were more numerous. The association also sent for the famous Wyoming wolf hunter, "Rattlesnake Jack" McIntyre, and his son, Jack, who was called "Little Rattle."

In 1915, a famous wolf, known as Two Toes, ravaged the North Park area with his pack. This wary animal had managed to survive several encounters with men, suffering only the loss of some toes in a trap. The Two Toes pack killed 50 head of cattle in 1915. Albert McIntyre finally killed him the following year.

Wolf bounties generally ran much smaller in other sections of the state, where the wolf-cattle ratio was more favorable to ranchers. However, many associations did pay substantial amounts, calculated to be enough when added to state bounties to make wolf hunting profitable. The Bent County Cattle and Horse Growers Association paid a bounty of $4.50 per scalp in the 1880's, stipulating that the animals must have been killed on the ranges of association members. Later, the bounty was changed to $5 for adult wolves, $2.50 for pups. In 1909, the association was billed for $550 in bounties, a sum which had to be carried over until there was sufficient money in the treasury to pay it.

The Logan County Cattle and Horse Protective Association in 1900 decided it would limit bounty payments in the future to members of the association, or to persons owning less than 25 head of cattle.

The coyote skulks somewhere between the saints and the sinners. Cattlemen have never agreed on the location of his particular niche. The coyote has more enemies than friends, more prosecutors than defenders, it's true, but an audible minority of stockmen insist that the coyote does more good than harm. This group maintains that the coyote preys on jackrabbits, prairie dogs and other small pests, and that the only larger animals he ever kills are the crippled, sick and diseased.

Through the years, the coyote has been a bounty animal more often than not, but there has never been a very high price on his head. Private citizens and government hunters and trappers have hunted, trapped and poisoned him, but he bounces back like a hardy perennial.

Once, however, there was a general uprising against coyotes. That was in 1923, when cattlemen became alarmed at the spread of rabies among cattle in adjoining states, said to have been caused by bites from infected coyotes. Stockmen organized coyote drives, supplementing the work of the U.S. Biological Survey, which sent out parties of men to hunt and kill the animals.

The jackrabbit is another hardy perennial, whose ranks are thinned from time to time, yet burgeon and expand into a de-

structive pest a few seasons later. Rabbit numbers have usually
been controlled by community rabbit drives.

Cattle prices soared after the outbreak of World War I, col-
lapsing in 1919 and leading to several years of economic troubles
for the cattle industry in the ensuing decade.

Photo by Chas. J. Belden from the Franklin Collection.

CHAPTER ELEVEN

FUROR OVER FENCES

After nearly a century of existence, Colorado still remains legally a range state. Stockmen are not generally responsible for livestock damage to unfenced crops or other unprotected property.

For economic reasons, stockmen have fenced their pastures for many decades, and the state has long had a fence law which provides redress for damage done by livestock to crops or other property enclosed within a fence which meets the legal specifications defined by the law. All these effect the purpose of a herd law to a large extent, but there has never been a true herd law enacted.

Efforts to enact a herd law, or to restrict the action of livestock by other means, have been numerous in the state's history. In 1861, the first Territorial Legislature enacted a law which prohibited the importation of cattle, sheep, goats, mules, and horses into Huerfano, Pueblo, Fremont, Jefferson, Boulder, and Costilla counties for the purpose of grazing. This law did, however, exempt land owners of the territory and drovers who were trailing cattle through these counties to destinations beyond.

The original founding members of the Colorado Stock Growers Association were mostly small scale stockmen whose cattle were largely imported from the East or brought into the territory as work oxen. These men resented the invasion of disease-bearing herds from Texas and they instigated legislation to curb the activities of drovers and to prohibit the importation of more Texas cattle.

At one of its earliest meetings, in 1867, the Association named a committee to "wait upon the legislature." Minutes of subsequent meetings referred to "the bill" in the legislature, without explanation. "The bill" was a general livestock statute passed by the Seventh session of the Legislative Assembly of Colorado Territory.

Section One permitted non-residents to herd stock in Colorado Territory for one year upon payment of 50 cents per head for cattle, 20 cents per head for sheep, in lieu of taxes. *Section Two* required non-residents to file certificates with county recorders, showing the number and description of animals which they planned to graze in the territory. *Section Five* provided penalties for violating the law—a fine of two dollars per head for cattle, and one dollar for sheep. The county was to retain three-fourths, the state to receive one-fourth of all fines. *Section Ten* made it illegal "for any person or persons to import into the Territory of Colorado any bull, cow, ox, steer or cattle, of whatsoever description, known as 'Texas cattle' for the purpose of sale, stock-raising, growing, herding, or feeding, or for any purpose whatsoever." *Section Eleven* provided the penalties for violations—a fine of $50 to $200 for the first offense, $100 to $300 for the second offense, with further fines of $100 for every 24 hours the offender should unnecessarily delay the movement of cattle from the territory.

Only one attempt was ever made to enforce this ban on Texas cattle. In 1869, ranchers in Douglas County became alarmed at the increasing ravages of splenetic or Texas Fever, then thought to be communicated directly by Texas cattle. It was later discovered that the fever, so deadly to "American" animals, was actually transmitted by infected ticks that rode into the territory on the hides of the Texas Longhorns. These cattle were completely immune to the disease, however. Be that as it may, Douglas County cattlemen knew that the presence of Texas cattle meant Texas Fever, and they knew that they had lost more than 1,000 head of their American cattle in 1868 from the disease.

When Joe Curtis and John Dawson trailed the first herd northward into Douglas County the next spring, driving 1,600 head across the divide between Cherry Creek and Bijou Creek, a group of local stockmen attacked at night, shouting and firing revolvers in a successful effort to stampede the herd. They killed several head, wounded many more. Dawson and Curtis were arrested and fined $50.00 under the statute, but collected their scattered animals and continued on their way north.

As ranchers stocked the ranges with Texas cattle and more and more Texans settled in Colorado, Association sentiment changed. These newcomers were instrumental in having the law repealed by the 1870 Territorial Legislature.

In 1872, a different group of stockmen had become the leaders of the Colorado Stock Growers Association. They were open range cattlemen numbering many former Texans in their ranks. Their presence and the changing Association policies were reflected in new legislation which favored the development of the range cattle industry. Restrictive legislation after that was confined to local farming areas.

In 1881, the legislature enacted a law which required stockmen in Costilla, Huerfano, and Las Animas counties to keep their animals under the care of herders from the tenth of May through the twentieth of October each year. If livestock damaged growing crops in these counties during the restriction period, the owners of the crops could impound the offending animals and file suit for damages in a justice of the peace court. In any specific case, damages were to be assessed by three disinterested persons, each of whom received the sum of 25 cents for his services.

The year 1885 was a legislative milestone for the Colorado cattle industry and the cattlemen's Association. In this session, the legislature assumed responsibility for a statewide brand registration system, a function which had been maintained by the Association since 1867 for its members. The legislature also created the office of State Veterinarian and the State Veterinary Sanitary Board. It enacted a measure holding railroads responsible for cattle killed by trains, and it also enacted a statewide fence law.

This measure provided that any person who made and maintained a legal fence in good repair could obtain redress for damage done by livestock. He also could hold such animals as security until his claim had been satisfied.

The fence law spelled out in detail the specifications for a legal fence. Legal fences included post and board, pole, barbed wire, smooth wire, and a miscellaneous category of hedge, rock, stone, and other fences. It provided that a legal fence must be at least 54 inches high. A post and board fence must be supported by posts at least five inches in diameter, spaced not more than eight feet apart. There were separate specifications for three-board and four-board fences. A legal barbed wire fence could include either three wires, or two wires with a rail of posts on top. Posts for a barbed wire fence were to be not more than eight feet apart. More lenient provisions prevailed for fences of four "plain wires." Posts could be 100 feet apart, but must be augmented by stays placed every ten feet.

In later years, the legislature liberalized the specifications of this first fence law.

Sentiment for a herd law bubbled and sputtered through the years. Farmers in various parts of eastern Colorado complained bitterly when range herds destroyed their crops. However, they hesitated to act. Most farmers were also stockmen, and dependent on the "commons" or open range. They realized that a herd law might injure them as stockmen more than it would help them as farmers. Those who confined themselves strictly to farming were a distinct minority.

A difference in the legal philosophy of the two cultures which affected the settlement of Colorado also entered into any herd law controversy. English common law endorsed a "fence live-stock in" concept. This placed the burden of responsibility on the owner of stock in the event they broke through the fence or got out.

Spanish law, on the other hand, was essentially that of a live-stock and open range country. It followed the "fence 'em out" theory. The Spanish had traditionally held that the landowner had to fence his own land if he wished to protect his crops from destruction by livestock grazing on open range.

The latter was essentially more practical for the West and, because of this, it has prevailed to the present.

The herd law was, in effect, an attempt to change this idea. It offered another approach to the English concept of placing the responsibility for crop damage back on the owner of live-stock. In essence, it simply shifted the burden of who was going to build the fence.

In 1916, a herd law proposal was the major issue of the state's general election. It may have settled once and for all the fate of any Colorado herd law. The Denver Post, through its satel-lite, a weekly publication named The Great Divide, unveiled a herd law proposal of its own, which it sought to have enacted by the voters of Colorado through the initiated referendum system.

The proposed measure surpassed in severity anything enacted by any other Western state. It was successful only in uniting Colorado's agricultural interests—both those in favor of a herd law and those opposed to one—into a solid front against the measure. The bill made no differential between farming and grazing areas, no allowance for the fact that the state's 14,000,-000 acres of forest reserves could not legally be fenced, and it would have repealed the existing fence law. Its proponents re-fused to consider changes when approached by representatives of farm organizations who favored a herd law with a proposal to modify it by excluding the grazing areas, thus permitting the use of some 40 million acres of land which were adapted only to grazing.

Section One of the measure provided "The owner, person in possession or caretaker of any domestic animal or animals, shall hereafter be liable for all injury done by such domestic animals." The rest of the bill provided for impounding trespassing animals and selling them if the owner could not be located or refused to pay the damages claimed, and it provided for repeal of the existing fence law "and all acts and parts of acts in conflict therewith."

The editors of the Denver Record-Stockman believed that the motive behind the herd law proposal was found in the fact that "a Denver paper behind the herd law and its proprietors were interested in cheap Colorado lands which they proposed to colonize."

The Sterling Evening Advocate in an editorial expressed similar thoughts: "Anything advocated by The Denver Post and The Great Divide is open to suspicion, and careful reading of the initiated measure proposed by that outfit leads us to believe that they are attempting to hand the farmers of Colorado a gold brick. It is charged that the measure is framed to encourage the sale of lands held by non-residents in northeastern Colorado, and we think after reading this proposed law that this is probably the 'Nigger in the woodpile' here. It is our belief that if the law carries it will practically destroy the livestock industry of the state."

Instigator of the proposal was Volney T. Hoggatt, a big, brawling, colorful promoter. Ex-pugilist Hoggatt was editor of The Great Divide, a close friend of Denver Post publisher Frederick G. Bonfils, and a confirmed enemy of all cattlemen. Hoggatt was promoting homestead colonies at that time, among them the Great Divide Colony which lured hundreds of homesteaders into Moffat County in 1915 and 1916. This followed passage of the Grazing Homestead Act, which permitted a person to file on 640 acres instead of the previous limit of 160 acres. (Cattlemen and the cattlemen's Association, incidentally, had long supported a "grazing homestead" law, but had sought a unit large enough to maintain 100 head of cattle, recommending 3,000 acres of range land.)

When petitions for the herd law went into circulation, the cattlemen's Association went into action, mustering its own strength and that of farm organizations and civic groups throughout Colorado. When the smoke finally cleared away, the measure had been beaten resoundingly at the polls. The Association had pulled out every stop in its campaign against the herd law, and its treasury was in the hole $1,364.11, a deficit which was made up by contributions from individual stockmen and local associations. The successful campaign had cost the state organization $8,170.05, which did not include additional expenditures by local associations and by individuals.

While cattlemen's organizations, state and local, had spearheaded the fight, they were assisted by the Farmers Alliance, the Farmers Union, the State Board of Livestock Inspection Commissioners, Colorado State Grange, the Denver Chamber of Commerce, Denver Civic and Commercial Association, and other organizations. As Association minutes put it, "Even Mayor Speer and the City Hall people helped out."

The Farmers Union and the Grange had, in the early stages of the 1916 herd law movement, looked favorably on a law which would shift the responsibility for crop damage to the owner of livestock. When the Denver Post and Great Divide announced their herd law proposal, representatives of the Grange and Farmers Union approached Hoggatt and Bonfils with the suggestion that the measure be modified to make it both workable and acceptable. John Grattan, a representative of the Grange, said, "Prior to our conference with him (Bonfils) we held conference with Volney Hoggatt, editor of The Great Divide, in an endeavor to modify and rationalize this law. They deceived us, and we were convinced there was more to their attempts to put the law on the statute books than their apparent desire to aid the struggling farmers of the state."

The cattlemen's Association at its annual meeting, January 21, 1916, approved a request for an assessment of five cents per head on cattle and horses and one cent per head on all cattle and sheep in the state, to be sent to all local associations, with the information that the money would be used to defeat the herd law.

The Post's petitions bearing 20,959 names, were filed with the Secretary of State just before the deadline on July 7, 1916. Examination disclosed that 11,330 of the signatures had been obtained in Denver, practically all of them on July 6 and 7. A detective agency hired by the Association reported that the 11,330 signatures had been obtained in Denver by 113 circulators, who were paid three cents per signature. The agency in its report to the Association in August, 1916, stated that it could find no addresses for 24 of the circulators. One of the circulators had been out of the city for three months, four were never located, four others were non-residents, six were minors, and seven were aliens. One man admitted his wife did the work which he had sworn to have done himself. One woman said her mother did the work and another circulator was not a qualified voter.

This triggered a grand jury investigation which was terminated by the resounding defeat of the bill. Reporting on the grand jury's actions, the Rocky Mountain News said on November 2, 1916, that "The petitions showed page after page in which the signatures were apparently in the same handwriting and the grand jury is investigating to determine who wrote the names and how they were verified."

While the grand jury action was dropped following the election, its disclosures led to passage of a bill in the next session of the legislature which made it illegal for persons to circulate initiative referendum petitions for pay.

The livestock and agricultural bureau of the Denver Civic and Commercial Association, in an analysis of the proposed measure, pointed out it would repeal the existing fence law, thus relieving railroads of all liability for livestock killed by trains, would jeopardize the interest of stockmen grazing animals on forest reserves, which could not be legally fenced, and would have made stockmen liable for irresponsible claims of damage.

With the exception of The Denver Post, every newspaper in Colorado opposed the measure.

The issue was defeated overwhelmingly by a vote of 155,134

opposed, to 85,279 in favor. It carried in Kiowa, Logan, Morgan, and Washington counties and gained a tie in Lincoln County. All other counties defeated it.

In the same election, A. H. Kramer, business agent for the Colorado State Grange, was elected to the Colorado House of Representatives from Aurora. He introduced House Bill No. 318 in the 1917 session of the legislature. This bill provided for establishment of herd districts, boundaries to be fixed by county commissioners, giving these officials authority to prevent "certain animals" from running at large. This measure, known as a "local option" herd law, was referred without comment, to the House Committee on Stock for study. It died there.

In the closing days of the session, a cattlemen's association-sponsored bill to amend Colorado's fence law reached the floor of the House. Kramer, with the editorial backing of The Denver Post, attempted to have his bill substituted for it, without success. The new fence measure liberalized the specifications for a legal fence, reducing the minimum height from 54 to 44 inches, and providing for wider spacing of posts for a three-wire barbed wire fence. This measure had the support of the Farmers Alliance, the cattlemen's Association, the State Board of Stock Inspection Commissioners, and the Colorado State Grange. Kramer caused a heated controversy on the floor of the House when he charged that signatures of representatives of these four organizations had been forged, a charge that was disregarded.

The Denver Post and Great Divide made a renewed effort to put a proposal for a local option herd law on the ballot in 1918, but failed to get enough support. M. J. McMillin, secretary of the Bent and Prowers County Cattle and Horse Growers Association, at the annual meeting in February, 1918, reported, "The Denver Post and Great Divide have been trying all summer and fall to stir up trouble between stockmen and homesteaders and are now having petitions prepared for circulation to get signatures to another herd law initiated measure."

McMillin said that many complaints had been made to Governor Gunter during the latter half of 1917 of damage to homesteaders' crops, but investigation showed that "in almost every instance the depredation was caused by other homesteaders' stock. Not a single case was found where the homesteader had even a fair fence, which shows that if a lawful fence was erected there would be very few complaints."

Today, Colorado's fence statute is supported by the fact that the modern rancher has found it good business to keep his stock behind fences. The law in its present form provides indemnity for property enclosed behind a lawful fence, defining it in this manner: "The following shall be a lawful fence in the State of Colorado: A well-constructed three strand barbed wire fence with substantial posts set at a distance of approximately 20 feet apart, and sufficient to turn ordinary horses and cattle, with all gates equally as good as the fence, or any other fence of like efficiency. Railroad right-of-way fences constructed in compliance with the statutes in force on the date of construction and maintained in good condition shall be considered legal fences."

Where do we go from here? Photo by Dick Goff

CHAPTER TWELVE

BETWEEN THE WARS

The defeat of the Herd Law Proposal in 1916 left the Colorado Stockgrowers Association financially embarrassed but strong in spirit. The campaign had demonstrated the power of Colorado's cattlemen as an organized group and their ability to enlist statewide support from organizations and individuals outside the industry.

Just as local associations became units of the state organization in a statewide campaign, the Colorado Stockgrowers Association became a part of the American National Livestock Association in national programs. During the resolutions session of the annual meeting, members discussed current American National resolutions and projects. Occasionally, the state group disagreed with a national association proposal. In a case of this nature, the Colorado Stockmen either abstained from approval, or took a stand against it. In the main, however, the Colorado Association incorporated national association resolutions pertinent to the Colorado industry into its own convention resolutions, and frequently launched state projects to support the national association.

The Colorado Association wholeheartedly joined the national campaign of cattle and other livestock associations to combat the growing power of the major packing companies, which dominated the market so completely that they were able to control the actions of their competitors. As early as 1900, the five major packers—Armour, Swift, Cudahy, Wilson and Morris —were known as "The Beef Trust."

At the annual meeting of the Colorado Stockgrowers Association January 25, 1917, the principal speaker, James J. Sullivan, used the packing industry as a means of illustrating the value of organization. Sullivan charged that the packers used their control of the stockyard companies to amass complete detailed information on cattle numbers, prices, and conditions, as well as range conditions. "If the price happens to be good, the stockyards travelling representative comes to you and says the price is so and so in Denver or Kansas City, and you had better get your stock out. He does not tell you that every other travelling representative is telling the same thing to every man he can reach, but he is doing it. As soon as you have your stock loaded on the cars, they've got you. You have to pay the freight. You cannot send them back now. They do not feed the public from the packing house, they feed them from the cold storage room. You do not know how much meat is in there, but they do.

"If the stock in the warehouse is way down, they can handle a great many head of cattle more, and they are ready to buy a great many. If the stock in the warehouse is up, they do not want any more and if you are not satisfied with the price they offer you, you can ship them back to the range or to the next market. And if you do that, God help you! The telegraph key tells the story long before you get there."

Asked if the stockyards shouldn't be made a public utility and placed under the control of the Public Utilities Commission, Sullivan replied, "Not a public utiliy. They are a monopoly! They are so organized that they would present figures to prove they are not making any money or more than a measly five or six per cent, and there is no way in God's world that you could diagnose the figures."

Pressure against monopolistic practices in the processing and distribution of foods of all kinds mounted during World War I as prices climbed. Public opinion came to the support of the stockmen. President Woodrow Wilson on February 7, 1917, directed the Federal Trade Commission to "investigate and report facts relating to the production, ownership, manufacture, storage and distribution of foodstuffs . . . to ascertain the facts bearing upon the question whether there are manipulations, controls, trusts, combinations, conspiracies, or restraints of trade out of harmony with the law or the public interest," with a view that "proper remedies, legislative or administrative, may be applied."

On July 3, 1918, the commission submitted a report on the meat packing industry. It was a ringing indictment of the major packers.

"It appears that the five great packing concerns of the country —Swift, Armour, Morris, Cudahy and Wilson—have attained such a dominant position that they control at will the market in which they buy their supplies, the market in which they sell their products, and hold the fortunes of their competitors in their hands."

The report charged that the packers had not only gained control of their own industry, but "an almost countless number" of related and by-products industries and even non-associated enterprises. "The producer of live stock is at the mercy of these five companies because they control the market places, storage facilities, and, to some extent, the rolling stock which transports their products."

The report said the five firms had competitors at their mercy because they controlled the market places, storage facilities and refrigerator cars for distribution. Because neither the producer nor the competitor could bring relief to the situation, the consumer was also at the mercy of the monopoly.

The commission members commended Francis J. Heney, the chief investigator, for achieving conclusive results despite intense opposition from the packing firms. Heney had been condemned, misrepresented and severely criticized, the report stated.

"The commission, through Mr. Heney, had to meet deliberate falsification of returns properly required under legal authority; we had to meet schools for witnesses where employees were coached in anticipation of their being called to testify in an investigation ordered by you and by the Congress of the United States; we had to meet a situation created by the destruction of letters and documents vital to this investigation; we had to meet a conspiracy in the preparation of answers to the lawful inquiries of the Commission."

The nation's stockmen heartily endorsed the report up to this point, and they agreed with the immediate solution of the problem—rigid control by the railroad commission and food administration under emergency powers granted for the duration of the war.

Even before the commission's report had been made public, the President in a proclamation dated June 18, 1918, placed all stockyards under federal supervision and required the licensing of stockyards, packer buyers, commission men, traders and others handling livestock in the yards.

At its annual meeting January 24, 1919, the Colorado Stockgrowers Association commended the findings of the Federal Trade Commission and the emergency program established by the President's proclamation, but condemned the permanent solution proposed by the commission.

Emergency supervision and licensing of facilities and personnel, a resolution stated, "marks an important step in the rectification and supervision of oppressive market conditions and practices that have operated to the injury of the patrons of these markets, and thereby curtailed live stock production to the detriment of the meat-consuming public . . . the results already obtained during the few months of the operation of this control prove the necessity for its permanent establishment, with such added authority and facilities as may be required to insure the maintenance of open competition and fair practices in marketing of livestock and distribution of meat, and animal by-products."

The resolution urged Congress to act before the official end of the war terminated the President's emergency powers of supervision.

Although they approved of the work done by the Federal Trade Commission, cattlemen distrusted the proposed permanent solution even more than they did monopoly. The Commission had recommended government ownership and operation of public stockyards, rolling cars used for transportation of livestock, all privately-owned refrigerator cars and "such of the branch houses, cold-storage plants, and warehouses as are necessary to provide facilities for the competitive marketing and storage of food products in the principal centers of distribution and consumption."

At the same meeting, the Colorado Stockgrowers Association adopted a resolution which requested Colorado's representatives in Congress to use their influence in assuring the return of the management of the railroads to their owners, and made the following additional stipulation "that we request our representatives in Congress to oppose all legislation proposing government operation or ownership of marketing facilities of live stock and meat products, but favor such regulations as shall be adequate and necessary."

The Colorado Association united with other stock growers organizations and the American National in a two-year campaign for legislation to provide for supervision of marketing and packing facilities without government ownership or operation. On August 15, 1921, Congress passed the Packers and Stockyards Act, which left the ownership and operation of these facilities in the hands of private concerns, but gave the Department of Agriculture broad powers of supervision.

The act was amended May 5, 1926, August 14, 1935, August 10 ,1939, June 15, 1942, and July 12, 1943. It was revised completely in June, 1955. However, it still remains the "Packers and Stockyards Act of 1921, As Amended." The act and the regulations established by the Secretary of Agriculture under the provisions of the act provide the standards for behavior of all persons and concerns in the operation of stockyards and packing plants and related facilities.

The Packers and Stockyards Act is one of the milestones of achievement in the history of the nation's livestock organizations. With its passage, the Colorado Association turned its attention to other projects.

In the course of a century, there have been many tense and dramatic moments at meetings of the Colorado Cattlemen's Association. One was in 1868, when the secretary halted abruptly while reading aloud Detective Dave Cook's investigation report on cattle stealing, because he suddenly realized that the report named Association officers among the cattle thieves.

Equally dramatic was the moment during a meeting of the Executive Committee on August 31, 1920, when President John P. Klug of Greeley asked, "What is the next order of business?" Dr. Ike L. Gotthelf of Saguache replied, "I move that we read the charges and proceed with the impeachment of the president of this organization."

"You're plum out of order," Klug growled. "This committee doesn't have the power to oust me. No one but the Association members that elected me can. Let's take up some other business that the committee has authority to handle."

Dr. Gotthelf said an attorney had studied the by-laws and informed the Board of Control that the Executive Committee did have the power to remove the president and to transact almost any other association business it wished. Despite Klug's protests, he was over-ridden. Dr. Gotthelf read the specifications and charges brought against Klug by the Board of Control, which accused him generally of mis-using his office for private gain and of bringing discredit on the Association. The Board of Control, with three of its four members—Gotthelf, Field Bohart of Colorado Springs and C. T. Stevens of Gunnison—present for the occasion, then asked the Executive Committee to remove President Klug.

After a lengthy discussion, the Executive Committee requested Klug to resign. He emphatically refused to do so. Uncertain just how to proceed, the committee then passed a motion that declared the office vacant. Webb Whinnery refused to move up from the office of vice president to president. He pointed out that he had been among the very first people to suggest that Klug should not remain as president while also head of a cattle loan company. The other committee members then concurred with Whinnery's suggestion that they select as president M. J. McMillin of Carlton, a man who had taken no part in the controversy over Klug and his loan company promotion. Furthermore, Whinnery added, McMillin was a man of unquestioned integrity. He was fully dedicated to the Association, and had the complete confidence of its members.

Klug retained his aplomb, and later in the meeting, when other subjects were under discussion he suggested courses of procedure. At the same time, he was careful to address McMillin as "Mr. Assumed President."

Klug was a battler, a hard driver, a successful, self-made rancher, and man of tremendous energy. He must certainly be ranked among the more capable of the Association's many presidents. He homesteaded on Box Elder Creek 20 miles southeast of Greeley in 1891. He built up a cattle ranch of more than 20,000 acres, first by his own physical exertions and later by travelling throughout the Rocky Mountain area buying and selling cattle, dealing and trading wherever he could turn a dollar profitably.

Long active in the Colorado Stockgrowers Association, he was a member of the Board of Control in 1916, when the stockmen drove the Denver Post herd law proposal into the ground. In seconding Klug's nomination for president Field Bohart had said, "He has been working tooth and toenail for the Association ever since the herd law fight."

Klug became president in 1919, just before cattle prices nose dived. Drouth in the northwest in the summer of 1919, followed by an unusually severe winter throughout the state, pyramided the cattlemen's problems. Klug himself suffered the heaviest losses he ever incurred in the cattle business in a spring blizzard in 1920.

The Association treasury had been badly crippled by the

herd law campaign, and now its membership suffered because of the industry's economic troubles. Klug stumped the state throughout the year of 1919, bolstering courage, firing up enthusiasm by his own example, and restoring faith in the state association. He ramrodded numerous projects for the benefit of the cattle industry. At the annual meeting, January 16, 1920, he was able to report the following accomplishments to the cattlemen's Association:

Retained for the shippers of the state the feed-in-transit rates, on the railroad;

Established a state advisory board of forest service permittees to represent the cattle industry in negotiations with the federal government over forest grazing matters;

Succeeded in having reinstated the legislature's appropriation of $100,000 for destroying predatory animals;

Assisted in securing favorable reductions in freight rates on cottonseed cake into drouth stricken sections of the state;

Helped shippers on the western slope to secure additional stock cars from the Rio Grande railroad during the shipping season;

Sparked a series of newspaper articles and editorials which resulted in a 12½ cents per pound reduction in the retail price of meat in Denver stores;

Used its influence in a successful effort to secure coal which enabled Denver slaughter houses to continue operations;

Succeeded in adding 10 new local associations to the state organization.

The Colorado Stockgrowers Association at that time was a federation of local associations, although there were also provisions whereby stockmen could belong as individuals without being members of a local group.

At the annual meeting, delegates present elected the new officers. Each local association named a representative to the state Executive Committee. The Executive Committee, in turn, selected from its membership a four-man Board of Control to assist the officers in the active management of the association.

The Board of Control met once a month. The Executive Committee met at the call of the president, but the by-laws required it to sit at least twice a year, one meeting to be held three months before the annual membership meeting.

In recognition of his outstanding leadership in 1919, Klug was reelected president for 1920, but not without a contest.

In addition to his other activities during the year, Klug had become affiliated with a new livestock loan company, formed November 20, 1919. It was to provide a source of credit badly needed at this time. Banks throughout the nation had been calling cattle loans of this nature, and turning down new loan applications.

The name of the new organization was the Colorado Stockgrowers Loan Company. Its officers were: John P. Klug, President; Percy Houts, Secretary. These two men held identical offices in the Colorado Stockgrowers Association. The new loan firm helped the financially-embarrassed association by moving into the same office quarters, as a rent-paying roommate.

By the time of the Association's annual meeting in 1920, a number of cattlemen were becoming concerned. Professional promoters, it was reported, were using this apparent connection with the Association to sell stock. These salesmen, they heard, were hinting that the loan company was a project of the Association itself. They also heard that a substantial portion of the money received from the sale of stock—43 per cent—was being paid out as commission and bonuses for organizing the company.

This group of concerned members nominated Webb Whinnery of Lake City in opposition to Klug's candidacy for re-election. In accepting the nomination, Whinnery explained that despite his friendship and high regard for Klug, he disapproved of the close affiliation of the loan company with the Association, and believed that Klug should not serve as president of both groups. This would cause prospective investors to think that the loan company was endorsed by and affiliated with the stockmen's organization, he declared.

Klug answered Whinnery's remark in a sarcastic vein, saying, "I evidently have committed a crime, because in looking after the needs of the cowmen of the territory I found that the stockmen of the state could be enabled in some way to organize some company—a loan company, if you please—which it finally came to, whereby the stockmen could stand together as a unit."

He denied there was an connection or attempt at a connection between the Association and the loan firm. He added that the loan company owned by stockmen and operated for the benefit of the livestock industry, was sorely needed. "Because I have gone and interested myself in a loan company which, if the livestock men want to take advantage of, is one of the greatest things that ever happened, I have committed a crime in the eyes of some of you men."

Numerous leaders of the Association, including former President Isaac Baer, Delph Carpenter and John Grattan expressed their confidence in Klug and their faith that the loan company would prove an instrument of service to the industry. Grattan said Klug was attempting to provide a profit-making agency which on the one hand would serve the industry and on the other hand would provide income for it, similar to the commercial enterprises of the Farmers Union.

The rank and file members favored Klug. He was reelected by an almost two to one margin. Whinnery moved the election be made unanimous. Klug responded by nominating Whinnery for vice president, and the Gunnison County stalwart was elected by acclamation.

Four days later the Executive Committee met. The president announced that Secretary Percy Houts, who had been unable to attend the annual meeting because of illness, declined to serve again. The committee then elected Houts' office assistant, Mrs. Evelyn Castle, as secretary. A personable women who became popular with stockmen throughout the state because of her ability and personality, Mrs. Castle served the Association for several years.

As its next order of business, the committee elected the Board of Control: Field Bohart, Dr. I. L. Gotthelf, C. T. Stevens and Frank Squier of Riffle. The board was instructed to find new office quarters for the Association in the stockyards area and to prepare a budget for 1920. The next day the board rented Room 311 in the Stock Yards Exchange building.

The Board of Control transacted routine business during the

early part of the year. Representing the Association, it wired the forest service and Colorado's congressional delegation in protest to a proposed 300 per cent increase in national forest grazing fees, a raise which was cancelled in the face of a storm of opposition from grazing interests hard-hit by economic troubles. The Association also joined a nationwide campaign to encourage the use of front quarters of beef by the consuming public; helped establish and then conferred with a committee which Governor Shoup named to study an increase in the one-fifteenth of a mill levy on livestock to finance the state inspection service; endorsed the campaign to maintain open shop employment policies in Denver; met with representatives of the Denver stock yards and packing firms for an extended discussion of mutual problems and interests.

Meantime, the Colorado Stockgrowers Loan Company collapsed, with a loss of thousands of dollars to the stockmen who had invested in the scheme. The promoters disappeared. Members of the Board of Control then discovered that the Colorado Stockgrowers Association had been incorporated with authorization to loan money and transact other business. This action had taken place prior to the annual meeting in January. The incorporators were: Klug, Houts, Mrs. Castle and C. E. Platt, all well-known and active Association members or employees, plus C. W. Good and A. G. Campbell. The last two, it developed, were stock salesmen for the loan company. By this time, Good and Campbell had left the state.

At its meeting on May 21, 1920, the members of the Board of Control present—Bohart, Stevens and Gotthelf— introduced a resolution which charged that Klug had "involved the good name of our Association by using the same name for a loan company and likewise its office and officers, and thru the medium of his incumbency as president of both organizations has prejudiced our Association." The resolution also stated that Association members had been induced to buy stock in the loan company under misrepresentation by its solicitors. It concluded by requesting Klug to resign as Association president.

Klug entertained the motion, the second and the unanimous vote in favor of the resolution. Then he told the board, "This resolution was not passed by my consent, but under my protests." Asked to respond to it, he said, "You may say this, that I propose to stay at the head of this Association and hand it over to the State when my term expires."

Bohart then moved that the secretary be instructed to send out notices for a meeting of the Executive Committee to be held July 21, Klug, however, over-ruled the motion, with the comment, "The Executive Committee meeting will not be called until I call it."

In July, the Board of Control demanded that Klug dissolve the incorporation of the Colorado Stockgrowers Association, an action to which he readily agreed without comment. He promised to do this immediately. Klug also agreed to call a meeting of the Executive Committee for August 31. The minutes of the July meeting of the Board of Control read:

"There was much general discussion during the meeting that, summed up, amounted to perhaps a better understanding by those present of the real conditions and of the questions at issue, and while words were not minced, a spade was called a spade, and the main issue seemed to be the request of the Board of Control for the resignation of Mr. Klug, and he did not see fit at this time to hand his resignation in. When asked if he would resign if a majority of the Executive Committee approved the action of the Board of Control and desired it, he answered, "It depends on how I feel at that time."

Discussion during the meeting developed the fact that Klug himself had suffered heavy losses in the loan company collapse. He apparently convinced the Board of Control members that his gravest sin was lack of judgment and failure to investigate the loan scheme before becoming involved. However, as they told members of the Executive Committee a month later, they felt that Klug had certainly defaulted in his responsibility to the Association.

Klug's final comment at this meeting discloses something of the inner nature of the man and lends credence to his often repeated insistence that what he had done was intended for the best interests of the industry.

"If you gentlemen, members of the Board of Control, would

make as much of an effort to get behind this state Association
and work for its up-building and push matters of importance
to the stockmen with the same vim and pep that you are using
to oust me, I feel that the state Association would be the biggest
in the United States. I am for the up-building of this Association, to make it second to none, and I hope that we can all work
together in harmony for the benefit of the stockmen, and if at
your Executive Committee Meeting, you succeed in ousting
me . . . I am for you still." His subsequent actions indicated he
meant what he said.

At the Executive Committee meeting which unseated Klug,
the Board of Control members explained that the reason they
had requested resignation or removal was that infuriated stockmen over the state were holding Klug responsible for the debacle
which had cost them a great deal of money.

Questioned by Bohart, Mrs. Castle said officials of the Grand
Mesa Livestock Association of Glenwood Springs had notified
her that the group would not affiliate with the state organization
as long as Klug was its president. She said several other local
associations had indicated their intention of joining "as soon as
the differences are settled and harmony restored."

The real reason for removal, Bohart summed up, was that the
Association was at a standstill. Money had ceased to come in
from the local organizations. They refused to participate, and
Klug's presence had become a crippling handicap. To all of
this, Klug replied, "It's not me that put on the brakes, gentlemen. It's others that put on the brakes, not me."

C. A. Switzer of Piney asked him if he objected to the committee's voting upon his resignation, and Klug replied, "I don't
care a continental, but you can only do what the by-laws allow
you and it is not in the power of this board to dismiss a president."

Following the action which declared the office of president
vacant and subsequent election of McMillin, the Executive
Committee voted to present to the annual convention a revised
constitution and by-laws for its approval.

The revision followed the same general pattern of the existing
constitution and by-laws, but the language was more detailed

and specific. The constitution provided that "The Executive Committee in the interim between the Annual Conventions shall possess all the powers of the Association and the members of the Association, including the government, management and control of the affairs of the Association, and the removal for cause of all Officers, and likewise for cause the removal of all members of the Board of Control and Advisory Board . . ." The Executive Committee was also empowered to make changes in the by-laws which did not conflict with provisions of the constitution.

At the annual convention, December 21 and 22, in Denver, the Association approved the new constitution and by-laws, and affirmed the action of the Executive Committee by retaining McMillin as president for the year 1921. However, there seemed to be no ill feeling toward Klug. He remained active in the organization, and in 1925 was again elected a member of the Board of Control.

Klug's fortunes suffered a sharp reverse in 1930,when, after selling a major portion of his ranch and farm holdings for a reported $2,000,000 and purchasing control of a Denver bank, he lost almost everything when the bank failed. His death June 20, 1945, was like numerous incidents of his life—sudden and violent. Although 80 years old, he was attempting to saddle a stallion which he was breaking when the animal threw him against a fence, causing his death.

The impeachment faded into the background quickly as the cattlemen of Colorado struggled with new problems. In 1919, the price of cattle zoomed to a record high of $15.50 per hundred weight at Chicago. The average value per head of all cattle at the same time was $58.80 per head. Prices began to slip in July, 1921, continuing downward for seven years. They touched bottom at $26 in 1925, then rose for four years, reaching $55.30 in 1929, then plummeted for five more years, reaching this century's third low point of $14.50 per head in 1934.

The decline which started in 1919 became really serious later in 1921 when the rest of the economy started to recover from the post-war slump. Even the sheep industry made a comeback, but the cattle business remained in trouble. Credit for range cattle enterprises was almost non-existent, the necessary liquidation process was slow in developing, and operating expenses were rising.

The Colorado Cattlemen's Association had alternately fought, negotiated and fraternized with the railroads. They were virtually the only means of transportation other than trailing until the 1930's, when the development of good highways and high speed trucks ushered in a new era.

Cattlemen's complaints against the railroads fell into many categories: damages and claims arising from animals killed by trains; failure to settle or even to recognize claims; delays in supplying cars within a reasonable length of time during the fall shipping season; rough handling of cattle in transit; unsatisfactory facilities for feeding in transit; unsatisfactory or unworkable arrangements for free return transportation for stockmen who accompanied their cattle to market points; poor services in general, and high freight rates.

In 1921, the Association moved to secure rollbacks in freight rate increases, with partial success. State Senator R. C. Callen of Rifle, one of the Association's wheelhorses in legislative matters, represented the Association and western slope shippers in successful negotiations with the Denver and Rio Grande Western railroad. The ensuing rate reductions amounted to about $25 per car. A similar effort to secure reductions on the Denver and Salt Lake or "Moffat" railroad, was nullified by the Public Utilities Commission, because the road was operating at a loss. Requests for reductions in rates on other railroads "by informal conferences, communications and personal appeals" failed, because the other railroads insisted they could not make reductions unless they were sanctioned by the Interstate Commerce Commission. The American National stepped into the negotiations with the interstate carriers and succeeded in obtaining an emergency reduction in freight rates on southern cattle shipped to northern ranges.

In 1923, the Association obtained passage of a bill which required all railroads on livestock runs within the state to maintain an over-all average travel speed of not less than ten miles per hour between the point of shipment and the destination. The only time deductions permitted from the ten-mile limit were delays required for in-transit feeding and time lost through acts of God.

At the annual convention January 24-25, 1924, the Association did an about-face with the following resolution:

"Whereas, it has long been the custom of our Association, and also other organizations, to pass resolutions with reference to the railroads when we had a grievance or something to complain about; and whereas, a sense of fairness should prompt us to recognize their good acts;

"Therefore, be it remembered by the Colorado Stockgrowers Association in convention January 24 and 25, 1924, that we express our appreciation of the very generally satisfactory service rendered by the railroads operating in Colorado, to the livestock shippers during the year 1923.

"We are mindful of the sincere and energetic efforts of operating officials to supply cars without delays and to move stock after the cars were loaded."

In 1924 the Association began working with the contact committee of the Central Western Shippers Advisory Board to the American Railway Association to develop an orderly marketing program for the fall run of cattle. Throughout the season, September 15 through December 15, the shippers organization supplied advance information on the availability of cars to the Association, which saw that all stockmen received information. Association bulletins, personal calls, newspaper notices and radio announcements were used for this purpose. The organization also succeeded in getting a large number of stockmen to place their orders for cars early.

This program removed one of the principal causes of trouble between cattlemen and their railroads.

The Colorado Cattlemen's Association concentrated its efforts for its first 50 years on obtaining for its members and the industry needed services, even when the Association had to supply them; in drafting and securing passage of beneficial legislation and fighting off harmful legislation, and in combatting opposing interests. By the end of World War I it had added another important function—that of leading the industry in its economic battles. These were a series of harassing actions, too numerous for specific mention. The fight continues today.

In 1921, the Colorado Stockgrowers Association was able to effect substantial savings for stockmen when its officials persuaded the Denver Livestock Exchange to cancel an increase in commission charges which had been imposed the preceding year. The stock yards officials also agreed to reduce feed charges, and they accepted without protest a reduction in yardage charges which the Association obtained by petitioning the Department of Agriculture under the Packers and Stockyards Act.

As a result of these achievements and the Association's war on tax increases and railroad malfeasances, stockmen of the state willingly accepted a check-off system under which 25 cents per carload was deducted from the proceeds of livestock shipments to principal markets and forwarded to the Colorado Stockgrowers Association. The deductions were voluntary in that any shipper who objected to the deduction was repaid the entire amount which he had been assessed. Local associations heartily endorsed this method of financing activities. Apparently the individual stockmen also approved, as there were relatively few requests for rebates.

In the early days of Colorado's cattle business, taxes were a minor issue in a stockman's life, but by the 1920's he was becoming acutely aware of his tax bill. In 1921, the Association's tax committee went to work. Two of its members were legislators, the chairman, William Lambert, Jr., of Sedalia, a representative, and R. C. Callen of Rifle, a senator. The other member was J. W. Setters. These three teamed up with the legislative tax committee, whose members included two staunch stockmen, Senator John J. Tobin of Montrose and Representative Robert F. Rockwell of Paonia. The result was a 50 per cent reduction in taxes on cattle, horses and sheep.

At the same time Association members met with the State Land Board and asked for reduction of the lease charge on state-owned grazing lands from eight cents to five cents per acre. The board said it could not make a blanket reduction, but agreed to consider individual applications. A number of stockmen received reductions following this meeting.

In 1923, at the request of the Association, the State Board of Stock Inspection Commissioners reduced the cattle inspection fee from five cents to three cents per head.

When Dr. B. F. Davis started his 26-year career as secretary-manager of the Colorado Stockgrowers Association in 1923, he concentrated much of his efforts on tax relief for the industry. Davis was able to marshal an impressive array of figures to show that for many years assessed valuations of land, livestock and farming equipment had progressed steadily upward, while at the same time valuations of city property had remained relatively stable. Davis also launched a campaign to secure reduction in assessments on livestock in line with the sharp drop in livestock prices.

His double-barrelled assessment fight bore fruit in 1924, when the valuation of range cattle was reduced $3 per head and 49 counties of the state reduced their assessed valuations on land. The savings to land owners and stockmen was estimated at $600,000. In the years that followed, the Association was able to secure a number of assessment reductions.

Tuberculosis was the dominant animal disease in Colorado during the period between World Wars I and II, at least from the standpoint of activity, attention and public expenditures.

In 1921, the Colorado General Assembly appropriated funds and passed legislation which enabled the participation of the state government and all dairy and beef herd owners who wished to join in the federal government's tuberculosis eradication program. The campaign provided for testing of cattle by federal and state veterinarians and deputized private veterinarians, and for disposal of reactors. The state and federal governments paid part or all of the difference between the salvage value of the reactor and the market value of a comparable healthy animal.

The program was entirely voluntary. Two years later, the legislature enacted a similar measure which provided for the creation of tuberculosis eradication districts, in which testing, condemnation and disposal of reactors would be mandatory. A district would be created upon the receipt of petitions representing fifty-one per cent of the cattle in the area. Cities and counties were enlisted to participate on a cost-sharing basis. This measure increased the amount of the indemnity which could be paid to cattle owners who disposed of reactors.

The Colorado Stockgrowers Association participated actively in securing passage of the enabling legislation and carried on an educational program through bulletins, newspaper articles and the appearances of federal and state veterinarians at stockmen's meetings. In 1925 an Association resolution condemned the actions of some veterinarians in private practice who discovered reactors in herds but took no action to see that the reactors were promptly disposed of as required.

For the first 57 years of its existence, the Colorado Cattlemen's Association held its membership meetings in Denver, a central place and focal point for railroads and highways. Its annual meetings were held anywhere from late November to February, but more frequently, in January. This date enabled the Association to bring its members together with legislators for conferences on bills affecting the livestock industry. It also was a convenient means of enabling a large number of stockmen to visit individually with senators or representatives from their districts, when Association leaders felt they needed a reminder of their responsibilities to the industry.

In 1924, the Gunnison County Stockgrowers Association and the Gunnison Chamber of Commerce engineered the first midsummer meeting of the state Association—at Gunnison, of course. That community gave the cattlemen a rip-roaring, warm-hearted reception. The turnout was tremendous. The weather was fair and warm, the roads were clear throughout the state, and there were no bawling critters at home to be hand-fed every day, a decided contrast from many of the winter meetings. They had such a good time that at the close of the meeting, members voted unanimously to meet every summer at Gunnison. Later, the practice of passing the midsummer meeting around to different communities was instituted. In the early 1930's, the midsummer meeting became the annual convention. In the 1950's, the Association began alternating the site of the convention between eastern and western slope locations.

Plans for the 1925 Gunnison session headlined the winter convention in Denver, January 25 and 26. One reason for the popularity of the Gunnison meetings was their unusual nature. This was back before Colorado mountain towns had elaborate motels and other facilities for tourists.

"Be prepared to camp," read the invitation to the second Gunnison meeting, July 13, 14, and 15, 1925. "Bring the wife and children. A plate, cup, knife, fork and spoon for each. Towel, soap and comb for all, and a dutch oven. Start with a new shirt and two five-dollar bills, and if you are careful, you may only need to change one—a bill!"

The invitation stressed the "exclusive camp grounds" reserved for the cattlemen without further explanation. Many newcomers were amazed when they arrived to find that the city and county of Gunnison had turned over to the Association the beautifully-shaded, grassy courthouse square. "As to the grass," Mayor Jorgenson proclaimed in his address of welcome, "it's grown here. Step on it, sleep on it, use it!"

There were 196 men, 106 women and 57 children when they finally arrived, traveling in 90 cars and two round-up trucks. For three days the Colorado Stock Growers Association comprised a canvas community, formed in a hollow square about three sides of the courthouse. On the outer perimeter the stockmen parked their cars and set up kitchens. The tent village included white canvas teepees used by cowboys and sheepherders tending livestock on the range; half-tents pitched against the sides of open touring cars; old-fashioned side-wall tents, many of which accompanied the round-ups in the mountain parks; and new-fangled umbrella tents. Dominating this array were the Association's big headquarters pavillion, with Secretary "Doc" Davis' teepee next to it, and the Denver Record-Stockman's large hospitality tent. Publisher Art Johnson had raided Bill Gillaspey's art collection for framed photos of the Cattlemen's Days celebration at Gunnison in 1905, installed plenty of folding canvas chairs, and provided the Denver newspapers. This was the hang-out for a great many of the cattlemen.

By the end of the first day there were more than 25 tents pitched on the square, plus a miscellaneous variety of camp kitchens which ranged from small one-family "flivver outfits," to the elaborate chuck wagon outfits of the Southern Colorado and Chaffee County Associations.

The Southern Colorado Association had brought a lumbering round-up truck 300 miles, with old-time round-up cook, John Arnett, as head cook and Charley Hudson as his assistant. This association formed a caravan; each car bore the owner's brand in chalk. "It's the prize exhibit of the camp," publisher Art Johnson declared after the first of several free meals at the Southern Colorado wagon. He described the breakfast as "a spiffing hot meal of hamburger steak, fried potatoes, biscuits, stewed fruit and coffee, served in the cooks' inimitable style, which was 'Help yerselves, boys. There's the tools and here's the pots and kettles.' We sat cross-legged on the turf and 'put 'er away.'" Queen of this outfit was Mrs. S. J. Capps, mother of the state Association president, Harry Capps, and widow of one of the pioneer stockmen of the Walsenburg region. S. J. Capps had been one of the early leaders in association activities in Huerfano County.

The Southern Colorado wagon fed more than 50 of their own crew, as well as several "estrays" that wandered in at mealtime like Johnson. Johnson said he held a little appetite in reserve, because the Southern Colorado crowd planned to attack the Gunnison River in the afternoon and serve a supper of fresh trout.

In charge of this outfit were Harry Beirne, Frank Monroe, Hardy Roberts and "Tommy" Thompson.

The Chaffee County Association also trailed over Monarch Pass with a round-up wagon. Bill Fletcher cooked sizzling steaks and boiled delicious coffee on a stove "as big almost as the Gunnison post office." DeWitt brothers, W. J. Cogan and J. R. Mills ramrodded the Chaffee County outfit.

According to the Record-Stockman, "The George Greenes and the Paul Whites of the Gilpin-Jefferson Livstock Association were picking things off a cooking contraption that looked like a red-hot Christmas tree."

The first outfit to roll into camp was the Fremont-Park County Stock Growers Association. Mr. and Mrs. Ernest Guiraud, Mr.

and Mrs. H. J. Tharp, Jack Nunn and Dave Farr "were doing the elegant by cooking breakfast on the latest improved gasoline camp range."

Many of the cattlemen and their families cooked over open wood fires. A typical family traveled in a Model T touring car, with side curtains under the seat in case of rain. The camp outfit was contained in a wooden kitchen box mounted on the left running-board, a tent draped across the spare tire at the rear, with a kerosene lantern and the top from a three-hole kerosene stove tied to the tent. This latter, blocked up on stones, formed a grill over a wood fire. Canvas water bags were tied on the side of the car, partly for drinking water and partly to refill the boiling radiator as the car chugged up the steep, graveled mountain highways.

The broad grassy space within the circle of tents was the reception area, playground and gathering place. Convention meetings were held in the courthouse.

Among the feature entertainment events was the annual Gunnison County Cattlemen's celebration, which Dr. Davis advertised in advance as "a wild west show, frontier's day celebration, rodeo and stampede all combined." In the evening there was a street carnival, music, dancing, and a great deal of yarn spinning around campfires.

The highlight for the women was a tea at Western State College, the women of Gunnison serving as hostesses.

Among the hosts were two of the great leaders of the Colorado Cattlemen's Association during its century of existence— W. S. "Webb" Whinnery and W. A. "Bill" Gillaspey. Both of these men had given many years of unselfish service to the Association as officers, members of the Executive Committee, and committee workers.

Whinnery was bursting with pride when, as chairman of the resolutions committee, he digressed to say, "This is the best stock association meeting I have attended in 35 years, and I've attended every one of them." Whinnery probably attended more meetings of the Association than any other one person. Still active in 1959, he recalled that "In the old days we only had one disease that really worried us—starvation."

Even today, old-timers recall the Gunnison summer meetings and agree with the Record-Stockman's comment that "This Gunnison stunt beats hotel conventions all hollow."

Another reason why the Gunnison meeting in 1925 was so enjoyable was that, at last, things were beginning to look up in the cattle business. Business conditions generally were good. Cattle prices had bottomed out a few months earlier at $26 per head, after seven years of decline. An upswing appeared certain. A big corn crop was in sight in the Midwest, with prospects of a strong demand for quality feeders.

Good prices continued through the remainder of the decade, slipping slightly in 1930, then dropping steadily for the next four years. The average on all classes of cattle in 1934, was $14.50 per head. That was a time, one grizzled old cowman recalled, "when I hated to go out and look those old bossies in the face."

By 1930, cattle feeding was becoming an important factor in Colorado's livestock economy. It was concentrated generally in the irrigated valleys of northeastern Colorado and along the Arkansas River. Feeders comprised an increasing percentage of the Colorado Stock Growers Association membership. The organization began to devote more and more attention to growing problems of this expanding industry. In recognition of this development, the Association in 1930 went through another name change, this time to the Colorado Stock Growers and Feeders Association.

Livestock feeding as an industry in Colorado started with the introduction of alfalfa in the latter part of the 19th century. The beginning of the beet sugar industry in the early 1900's established the feeding of cattle or sheep as an almost universal practice on irrigated farms.

Sugar beets quickly became the most important irrigated cash crop in Colorado. They were produced for a guaranteed minimum price which assured the farmer of a greater gross income per acre than any other crop he could raise. The beet was a hardy plant which could produce at least a partial crop under adverse weather conditions.

However, it was an expensive crop to produce, requiring much special equipment, hand labor, irrigation water and plant food. It entailed a rotation with soil-building crops and heavy applications of manure to restore soil fertility. A very common rotation was to follow beets with corn, then seed the ground to oats or barley as a nurse crop for alfalfa. After the ground had been in alfalfa for three years, the ground was plowed for potatoes, and on the following year went back to beets. Some farmers shortened this rotation by omitting potatoes or corn. Others made it a four-year rotation by planting sweet clover instead of alfalfa and plowing the clover under as green manure for potatoes the spring after the grain crop had been harvested.

The availability of farm-grown grain, corn, hay and sugar beet tops, together with low-cost beet pulp which a grower could purchase at the sugar factory in his community, made livestock feeding a natural partner of sugar beets. Most beet farmers figured that if the only profit from their feeding operation was the manure it was a worthwhile venture. The farmer with livestock "sense" and good judgment, however, often found feeding his most profitable enterprise.

To these farmer-feeders, livestock feeding was as important, as interesting and as profitable as the production of crops. They became skilled technicians in the fine art of obtaining maximum gain for minimum cost. With the advent of mechanized agriculture, larger farms, bigger machines, highly specialized enterprises and mass production methods in farming, these men changed from cash crops to feed production. A great many of them became commercial feeders. They purchased the cattle, grain and other feeds. Most of the actual physical labor was done by employees. The commercial feeder depended on his feeding knowledge and his management ability for a return on his investment in livestock. Some of these commercial feeders found it profitable to custom feed cattle for others, relieving themselves, in part, at least, of the need for large amounts of operating capital.

Men of this type were active in the Colorado Cattlemen's Association from the mid-1920's until 1955. A few of them, like W. C. Harris of Sterling, who began livestock feeding in 1902, I. W. Bennett of Fort Collins and J. C. Evans of Greeley were prominent in the Association as early as 1900. By 1955, the problems of the cattle feeder had become so specialized that they formed a separate organization, the Colorado Cattle Feeders Association. Most of its members are still active in the Colorado Cattlemen's Association and the two groups work together on many projects for the benefit of the beef industry as a whole.

The universal economic depression and the terrible Western drouths overshadowed everything else during the 1930's. The Association concentrated its efforts toward securing reductions in taxes, transportation charges, commissions and other costs, in order to reduce the drastic losses in income suffered by stockmen. In 1932, the resolutions committee commended the state board of equalization for ordering a rollback of 20 per cent in assessed valuations for 1931, but pointed out that farm income had dropped 50 per cent, so agriculture still was bearing an unfair share of the tax burden. They opposed the railroads' request for an increase in freight rates, pointing out that railroads had suffered a mere 16 per cent loss of income while its agricultural shippers had lost half.

Throughout the early 1930's, the Association fought for reduced expenses and for assistance to the industry on every front. It asked for increases in protective tariffs on goods competitive with livestock and livestock products; for reduction in lease charges on state lands; for economy measures at all levels of government, including a 15 per cent reduction in salaries of county officers; for a reduction in delinquent tax penalties and an extension of time for redeeming tax-foreclosed property.

The Colorado Stock Growers and Feeders Association operated on a bare bones budget in the lean years. The Association retained the support of most of the local associations, but all of these had trouble keeping their dues paid. There just wasn't enough money. At the very worst time, Dr. Davis, the Association's secretary-manager, mortgaged his home and borrowed money on his life insurance, then loaned the money to the organization to keep it going. Dr. Davis and a Denver newspaper reporter rode a freight train to Sterling for the midsummer meeting in June, 1934.

Partly as a result of Association efforts, cattle were included as a basic commodity under the Agricultural Adjustment Act of 1934. Under the provisions of this act, the Department of Agriculture used funds provided by the Jones-Connally Act to purchase and destroy some 8,000,000 cattle, 4,000,000 ewes and 250,000 female Angora goats in drouth-stricken areas of the West.

The Association also approved the results of the Land Utilization Act, under which the government re-purchased thousands of acres of marginal farm land from farmers who couldn't make them pay out in drouth years, relocated the farmers on good land in other areas and turned the re-purchased lands back to pasture for use as grazing districts.

The Association pressed for relief measures, particularly low interest loans from government agencies, but fought strenuously against government controls for the beef industry.

In 1937, at the annual convention in Steamboat Springs, the Association spelled out its attitude toward government programs for agriculture in a resolution endorsing the soil conservation program. After commending the principle of soil conservation and the voluntary program, it added:

"Whereas, the cattle men of Colorado do not subscribe to the theory of regimentation or to any plan of government control of agricultural production.

"Therefore, Be It Resolved, that we endorse all voluntary efforts toward soil conservation, but are opposed to any program of regimentation or government control of the production of livestock, feed and grains."

A resolution opposing government controls has been included in every set of resolutions adopted by the Association since that time.

Stockmen attending the Steamboat Springs meetings also commended the Farm Credit Administration, its lending agencies and the Colorado production credit associations and national farm loan associations "for valuable services rendered to our livestock producers and feeders."

At this session, the Association commended research work being conducted in detection and prevention of Bang's disease, also known as brucellosis and contagious abortion, but expressed the opinion this work had not advanced to the point where control programs were practical for range and semi-range areas. Within five years, however, the Association gave its approval to control programs. A 1942 resolution asked the Colorado Legislature to appropriate funds for a state-federal program.

Colorado's cattle population remained fairly constant from 1900 until World War II. The peak years were 1919 with 1,881,000 head, 1920 with 1,757,000 and 1934 with 1,745,000 unsalable animals. The low points occurred in 1928, when there were 1,377,000; 1939, when there were 1,400,000; and 1926 and 1927, when numbers were exactly the same, 1,406,000.

Wartime conditions stimulated cattle prices and production. The average price for all cattle in 1942, was $54.00 per head, only $4.80 below the 1919 peak. In 1943, it rose to $71.30, dipped to $63.40 and $61.30 in 1944 and 1945, then in 1946, started a long upward climb under the pressure of postwar expansion and inflation.

The Association emphasis during the war years was on efforts to stimulate production to meet the needs of the nation and its allies for beef, and it battled red-tape to remove war-imposed obstacles to production.

At a special 90th Anniversary Convention at Glenwood Springs in 1957, the Association paid tribute to the officers who had served in the nine previous decades. In the group above are the past presidents who attended. Left to right: Robert Schafer, Robert Burghart, Howard Linger, Floyd Beach, Leavitt Booth, Harry Capps, Charles Lilley, Frank Fehling, Francis Murphy, and the late Tom Field. Photo by Dick Goff.

CHAPTER THIRTEEN
THE OUTFIT TODAY

The Colorado Cattlemen's Association almost became one of the casualties of World War II. Wartime conditions and restrictions slowed up its activity. At times, the organization could not obtain permission to hold meetings because of the travel involved for members. The Association continued its routine business, kept working for favorable legislation and fought to free the stockman from fetters to production. However, there was a definite slacking off of interest on the part of individual members and affiliated local associations. Many of these latter ceased to function.

Soon after the war ended, a vague rift developed between the stockmen of the eastern and western slopes. Western slope associations, by then locked in bitter combat with the United States Forest Service, felt that the easterners were holding the Association back from a more active participation in this conflict. Eastern slope members believed that the westerners wanted to run matters entirely from that side of the mountains and to restrict Association activities entirely to the forest service troubles.

As a result, cattlemen of the western slope neglected the state organization and rallied around their local associations, which were strong and active. The Uncompaghre Cattle and Horse Growers Association, at that time, was larger than the state organization. Eastern stockmen drifted away, and the Association floundered. It was in much the same condition as it had been in the early months of 1900, when the Western Range Stockgrowers Association brought about a revival.

Throughout the state, however, thoughtful cattlemen realized that a strong, united and representative statewide association was vital to the industry.

When Dr. B. F. Davis retired in the fall of 1949 after 26 years of dedicated service, during which the Association experienced many of its most fruitful years, the Executive Committee members carefully weighed the choice of his successor. They finally decided upon a man who had been born and raised in the cattle business, educated in agriculture at Colorado State University, and had been a successful county agent on both sides of the mountains—David G. Rice, Jr.

Rice is a tall, gangly, individual with Lincolnian features. He stands six feet, two, wears an 7½ boot, smokes a straight-stemmed pipe and usually has his crossed feet resting on his desk on those rare occasions when he pauses long enough to sit. He has a seemingly infinite capacity for work, but always appears as if he were resting between rounds of golf. He must actually be as completely relaxed at work as he seems to be. Otherwise, no individual could survive a continual round of 20-hour days and seven-day weeks.

People in the lobby of the Shirley-Savoy Hotel were amused once to watch Dave at a bank of three telephones, carrying on a double-barreled conversation with a phone at each ear. He had been called from a committee meeting to talk over a matter of Association business. He dialed a third party involved in the matter. By listening to both men and relaying their remarks to each other, he was able to return to his committee meeting with that particular business completed and off his list of worries.

Rice's grandparents were early settlers and cattle raisers in Fremont County, where they settled in 1881. Rice Mountain, northeast of Canon City, is named for his grandfather, W. A. Rice. In 1884, the W. A. Rices moved on to Grand Junction, then a village with three frame houses and a cluster of log cabins. David Rice, Jr., was raised in this community.

Throughout the years, Dave Rice has proved himself a master of indirect methods. When he went to Elbert County as a fledgling county agent, he knew he was going to need a lot of cooperation from farmers and ranchers, but he didn't ask for it. "I sort of stuttered and stammered around at the meetings, and they began to feel sorry for me, and they offered to help out and began making suggestions. Pretty soon, they were all working."

As county agent in Delta County, Rice had his baptism of fire in the forest service war. He came under the guiding influence of a group of cattlemen whose leader was Art Starr of Austin. Starr was the man behind the scenes in many cattlemen's projects. He was the ringleader of the Western Slope Livestock Committee, for instance. This self-appointed, non-affiliated, and legally non-existent group included Chet Blake, Floyd Beach and Kelso Musser of Delta, J. B. Claybough of Whitewater, and Roy Case of Montrose in its ranks. There were no dues, no meetings, no membership list, but lots of resolutions, lots of phone calls, telegrams and personal contacts. Each man paid his own expenses. Colorado senators and representatives in Congress and government officials were under a continuous bombardment of telegrams on forest service issues. "They'd write just as big as they could sound," commented Rice. "After I became secretary of the Association, whenever I needed some fast action, I'd call Floyd Beach and ask him to get the Western Slope Livestock Committee together."

An outstanding achievement of this committee was the telephone campaign which it triggered the night after Republican Governor Ralph Carr died, leaving the party without a candidate in the imminent election. The committee enlisted leaders of the Colorado Cattlemen's Association in every part of the state. With this assistance, they contacted every member of the state Republican vacancy committe. By two o'clock the following morning, the vacancy committee was committed to select cattleman Dan Thornton of Gunnison, as the party's substitute nominee for governor.

Art Starr was a member of the Colorado Stockgrowers and Feeders Association when Rice was named executive secretary. Its chairman was Walter Crew of Denver. Henry Bledsoe of Cheraw, was serving his second term as Association president. The headquarters at that time was in the Cooper Building, 17th and Curtis Streets, a structure erected by one of the Association's great early leaders, Governor Job A. Cooper.

Rice was employed at a salary of $3,000 a year, with the understanding that if he could boost the membership to 1,000 by June 1, 1950, his salary would be automatically increased to $4,000. This was in October, 1949. The name of the Association was also changed to its present one, the Colorado Cattlemen's Association.

Rice's first action was to ask the office girl for a mimeographed list of members. She smiled and said, "We don't have one, but if you'll wait five minutes, I'll type one for you." It developed that the Association had exactly 22 paid-up individual members. Local associations were providing some support, but they had fallen into the practice of paying whatever amount they wished, and their contributions had been dwindling every year.

Rice started making the rounds of the existing local associations. He also succeeded in stirring up interest in reactivating many of the locals which had fallen by the wayside. By June 1, he was able to present a list of more than 1,200 bona fide, dues-paid, individual members.

The Executive Committee called the presidents of all the local associations together in Denver in the fall of 1950 for a reorganization meeting. Frank Fehling of Nathrop, was chairman of the session, which was long, controversial and, at times, noisy. Eventually, there was a meeting of the minds and the policies and framework which exist today were shaped.

In the fall of 1951, the Association established its present program of active standing committees. Previously, committees had met only once a year, during the conventions, or on very special occasions. "The idea of the new system was to have enough projects to keep everyone busy," Rice explained.

From that time on, committees met regularly, Secretary Rice served as the secretary of each committee. "We'd have a planning session with the chairman and a few others so we'd know where we wanted to go, and so everyone would have a job." Planned discussions kept committee meetings on the scheduled topics and served to brief members. "After each meeting, we sent written reports to the committee members and Board of Control. That way, they knew where they'd been after they got there."

The committee system and a close affiliation with the local associations are probably what held the organization together during the fall of 1950. Committee activity also kept many of the Association's ablest members active after they had completed their terms as president. The committee system continues today to keep the Association effective in many spheres of action. It eliminates the danger of neglecting important but prosaic matters during the stress of campaigns for short-lived, emergency projects.

As Rice pointed out, "Everyone has as least one point of interest. The leaders' job is to tie a good man to his particular interest in the Association. When you've got him going on this, pretty soon he's interested in the whole outfit."

Except for the professional, full-time staff, no one is paid for his services. In 1955, an Association employee interviewed a number of past presidents, then estimated that it cost a stockman between $5,000 and $6,000 in traveling expenses alone for the privilege of heading the Colorado Cattlemen's Association.

In the light of present prices, this estimate is conservative for the 1960's. Yet, through the years, smaller operators have accepted the responsibilities and expenses of the presidency, even when it meant borrowing money at the bank for traveling and other direct expenses, and for hiring help to do the work at home.

This feature alone insures business-like approach to Association affairs. A Board of Control member from Craig, Cortez, Springfield or Julesburg isn't likely to be traipsing to Denver at his own expense for non-essentials.

As impressive as the sacrifices made by the presidents and other officers is the dedication of committee members.

Robert Schafer of Boyero is a successful cattle producer who is thoroughly convinced that a strong state association is essential to the continued progress of the industry and to the success of the individual cattleman.

As chairman of the Association's membership committee, Schafer drove 12,000 miles from October 30, 1955 to May 1, 1956, to tell the story of the organization and help local stockmen enlist members. He devoted nearly five months of the six-month period to this activity, paying all of his traveling expenses out of his own pocket.

He attended regional meetings, meetings of nearly every local association in the state, and barnstormed through the range areas to contact individual producers and sign them up. Day after day he talked to ranchers about their industry, their ideas and the things they felt could be done to help the industry.

In the spring of 1957, Schafer held a series of regional meetings and organized a membership team with representatives from every local association, a responsible leader being named for each region. Otto Maul of Kiowa proved himself then and for years after the Association's Number One membership salesman.

Robert Burghart, Jr., of Colorado Springs, took up the good work when Schafer relinquished the chairmanship to become president. In 1960, Burghart established a five-year program to bring the Association's membership to 5,000. Under Burghart and Vic Hanson, Jr., of Walden, who succeeded him, the membership campaign reached its goal in July, 1965. By 1966, the Archuleta County Stockgrowers Association and the Custer County Stockgrowers Association were able to announce that every cattleman, large or small, within their respective counties, was a member of the Colorado Cattlemen's Association.

Committees occasionally have a habit of outgrowing their original framework.

In 1951, the organization had a feeders committee. This mushroomed into the Colorado Cattle Feeders Association.

In the same year, the Association established a youth committee to provide something of interest for children of Association members and lead them into eventual active participation. Under the successive leadership of Robert Hogsett of Fort Morgan, Carl Carlson of Denver, Ray Burke of Timnath and John Boyd of Broomfield this small committee developed by stages into the very active Junior Colorado Cattlemen's Association of today.

Early projects for the youth committee included choosing a Junior Cattleman of the Month. Its sponsors stressed the importance of management in cattle production. Every summer, the young stockmen would attend a seminar on ranch and range management at the headquarters of some successful Association members. Today, the juniors run their own show. They select projects, plan tours and other activities, and follow them through to completion. One of their annual projects is to raise money for the Association's Endowment Trust Fund.

The junior organization in 1966 cited an Association member, Raymond McMillin of Carlton, for his great interest in and support of juniors. McMillin established the Calf Foundation of the Bent-Prowers Association. He presented six two-year-old cows with calves by the side to the foundation and secured similar contributions later from other cattlemen. The foundation presents young cows or bred heifers each year to boys and girls at a drawing. The program has enabled a number of youngsters to get started in the cattle business. McMillin is a son of M. J. McMillin, pioneer southeastern Colorado cattleman who played a prominent part in the development of both the

Colorado Cattlemen's Association and the Bent-Prowers Association.

While specific programs to encourage the breeding and use of quality, purebred cattle have been a part of Colorado Cattlemen's Association activity in recent years only, the Association has always been identified with the improvement of beef animals.

Early leaders in the organization included the first leaders in the purebred cattle business. Samuel Hartsel, Jared Brush, John Prowers, for example, were leaders in the state Association and each was among the first stockmen in his particular area to use purebred Shorthorn bulls. Brush, John Routt and Prowers were early Angus feeders.

The Association's early and repeated efforts to eliminate inferior and dairy-type bulls from the public domain, and its sponsorship of legislation making it illegal to run anything but a purebred beef bull at large were its first specific projects for cattle improvement.

The Association was instrumental in securing legislation which removed restrictions on the importation of purebred cattle into Colorado. In the 1920's and 1930's, the Association fought successfully for lower assessments on purebred animals.

The Association annually awards the grand championship trophy in junior college livestock judging competition at the National Western Stock Show in Denver.

In 1951, the Association's cattle improvement committee investigated the possibility of an Association-sponsored sale of registered range bulls. The committee's chairman, Lars Prestrud of Littleton, with Murray Giffin of Nunn, and Dave Rice attended the California association's annual sale at Red Bluffs, and returned with ideas. Out of this grew the Bullanza Bull Sale, which has developed into a major institution under the management of the Colorado Hereford Association. This sale has been the climaxing feature of the Association's annual midwinter meeting in Colorado Springs for many years.

The Association also sponsors the annual Shorthorn Bull Sale jointly with the Western Shorthorn Association. Like the

Hereford sale, this event was inaugurated to help improve the quality of range bulls.

In 1953, the cattle improvement committee introduced and obtained appropriations for a bull fertility testing program at Colorado State University. It worked with Colorado Livestock Conservation, Inc., in a bruise control program and on similar projects.

In 1958, the committee co-sponsored with Colorado State University the first statewide grub control program, and the next year joined the university in establishing the Record of Performance service. Under this latter project, extension service specialists weighed and graded calves for commercial and pure-bred breeders to assist them in establishing the worth of individual sires and dams. The success of this venture led to the foundation of the Colorado Beef Cattle Improvement Association, with the committee as its sponsor. This is a self-financing organization which utilizes the services of extension livestock specialists in the weighing and grading of calves and the university's electronic accounting machines in processing all data. These records make it possible to determine accurately the impact of a particular sire on a group of cows and the value of an individual cow as a dam, by measuring the quality, size and gaining ability of the progeny.

More recently, the cattle improvement committee has followed Colorado cattle into the feed lots, the packing plants and the retail stores to find means of improving the product of Colorado ranges and to market more salable beef for the same investment per animal. A series of tests in conjunction with the Colorado Cattle Feeders Association, Colorado State University and the Adolph Coors Company Feed Lot of Longmont compares the quality of Colorado feeder cattle with southern stock. This project arose from a contention by cattle feeders that the lighter-framed, less "typy" southern cattle can be upgraded by feeding and a contrary insistence by cattle producers that an animal must have good quality from the outset to produce good quality beef. To date, tests are not conclusive, but committee members point out that the outstanding individual animals in the comparisons have all been Colorado cattle, and that the tests indicate that only good quality southern cattle can be measurably upgraded through feeding.

Another test, sponsored by the committee in cooperation with Colorado State University, Coors Feed Lot, the Monfort Feed Lots and Monfort Packing Company of Greeley and Safeway Stores follows selected progeny of specific sires through the feed lots to determine their efficiency as feeders, and from there into the packing plants and the stores to determine the amount of salable beef obtained from the progeny of any particular bull. One purpose of both these comparisons is to impress upon the cattleman the importance of producing cattle which will satisfy the feeder's demand for efficient gains and the packers' and retailers' demand for a high percentage of desirable meat.

Nate Patton of Canon City has headed the cattle improvement in its active program during recent years.

The Association's research committee worked closely with officials at Colorado State University and with legislative committees in a program which resulted in a complex of livestock research facilities at the university. The entire "Foothills Complex" for veterinary research resulted from a campaign instigated and promoted by the Association committee.

In 1953, the research committtee established the Floyd Cross Foundation for the advancement of cattle research at Colorado State University. The foundation is financed jointly by the Colorado Cattlemen's Association and local associations. John Holtorf of Akron, and Ben Ferguson, then county agent at Monte Vista, spearheaded the move to establish the foundation, which honors a former dean of the veterinary college at the Fort Collins institution. In recognition of his services to the industry, Cross also was named a life member of the Colorado Cattlemen's Association.

Specific achievements fail to tell the story of some of the Association's most important committees. During the last 15 years, probably more time has been devoted to taxes and legislation than to any other specific programs, yet it would require listing a multitude of projects to accurately illustrate the accomplishments of the tax and legislation committees.

By the early 1950's, legislation was affecting the cattle industry to the extent that not only did the executive secretary devote a substantial portion of his time to legislation, but an Association officer also spent most of his days at the capitol when the legislature was in session. Since the standing committees were first organized, Francis P. "Pat" Murphy of Walden, has kept a vigilant eye on the activities of the Colorado General Assembly. In 1965, the position of vice chairman was created for the committee, with Robert A. Burghart, Jr., of Colorado Springs, delegated to assist Murphy and Rice. Frequently, all three are on duty at the capitol at the same time, each man attending a different session, committee meeting or buttonholing assignment. Murphy served his apprenticeship as a watchdog of the legislature under his cousin, the late Charles P. Murphy of Spicer, who was a powerful figure in the Colorado General Assembly and a leader in the Association during the 1940's. Both Murphys headed the Colorado Cattlemen's Association, Charles P., in 1942, 1943 and 1944, Francis P., in 1954 and 1955.

By teaming up with lobbyists for other rural interests, the Association's efforts have remained effective in spite of the increasing population shift to urban centers. On more than one occasion, the capitol press corps has named Dave Rice the most proficient lobbyist at a particular session of the legislature.

By 1963, the demands on the Association's tax committee had become so heavy that Jack Owen of Karval and Jim Lillpop of Alamosa were named co-vice chairmen to assist Chairman John Benton of Burns. This committee works at all levels of government in the state to protect the interests of the cattle industry in assessment and taxation.

The committee was able in 1964 to remove the bugaboo of sales ratio from the fears of rural landowners. Under the sales ratio plan devised by certain urban interests, the assessment of lands would have been determined by the prices received in actual transactions, regardless of special conditions affecting the sale prices of the lands. The Association was influential in drafting, then active in securing, passage of the 1964 act, which prescribed as the yardstick for assessment of any piece of land the ability of that land to produce livestock, crops or any other form of income, rather than the selling prices of similar lands.

If the sales ratio theory had prevailed, the assessed value of lands owned by CCA members would have doubled or tripled.

The committee represented the cattle industry during the period when the entire assessment system of the state was overhauled. One of its achievements was the development of a formula for assessing livestock. This formula is based on the ratio between cattle prices and the parity index of livestock prices.

The livestock sanitation committee continues a work which began in 1868 with efforts to fight "Texas fever" by excluding Texas cattle from Colorado ranges. A major project in recent years has been to assist Colorado counties in obtaining their original certification and later re-certification as "modified certified" brucellosis-free areas. The Colorado committee also spearheaded a successful national drive for the approval of calfhood vaccination as a means of obtaining re-certification.

In the fall of 1964, this committee was called into action by the threat of an epidemic of vesicular stomatitis in cattle. To forestall an epidemic, it was necessary to prevent the assembly of cattle at purebred shows and fairs for a time while the individual cases were located and treated. Fearful of a panic, the Association quietly asked officials of purebred organizations to attend a meeting where control plans would be discussed. Despite elaborate precautions to prevent the situation from becoming known to the general public, more than 100 stockmen appeared for the small "confidential" gathering, some of them quite perturbed.

Because of the extensive use which the cattle industry makes of public lands, and the important role which they play in the affairs of the Association, there are separate committees for federal lands and for lands owned by the state, schools and local echelons of government.

At times, particularly in the drouth years of the 1930's, state and school grazing lands often went begging. The state land board enlisted the support of the Colorado Stockgrowers and Feeders Association to find stockmen who would lease the vacant lands. By the 1950's, however, thanks to the work of the land board and greatly improved economic conditions, state lands were virtually all under lease, and returning a substantial income to public educational funds.

In 1960, urban interests started a hue and cry for increased state land fees and/or the sale of the lands to private individuals. Occasionally a desirable location for real estate development had caused a particular tract of state land to command a potential price many times its value for agricultural uses. Such instances were cited as evidence that all state lands could be leased for much higher rates than the existing ones. Another device used by metropolitan newspapers and backers of increased lease fees was to point to an incident where a non-leaseholder offered a much higher rental for a particular piece of state land, ignoring the fact that the tract was part of a much larger block in which the bidder had no interest but which could be leased principally because it included the desirable tract.

The result of the agitation was a series of public hearings throughout the state which vindicated the existing administrative policies. The Association's state lands committee assisted stockmen in presenting their views. The Colorado Education Association commended the substantial annual income which schools received while retaining ownership of lands which were increasing in value each year. This and a provision under which lease prices are kept at a realistic level by a bid system helped win the case for the rural areas. Whenever a state lease expires, the leaseholder has the option to renew it, but he must match any bona fide bid which is made to purchase the lease.

The work of the Colorado Cattlemen's Association federal lands committee is almost as well known in other Western states as in Colorado, because of the committee's success in establishing and maintaining a satisfactory working agreement with the United States Forest Service, the Bureau of Land Management and other users of the public lands, as well as for the committee's work in range improvement on the public domain. The committee cooperates with the other user groups in conservation programs, and in meeting the threat of adverse provisions of wilderness legislation.

The Association's federal lands committee dates back to 1907, when the organization joined Fred Light of Snowmass in defending the first trespass suit brought against a Colorado rancher by the United States Forest Service. In the next 40 years, the committee's activity expanded and contracted as the Association's relations with the forest service waxed and waned. When the feud with the federal agency reached its peak in the late 1940's, the committee was revitalized into one of the Association's most active units.

With the late Russell Rose of Pueblo as its chairman, the group developed the cooperation concept which finally brought the Association and the forest service together as partners in improving the forest ranges. It created the present-day range improvement committee as one of its sub-committees. This unit, under the chairmanship of Leonard Horn of Wolcott, has been frequently cited for its achievements.

Ed Cliff, chief forester of the United States, called the Colorado program an outstanding example of a cooperative range improvement project. The American National Cattlemen's Association reviewed in detail the work done on the Grand Mesa and Uncompaghre national forests and recommended that this type of work be done in other western states.

Another enthusiastic supporter of the Colorado range program on public lands is Paul Friggens, roving editor of The Readers Digest magazine and formerly an editor of Farm Journal magazine who said:

> "The Colorado Cattlemen's Association pioneered the effort to bring the federal government and the users of the public lands together on common ground. The result has been more effective conservation of these resources and a demonstration of the soundness of the multiple-use program."

Stockmen as individuals and the Colorado Cattlemen's Association as a group are enjoying relatively friendly relations these days with the Colorado Game, Fish and Parks Department, and with hunters and fishermen. Much of the credit for the change from a state of near hostility is due to the work done during the last 16 years by the Association's game and fish committee and to the leadership of Cattleman-Senator Fay DeBerard of Kremmling in the Colorado General Assembly. Orris Albertson of Burns, was chairman of the committee for five years, during which time the group implemented "Operation Respect," settled a serious controversy with state officials and sportsmen over the right of access to public lands across private property, and solved a long-standing problem caused by the conflict of big game hunting seasons with the movement of cattle off the forest ranges for the year. Numerous other problems were settled which had caused a barrier between stockmen on the one side and game and fish officials, hunters and fishermen on the other. More recently, with Kenneth Buckley of Craig as chairman, the committee helped to develop a liaison trouble-shooting committee to investigate major differences before they grow into outright controversies. This committee includes the executive heads of the following organizations:

Colorado Cattlemen's Association, Colorado Wool Growers Association, Colorado Department of Agriculture, Colorado Farm Bureau, Colorado County Commissioners Association and the Colorado Game, Fish and Parks Department.

The work of the Association's transportation committee is complex and technical. Members have had to virtually become experts in the fields of transportation, rates, taxes and regulations. Its major accomplishments have meant savings of thousands of dollars over the years. Much of this resulted from constant attention to small details of legislation and negotiation. The committee works in close cooperation with shipper organizations and transportation firms. This committee is headed by Leavitt Booth of Lakewood, a former Association president and chairman of the Colorado Cattlemen's Centennial Executive Committee.

A century ago, a cattleman's marketing program consisted of holding a beef round-up in the fall, then driving the beef animals to market or to a loading point, where they were loaded in railroad cars for shipment to stockyards. Aside from price, his principal concern was whether or not the railroad would have cars waiting on the siding when he was ready to load.

As the business became more complex, the cattleman extended his marketing activities to negotiations with stockyards companies, commission firms and packing houses for more favorable prices and conditions. By the 1960's the Colorado Cattlemen's Association marketing committee had become international in its activities.

Today, the marketing of beef is emphasized even more strongly than the marketing of live animals. The committee concentrates much of its effort on three objectives: solving the problem of beef imports, improving the cattle producer's position in the retail marketing field, and relieving the retail market of downward pressure on prices caused by excessive tonnage.

Since its formation, the committee has fought for adequate legislation to control beef imports. In 1963 and 1964, the domestic beef industry suffered severe losses when Australia and New Zealand sharply increased their imports to the United States, taking advantage of a token tariff of only three cents per pound. The committee worked with Governor John Love and his staff in efforts to organize governors and congressional delegations of Western states in a unified movement to seek beef import legislation which would protect the domestic industry and require the labeling of all foreign beef sold in the country. It also worked successfully for the passage by the Colorado General Assembly of a resolution demanding the enforcement of Colorado's foreign meat labeling statute.

The committee was active, too, in the national movement which resulted in altering government carcass beef grades. This permitted the inclusion of younger, smaller animals in the "choice" grade, by reducing the amount of fat necessary to qualify these cattle as U.S. Choice.

A continuing program has been to sponsor and participate in studies and hearings which will develop information on factors which affect the prices of cattle and beef. The committee has teamed with the Denver Better Business Bureau to expose and make known to the general public misleading unethical practices by racketeering meat retailers.

The committee also works with local associations in sponsoring sales of feeder cattle, directs the publication of the annual Feeder Edition of the Association's Cattle Guard magazine, and takes a prominent part in conferences with stockmen throughout the state on marketing problems.

The Colorado Cattlemen's Association beef promotion committee achieved one of its long-sought objectives in October, 1965, when the Colorado Beef Promotion Board was established as an agency of the state government, financed by a legislative appropriation and empowered to carry on an aggressive program to promote Colorado beef. The board includes representatives of producers, feeders, processors and distributors.

The committee fought for many years for an adequate beef promotion program in the state. From its start, it teamed up with the Colorado Cowbelles in a variety of promotional projects. Lars Prestrud and Mrs. Al Atchison of Littleton, as individuals and as a team, turned great quantities of the energy and leadership of both organizations into this work. In 1956, the beef promotion committee organized the Colorado Beef Council, which united the various segments of the beef industry in promotional enterprises. The Colorado committee launched a drive which also helped in the formation of the National Beef Council, of which Robert A. Burghart, Sr., of Colorado Springs, was the first secretary. The committee sponsors Colorado Beef Week in conjunction with National Beef Month, in January; Beef for Father's Day, the program originated in Colorado by the Cowbelles; the Beef for Summer Barbecue promotion and Beef for Christmas Day promotion originated by Mrs. Tom Currier of Collbran. She carried on an aggressive individual campaign, then enlisted the active assistance of the Plateau Valley Cowbelles and the Western Slope Cowbelles council. These groups sold the idea to the Colorado Cowbelles. Mrs. Atchison and Prestrud took it up at that point and it became a major project, now a national program.

Other projects which the committee originated or participated in actively include a roadside sign campaign with the theme, "Watch Your Curves—Eat Beef," begun in 1955 and beef advertising as a part of the publicity projects of the Colorado Division of Commerce and Development. The sign campaign spread into several states. As a result of a promotion launched in 1955, 50 processing plants in Colorado now manufacture beef sausage and beef bacon.

The efforts of this committee and the Colorado Cowbelles have been recognized nationally on several occasions. Beef for

Father's Day is now an American CowBelles project. Otto Maul of Kiowa and Mrs. Robert A. Burghart, Sr., have both served as directors of the National Beef Industry Council of the National Livestock and Meat Board.

A recent project originated by former Governor Dan Thornton and sponsored jointly by the Colorado Cattlemen's Association and the Colorado Cattle Feeders Association has been the Colorado Beef Club. Under this program, feeders and producers supply beef for training tables of Colorado University and Colorado State University athletic teams. In return, the athletes help to publicize the state's great beef industry.

Public relations had little meaning to the average cattleman of the 1870's and 1880's. However, Secretary William Holly of the Colorado Stockgrowers Association, organized excursions which brought Denver people out to the range country by special train to see the round-ups first-hand. By the early 1900's, the Association was becoming aware of the need for enlisting the assistance and Cooperation of people outside the organization in many of its projects.

In electing Fred P. Johnson, editor of the Denver Record-Stockman, as secretary in 1901, a position which he held for 16 years, the Association provided itself with an ideal public relations representative. Johnson was enthusiastic, energetic and diplomatic. His news and editorial columns and his personal contacts did much to create a favorable attitude toward stockmen on the part of other branches of the industry and the general public.

Association officials didn't think of it in this light, but the strong statewide support the organization obtained in the 1916 Herd Law Fight was a triumph for public relations. In 1921, the officers met with officials of the Denver stockyards and commission firms and persuaded them to voluntarily cancel increases in commissions, yardage fees and feed costs, another victory for good public relations.

While they practiced the art to a lesser or greater extent for many years, Colorado cattlemen didn't recognize it officially until 1951, when a public relations unit was included among the standing committees. This group has launched numerous public relations projects of its own and assists other committees in developing those phases of their activities which foster good public relations.

Operation Respect, begun by the Moffat County Cowbelles, under the leadership of Mrs. A. R. Lyons of Craig, and sponsored since by the Association's game and fish committee, has done much to promote good feeling between stockmen and sportsmen. A new color movie, "Ranchers and Rangers," produced by the United States Forest Service, Bureau of Land Management, Colorado Game, Fish and Parks Department, Colorado State University and the Colorado Cattlemen's Association, emphasizes the important contributions to conservation which resulted from a cooperative range improvement program. It also reflects the feeling of good will which now exists between the various agencies and the cattlemen of Colorado.

The Association's public relations committee cooperates in sponsoring the annual agricultural and livestock luncheon which honors representatives of all news media in the state. The committee participates in many other activities designed to improve the image of agriculture and the cattle industry in the eyes of the general public.

At present, the public relations committee is engaged in the most ambitious project it has ever undertaken. This is the job of coordinating all programs of the Colorado Cattlemen's Centennial celebration, and using this event as a means of impressing the people of the state and the nation with the economic and historic importance of the cattle industry. In this connection, as one of its earliest Centennial projects, the Association gave a group of newspaper, magazine, radio and television editors from various parts of the United States a four-day intimate view of cattle country. The visitors ate ranch grub, indoors and out; watched the branding, dehorning, vaccination and castration of calves: the preparation and fitting of registered bulls for shows and sales; haying operations on the mountain meadows; slept under canvas in sleeping bags, and took part in typical Saturday night activities in a small cowtown.

The Association's newest committee is the water committee. Water has always played a major role in the cattle business.

In the open range days, a man controlled the land to the exact degree that he controlled water for the stock grazing the land. If a man put cattle on the open range without control over an adequate water supply for his stock, he was considered a range pirate.

Western novels, movies, and television shows to the contrary, far more men were killed in the early West over water than over whiskey.

What is known as the Lake County War was a bloody conflict in present-day Chaffee County which started in 1875 when Eli Gibbs and an Englishman named Harrington quarreled over irrigation water. The Nathrop community split into two factions when Harrington was slain, presumably by Gibbs. A number of men were killed in ensuing battles between vigilantes and anti-vigilantes, estimates reaching as many as 100. Probate Judge Ellis F. Dyer was shot while presiding at Granite over a trial of several of the participants who had been charged with felonious assault.

This is one of the more dramatic of many incidents which illustrate the important role which water has always played in the range country. While the Colorado Cattlemen's Association has frequently been interested in controversies and legislation over water, it did not handle these matters through a special committee. By 1966, however, water and the competition for its use had become a major factor in the future growth and development of the state. This led to the establishment of the Association's water committee, under the leadership of Carl Breeze, Kremmling rancher, banker and water authority.

Last on the list of standing committees of the Colorado Cattlemen's Association, because it was the first in existence, is the brand and theft committee. The modern committee's functions include most of the activities for which the Colorado Stockgrowers Association was formed November 30, 1867.

Despite 100 years of relentless activity and expenditures reaching into millions, cattle theft remains today a major problem. The cattle and horse thief of the 19th century has been dignified into the rustler of the 20th century. The long loop, running iron and fast horse have given way to high-powered rifles, fast trucks, high-speed trailers and paved highways. These advances in transportation now make it possible for thieves to be hundreds of miles away before a rancher has discovered his loss. The vast number of retail meat outlets and locker plants, and millions of home freezers in use today make it difficult to locate stolen beef.

As a result, the brand and theft committee remains one of the Association's most active working groups, despite its tremendous efforts and achievements to solve the problem of cattle stealing. In recent years, the committee's principal activities have been to assist local associations in obtaining convictions and conducting brand conferences throughout the state in order to draw the brand board, sheriff's officers, state patrol, ports of entry officials, game and fish officials, and members of state and local associaitons into a unified theft control team. The committee has also written and sponsored legislation to improve brand inspection procedure. In 1955, committee members worked in cooperation with the state civil service commission to develop a new and more practical system for brand inspector examinations. The resulting regulations require that the examining board be composed of stockmen. The committee assisted the state brand board in preparing a detailed manual to guide the state patrol in enforcing brand and theft laws.

The rank and file of the Colorado Cattlemen's Association have always disliked government intervention and control more than they have welcomed government assistance. This attitude has been obvious since the beginning of the organization. At times, however, a group of members has urged efforts to secure government benefits even at the cost of accepting government controls.

After cattle prices collapsed in 1952, men of this type clamored for government supports to assist the stricken industry. Most of the leaders were men who combined cattle production with wheat farming. At a regional meeting in Canon City, in September, 1953, a resolution recommending supports for the beef cattle industry was brought before the Association. Noting a number of unfamiliar faces, the meeting's chairman, Lars Prestrud of Littleton, called for a check of membership cards before consenting to a vote. It was discovered that several who spoke loudly in favor of supports were not members of the Association. The motion was disqualified.

A more determined effort occurred at a regional meeting in Craig the following November. This session received nation-wide attention. Advance publicity indicated that the cattle-men would ask for supports.

Both sides anticipated a struggle and came prepared. Before the meeting convened, all voting delegates were registered, their credentials checked, and it was ascertained how many votes each delegate was authorized to cast for his association.

The meeting degenerated into a heated political donnybrook. Peacemakers prevented actual fisticuffs, but the air was charged with hostility. At one point, a rugged exponent of untrammeled free enterprise began walking across the seats of the auditorium in an effort to reach a belligerent advocate of government pro-grams. Finally, the proposed resolution recommending price supports for the beef industry came to a vote. It lost, by a vote of 2,250 to 240.

A herd law proposal reared its ugly head again in the 1950's, when sheepmen of Moffat County, in coalition with wheat growers and landowners in the Denver area, presented what was for a time a serious bid for a herd law. The law did not pass. Owners of land in the Denver metropolitan area who joined this movement were not concerned about cattle. They were outraged by horsemen who turned their animals loose to forage in the fields in the winter months. Passage of an abandoned animal act solved their problem.

As the Association's membership mounted and its programs broadened in scope, officials felt a need for a voice to keep members informed at regular intervals of developments in the Association and the industry. In 1955, under the leadership of President Robert A. Burghart, Sr., the Cattle Guard magazine was established. Dick Goff, Denver livestock advertising man, was the editor of the new publication, which appeared for the first time in November, 1955.

Association members greeted the new publication enthusias-tically. Not only did it provide a medium for news of particular interest to them, but proved a choice advertising vehicle for business firms selling products and services to cattle producers. Within three years, the Cattle Guard was paying its own way and returning a profit to the Association.

"Dick, I sure want to be in that first issue," Stafford C. Painter, Roggen Hereford breeder, told Goff when plans for the new magazine were announced. Painter, who was Association president in 1951-1952, said he would advertise some Hereford bulls for sale. He was "in" the first issue, but not as planned. A black-bordered story reported his tragic death in an automobile accident October 25, 1955.

Goff produced the Cattle Guard until 1958, when he resigned to devote his full time to his growing advertising agency. Tom Lawrie served as editor on a part-time basis until 1961, when the Association employed John Boyd as a full-time staff member. Boyd divides his time between assisting Dave Rice, in promoting membership programs and editing the magazine. In 1966, the Cattle Guard received the Western States Business Publications Association award for achievement.

In 1963, when Dave Rice was promoted to executive vice president, Boyd became executive secretary, continuing his three-phase occupation.

The Colorado Association changed its address three times during the 1950's. In 1950, headquarters were removed from the Cooper Building downtown to the Livestock Exchange Building in the stockyards. In 1953, the office of the Association was moved "upon the hill" in the stockyards area, to 4651 Lafayette Street. In September, 1956, the organization occupied its present quarters at 4675 Lafayette Street.

Eminent domain, the power sought by the Colorado Game and Fish Department to acquire land whether or not the owners wished to sell, and to acquire routes across private property as access roads to public hunting and fishing lands, caused the Colorado Cattlemen's Association concern through the latter part of the 1950's and into the next decade. A campaign to defeat a constitutional amendment which would have established the game and fish department as an autonomous agency of the state, was successful, but at considerable expense and effort to the Association.

Reapportionment of the state senate became a matter of vital concern to rural Colorado in 1956, when Mayor Will Nicholson of Denver, spearheaded a drive to reapportion both houses of the legislature strictly on a population basis. This would have caused a substantial shift of representation in the senate from the rural areas to the cities, particularly Denver. Rural residents, stockmen included, had agreed in the past to reapportion the house of representatives but opposed any change in the senatorial districts, in order to protect themselves from complete domination by the cities. The Colorado Cattlemen's Association was one of the leaders in the campaign which defeated the Nicholson plan at the polls in November, 1956.

Six years later, reapportionment was a hotter issue than ever. There were two opposing reapportionment plans on the ballot. Constitutional Amendment Proposal Number Seven had the support of all rural interests and substantial backing in the cities as well. It proposed to model the Colorado General Assembly after the United States Congress, with the house of representatives apportioned strictly on a population basis, the senate maintaining fixed districts despite population changes. It was called the federal plan. Constitutional Amendment Proposal Number Eight was strongly backed by organized labor. It would have prescribed the reapportionment of both houses of the legislature strictly on a population basis.

The Colorado Cattlemen's Association threw its entire weight behind Amendment Seven. Ed C. Johnson, former governor and senator, a staunch friend of the cattlemen for many years, led the fight. Amendment Seven won a smashing victory. It carried by almost as big a margin in the metropolitan areas as it did in the country. Amendment Eight was beaten almost as badly as the other proposal had won. Ed Johnson said it was the only time he had ever known a controversial constitution amendment to win a clear-cut majority in every county in the state.

Some weeks later, Colorado residents were stunned when the United States Supreme Court in a 5-4 decision declared invalid the plan which voters of the state had overwhelmingly approved.

The federal tribunal then ordered the Colorado Legislature re-apportioned on exactly the same lines as Amendment Eight had proposed. Declared invalid, along with the rest of the federal plan, was a provision for sub-districting those counties in the state which elected more than one senator or representative. As a result, a Denver voter, for instance, went to the general election with the task of selecting from a slate of 36 people nominated by the two parties the 18 for whom he wished to vote.

In 1966, Colorado voted by a substantial margin to sub-district large counties, so that each man in the legislature would represent a particular district and no district would have more than one representative or senator. Once again, the Colorado Cattlemen's Association had gone all out for the election victory, lined up with a rural team headed by Ed C. Johnson.

The election battles are representative of some of the campaigns which through the years have strained the treasuries of the state and local associations to the utmost. Pondering over the financial drain occasioned by these hectic, emergency projects, Association leaders in general and Robert Johnston, Jr., of Fowler in particular, decided the Association needed a permanent war chest or fund which would produce enough income each year to assist the organization in its work. In June, 1959, the Association voted to establish the Colorado Cattlemen's Endowment Trust Fund. Its trustees selected Johnston as chairman and mapped a five-year plan to raise a permanent fund of $100,000.

For a few years, Johnston became a crusader. He barnstormed the state, carrying everything before him by the force of his effervescent enthusiasm. Local associations, individual members and friends of the organization donated calves and contributed money as the fund mounted rapidly. Henry Mitchell, a retired livestock banker, took over the job of investing the funds.

When he was elected president of the Colorado Cattlemen's Association in July, 1963, Johnston yielded his position as chairman of the board of trustees to Robert A. Burghart, Sr., who carried the ball for the final touchdown. At the close of the five-year period, July 12, 1964, during the annual convention at Pueblo, the fund passed the $100,000 mark. It has continued to grow each year since.

Cattlemen and their women folks work hard and play hard. They put the same enthusiasm into horseplay as they do into cow work. After a spell of serious business, they like to relax and enjoy the lighter side of life.

Past President Si Berthelson of Rio Blanco, had them rolling in the aisles at the 1962 convention banquet in Sterling with his remarkably true-to-life imitation of President Robert Parsons of Weston, making a fiery, voluble, fist-swinging speech.

Stockmen can also be very sentimental. Consider the time when they rang the wedding bells at Glenwood Springs in 1963.

The 96th convention was nearly over. In the banquet hall of the Colorado Hotel at Glenwood Springs, cattlemen and their wives had finished the banquet and were waiting for the floor show to start when Master of Ceremonies Homer Young of Glenwood Springs called for attention. It seemed there was a special announcement. Executive Vice President Dave Rice, hunched over the microphone with his left hand in his hip pocket, read an invitation. Composed by Rice's personable and capable secretary, Miss Dixie Savio, it invited everyone present to attend a wedding—at that place, at that moment.

Chairs were pushed back to form an aisle to the speakers' table. Mrs. Paul Budin of Sterling, struck up the strains of a suitable organ prelude. Murray Giffin of Nunn, sang "The Lord's Prayer," then Mrs. Budin played the wedding march as Edna Bender of the CCA office staff, beautifully attired and radiant, marched down the aisle to the improvised altar, where her fiance, John Martin of Denver, waited. Reverend Walter K. Klein of New Castle, who had pronounced the invocation for the banquet, performed the ceremony. Mr. and Mrs. Leonard Horn of Wolcott and Mr. and Mrs. Robert Parsons of Weston stood up with the bridal couple, and everyone lived happily, at least for the balance of the evening. (Treasurer John Holtorf, of Yuma, was somewhat distressed when he discovered that the newlyweds, after occupying the bridal suite as guests of the Association, had forgotten to check out when they left. As a result, the Association received a bill for four extra days in the most expensive suite in the hotel. Hotel officials, however, made John smile by telling him to forget that part of the bill.)

The wedding was arranged on very short notice. Edna Bender, a member of the office staff for ten years, attended the membership committee meeting as stenographer. Bob Parsons, one of several who knew she was planning to be married very soon, broached the idea of a public wedding to her. At first she demurred, but Parsons, never bashful and never one to give up easily, finally persuaded her. He pointed out what a wonderful memory it would be—a wedding attended by 400 people whom she had known and worked with for so long.

When the membership committee meeting adjourned, she consulted Dave Rice and Dixie Savio, then made her decision. "After all," she told Dixie, "most of my real friends are the Association members and all the people I would want to invite are right here." Her fiance had come to Glenwood Springs to be near her during the convention. He and Dave Rice drove to Denver and back that night, returning with rings and his best suit.

At the close of the first century, the Colorado Cattlemen's Association was still wrestling with some of the same general problems that had confronted it for 100 years—cattle stealing, the fight to retain an adequate supply of stock water and increasing competition for the use of the land.

As the development of the industry and the state progressed into more and more complex stages, the Association faced an ever-increasing myriad of complicated, puzzling, highly technical problems. These were both challenges and opportunities. The modernization of the organization's machinery in the early 1950's, which established 15 standing committees, enabled it to carry on many projects simultaneously. This made it possible to utilize the leadership, abilities and services of the entire membership to a much greater extent than ever before. As the membership hit the 5,000 mark in the mid-1950's and continued to climb, the Association became more representative of the rural areas. In later years, it has allied itself with other organizations whose primary concern is the welfare of non-metropolitan enterprise in Colorado, thus retaining a powerful voice for the rural sections in spite of the urbanization of the state.

The cattleman of 1967 differs from the cattleman of 1867 to an even greater extent than today's purebred beef cattle differ from the lanky, semi-wild Longhorns. One hundred years of growth and development have transformed the cattle business from a way of life into a business whose success depends upon a delicate balancing of many complex factors. A successful cattleman today must combine the skills of a scientist, a technician and a business executive. He must be a veterinarian, nutritionist, marketing expert, politician, accountant, salesman, range technician, machinist and animal husbandman, all in one package. He must keep up to the minute on cattle and beef price and supply trends, government regulations, world politics, transportation problems and developments, carcass yield and grade data, feed conversion ratios and grain markets. He must concern himself with water control programs, housewives' reactions at the meat counter, government wage-hour programs, the gross national product and disposable income of industrial workers, because all of these things may affect his future operations and the prices which he will receive for his product.

His predecessor, the old-time cowman of the open range days, had a few major problems—weather, prices, theft, transportation and livestock diseases. The old-timer's problems were major ones, but they were simple. They did not usually require any great amount of technical ability or specialized knowledge. Determination, courage and stamina were his stock in trade. His production costs were low. He usually had the advantage of a wide spread between the price he paid for his cattle and the price which he received. If he could keep a substantial percentage of his cattle alive and in good condition for market, he could expect substantial profits.

By contrast, the modern stockman operates on a very slim margin. His costs are high and going higher. To realize a net profit he must make no serious mistakes at any stage of the production process.

Today's highly skilled cattle feeder, for example, has reduced his business to such a fine art and expanded his enterprise to such a large volume that he is able to operate profitably on a minus spread—receiving less per pound for his finished cattle than he paid for them. He normally realizes a very small profit per animal, offsetting this by fattening the absolute maximum number which he can without increasing fixed costs.

In a sense, the history of the cattle business for the last 100 years has been an account of the cattleman learning more and more as the requirements of that business demanded progressively more knowledge and ability.

In rising to meet this challenge, the cattleman has earned the respect of industrial, trade and professional leaders, who now recognize him as a fellow businessman, with many of the same basic problems.

The Association is ending a century of tremendous service to the beef industry. Probably the greatest single factor in its success has been the dedication of hundreds of men and women who served long and faithfully, rewarded only by the knowledge that they were performing a needed function which would benefit the industry as a whole.

"You've often heard there's no limit to the amount of good you can do if you don't care who gets the credit," commented Wad Hinman, the Association's Centennial president. "That's the reason why we got where we are now, and why we are getting so much done today. There's a whole lot of people doing lots of hard work for the Association. Many of them don't get the credit they deserve, and they don't ask for it. They're just interested in getting the job done. The spirit of these people, as leaders and as workers, is what makes the Colorado Cattlemen's Association the great outfit it is."

This Fulton Meat Market in Bayfield, Colorado, was an up-to-date place in the 1880's, but the modern supermarket is far removed from the merchandising ideas displayed here. Photo loaned by Frank Wommer, Jr.

CHAPTER FOURTEEN
WHAT PRICE BEEF?

The cowman in Colorado, and most of the West, is living in a dilemma. He is caught between political groups that compete for the use of his land, and the economic pressure of mass selling, buying and merchandising. The result is a trend that has forced land prices, taxes and operating costs beyond the reach of agricultural production.

He is essentially a small, independent businessman with an abnormally large financial investment, operating in a world of organized labor, organized politics, and possibly in the future, organized consumers.

He is tied financially, historically and emotionally to a beef

306

critter whose physiology is a major handicap in today's economic world. Unfortunately, neither the cowman nor the beef cow adapt very readily to the requirements of mass production.

Today the cow-calf man in the West is literally fighting for survival.

Yet, the beef cow and her progeny have, over the past century, created more new wealth for the state, paid more taxes and sent more children to school than any other single product or industry. It is the largest single cash crop in all agriculture, contributing more than half of the total agricultural income within the state. In 1966, for example, the gross farm income in the state was $975 million. Income from cattle and calves amounted to $534 million of that.

In a hundred years, beef cattle marketing in the state has produced a total income in *new wealth* of more than 7½ BILLION dollars—an average of more than 75 million dollars each year for a full century. No other industry in the state can match that.

This is roughly about three times as much, for example, as all the gold, silver, lead, zinc, iron and other minerals taken from all the mines in the state during that same century. This is not to infer that mining is not important. It is, vitally so, especially in this state. But, it is still only a fraction of the dollar value of the beef industry.

The true picture of the Colorado cattleman can best be told in the cold, harsh columns of prices, numbers and cash values.

Unfortunately, although his total dollar production has soared, his own net income has steadily declined since the end of World War II. Today most Colorado cattlemen are living on an equity derived mainly from the increased collateral value of their land.

Wrapped up in the array of figures listed in this chapter, is a graphic picture of what has happened to the industry during that period.

As previously explained, the price level of cattle (or beef) has seldom reflected the net position of the cattle producer. The three periods when cattle values dropped to less than $15 per head (1879-1895-1934) were vastly different in their effect on the cowman.

In the period of 1879-80, when values hit their first low of $14.30 per head, costs were extremely low and the cowman could easily retrench and sit tight.

Then in the depression following the panic of 1893, when cattle hit a 100-year low of $14 per head, the cowman was much more vulnerable. He had a much higher investment in land, cattle and improvements. A large number of producers folded during this critical time.

In the severe period of the Great Depression during the 1930's, the price decline was further complicated by a severe drouth which drastically cut feed production in the grazing and farm areas. Just how severe this was is shown in the startling decline in cattle numbers over the years 1929 to 1934—a decrease of some two-thirds of the total state beef herd. This was one of the most disastrous periods of all to the cowman—as well as a severe blow to the membership and influence of the Association.

Economically speaking, however, the cattle industry today is a far different world than it was during the first 75 years of the cattle Association's existence. It has just enough of the old trappings left, however, to delude many people into thinking that the cow business is still much the same as it always was. Nothing could be further from the truth.

A study of the price-number-income columns following will show a remarkable change in the industry within the last ten yeas. Despite the fact that the total inventory value of all cattle in the state is greater now than ever before—$375,839,000—the average value per head is still considerably below the average of $177 for 1952. Today's average of $131 is not quite up to the high point of the 1940's when cattle reached $134 in 1949. It is, however, considerably above the low point of $82 for 1957.

Note that in two years, from 1952 to 1954, the average value per head dropped roughly 50%. The drastic economic effects of this latest slump hit many of the Colorado producers extremely hard—and they have not yet recovered. This was especially critical because it appeared at a time when the rest of the

COLORADO CATTLE INDUSTRY SUMMARY
100 Years — 1867 thru 1966

Total Numbers—all cattle—Average value per head—Total Inventory Value and Annual Cash Recipts from Cattle Marketings.

Year	Number	Av pr. hd.	Total Inventory Value	Year	Number	Av pr. hd.	Total Inventory Value	Annual Cash Sales
1867	147,000	$22.10	$3,250,000	17	1,745,000	$48.20	$84,165,000	Not available prior to 1924
68	184,000	24.10	4,440,000	18	1,865,000	54.00	100,746,000	
69	225,000	24.20	5,436,000	19	1,881,000	58.50	109,987,000	
1870	291,000	25.20	6,825,000	1920	1,757,000	49.70	87,323,000	
71	313,000	26.20	8,210,000	21	1,683,000	36.90	62,103,000	
72	355,000	26.30	9,330,000	22	1,680,000	29.40	49,392,000	
73	410,000	23.40	9,574,000	23	1,614,000	28.30	45,676,000	
74	452,000	19.50	8,798,000	24	1,540,000	27.70	42,658,000	$31,527,000
75	488,000	18.40	9,000,000	25	1,465,000	26.00	38,090,000	38,103,000
76	532,000	16.30	8,692,000	26	1,406,000	32.00	44,992,000	34,642,000
77	598,000	16.30	9,722,000	27	1,406,000	36.20	50,897,000	48,524,000
78	666,000	16.50	10,987,000	28	1,377,000	46.70	64,306,000	47,198,000
79	734,000	14.30	10,468,000	29	1,421,000	55.30	78,581,000	46,372,000
1880	809,000	14.30	11,551,000	1930	1,454,000	50.90	74,009,000	35,253,000
81	813,000	16.30	13,283,000	31	1,541,000	37.80	58,250,000	27,462,000
82	827,000	20.50	16,956,000	32	1,555,000	22.50	34,988,000	19,325,000
83	963,000	27.30	26,328,000	33	1,614,000	16.10	25,985,000	14,435,000
84	1,141,000	26.90	30,687,000	34	1,773,000	14.50	25,760,000	23,185,000
85	1,240,000	27.30	33,828,000	35	1,590,000	16.30	25,914,000	29,801,000
86	1,300,000	26.20	34,010,000	36	1,478,000	30.30	44,783,000	27,333,000
87	1,340,000	22.70	30,427,000	37	1,510,000	32.20	48,622,000	40,788,000
88	1,350,000	20.50	27,696,000	38	1,430,000	31.40	44,902,000	33,810,000
89	1,295,000	20.60	26,620,000	39	1,400,000	34.90	44,860,000	39,776,000
1890	1,176,000	17.40	20,505,000	1940	1,400,000	38.10	53,340,000	38,603,000
91	1,119,000	16.40	18,357,000	41	1,442,000	42.10	60,716,000	45,182,000
92	1,064,000	17.00	18,098,000	42	1,586,000	54.00	85,622,000	60,331,000
93	1,012,000	17.40	17,619,000	43	1,745,000	71.30	124,407,000	72,732,000
94	942,000	16.00	15,057,000	44	1,920,000	63.40	121,798,000	82,433,000
95	925,000	14.00	12,987,000	45	1,843,000	61.30	112,976,000	91,437,000
96	940,000	17.70	16,659,000	46	1,861,000	72.30	134,550,000	127,102,000
97	965,000	20.00	19,279,000	47	1,731,000	90.20	156,136,000	149,803,000
98	991,000	26.60	26,326,000	48	1,800,000	118.00	212,400,000	197,438,000
99	1,111,000	26.40	29,278,000	49	1,800,000	134.00	241,200,000	182,932,000
1900	1,223,000	28.30	34,600,000	1950	1,800,000	125.00	225,000,000	214,915,000
01	1,380,000	25.70	35,492,000	51	1,890,000	168.00	317,520,000	259,044,000
02	1,510,000	23.50	35,430,000	52	2,098,000	177.00	371,346,000	263,827,000
03	1,480,000	20.00	29,540,000	53	2,161,000	117,00	252,837,000	178,325,000
04	1,461,000	17.30	25,330,000	54	2,096,000	88.00	184,448,000	191,583,000
05	1,462,000	18.40	26,885,000	55	2,054,000	88.00	180,752,000	184,673,000
06	1,435,000	18.90	27,161,000	56	2,027,000	84,00	170,268,000	191,594,000
07	1,370,000	21.30	29,160,000	57	1,971,000	82,00	161,622,000	190,770,000
08	1,292,000	21.50	27,778,000	58	2,021,000	123.00	248,583,000	285,047,000
09	1,211,000	21.10	25,534,000	59	2,164,000	158.00	341,912,000	293,538,000
1910	1,102,000	25.10	27,614,000	1960	2,267,000	131.00	296,977,000	289,571,000
11	1,107,000	27.10	30,015,000	61	2,282,000	135.00	308,070,000	308,585,000
12	1,085,000	30.00	32,584,000	62	2,394,000	144.00	344,736,000	337,228,000
13	1,225,000	36.40	44,550,000	63	2,590,000	147.00	380,730,000	358,120,000
14	1,360,000	42.70	58,126,000	64	2,616,000	125.00	327,000,000	349,255,000
15	1,564,000	46.30	72,478,000	65	2,600,000	109.00	283,400,000	424,445,000
16	1,601,000	48.10	77,024,000	66	2,869,000	131.00	375,839,000	534,900,000

nation was experiencing an unprecedented increase in net income and wages were setting new high records almost yearly.

As a result, taxes, equipment and supplies went up while the dollar income of the cowman dropped as much as 50%.

Today the cattle producer faces this contradictory position. The wholesale price of beef and fat cattle were at about the same level at the beginning of 1967 as they were 20 years earlier, yet operating costs in that period increased greatly—one economist said an average of 65%. Actually, this may be lower than individual experience would show. The cost of farm machinery has gone up considerably more than 65% in the period, for example.

Taxes have increased much more than this amount. One former president of the Association figured his taxes in 1944 amounted to the sale price for three steers that year. In 1954 it took eight steers, and in 1964, it required 15 steers to pay his taxes. In the face of this it is interesting to compare the relative values of cattle for those years—$63.40 for 1944; $88.00 for 1954; and $125.00 for 1964. If his cow herd remained at approximately the same size, the percentage of its value paid out in taxes would have increased by nearly 1,000%!

Another North Park rancher reported 1945 taxes on his ranch amounted to $321.60, on a mill levy of 26.47. His steer calves that year bought $105 per head. His 1965 taxes were $1,436.55, with a mill levy of 50.01. His calves in 1965 brought $120. On a "steer unit" basis his taxes increased from slightly over three head in 1945 to about 12 head in 1965.

But, this isn't all. One of these ranchers pointed out that he could hire a good hand in 1945 for $50 per month, plus furnishing a house, meat, milk and eggs. Today he pays his hand $450 per month, plus a much better modern house, plus the same beef, milk, eggs, etc.

Most cattlemen have tried to offset some of these increasing costs by adding more land so that they could increase cow herd size and thus try to cut production costs on a cow unit basis. Fortunately, most of this land has gone up in value, so the investment has been a good one. But the net income, if any, from each individual cow has continued to drop.

One rancher in Huerfano County said taxes on a piece of unimproved pasture land purchased in 1945 had increased from $8.91 in 1945, to $21.80 in 1952, and then to $40.73 in 1965.

It is difficult to get accurate comparative tax statements because very few cattlemen operating today are on exactly the same ranch acreage or location that they were 20 years ago. However, these rough comparisons will give some indication of the cost squeeze for the present-day cattle producer.

By the same token, the consumer has increased her buying power by a considerable amount. Figured on today's average wage, it takes only 18 minutes of work to buy a pound of beef today, its lowest point in history, and about half of the amount required to buy a pound of beef in 1929.

In comparison with other ranch supply items, a roll of barbed wire cost $4.85 in 1945, the same wire in 1965 cost $9.00. A block of salt went from 52 cents to 92 cents, and a small tractor that cost $900 in 1945 had increased to $2,800.00 in 1965.

From these few examples, it is easy to understand the apprehension with which the average Colorado cattleman looks toward the future.

As an employer, he is appalled at the prospect of increasing wages when he is unable to increase the selling price of his own product—feeder cattle. Whether he can change this in the future remains to be seen. Certainly some form of coordinated group action through his associations, local, state and national, appear to be his only means of defense.

He looks at the feeder, the packer, the processor and the retailer with growing concern. His main problem today is that he has concentrated almost entirely on the production end of the business. At least this is where his time and his money is spent. For almost a century he has left the marketing end of his feeder cattle to others.

The development of the railroads made possible the large central markets. They, in turn, were stimulated by the large centralized packing plants who needed cattle in large quantities to keep their huge work forces busy.

Then the development of paved highways, high-speed trucks, and fast automobiles made the ranches and feedlots much more accessible to cattle buyers and traders. The numbers of local auction markets began to increase after World War II, adding to the decentralizing trend of livestock marketing.

Gradually, buying began to move away from the central markets. High operating costs, principally increasing labor demands, made the big packing plants obsolete. Small, more efficient plants were built in the country. They could kill and process beef cattle at costs far below the unit cost of the big name packers that built the industry—Swift, Armour, Cudahy, Morrell—all these once great titans of the meat trade began to close down their huge plants. They continue to be a factor in the business because they began to buy up some of the small plants in the country and build others. In addition, they had an efficient sales force and distributing system. Through this they maintained a large measure of control of the wholesale trade.

Another big development of the post-World War II era were the supermarkets. These were the result of mass merchandising techniques, based on rapid turnover and a small margin of profit. The consumer liked them, and still does. From all indications today, the bigger they are the better she likes them. Without question, they are here to stay. They handle an ever-increasing percentage of the retail sales of beef.

But beef and the cowman are worlds apart, despite a natural affinity for this end product. The cattle producer sells no beef—only cattle. His marketing problem lies right there. If he gets a better price for Colorado feeder cattle, the beef that is produced from their carcasses will price itself.

Cowmen have begun to realize, too, that the price of cattle is not as directly affected by the price of beef as it once was. Supply and demand, of both beef and cattle are still factors in determining price trends, but new elements have come into the picture.

Today the price of beef, and to a lesser extent, the price of cattle are becoming political issues. A decrease in the supply of cattle may not necessarily be reflected by an increase in price. A treaty signed in Switzerland by U.S. State Department officials could increase the import of foreign beef. Beef produced on land in Australia, for example, carries only a fraction of the tax load that our land now has. Labor costs there are also lower.

There is every indication that the price of beef may become still more of a political issue—as it is in many foreign countries. Nor can the beef producer look to government for help in his dilemma. Even the Department of Agriculture has added a rapidly growing new "consumer division" to protect the buyer—a sign of the new trend to go where the votes are.

This, then, leaves the cowman and his Association to fight for a measure of better market conditions. Some of the old-time cattle growers are inclined to be bitter about the trend of events in this rapidly changing world. They resent the fact that others seem to be making a profit in processing beef from the cattle they produce at a loss. At first they felt that a concerted effort toward beef promotion would help to improve the demand and thus prices. Some of the benefits, they thought, would filter back down the long chain of distribution to them.

Now, they are not so sure. One skeptical cowman expressed his feeling in a wry comment.

"Hell," he drawled, "it's about like asking a consumer to use toilet paper made from Colorado trees."

A few worried cowmen have condemned the retailing industry as the principal culprit in the unprofitable price picture. The large supermarket companies, they say, have such a great volume of sales that they can dictate the prices they pay for beef. Thus, these people believe, the price is passed down the chain to the cowman.

Officials of the retail food industry deny this. They point to the highly competitive nature of the food business. They, too, are caught in the maze of government regulations, higher taxes and increasing labor costs. One store executive said wages for his head meat cutters had increased 55% in the past ten years. Meat wrappers had received increases amounting to 57% of the 1955 level. In addition, he declared, fringe benefits added another 18% to labor cost today. Labor now accounts for half of their entire operating margin, he added.

This same picture is reflected in all business today. It is part of the inflationary spiral. It is significant, however, that the huge increase in per capita beef consumption over the past 30 years parallels the growth of the supermarket. Certainly, the cattle producer can expect no change in this trend toward mass merchandising of his end product. He can only hope that the retailer continues to make enough money on beef to continue pushing it. What would happen if the retail industry found beef unprofitable to handle might be a decline that could be catastrophic to the cattleman.

In the meantime, wiser heads have counseled the trend to first things first. The Association marketing committee is supporting the recent efforts of the American National Cattlemen's Association to develop a coordinated marketing program for slaughter cattle. They hope that more orderly marketing and better communications on trends within the wholesale beef trade will help prices back to the producer level. Here again the unpredictable effects of weather and politics will have to be part of the risk.

The problem of getting feeder cattle sold at a better price level is doubly perplexing. Since World War II, Colorado has become one of the biggest Western states in cattle feeding. Some of the nation's largest and most efficient feedlots are located here. These huge, industrial-type operations have changed the entire balance of income for the cattle industry in the state.

Study the figures on inventory and income from cash sales in the following table. For nearly 75 years, annual cash sales from the total state cow herd represented about two-thirds of the inventory value of our cattle population. After the war this began to change. Within the last decade cash sales climbed to a point that was half again as large as our total state inventory value.

This is the result of the burgeoning feedlot industry. Thousands of cattle are brought in from outside the state, put on feed for a few months, then sold for slaughter. The sales show up on our total state cattle sales, but few are added to our inventory. Tax-wise, they are figured on an average inventory basis, and the feeder may run as many as three lots per year through his pens.

The size of this end of the cattle industry is best indicated by a dollar comparison. In 1951, total cattle inventory value was $317 million, the annual cash sales amounted to $259 million. In 1961, they were almost even—inventory value was $308 million, cash sales $308.5 million. By 1966, the sales had soared in proportion—inventory $375 million, cash sales $534 million. The difference is largely the contribution of the state's large feedlot operations.

To the Colorado cow-calf man, however, this new market for feeder cattle is unprofitable. Commercial feeders can buy "southern" cattle in Texas, Oklahoma and the Gulf states and ship them to Colorado, for less money than the Colorado producer can grow the bigger, high-quality calves for which the state became famous years ago. The fancy end of these cattle are largely sold east of here, some a thousand miles or more from the feedlots of our own state.

The modern commercial feeder has based his operation on scientific controls, big volume and a relatively short margin. His is the first part of the industry to adapt to mass production techniques. He is, however, geared to the cheaper cattle produced in the south where costs are considerably lower than Colorado.

How these production costs can be lowered with Colorado's high taxes and soaring land costs is another problem facing the producer here.

There was an old rule of thumb in the cow business which held that any time a man had more money invested in his ranch on a cow unit basis than a cow would bring on the market, he was in trouble. Today a good young commercial cow will bring $200 to $250, while the average Colorado ranch in the 250 to 500-cow size will sell for as much as $1,000 per cow unit, and considerably more where a good location for recreation, development or speculation is involved.

If there ever was any basis to the old maxim, then the entire industry today is in trouble. But, of course, the world is different now. The new economics like the "new" mathematics that is taught in our schools, comes up with some astonishing answers. Some of the new math problems don't even have answers, we are told.

Whether the cattle industry economics in Colorado has reached this point as yet remains to be seen.

Certainly the present condition cannot continue much longer. Today the Western cattle producer is taking a new look at his century-old industry. He is beginning to realize for the first time that marketing is the key to the success of his entire operation.

Wad Hinman had this to say about the changing attitude in the range country after a meeting with a local association on the Western Slope early in 1967.

"Marketing is now the problem that is of greatest concern to every Colorado cattleman. There is a growing feeling that our traditional marketing methods are inadequate for the industry today. One small local in the state recently offered $500 to help launch a study project in this field. It could be used for research, experimental work or promotion, as long as it was pointed toward this problem. Other groups have also urged something along this line, and will back such an effort with cash. There is no doubt that this will be our top priority project for a long time to come."

In this he feels the Association faces one of the most difficult problems in its 100-year history, but he is not pessimistic.

"We know that we can't lick this situation overnight," he said, "But we have a century of experience in this kind of group project work behind us and a large number of capable and dedicated men to draw on. I think there is no limit to what we can do if we all buckle down and work together, on both a state and national basis."

If any one phrase could describe the condition of the cattle industry at the time the Association starts into its second century, it could be called an "era of change."

History has shown that such a time of change can also be a time of great opportunity.

The End

New developments in transportation over the past century have made dramatic changes in the marketing pattern of Western cattle and beef. Jet transports like this new Boeing 747 and the Lockheed C5 will carry more than 110 tons of perishable commodities at more than 600 miles per hour—at freight rates which are expected to compare with present surface transportation costs by refrigerated trucks. This type of equipment will make possible overnight delivery of Colorado pre-packaged beef to such major world markets as London, Paris and Rome. Delivery on this plane will begin in 1969 to nearly every major airline.

Photo by the Boeing Company

APPENDIX A
OFFICERS AND DIRECTORS 1867—1967

1867
COLORADO STOCK GROWERS ASSOCIATION
November 30, 1867
President : Capt. Allen G. Reed
Vice Pres.: Andrew Slain
Secretary : A. J. Williams (first meeting)
Secretary : Alex Davidson (Dec. 7, 1867 to April, 1868.)

(No photo available)

1868
COLORADO STOCK GROWERS ASSOCIATION
April 30, 1868
Reed, Slain and Davidson resigned.
President : Dr. John Parsons
Vice Pres.: Joseph Block
Secretary : Robert S. Wilson

1869
COLORADO STOCK GROWERS ASSOCIATION
(No photo available)
President : Dr. John Parsons
Vice Pres.: Joseph Block
Secretary : Robert S. Wilson

1870
COLORADO STOCK GROWERS ASSOCIATION
President : A. J. Williams
Vice Pres.: Joseph Block
Secretary : Robert S. Wilson

1871
COLORADO STOCK GROWERS ASSOCIATION
President : A. J. Williams
Vice Pres.: Joseph Block
Secretary : H. W. Brownell

A. J. WILLIAMS

JOHN G. LILLEY

1872
COLORADO STOCK GROWERS ASSOCIATION
President : John G. Lilley
Vice Pres.: Joseph L. Bailey
Secretary : William Holly
Treasurer: A. J. Williams
Executive Committee: W. W. Roberts, Chairman

JOSEPH L. BAILEY

1873
COLORADO STOCK GROWERS ASSOCIATION
President : Joseph L. Bailey
Vice Pres.: W. W. Roberts
Secretary : William Holly
Treasurer : A. J. Williams
Executive Committee: Jared L. Brush, Chairman

1874
COLORADO STOCK GROWERS ASSOCIATION
President : Joseph L. Bailey
Vice Pres.: James M. Wilson
Secretary : William Holly
Treasurer : A. J. Williams
Executive Committee: Jared L. Brush, Chairman

1875
COLORADO STOCK GROWERS ASSOCIATION
President : James M. Wilson
Vice Pres.: C. C. Gird
Secretary : William Holly
Treasurer : A. J. Williams
Executive Committee: Alfred Butters, Chairman; Joseph W. Bowles, P. P. Wilcox, John W. Prowers, Judge Douglas

1876
COLORADO STOCK GROWERS ASSOCIATION
President : James M. Wilson
Vice Pres.: A. D. Wilson
Secretary : William Holly
Treasurer : A. J. Williams
Executive Committee: Jared L. Brush, Chairman

JAMES M. WILSON

JOSEPH P. FARMER

1877
COLORADO CATTLE GROWERS ASSOCIATION
President : Joseph P. Farmer
Vice Pres.: Jacob H. Scherrer
Secretary : Samuel E. Wetzel
Treasurer : Alfred Butters
Executive Committee: Finis P. Ernest, Chairman
W. J. Wilson, J. L. Brush, R. G. Webster, H. B. Tuttle

1878-1879
COLORADO STOCK GROWERS ASSOCIATION
President : Alfred Butters
Vice Pres.: Jacob H. Scherrer
Secretary : Samuel E. Wetzel
Treasurer : James M. Wilson
Executive Committee: J. G. Benkleman, R. G. Webster, Finis P. Ernest, J. W. Barron, W. J. Wilson

1879
Executive Committee: J. G. Benkleman, R. G. Webster, Finis P. Ernest, W. J. Wilson, N. S. Harrison

ALFRED BUTTERS

1880
COLORADO CATTLE GROWERS ASSOCIATION
President : Alfred Butters
Vice Pres.: R. G. Webster
Secretary : Samuel E. Wetzel
Treasurer : James M. Wilson
Executive Committee: J. G. Benkleman, A. A. Knee-land, Joseph W. Bowles, M. Fulwider, R. G. Webster

1881-1882 (2 years)
COLORADO CATTLE GROWERS ASSOCIATION
President : James M. Wilson
Vice Pres.: Jacob H. Scherrer
Secretary : Samuel E. Wetzel
Treasurer: Job A. Cooper
Executive Committee: Jared L. Brush, R. G. Webster, J. G. Benkleman, J. F. Brown, F. L. Cochran

1882
Executive Committee: R. G. Webster, Joseph W. Bowles, Henry H. Metcalf, J. W. Snyder, W. H. H. Cranmer

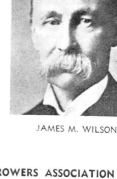

JAMES M. WILSON

1883-1884
COLORADO CATTLE GROWERS ASSOCIATION
President : Jacob H. Scherrer
Vice Pres.: J. F. Brown
Secretary: L. R. Tucker
Treasurer : Job A. Cooper
Executive Committee: R. G. Webster, W. H. H. Cranmer, Joseph W. Bowles, Henry H. Metcalf, J. W. Snyder

1884
Executive Committee: S. H. Standart, Henry H. Metcalf, J. W. Snyder, W. H. H. Cranmer, S. C. Haver

JACOB H. SCHERRER

1885-1886
COLORADO CATTLE GROWERS ASSOCIATION
President : Job A. Cooper
Vice Pres.: J. F. Brown
Secretary : S. H. Standart
Treasurer : James M. Wilson
Executive Committe: Henry Gebhard, Henry H. Metcalf, R. G. Head, J. W. Snyder, W. H. H. Cranmer

1886
Executive Committee: Jacob H. Scherrer, Henry H. Metcalf, W. H. H. Cranmer, M. W. Jones, David C. Wyatt

JOB A. COOPER

1887
COLORADO CATTLE GROWERS ASSOCIATION
President : John L. Routt
Vice Pres.: Alfred Butters
Secretary : Henry H. Metcalf
Treasurer : Job A. Cooper
Executive Committee: S. H. Standart, Henry H. Metcalf, Jacob H. Scherrer, David C. Wyatt, Job A. Cooper, Hiram S. Holly, J. F. Brown

JOHN L. ROUTT

HIRAM S. HOLLY

1888
COLORADO CATTLE GROWERS ASSOCIATION
President: Hiram S. Holly
Vice Pres : L. R. Tucker
Secretary : Henry H. Metcalf
Treasurer : Job A. Cooper
Executive Committee: William Withers, Henry H. Metcalf, David C. Wyatt, Thomas Niblock J. G. Benkleman, W. H. H. Cranmer, Jacob H. Scherrer

1889
COLORADO CATTLE GROWERS ASSOCIATION
President : Jacob H. Scherrer
Vice Pres.: George W. Ballantine
Secretary : Henry H. Metcalf
Asst. Secy: H. B. Cullum
Treasurer : Job A. Cooper
Executive Committee: George W. Ballantine, Henry H. Metcalf, Thomas Niblock, David C. Wyatt, William Withers, George K. Peasley

JACOB H. SCHERRER

JARED L. BRUSH

1890-1891-1892
COLORADO CATTLE GROWERS ASSOCIATION
President: Jared L. Brush
Vice Pres.: A. V. Sherrer
Secretary: Henry H. Metcalf
Treasurer: J. G. Benkleman
Executive Committee: David C. Wyatt, Henry H. Metcalf, M. Fulwider, Thomas Niblock, M. W. Jones, William Arthur, A. A. Mermoch
Vice Pres. 1891 and 1892: Joseph W. Bowles

1891-1892
Executive Committee: David C. Wyatt, Henry H. Metcalf, Thomas Niblock, M. Fulwider, William Withers, C. M. Hampson, George K. Peasley

1893-1894-1895-1896-1897-1898-1899
COLORADO CATTLE GROWERS ASSOCIATION
President : David C. Wyatt
Vice Pres.: Joseph W. Bowles
Secretary : Henry H. Metcalf
Treasurer : J. G. Benkleman

1893-1896
Executive Committee: M. Fulwider, Henry H. Metcalf, E. J. Temple, J. K. Mullen, George K. Peasley, Joseph W. Bowles
J. S. Brown and J. O. Dostal added to committee in 1897

1899
Executive Committee: Conrad Schaefer, A. Beuck, H. H. Robinson, J. E. Painter, Joseph W. Bowles, Henry H. Metcalf

DAVID C. WYATT

(No photo available)

1900
WESTERN RANGE STOCK GROWERS ASSOCIATION
President : William Lloyd Grubb, Garfield Co.
Secretary : H. D. Williamson, Eagle Co.
Treasurer : A. A. McIntyre, Lincoln Co.
Corr. Secy: Robert A. Palmer, Douglas Co.
Executive Committee: C. M. Hammond, A. B. Foster, Charles W. Bowles, J. O. Dostal

1901
CATTLE AND HORSE GROWERS ASSOCIATION OF COLORADO
President : William Lloyd Grubb, Carbondale
Vice Pres.: Conrad Schaefer, Duel
Secretary : Charles W. Bowles, Littleton
Treasurer : T. S. Harper, River Bend
Asst. Secy: Fred P. Johnson, Denver
Executive Committee: William Lloyd Grubb, Charles S. Bowles, T. S. Harper, W. A. Gillaspey, A. B. Foster, Arnold Powell, Don C. Crampton, I. W. Bennett, J. A. Lockhart

1902-1903
CATTLE AND HORSE GROWERS ASSOCIATION OF COLORADO
President : William Lloyd Grubb, Carbondale
Vice Pres.: Conrad Schaefer, Duel
Secretary : Fred P. Johnson, Denver
Treasurer : T. S. Harper, River Bend
Executive Committee: Conrad Schaefer, Fred P. Johnson, T. S. Harper, J. E. Painter, W. A. Gillaspey, E. Scott Robertson, W. T. Ashley, Samuel Hartsel, Thomas H. Iles
Board of Control: Conrad Schaefer, Fred P. Johnson, I. W. Bennett

1903
Executive Committee: W. A. Gillaspey, W. T. Ashley, M. A. Lee, H. S. Tomkins, I. W. Bennett, James Taylor, Thomas H. Iles
Board of Control: Conrad Schaefer, Fred P. Johnson, I. W. Bennett

CONRAD SCHAEFER

1904
COLORADO CATTLE AND HORSE GROWERS ASSOCIATION
President : Conrad Schaefer, Duel
Vice Pres.: W. A. Gillaspey, Gunnison
Secretary : Fred P. Johnson, Denver
Treasurer: T. S. Harper, River Bend
Executive Committee: John A. Edge, S. Price Sloss, W. A. Gillaspey, W. T. Ashley, J. R. Smith, Samuel Hartsel, Conrad Schaefer, T. S. Harper, I. W. Bennett, James Taylor
Board of Control: Conrad Schaefer, Fred P. Johnson, I. W. Bennett

1905-1906
COLORADO CATTLE AND HORSE GROWERS ASSN.
President : Elias M. Ammons, Douglas Co.
Vice Pres.: Fred Light, Garfield Co.
Secretary : Fred P. Johnson, Denver
Treasurer: T. S. Harper, River Bend
Executive Committee: J. R. Smith, W. H. Gerdts, D. W. Amos, E. McCrillis, T. T. Younger, Fred Light, H. B. Means, A. F. Crow, Cris Manhart, E. R. Creighton, C. E. Ayer, J. E. Painter, A. W. Heyser, E. E. Paddock, E. E. Metzel, Samuel Hartsel, H. H. Robinson, J. R. Sullivan, John Welch, I. W. Bennett, Arnold Powell, B. F. Duffy

ELIAS M. AMMONS

JOHN W. SPRINGER

1907
COLORADO CATTLE AND HORSE GROWERS ASSN.
President : John W. Springer, Denver
Vice Pres : James D. Husted, Denver
Secretary : Fred P. Johnson, Denver
Treasurer: T. S. Harper, Colorado Springs
Executive Committee: John W. Springer, J. E. Painter, T. S. Harper, W. A. Gillaspey, S. Price Sloss, I. W. Bennett, Elias M. Ammons

1908
COLORADO CATTLE AND HORSE GROWERS ASSN.
President : James D. Husted, Denver
Vice Pres : W. A. Gillaspey, Gunnison
Secretary : Fred P. Johnson, Denver
Treasurer: T. S. Harper, Colorado Springs

1909
COLORADO CATTLE AND HORSE GROWERS ASSN.
President : James D. Husted Denver
Vice Pres.: W. A. Gillaspey, Gunnison
Secretary : Fred P. Johnson, Denver
Treasurer: Isaac Baer, Meeker

JAMES D. HUSTED

W. A. GILLASPEY

1910-1911
COLORADO CATTLE AND HORSE GROWERS ASSN.
President : W. A. Gillaspey, Gunnison
Vice Pres.: I. W. Bennett, Ft. Collins
Secretary : Fred P. Johnson, Denver

FRANK D. SQUIER

1912-1913
COLORADO CATTLE AND HORSE GROWERS ASSN.
President : Frank D. Squier, Rifle
Vice Pres.: J. P. Adams, Denver
Secretary : Fred P. Johnson, Denver
Treasurer : S. Price Sloss, Basalt

1914
COLORADO CATTLE AND HORSE GROWERS ASSN.
President : Frank D. Squier, Rifle
Vice Pres.: Frank Jones, Middle Park
Secretary : Fred P. Johnson, Denver
Treasurer : Raymond S. Husted, Denver

1915
COLORADO CATTLE AND HORSE GROWERS ASSN.
President : Frank D. Squier, Rifle
Vice Pres.: Frank Jones, Middle Park
Secretary : Fred P. Johnson, (retiring) Denver
Secretary : Raymond S. Husted (acting) Denver
Treasurer : Raymond S. Husted, Denver
Executive Committee: Frank D. Squier, Raymond S.
Husted, J. H. Neal, S. Price Sloss, T. W. Monell, C. T.
Stevens, W. S. Whinnery, M. J. McMillin, J. R. Smith,
W. H. Gerdts

1916
COLORADO CATTLE AND HORSE GROWERS ASSN.
President : Frank D. Squier, Rifle
Vice Pres.: Isaac Baer, Meeker
Secretary : Raymond S. Husted, (pro tem) Denver
Secretary : John B. Calkins, Delta
Treasurer: W. E. Schoolfield, Delta
Executive Committee: Frank B. Keys, W. E. School-
field, J. H. Neal, H. J. Capps, J. C. Temple, F. D.
Squier, Isaac Baer, W. L. Girdner, D. P. Van Buskirk,
Field Bohart, F. R. Carpenter, John P. Klug, Charles
Meyers, Raymond S. Husted, Sam Wasson, Thomas
Iles, George H. Watson, J. R. Smith

ISAAC BAER

1917
COLORADO CATTLE AND HORSE GROWERS ASSN.
President : Isaac Baer, Meeker
Vice Pres.: John P. Klug, Greeley
Secretary : John B. Calkins, Delta
Treasurer: John B. Calkins, Delta

1918
COLORADO CATTLE AND HORSE GROWERS ASSN.
President : Isaac Baer, Meeker
Vice Pres.: John P. Klug, Greeley
Secretary : Field Bohart, Colorado Springs
Treasurer: W. E. Schoolfield, Delta
Executive Committee: J. R. Smith, John Grattan,
Howard Sneddon, A. E. Wright, Charles E. Collins, W.
Boucher, F. D. Squier, T W. Gray, J. C. Temple,
Charles W. Griffith, W. S. Whinnery, F. C. Jones,
Harry Pyle, Frank W. Murphy, Hollis R. Mills, Ray-
mond Husted, Edmund Pauls, Fred Light, R. E. Ewing,
Fred A. Diez, S. Price Sloss, S. W. Nay, J. H. Neal,
Harry J. Capps, George H. Watson, C. C. Crismer, J.
P. Sanchez

1919-1920
COLORADO STOCK GROWERS ASSOCIATION
President : John P. Klug, Greeley
Vice Pres.: W. S. Whinnery, Lake City
Secretary : Percy Houts, Denver
Treasurer: W. E. Schoolfield, Delta
Board of Control: J. N. McWilliams, R. C. Callen,
Harry J. Capps, C. J. Farr, C. T. Stevens, Frank Fos-
dick
Advisory Board: Robert F. Rockwell, Hollis R. Mills, S.
Price Sloss, A. H. Webster, J. C. Temple

1920
Board of Control: Field Bohart, Dr. Ike Gotthelf, C. T.
Stevens, Frank Squier
Advisory Board: Hollis Mills, R. F. Rockwell, S. Price
Sloss, A. H. Webster, J. C. Temple

JOHN P. KLUG

M. J. McMILLIN

1920-1921
COLORADO STOCK GROWERS ASSOCIATION
October 19, 1920
(Second set of officers.)
President : M. J. McMillin, Carlton
Vice Pres.: W. S. Whinnery, Lake City
Secretary : Evelyn D. Castle, Denver
Treasurer: W. A. Snyder, Denver
Board of Control: Field Bohart, Dr. Ike Gotthelf, C. T.
Stevens, Frank Squier
Advisory Board: Hollis Mills, R. F. Rockwell, S. Price
Sloss, A. H. Webster, J. C. Temple

1921 (Same Officers)
Board of Control: W. J. Rowe, W. H. Haley, Richard
Dillon, Claude H. Reese
            (Same Advisory Board)

1922
COLORADO STOCK GROWERS ASSOCIATION
President : Ben M. White, Eagle
Vice Pres.: Harry J. Capps, Walsenburg
Secretary : Evelyn D. Bleasdale
Treasurer: W. H. Haley, Elizabeth
Board of Control: Richard Dillon, J. H. Neal, J. C. Temple, C. T. Stevens

BEN M. WHITE

HARRY J. CAPPS

1923-1927 (first half)
COLORADO STOCK GROWERS ASSOCIATION
President : Harry J. Capps, Walsenburg
Vice Pres.: Richard Dillon, Sedalia
Secy-Man: B. F. Davis, Denver
Treasurer: Richard Dillon, Sedalia (1923 only)
Treasurer: J. H. Neal, Denver 1924-1927
Board of Control: C. T. Stevens, Frank Parsons, Field Bohart, W. T. Lambert
Executive Committee: George Lucero, Field Bohart, Harvey Witwer, J. W. Setters, J. D. Conway, Joseph N. Neal, W. J. Rowe, Waite Phillips, T. W. Monell, C. J. Farr, James L. C. Painter

1924-1925
Board of Control: Frank Parsons, James I. Alfred, J. H. Neal, John P. Klug

1925-1926-1972
Board of Control: Frank Parsons, Field Bohart, C. T. Stevens, Kenneth Chalmers

1927-1928
COLORADO STOCK GROWERS ASSOCIATION
President : J. W. Goss, Avondale
Vice Pres.: William L. Curtis, Gunnison
Secy-Man: B. F. Davis, Denver
Treasurer: J. H. Neal, Denver
Board of Control: Frank Parsons, Field Bohart, C. T. Stevens, M. J. McMillin
Executive Committee: G. E. Anderson, Field Bohart, Joseph N. Neal, Henry L. Beirne, W. A. Hobson, A. A. Curtis, George Green, E. W. Gregg D. J. Davis, Earl Van Tassle, Ezra K. Baer, W. S. Whinnery, R. A. Maxfield

J. W. GOSS

1928-1929-1930
COLORADO STOCK GROWERS ASSOCIATION
President : Joseph N. Neal, Meeker
Vice Pres.: J. W. Goss, Avondale
Secy-Man: B. F. Davis, Denver
Treasurer: J. H. Neal, Denver
Board of Control: Field Bohart, Frank Parsons, M. J. McMillin, C. T. Stevens

JOSEPH N. NEAL

1930-1931-1932
COLORADO STOCK GROWERS ASSOCIATION
President : William L. Curtis, Gunnison
Vice Pres.: Field Bohart, Colorado Springs
Secy-Man: B. F. Davis, Denver
Treasurer : J. H. Neal, Denver
Board of Control: M. J. McMillin, C. T. Stevens, Frank
Parsons, L. A. Edmundson, A. A. Smith, Ray Reynolds,
A. W. Hahn

W. L. CURTIS

1932-1933
COLORADO STOCK GROWERS ASSOCIATION
President : Field Bohart, Colorado Springs
Vice Pres.: Thomas McQuaid, Hartsel
Secy-Man: B. F. Davis, Denver
Treasurer: J. H. Neal, Denver
Board of Control: C. T. Stevens, Frank Parsons, L. A.
Edmundson, A A. Smith, A. W. Hahn, Ray Reynolds,
Wilbur L. Curtis

FIELD BOHART

1933-1934
COLORADO STOCK GROWERS AND FEEDERS ASSN.
President : Thomas A. McQuaid, Hartsel
Vice Pres: A. A. Curtis, Steamboat Springs
Secy-Man: B. F. Davis, Denver
Treasurer : J. H. Neal, Denver
Board of Control: C. T. Stevens, Frank Parsons, L. A.
Edmundson, A. A. Smith, A. W. Hahn, Ray Reynolds,
Wilbur L. Curtis

TOM McQUAID

1934-1935-1936
COLORADO STOCK GROWERS AND FEEDERS ASSN.
President : A. A. Curtis, Oak Creek
Vice Pres.: L. A. Edmundson, Pueblo
Secy-Man: B. F. Davis, Denver
Treasurer : J. H. Neal, Denver
Board of Control: C. T. Stevens, Frank Parsons, A. A.
Vickers, A. A. Smith, M. M. Simpson, Ray Reynolds,
W. L. Curtis

A. A. CURTIS

1936-1937-1938
COLORADO STOCK GROWERS AND FEEDERS ASSN.
President : L. A. Edmundson, Pueblo
Vice Pres.: Charles W. Lilley, Virginia Dale
Secy-Man: B. F. Davis, Denver
Treasurer : J. H. Neal, Denver
Board of Control: C. T. Stevens, Frank Parsons, A. A.
Smith, M. M. Simpson, J. H. Dickens, George S. Green,
A. A. Blakley

L. A. EDMUNDSON

1938-1939
COLORADO STOCK GROWERS AND FEEDERS ASSN.
President : Charles W. Lilley, Virginia Dale
Vice Pres.: A. A. Smith, Sterling
Secy-Man: B. F. Davis, Denver
Treasurer: George S. Green, Golden
Board of Control: Joseph N. Neal, Charles P. Murphy,
Alfred M. Collins, Walter Sanburg, Elmer Mourning,
Albert V. Berg, A. A. Blakley

CHAS W. LILLEY

1939-1940
COLORADO STOCK GROWERS AND FEEDERS ASSN.
President : A. A. Smith, Sterling
Vice Pres.: Howard K. Linger, Hooper
Secy-Man. B. F. Davis, Denver
Treasurer: George S. Green, Golden
Board of Control: Joseph N. Neal, Charles P. Murphy,
Alfred M. Collins, Walter Sanburg, Elmer Mourning,
Albert V. Berg, A. A. Blakley

A. A. SMITH

1940-1941
COLORADO STOCK GROWERS AND FEEDERS ASSN.
President : Howard K. Linger, Hooper
Vice Pres.: Albert V. Berg, Morley
Secy-Man. B. F. Davis, Denver
Treasurer: George S. Green, Golden
Board of Control: Joseph N. Neal, Charles P. Murphy,
Alfred M. Collins, Walter Sanburg, Albert V. Berg, A.
A. Blakley

HOWARD K. LINGER

1941-1942
COLORADO STOCK GROWERS AND FEEDERS ASSN.
President : Albert V. Berg, Morley
1st Vice P: Charles P. Murphy, Spicer
2nd Vice P: Frank Fehling, Nathrop
Secy-Man: B. F. Davis, Denver
Treasurer: George S. Green, Golden
Board of Control: Joseph N. Neal, Alfred M. Collins,
Walter Sanburg, Elmer Mourning, Paul W. Henerson,
A. H. Norell, A. A. Blakley

ALBERT V. BERG

CHAS. P. MURPHY

1942-1943-1944
COLORADO STOCK GROWERS AND FEEDERS ASSN.
President : Charles P. Murphy, Spicer
1st Vice P: Frank Fehling, Nathrop
2nd Vice P: Neil M. Andrews, Gunnison
Secretary : B. F. Davis, Denver
Treasurer : George S. Green, Golden
Board of Control: Paul W. Henerson, Elmer Mourning, A. H. Norell, W. R. Shellabarger, Arthur R. Amick, O. S. Perry, A. A. Blakley

1944-1945-1946
COLORADO STOCK GROWERS AND FEEDERS ASSN.
President : Frank Fehling, Nathrop
Vice Pres.: Neil M. Andrews, Gunnison
Exec. Secy: B. F. Davis, Denver
Treasurer : George S. Green, Golden
Board of Control: Paul W. Henerson, Elmer Mourning, A. A. Blakley, Arthur R. Amick, O. S. Perry, W. R. Shellabarger, A. H. Norell

FRANK FEHLING

NEIL M. ANDREWS

1946-1947
COLORADO STOCK GROWERS AND FEEDERS ASSN.
President : Neil M. Andrews, Gunnison
Vice Pres.: A. Elmer Headlee, Canon City
Exec. Secy: B. F. Davis, Denver
Treasurer : George S. Green, Golden
Board of Control: A. H. Norell, Elmer Mourning, W. R. Shellabarger, Arthur R. Amick, O. S. Perry, A. A. Blakley, A. T. McCarty

1947-1948
COLORADO STOCK GROWERS AND FEEDERS ASSN.
President : A. Elmer Headlee, Monte Vista
Vice Pres.: Henry Bledsoe, Cheraw
Exec. Secy: B. F. Davis, Denver
Treasurer : George S. Green, Golden
Board of Control: A. H. Norell, Don Collins, Lucas Mc-Cullough, O. S. Perry, A. T. McCarty, Frank Fehling, A. A. Blakley

A. ELMER HEADLEE

1948-1949-1950
COLORADO STOCK GROWERS AND FEEDERS ASSN.
President : Henry Bledsoe, Cheraw
Vice Pres.: A. T. McCarty, Trinidad
Exec. Secy: B. F. Davis, Denver
Treasurer: George S. Green, Golden
Board of Control: A. H. Norell, Don Collins, Lucas McCullough, O. S. Perry, A. P. Starr, Frank Fehling, A. A. Blakley

1950
Board of Control: W. C. Crew, Arthur R. Amick, R. J. Lamborn, A. P. Starr, M. McAlpine

HENRY BLEDSOE

1950-1951
COLORADO CATTLEMEN'S ASSOCIATION
President : A. T. McCarty, Trinidad
Vice Pres.: Stafford Painter, Roggen
Exec. Secy: David G. Rice, Jr., Denver
Treasurer: Leavitt Booth, Arvada
Board of Control: W. C. Crew, Arthur R. Amick, R. J. Lamborn, A. P. Starr, M. McAlpine

A. T. McCARTY

1951-1952
COLORADO CATTLEMEN'S ASSOCIATION
President : Stafford Painter, Roggen
1st Vice P: Floyd Beach, Delta
2nd Vice P: Don Collins, Kit Carson
2nd Vice P: Milton Nelson, Longmont
Exec. Secy: David G. Rice, Jr., Denver
Treasurer: Leavitt Booth, Arvada
Board of Control: Willard Simms, R. E. Jones, R. J. Lamborn, A. P. Starr, M. McAlpine, A. T. McCarty

STAFFORD PAINTER

1952-1953
COLORADO CATTLEMEN'S ASSOCIATION
President : Floyd Beach, Delta
1st Vice P: Leavitt Booth, Arvada
2nd Vice P: Robert Hogsett, Ft. Morgan
2nd Vice P: Francis P. Murphy, Spicer
Exec. Secy: David G. Rice, Jr. Denver
Treasurer: Robert A. Burghart, Colorado Springs
Board of Control: Lars Prestrud, R. E. Jones, Noble M. Love, Terry Robinson, M. McAlpine, Stafford Painter

FLOYD BEACH

LEAVITT BOOTH

1953-1954
COLORADO CATTLEMEN'S ASSOCIATION
President : Leavitt Booth, Arvada
1st Vice P: Francis P. Murphy, Coalmont
2nd Vice P: Robert A. Burghart, Colorado Springs
2nd Vice P: A. P. Starr, Austin
Exec. Secy: David G. Rice, Jr., Denver
Treasurer : M. McAlpine, Redwing
Board of Control: Tom Field, R. E. Jones, Noble M. Love, Terry Robinson, Russell Rose, Floyd Beach

1954-1955
COLORADO CATTLEMEN'S ASSOCIATION
President: Francis P. Murphy, Coalmont
1st Vice P: Robert A. Burghart, Colorado Springs
2nd Vice P: Tom Field, Gunnison
2nd Vice P: Robert Schafer, Boyero
Exec. Secy: David G. Rice, Jr., Denver
Treasurer : Lars Prestrud, Littleton
Board of Control: M. McAlpine, R. E. Jones, Martin Domke, J. T. Wadlow, Russell Rose, Leavitt Booth

FRANCIS P. MURPHY

ROBERT A. BURGHART

1955-1956
COLORADO CATTLEMEN'S ASSOCIATION
President : Robert A. Burghart, Colorado Springs
1st Vice P: Tom Field, Gunnison
2nd Vice P: Robert Schafer, Boyero
2nd Vice P: R. E. Jones, Yampa
Exec. Secy: David G. Rice, Jr., Denver
Treasurer : Otto A. Maul, Kiowa
Board of Control: Arthur Brown, Leonard Horn, J. T. Wadlow, Robert Parsons, John Holtorf, Francis P. Murphy

1956-1957
COLORADO CATTLEMEN'S ASSOCIATION
President : Tom Field, Gunnison
1st Vice P: Robert Schafer, Boyero
2nd Vice P: R. E. Jones, Yampa
2nd Vice P: M. McAlpine, Redwing
Exec. Secy: David G. Rice, Jr., Denver
Treasurer : J. T. Wadlow, Whitewater
Board of Control: Robert A. Burghart, Leonard Horn, John Holtorf, Robert Parsons, Gerald Greeman, Victor Hanson, Jr., Francis P. Murphy, Leavitt Booth, Floyd Beach

TOM FiELD

1957-1958
COLORADO CATTLEMEN'S ASSOCIATION
President : Robert Schafer, Boyero
1st Vice P: R. E. Jones, Yampa
2nd Vice P: J. T. Wadlow, Whitewater
2nd Vice P: Robert Parsons, Weston
Exec. Secy: David G. Rice, Jr. Denver
Treasurer: Otto Maul, Kiowa
Board of Control: J. T. Wadlow, Si Berthelson, John Holtorf, Victor Hanson, Jr. Gerald Greeman, Bob Johnston, Jr., Tom Field, Robert A. Burghart, Francis P. Murphy, Leavitt Booth, Floyd Beach

ROBERT SCHAFER

R. E. JONES

1958-1959
COLORADO CATTLEMEN'S ASSOCIATION
President : R. E. Jones, Yampa
1st Vice P: M. McAlpine, Redwing
2nd Vice P: J. T. Wadlow, Whitewater
2nd Vice P: Otto A. Maul, Kiowa
Exec. Secy: David G. Rice, Jr., Denver
Treasurer: John Holtorf, Akron
Board of Control: J. T. Wadlow, Si Berthelson, Jack Bain, George McClave, Melvin Coleman, Bob Johnston, Jr., Robert Schafer, R. A. Burghart, Francis P. Murphy, Leavitt Booth

1959-1960
COLORADO CATTLEMEN'S ASSOCIATION
President : Otto A. Maul, Kiowa
1st Vice P: Si Berthelson, Rio Blanco
2nd Vice P: Robert Parsons, Weston
2nd Vice P: Orris Albertson, Burns
Exec. Secy: David G. Rice, Jr., Denver
Treasurer: John Holtorf, Akron
Board of Control: Francis P. Murphy, Arthur Hudspeth, Bob Johnston, Jr., Melvin Coleman, Jack Bain, George McClave, R. E. Jones, Robert Schafer, Robert A. Burghart

OTTO A. MAUL

SI BERTHELSON

1960-1961
COLORADO CATTLEMEN'S ASSOCIATION
President : Si Berthelson, Rio Blanco
1st Vice P: Robert Parsons, Weston
2nd Vice P: Bob Johnston, Jr., Fowler
2nd Vice P: Orris Albertson, Burns
Exec. Secy: David G. Rice, Jr., Denver
Treasurer: John Holtorf, Akron
Board of Control: Otto A. Maul, Arthur Hudspeth, Melvin Coleman, Jack Bain, Norman King, Robert Schafer, R. E. Jones, Robert A. Burghart

ROBERT PARSONS

1961-1962
COLORADO CATTLEMEN'S ASSOCIATION
President : Robert Parsons, Weston
1st Vice P: J. T. Wadlow, Whitewater
2nd Vice P: Bob Johnston, Jr., Fowler
2nd Vice P: Arthur Hudspeth, Steamboat Springs
Exec. Secy: David G. Rice, Jr., Denver
Treasurer : John Holtorf, Akron
Board of Control: Si Berthelson, Otto A. Maul, Wad Hinman, Melvin Coleman, Jack Bain, Robert Smith, Orris Albertson, Robert Schafer, R. E. Jones

1962-1963
COLORADO CATTLEMEN'S ASSOCIATION
President : J. T. Wadlow, Whitewater
1st Vice P: Bob Johnston, Jr., Fowler
2nd Vice P: Arthur Hudspeth, Steamboat Springs
2nd Vice P: Jack Bain, Ft. Morgan
Exec. Secy: David G. Rice, Jr., Denver
Treasurer : John Holtorf, Akron
Board of Control: Robert Parsons, Si Berthelson, Otto A. Maul, Wad Hinman, Norman King, Carl Meline, Robert Smith, Jim Shoun, Robert Schafer, R. E. Jones

JACK WADLOW

BOB JOHNSTON, JR.

1963-1964
COLORADO CATTLEMEN'S ASSOCIATION
President : Bob Johnston, Jr., Fowler
1st Vice P: Arthur Hudspeth, Steamboat Springs
2nd Vice P: Jack Bain, Ft., Morgan
2nd Vice P: Wad Hinman, Yampa
Exec. Secy: David G. Rice, Jr., Denver
Treasurer : John Holtorf, Akron
Board of Control: J. T. Wadlow, Robert Parsons, Si Berthelson, Otto A. Maul, Ken Buckley, Norman King, Carl Meline, Ralph Yoder, Jim Shoun, R. E. Jones

1964-1965
COLORADO CATTLEMEN'S ASSOCIATION
President : Arthur Hudspeth, Steamboat Springs
1st Vice P: Jack Bain, Ft. Morgan
1st Vice P: Wad Hinman, Yampa
2nd Vice P: Beverly Bledsoe, Hugo
Treasurer : John Holtorf, Yuma
Exec. V. P: David G. Rice, Jr., Denver
Exec. Secy: John Boyd, Denver
Asst. Exec. Secy: Dixie Savio, Denver
Board of Control: Bob Johnston, Jr., J. T. Wadlow, Robert Parsons, Si Berthelson, Ken Buckley, Norman King, Carl Meline, Ralph Yoder, Nate Patton, Otto A. Maul

ARTHUR HUDSPETH

1965-1966
COLORADO CATTLEMEN'S ASSOCIATION
President : Jack Bain, Ft. Morgan
1st Vice P: Wad Hinman, Yampa
2nd Vice P: Beverly Bledsoe, Hugo
2nd Vice P: Victor Hanson, Jr., Walden
Treasurer : Robert Smith, Rush
Exec. V. P. David G. Rice, Jr., Denver
Exec. Secy: John Boyd, Denver
Asst. Exec. Secy: Dixie Savio, Denver
Board of Control: Arthur Hudspeth, Bob Johnston, Jr.,
J. T. Wadlow, Robert Parsons, Jack Orr, Norman King,
Ralph Yoder, Ken Buckley, Nate Patton, Carl Meline

JACK BAIN

1966-1967
COLORADO CATTLEMEN'S ASSOCIATION
President : Wad Hinman, Yampa
1st Vice P: Beverly Bledsoe, Hugo
2nd Vice P: Victor Hanson, Jr., Walden
2nd Vice P: Nate Patton, Canon City
Treasurer : John H. Smartt, McClave
Exec. V. P: David G. Rice, Jr., Denver
Exec. Secy: John Boyd, Denver
Asst. Exec. Secy: Dixie Savio, Denver
Board of Control: Jack Bain, Arthur Hudspeth, Bob
Johnston, Jr., J. T. Wadlow, Robert Parsons, Jack
Orr, Norman King, Ralph Yoder, Ken Buckley, John
Sondstead

W. P. "WAD" HINMAN

C. BEVERLY BLEDSOE

CCA ACTIVE STANDING COMMITTEES

Beef Promotion	Otto A. Maul, Kiowa
Brand and Theft	Lewis Edmundson, Walsenburg
Cattle Improvement	Nate Patton, Canon City
Federal Lands	Lawrence Phelps, Gunnison
Game and Fish	J. K. Buckley, Craig
Legislation	Francis P. Murphy, Walden
Livestock Sanitation	Beverly Bledsoe, Hugo
Marketing	Jack Orr, Kremmling
Membership	Victor Hanson, Jr., Walden
Public Relations	Melvin Coleman, Saguache
Research	John Holtorf, Yuma
State Lands	Joe Hatton, Colorado Spgs.
Tax	John Benton, Burns
Transportation	Leavitt Booth, Arvada
Water	Carl Breeze, Kremmling

Dr. B. F. Davis
Executive Secretary 1923-1949

David G.. Rice, Jr.
Executive Vice President 1949-

Benjamin Franklin Davis was born March 15, 1878, at Fort Scott, Kansas, attended school there and was graduated from Kansas City Veterinary College in 1907. In the meantime, he had crammed a lifetime of adventure into the preceding decade. He joined the gold rush to Alaska in 1898 and 1899, spent three years with the U. S. Army in China and the Pacific Islands during the bloody Boxer Rebellion, and worked as a performer and veterinarian for a circus touring the U. S. After graduating from veterinary college, he worked as a meat inspector and field veterinarian for the U. S. Department of Agriculture in Nebraska, Colorado and Wyoming.

In 1911, he was appointed State Veterinarian for Wyoming and served for several years in this office. At one point he bought horses under contract for the British Army during World War I, was President of the Wyoming State Fair Board, Manager of Cheyenne's Frontier Days, and Secretary of the Wyoming Stock Growers Association. He resigned the latter post to become Secretary-Manager of the Colorado Stockgrowers Association in the fall of 1923.

Dr. Davis managed and directed the Colorado cattle growers organization until he retired in 1949. He died, at the age of 79 after a long illness, on Monday, December 23, 1957. He carried the organization through some of its most difficult years—the Depression of the 1930's and World War II, and contributed more than a quarter century of service to the Association and the livestock industry.

Born April 21, 1916 on the family farm near Grand Junction, Colorado, Dave attended high school in Grand Junction and graduated from Colorado State University in 1939 with a degree in Animal Husbandry. He was a member of Sigma Alpha Epsilon social fraternity and Alpha Zeta and Alpha Tau Alpha honorary fraternities. He was President of the University Livestock Club, directed the Little National Western Stock Show and was assistant manager of College Rodeo Days.

He served as County Extension Agent in Elbert County, where he assisted in reorganizing the Elbert County Livestock Association and the Big Sandy Woolgrowers Association. He also directed the formation of five soil conservation districts in the county.

Following service in World War II, he was County Agent in Delta County, Colorado, and helped to organize the North Fork Stockgrowers Association, the Delta County Agricultural Planning Committee, and served as Director of the Delta County Fair Board.

He was named Executive Secretary of the Colorado Cattlemen's Association in October, 1949. Within a few years he had increased the membership from 22 individuals and 31 affiliated local associations to the present membership of approximately 5,000 individuals and some 71 local associations.

In the past 18 years, Dave has become a recognized spokesman for the livestock industry in Colorado and has received numerous citations and awards for his contributions to Agriculture.

Governor John A. Love receives the first Cattlemen's Centennial Honorary Membership Award from CCA president Wad Hinman, right. Four other former Governors of Colorado assist; left to right, Dan Thornton, Walter Johnson, Ed C. Johnson, Love, and Steve McNichols.

Honorary Centennial Commission Officers

President: Former U.S. Senator Edwin C. Johnson
Vice Presidents: Governor of Colorado John A. Love
Former Governors Stephen L. R. McNichols, Dan Thornton, Walter W. Johnson, Teller Ammons

Centennial Commission Executive Committee

Executive Director: David G. Rice, Jr., Denver
Chairman: Leavitt Booth, Arvada
Mrs. Alfred P. Atchison, Englewood
Jack Bain, Fort Morgan
R. A. Burghart, Sr., Colorado Spgs.

W. P. Hinman, Yampa
Francis P. Murphy, Walden
Willard Simms, Denver

Centennial Commission Board of Trustees

Chairman: W. P. Hinman, Yampa

Past Presidents of CCA:

Neil M. Andrews, Gunnison
Jack Bain, Fort Morgan
Floyd Beach, Delta
H. G. "Si" Berthelson, Rio Blanco
Henry Bledsoe, Sr., Yuma
Leavitt Booth, Arvada
R. A. Burghart, Sr., Colorado Spgs.
Harry J. Capps, Pryor
Frank Fehling, Nathrop
Arthur Hudspeth, Steamboat Spgs.
R. E. Jones, Yampa

Bob Johnston, Jr., Fowler
Charles W. Lilley, Broomfield
Howard K. Linger, Amarillo, Texas
Otto A. Maul, Kiowa
A. T. McCarty, Trinidad
Francis P. Murphy, Walden
Joseph N. Neal, Meeker
Robert Parsons, Weston
Robert Schafer, Boyero
J. T. Wadlow, Whitewater

Other Members:

Mrs. Alfred P. Atchison, Englewood, Colorado Cowbelles
Mrs. Alvin Black, Cotopaxi, Colorado Cowbelles
Carl B. Bledsoe, Hugo, CCA Board of Control
Willard Simms, Denver, Manager, National Western Stock Show

APPENDIX B
COWBELLES AND JUNIORS

Colorado's stockmen have demonstrated that they are as progressive as any in the business, and the Colorado Cattlemen's Association has often been held up to other groups as an example of what a state association should be. Yet for years, the Association and its members overlooked one of its greatest assets—the women.

They didn't neglect them. They merely failed to capitalize on the tremendous amount of energy, ideas and forceful activity represented by their wives. At each of the annual conventions from the 1920's on, there were special events to amuse and entertain the womenfolks, but the ladies—even those who opened gates, heated branding irons, served as spare cowhands and tended sick calves in the kitchen—weren't officially considered a part of the serious cow business.

In 1941, the ladies decided to do something about the situation. They organized and quickly triggered the Association's beef promotion program. The Beef for Father's Day program initiated by the Colorado Cowbelles has gained nationwide recognition.

To Mrs. George Green of Golden, Mrs. Don Collins of Kit Carson and Mrs. Forrest Bassford of Denver must go much of the credit for the existence of the organization. Mrs. Bassford, then editor of the Ranch Home page of the Record-Stockman, appealed to her readers, and especially to the women who accompanied their husbands to the annual meetings of the Colorado Stock Growers and Feeders Association to organize an auxiliary group. Mrs. Green and Mrs. Collins spent many hours in planning and writing letters to get the new venture started.

The organization was formed at a planning dinner in the Log

Inn Cafe at Alamosa, June 21, 1941. The stated purpose of the new entity was a social one—to help women to become better acquainted with each other at conventions, to organize entertainment for the meetings and to lend moral support to the men's association.

The 72 charter members elected as their first officers: Mrs. George S. Green of Golden, president; Mrs. Howard Linger of Hooper, vice president; Mrs. Marshall Nay of Steamboat Springs, secretary; Mrs. Albert Berg of Morley, treasurer.

The committee which arranged this meeting, included Mrs. Howard Linger, whose husband was then president of the Colorado Stock Growers and Feeders Association; Mrs. William A. Shellabarger of Saguache, whose husband was president of the San Luis Valley Cattlemen, Mrs. Louis Higel and Mrs. Earl O. Linger, both of Alamosa.

Mrs. George Green, the first president, had missed only two meetings of the Colorado Stock Growers and Feeders Association in the preceding 30 years. She had actively assisted her husband as treasurer of the Association for several years.

A touch of sadness accompanied the organization of the women's auxiliary. Mrs. Albert Berg, the treasurer, died during the first year.

Objectives of the Colorado Cowbelles today are two-fold: First, to promote beef and the beef industry; second, to promote better public relations within the industry, with other industries and with the public in general.

Beef for Father's Day is the organization's major activity at present. It originated with western Colorado women in 1953. So successful was the state-wide promotion of the event by the Colorado Cowbelles, that it became the main project of the American National CowBelles. For this event, the Colorado Cowbelles supplied colorful posters, counter strips, bumper stickers, table tents, menu clip-ons and other materials. They followed through aggressively, seeing that these materials were used in stores, meat markets, hospitals, nursing homes, restaurants and elsewhere. They also stimulated newspaper, magazine, radio and television advertising of Beef for Father's Day.

The Colorado Cowbelles have contributed hundreds of dollars to the American National CowBelles for beef promotion, and to the national and Colorado beef councils. Their projects include beef promotion booths at the National Western Stock Show in Denver and the Colorado State Fair at Pueblo. They have encouraged local Cowbelle organizations to provide similar exhibits at county fairs, rodeos and other public events.

The Colorado Cowbelles developed and distributed place mats, three sizes of napkins and coasters, steak sticks, bumper stickers, hostess aprons, cook books and the familiar "Watch Your Curves—Eat Beef" bumper stickers. Outstanding Colorado men who won "Father of the Year" awards sponsored by the women's association have been proud to participate and remain staunch supporters of the Cowbelles.

In the "Recipe of the Week" campaign, local Cowbelle associations supplied tested beef recipes and suggested menus, which were then re-tested at Colorado State University. Printed copies of these menus and recipes were distributed to newspapers and other media throughout the state, and placed in grocery stores and meat markets for free distribution. Later, these recipes were compiled into a cook book, "Colorado Cattlemen's Favorite Recipes." It has been necessary to reprint editions of the cook book twice.

To date, Colorado Cowbelles have distributed the following materials:

3,105,000	Place Mats
1,848,000	Dinner Napkins
800,000	Luncheon Napkins
300,000	Petite Napkins
100,000	Coasters
15,000	"Colorado Cattlemen's Favorite Recipes" cook books
12,000	Weight Watcher Menus ("Eat Steak for Breakfast").

Under the sponsorship of the Cowbelles, seventh and eight-grade children throughout the state have competed in essay contests with such titles as "The Story of Beef—From Calf to Counter", "The Romance of Brands" and "Colorful Colorado Cattlemen".

Another successful Cowbelles project was an indoor and outdoor beef cookery contest, "Entertaining with Beef," conducted in cooperation with officials of Colorado State University, where the final cook-offs were held. This event had great public appeal.

On several occasions the Colorado Cowbelles have received recognition from the American National CowBelles for beef promotion activity. In 1959, the national group presented to the Colorado women, a leather facsimile of a steer, upon which were branded the Colorado organization's beef promotions for the year. In 1962, the Colorado association received the Community Service award, and in 1964, the Roan Creek Cowbelles of Debeque won the national organization's Top Hand award for beautifying school grounds.

In 1960, the Colorado Game and Fish Department saluted the Colorado Cowbelles for their hunter-landowner program to promote conservation.

The Cowbelles co-sponsored the College Rodeo World Championship Finals at Littleton in 1963, and presented a saddle to the contestant who was acclaimed high point all-around girl.

Each year the organization sponsors the ringing of Freedom Bells on the Fourth of July.

Its donations include $1,000 to help rural areas in their legislative reapportionment fight, $2,000 to the Colorado Cattlemen's Endowment Trust Fund, $2,000 to the Colorado Cattlemen's Centennial celebration.

A few of its less-prominent projects have been to supply promotional materials and support the following: Colorado Boys' Ranch; national and state beef councils; National Advertising Men and Women's convention; National Soil and Water Conservation Association convention; annual meetings of local and state conservation organizations; state teachers' conventions; national county commissioners and county officials conventions, Mrs. America contest at St. Petersburg, Florida.

Membership in the Colorado Cowbelles exceeded 1,500 at the end of 1965. Since 1953, the state organization has been affiliated with the American National CowBelles, and 391 of its members also belong to the national organization.

For nearly a quarter of a century, the Cowbelles raised all of the funds for their projects. When the Colorado Beef Board was created by the legislature in 1965, the Cowbelles were able to work in cooperation with the new agency on beef promotion. The first joint project was a beef promotion booth at the National Western Stock Show in January, 1966.

Cowbelles manned this booth for ten days. They gave bite-sized pieces of choice roast beef to more than 26,000 persons, discussed with the public the desirability of beef produced, fed and processed in Colorado, and displayed a number of cuts of fresh beef in a refrigerated showcase in the booth.

During the state convention at Lamar in June, 1966, the Colorado Cowbelles celebrated their silver anniversary. Past presidents received special honors.

The Colorado Cowbelles have played an important part in planning and preparations for the Centennial celebration of the Cattlemen's Association.

PRESIDENTS of the COLORADO COWBELLES 1947-1967

1941-1942—Edna Green
1942-1943—Doris Linger
1943-1944—Marie Murphy
1944-1946—Minniebell Fehling
1946-1947—Patty Amick
1947-1948—Blanche Collins
1948-1949—Daisy Bledsoe
1949-1950—Wanda Downing
1950-1951—Jewel McCarty
1951-1952—Mildred Beckstead
1952-1953—Jo Bledsoe
1953-1954—Sue Field

1954-1955—Murva Booth
1955-1956—Yodie Burghart
1956-1957—Magaret Rose
1957-1959—Mary Wadlow
1959-1960—Helen Bonnell
1960-1961—Bernice Money
1961-1962—Joanna Zazislan
1962-1963—Mona Berthelson
1963-1964—Ersley Hart
1964-1965—Ruth Bain
1965-1966—Zella Black
1966-1967—Rilla King

COLORADO JUNIOR CATTLEMEN'S
ASSOCIATION
1950-1967 Officers

1950-51
Pres. Thaine Sussex, Ft. Morgan

1951-1953
Pres. Virginia Painter, Roggen

1953-54
Pres. Leonard Austin, Julesburg

1954-55
Pres. Robert "Mac" Johnson, Sugar City

1955-56
Pres. Danny Alt, Akron
Treas. Mary Helen Holtorf, Akron

1956-57
Pres. Thomas Dorr, Steambort Springs
V. Pres. Alma Ann McArthur
Secy. Mary Helen Holtorf, Akron

1957-58
Pres. Bernard Parsons, Weston
V. Pres. Alma Ann Loflin, Utleyville
Secy. Joan Burke, Timnath

1958-59
Pres. Mary Helen Holtorf, Akron
V. Pres. Don Moor, Lamar
Secy. John Burke, Timnath

1959-60
Pres. Jay Bain, Ft. Morgan
Secy. Cheryl Bain, Ft. Morgan
Treas. Larry Austin, Julesburg

1960-61
Pres. Larry Austin, Julesburg
V. Pres. Lewis Edmundson, Walsenburg
Secy. Cheryl Bain, Ft. Morgan

1961-62
Pres. Lewis Edumundson, Walsenburg
V. Pres. John Burke, Timnath

1962-63
Pres. John Burke, Timnath
V. Pres. Jimmy Shoun, Canon City
Secy. Sandy Bledsoe, Wray

1963-64
Pres. Gary Shoun, Canon City
V. Pres. Wiley Berthelson, Rio Blanco
Secy. Sandy Bledsoe, Wray

1964-65
Pres. Wiley Berthelson, Rio Blanco
V. Pres. John Cadwell, Pueblo
Secy. Mary Ann Bledsoe, Wray

1965-66
Pres. John Cadwell, Pueblo
V. Pres. Steve Shoun, Canon City
Secy. Terry Hanna, Pueblo

1966-67
Pres. Steve Shoun, Canon City
V. Pres. Sally Lou Johnson, Rio Blanco
Secy. Debbie Bain, Ft Morgan
Board of Control: John Cadwell, Bill McEndree, Gary Shoun , Clifford Van Campen Parlimentarian: Richard Robbins
Reporter: Cheryl Preisser

APPENDIX C
THE LOCAL ASSOCIATIONS

Archuleta County Stockgrowers Assn.
1966 Officers:
Pres: H. Ray Macht, Pagosa Springs
V.P.: Olen W. Crowley, Chromo
Sec'y: Jim Cloman, Pagosa Springs
Organized at Pagosa Springs as Treasure Mountain Stock Growers Assn., original date not known. Reorganized in 1930; at one time called Archuleta County Cattlemen's Assn.
Original Officers: Pres. Harry C. Macht, Sec'y. Louis Montroy

Bent-Prowers Cattle & Horse Growers Assn.
1966 Officers:
Pres: Dan Sniff, Hasty
1st V.P.: Russel Reyher, Lamar
Sec'y: John A. Smartt, McClave
Treas: Marshall Dean, Las Animas
Dir.-Norris Anderson, R. D. Bamber, A. P. Brown, Kenneth Clark, Eddie Dunlap, Lyman Edgar, Bob Emick, Charlie Fletcher, Phil Gilbert, Lewis Mathews, Clyde McEndree, H. H. Mendenhall, Robert Morrison, Robert Mundell, Wm. E. Rose, Alvin Spady
Organized Mar. 1870 as Bent County Stock Assn. at Las Animas (Old Town); became defunct Apr. 1871. Reorganized Feb., 1874 at West Las Animas with Pres. John W. Prowers, V.P. James C. Jones, V.P. H. S. Holly, Sec'y. R. M. Moore, Treas. Mark B. Price. Later called The Bent-Prowers.
Original Officers: Pres. Stephen P. Jones, V.P. John W. Prowers, Sec'y. R. M. Moore, Treas. Mark B. Price

Black Mesa Cattle Association
1966 Officers:
Pres: Carton Meek, Maher
V.P.: Wallace Klaseen, Crawford
Sec'y: Robert L. Kraai, Crawford
Treas: Oscar Leinnan, Crawford
Organized Jan. 24, 1935 at Crawford.
Original Officers: Pres. George L. Tracy, V.P. Glenn Davis, Sec'y-Treas. Nelle Zeldenthuis

Boulder South-Larimer Livestock Assn.
1966 Officers:
Pres: E. Louden Buster, Lyons
V.P.: Hiram Fullen, Boulder
Sec'y-Treas: James D. Tatum, Boulder
Organized May 19, 1917 at Longmont as Boulder County Stockgrowers Assn.; second association formed Feb. 4, 1919 at Boulder as Cattlemen's Protective Assn. of Boulder with Pres. A. R. Weaver, V.P. Glenn Martin, Sec'y-Treas. Sam R. Fowler, Exec. Comm.-Arthur W. Crews, Wesley Hetzer, Charles E. Kohler, E. E. Scholfield. Both merged May 16, 1951, as Boulder South-Larimer County Stockmans Assn. with Pres. Leslie Kuhn, V.P. Frank Bruning, Sec'y-Treas. Boyd Bruning, Adv. Board-Harold Alps, Frank Bruning, L. E. Cushman, Leslie Kuhn, Lyman Linger.
Original Officers: Pres. C. W. Pace, V.P. E. L. Montgomery, Sec'y-Treas. V. O. Coffin, Exec. Comm.-John E. Burns, James Churnside, V. O. Coffin, J. B. Edmunds, C. W. Pace

Central Colorado Cattlemen's Association
1966 Officers:
Pres: Jim Settele, Fairplay
V.P.: Walt Ford, Lake George
Sec'y: Leland R. Barden, Fairplay
Treas: Marie Chisholm, Fairplay
Dir.-Jack Eavenson, Shorty Holmes, Don Jones, Dave Rowland, Lyle Werley, Don White
Organized May 16, 1950 at Fairplay.
Original Officers: Pres. J. B. Fitzsimmons, V.P. Tom Campbell, Sec'y-Treas. J. T. McDowell, Bd. of Con.-John Buyer, Frank Fehling, Clyde Gilley, Thomas McQuaid, J. L. Settele, Lee Wallace

Chaffee County Cattlemen's Association
1966 Officers:
Pres: Glen Morrison, Buena Vista
V.P.: Lester Peters, Nathrop
Sec'y: R. (Ray) L. Sailor, Buena Vista
Treas: George Tegeler, Buena Vista
Organized Feb. 12, 1916 at Buena Vista

345

as Chaffee County Cattle and Horse Growers Assn. Two prior associations were United Rocky Mountain Cattlemen's Assn. founded in 1883 at Poncha Springs and Chaffee County Cattlemen's Assn. formed a few years after the first became defunct at Buena Vista with Pres. Max Dickman, V.P. P. C. Bond, Sec'y. Howard Sneddon, Treas. W. P. Blanchard, Bd. Mem.-T. J. Ehrhart, A. E. Wright. This association became defunct about 1912-13.

Original Officers: Pres. Mel DeWitt, V.P. Chris Nachtrieb, Sec'y. A. A. McLennan, Treas. William Hallock, Bd. Mem.-Bert DeWitt, Frank Fehling, Myron J. Tomkins, Edward Wright

Cheyenne County Livestock Association

1966 Officers:
Pres: Byron Hudson, Cheyenne Wells
V.P.: Bill Evans, Kit Carson
Sec'y-Treas: Burr Keller, Kit Carson
Dir.-Benny Gibbs, Conrad Hogan, Frank Howard, Ed Kimmel, Lowell Reynolds
Organized May 25, 1950 at Cheyenne Wells.
Original Officers: Pres. Don C. Collins, V.P. M. K. White, Se'y: C. S. Miles, Treas. Byron Hudson, Dir.-C. A. Harms, J. A. Oswald, A. A. Pelton, Julius Peterson, L. G. Wilson

Crowley-Kiowa-Lincoln Stockgrowers Assn.

1966 Officers:
Pres: Kenneth Carter, Ordway
V.P.: Virgil Trotter, Sugar City
Sec'y-Treas: Don Hendrix, Ordway
Exec. Comm.-Bill Hagans, "Hap" Raith, Harley Rusher.
Organized March 10, 1928 at Ordway.
Original Officers: Pres. M. Joe Trainor, V.P. W. F. Bean, Sec'y-Treas. Ed C. Tritt, Exec. Comm.-Charles R. McCabe, L. D. Watts

Crow Valley Livestock Co-Operative Inc.

1966 Officers:
Pres: Russell E. Peterson, Nunn
V.P.: H. M. Moore, Grover
Sec'y-Treas: Clyde S. Diehl, Ault
Dir.-W. A. Barnett, Charles Jones
Organized May 20, 1936.
Original Officers: Pres. J. E. Reno, V.P. H. B. Pollock, Sec'y. Anna K. Rosey, Treas. Earl J. Anderson, Dir.-R. B. Golden, M. L. McIntosh

Custer County Stockgrowers Association

1966 Officers:
Pres: George A. Vickerman, Westcliffe
V.P.: Harold G. Vickerman, Westcliffe
Sec'y-Treas: Stanley Coleman, Westcliffe
Bd. of Dir.-William Frank, Tom Hook, Ashley Rich, Lisle Vahldick
Organized July 22, 1895 at Westcliffe
Organized July 22, 1895 at Westcliffe, as Custer Co. Cattle Growers Protective Assn.; was inactive from 1905 until reorganized July 27, 1945, as Wet Mtn. Valley Livestock Assn. with Pres. Earl E. Cress V.P. E. H. Georges, Sec'y-Treas. Leon A. Hemenway. Present name adopted June, 1956.
Original Officers: Pres. T. L. Kennicott, Sec'y. W. H. Hall, Treas. John L. Schwab

Douglas County Cattlemen's Association

1966 Officers:
Pres: Frank Christensen, Castle Rock
V.P.: Joe Bain, Castle Rock
Sec'y-Treas: David A. Curtis Sedalia
Dir.-Frank Allen, Clay Keene, John Lowell, Jim Marr, Bill Sinclaire, Vernon Wyatt
Organized March, 1918, as Douglas County Livestock Association.
Original Officers: Pres. H. H. Gordon, V.P. Fred Kuehster, Sec'y-Treas. Daniel N. Ball, Exec. Comm.-W. H. Childers, Frank Dakan

Eagle County Cattlemen's Association

1966 Officers:
Pres: Glen Norman, Eagle
V.P.: John Benton, Burns
Sec'y-Treas: Nick Strubi, Burns
Organized about 1940 or previous.
Original Officers: Pres. Chester Mayer, Sec'y. D. O. Johnson

Elbert County Livestock Association

1966 Officers:
Pres: Walter R. Maul, Kiowa
V.P.: Jack Fletcher, Agate
Sec'y: Kelby Myers, Calhan
Organized originally in the 1880's; disbanded after it had served its purpose. Reorganized Oct. 23, 1935.
Original Officers: Pres. Elmer Mourning, V.P. W. J. Park, Sec'y. A. G. Cornforth

The Fremont Cattlemen's Association

1966 Officers:
Pres: Carl Dilley, Canon City

V.P.: David Nash, Canon City

Sec'y-Treas: Clarence Canterbury, Canon City

Dir.-Grant Adkisson, Bob Dilley, R. N. Patton, Vern Pease, Dawson Reid, Tom Robb

Organized Dec. 28, 1897, at Canon City as The Fremont Co. Cattlegrowers Protective Assn. Renamed Fremont Co. Stockgrowers Assn. on May 27, 1911. In 1921, merged with Park Co. Assn., became The Fremont-Park Co. Stockgrowers Assn. Present association organized July 19, 1934, at Canon City, with Jres. W. A. MacKenzie, V.P. Paul Huntley, Sec'y-Treas. E. C. Higgins, Dir.-Walter Alexander, Clyde Chess, Al Griffin, H. C. Rathke, Eugene Rowe. Current name adopted 1961.

Original Officers: Pres. Robert W. Pope, Sec'y. Don C. Crampton, Treas. Jesse Rader, Exec Comm.-R. L. Reed, W. A. Stump, T. Witcher

Gilpin-Jefferson Livestock Association

1966 Officers:

Pres: John Boyle, Golden

V.P. Dick Johnson, Golden

Sec'y-Treas: John Lutz, Golden

Adv. Bd.-Paul Pattridge, Tom Pearce, Art Ranson

Organized about early 1919 at Black Hawk; reorganized Feb. 26, 1921 as Gilpin-Jefferson County Stock Assn. with Pres. Geo S. Green, V.P. Guss Brumm, Sec'y. Arthur Nicholls, Treas. James Young, Adv. Bd.-Wm. Allgood, Tom Pearce, Wm. Stearns, Paul White.

Original Officers: Pres. C. S. Taylor, V.P. Geo. Snyder, Sec'y. Arthur Nicholls, Treas. James Young, Exec. Comm.-Geo. S. Green, H. B. McGammon

Grand Mesa Stock Growers Association

1966 Officers:

Pres: Nat Hart, Austin

V.P.: Clarence Hawkins, Austin

Sec'y-Treas: Josephine McCoy, Cedaredge

Adv. Bd.-Bob Cockroft, Clarence Hawkins, George Lewis, Harold McCoy, Jim Vela

Organized Jan. 8, 1916 at Cedaredge.

Original Officers: Pres. John E. Shelledy, V.P. B. L. Bertram, Sec'y-Treas. Parker M. Hart, Adv. Bd.-B. L. Bertram, H. K. Ferguson, Parker M. Hart, J. E. Shelledy, W. B. Stockham

Gunnison County Stockgrowers Assn.

1966 Officers:

Pres: Lee Spann, Gunnison

V. P.: Duane Phelps, Parlin

Sec'y-Treas: Mrs. Peggy Lue Reece, Gunnison

Dir.-Fred Field, Craig Goodwin, Dave Howard, Bernard Irby

Organized June 30, 1894 at Gunnison.

Original Officers: Pres. A. Hartman, V.P. J. H. Andrews, Sec'y. C. L. Stone, Treas. A. E. Hyzer, Exec. Comm. H. C. Bartlett, William A. K. Stevens Snyder

Holy Cross Cattlemen's Association

1966 Officers:

Pres: Rex Coffman, Carbondale

V.P.: Frank Starbuck, Silt

Sec'y-Treas: Deyoe Green, New Castle

Organized in 1898 as Grand River Stock Growers Assn. Present association or organized 1955 at Glenwood Springs

Original Officers (1955): Pres. Humbert Rees, V. P. James Conto, Sec'y-Treas. Deyoe Green

Huerfano Basin Stockgrowers Assn.

1966 Officers:

Pres: Homer McKinley, Walsenburg

V.P.: Bill Baker, Walsenburg

Sec'y-Treas: Lowell Goemmer, La Veta

B.-C. E. Bauer, Joe Crump, Bob Drury, Dr. John Goemmer, John Kimbrel

Organized in 1895, at Gardner as Cuerno Verde Roundup Assn., then became Cuerno Verde Livestock Assn. with Pres. Gus Meyer. From this Upper Huerfano Basin Assn. In 1952, association split; became Huerfano Co. Livestock Assn.; the Huerfano Basin Livestock Growers Assn.; current name adopted about 1962.

Original Officers: John MsKinley, John Meyer, John Schwab, Sec'y. Fred Dietz

Kit Carson County Cattlemen's Assn.

1966 Officers:

Pres: Harley Rhoades, Burlington

V.P.: Joe Hendricks, Stratton

Sec'y-Treas: Paul Short, Flagler

Rec. Sec'y: Avis Bader, Burlington

Organized about 1900 at Stratton as Kit Carson Assn.

Original Officers: Pres. J. J. Pugh, Sec'y. C. S. Wellman.

La Plata County Cattlemen's Association

1966 Officers:

Pres: Charles Lemon, Durango

V.P.: Lawrence Huntington, Hesperus
Sec'y-Treas: James Mars, Bayfield
Bd. of Dir.-Jim Cole, Roger Edwards, Bruce Fassett, John Horrath, Lawrence Huntington, David James, Jim Mars, Joe Salmon, David S'·llivan
Organized May 22, 1950 at Durango.
Original Officers: Pres. Frank Wommer, Sr., V. P. Louis Campbell, Sec'y-Treas. A. F. Hotter, Dir.-Mike Bodo, Jr., John Lechner, Charles Lemon, Paul Martin, Gerald Mitchell, Philip Schalles, Hon. Dir.-Bernie Williams

Larimer County Stockgrowers Association
1966 Officers:
Pres: M. A. "Pat" Ferree, Livermore
V.P.: Edward Hansen, Livermore
Sec'y-Treas: Lester Rivers, Livermore
Bd. of Dir.-Lawrence Griffith, Robert Hohnholz, Dennis Steinhoff, William Tibbits
Organized Aug. 20, 1884 at Livermore.
Original Officers: Pres. T. A. Gage, V.P. Frank Kibler, Sec'y-Treas. S. B. Chaffee, Exec. Comm.-T. B. Bishopp, J. H. Bristol, C. N. Campbell, F. L. Carter-Cotton, Fred Christman, Russell Fisk, A. H. Haygood, A. H. Morgan, C. E. Roberts, F. J. Spencer, John S. Williams

Leroux Creek Pool Association
1966 Officers:
Pres: Harry Wood, Jr., Hotchkiss
V.P.: Shirley Smith, Hotchkiss
Sec'y-Treas: Lee Gray, Hotchkiss
B.-U. S. Hendrickson, Jim Patterson, Keith Pfeiffer, Sheldon Smith, Marvin Taylor, Leo Ward
Organized Feb. 25, 1936 at Hotchkiss.
Original Officers; Pres. Harry S. Wood, Sr., V.P. Carl Smith, Sec'y-Treas. Lee Gray, Bd.-Ollie Buzzard, Jim Hill

Lincoln County Stockmen's Association
1966 Officers:
Pres: Pat Holland, Boyero
V.P.: Lawrence H. Withers, Hugo
Sec'y-Treas: Robert Palmer, Boyero
Organized June 15, 1898 at Hugo, as Lincoln County Cattle Growers' Assn.
Original Officers: Pres. Colin C. Sutherland, V.P. Dan C. Barksdale, Sec'y-Treas. John P. Dickinson

Mancos Cattlemen's Association
1966 Officers:
Pres: George Eppich, Mancos

V.P.: Bill Crader, Mancos
Sec'y-Treas: Mrs . Dwight Wallace, Mancos
Adv. Bd.-George Mauler, Fred Reddert, Dwight Wallace
Organized Feb. 16, 1918 at Mancos.
Original Officers: Pres. George Mennefee, V.P. A. M. Decker, Sec'y-Treas. W. W. Wallace, Adv. Bd.-E. K. McGalliard, A. M. Puett, Joe Sponsel

Middle Park Stockgrowers Association
1966 Officers:
Pres: Rod Hinman, Kremmling
V.P.: Jack Horn, Granby
Sec'y-Treas: Grady Culbreath, Kremmling
Past Pres: Jacko Orr. Kremmling
Dir.-Rusty Evans, Redwood Fisher, Wayne Harbert, Will Ingram, Lynn Matheson, Jim Murphy, Ted Orr, Jr., Ted Orr, Sr., Dick Smith
Organized early 1900; other local associations, including Williams Fork, Troublesome and Blue Valley Stockgrowers, have since merged with present organization.
Original Officers: Pres. F. C. Jones, V.P. J. A. McNamara, Sec'y. W. O. Howe, Treas. T. E. Pharo

Mile-Hi Cattlemen's Association
1966 Officers:
Pres: E. Proctor Nott, Denver
V.P.: F. M. Petersen, Denver
Sec'y-Treas: Vince Dwyer, Denver
Directors—Al Atchison, James Gammon, R. H. Heckendorf, Roy Johnson, William Mason, Robert Nunemacher, Willard Simms
Organized March 12, 1958 at Denver.
Original Officers: Pres. R. H. "Dick" Heckendorf, V.P. Jess Egurrola, 2nd V.P. E. Proctor Nott, Sec'y-Treas. Willard Simms

Moffat County Cattle Association
1966 Officers:
Pres: Earl Van Tassel, Jr., Craig
V.P.: Kenneth Osborn, Hamilton
Sec'y-Treas: Otis Lyons, Craig
Organized May 3, 1952 at Craig. (Two earlier associations, one headed up by Matt Rash of Brown's Park.)
Original Officers: Pres. Earl Wilson, V.P. O. E. (Elbert) Mock, Sec'y-Treas. A. R. (Ray) Lyons, Bd. of Dir.-Harry Durham, Sr., Clifford "Stubb" Leggett, George Mock, Guy Ramsey, Dewey Sheridan, Sr., Robert Van Dorn

Morgan County Cattlemen's Association

1966 Officers:
Pres: Gene Mitchell, Brush
V.P.: Ed Rigsby, Weldona
Sec'y-Treas: W. H. August, Brush
Organized June 21, 1939 at Brush.
Original Officers: Pres. J. A. Fries, V.P. Edward Hellstern, Sec'y-Treas. Robert Hogsett

Northeastern Colorado Cattlemen's Assn.

1966 Officers:
Pres: Thomas De Soto, Sterling
V.P.: William M. Wooters, Sterling
Sec'y: J. T. "Ted" Haddan, Atwood
Dir.-Galen Bamford, Darrel Bonham, Kenneth Brammer, Arthur Marquardt, Charles McRea, Carl Meline
Organized Feb. 4, 1899 in Logan County as Logan County Cattle & Horse Protective Assn. Reorganized Aug. 28, 1951, at Sterling, as Northeastern Cattlemen's Assn. with Pres. Bill Seckler, V.P. Jack Casement, Sec'y-Treas. Edgar Tunison
Original Officers: Pres. J. J. Cheairs, V.P. E. A. Harris, Sec'y. M. H. Smith, Dir.-Gene Buchanan, R. T. Patterson

North Fork Livestock Association

1966 Officers:
Pres: Henry Hamilton, Crawford
V.P.: Dick Mott
Sec'y-Treas: C. A. Bailey, Paonia
Dir.-Clint Roeber, Marion O. Sell, Theodore Simmeo, Ross Taylor
Organized 1918 at Paonia.
Original Officers: Pres. Guy Hammond, Sec'y-Treas. Inez Brown

North Park Stockgrowers Association

1966 Officers:
Pres: Owen Geer, Coalmont
Sec'y: Don Hanson, Walden
Dir.-Oley Kohlman
Organized March 15, 1899 at Hebron.
Original Offices: Pres. Hubert Chedsey, Sec'y-Treas. James Marr, Bd. of Dir.-Fletcher Campbell, Alex K. Marr, Andrew Peterson

Nucla Cattle Growers Association

1966 Officers:
Pres: O. J. Cooper, Nucla
V.P.: Benton Blackburn, Nucla
Sec'y-Treas: John A. Galley, Jr.
Organized Oct., 1918 at Nucla.
Original Officers: Pres. J. N. Langworthy, V.P. A. R. Payson, Sec'y-Treas. M. D. Bowen

Ouray County Cattlemen's Association

1966 Officers:
Pres: Lloyd Berryman, Ridgway
V.P.: Derrell Kenney, Ridgway
Sec'y: D. A. "Bud" Masden, Montrose
Treas: Verel Smith, Montrose
Organized 1953 at Ridgway.
Original Officers: Pres. Bryan Fisher, V.P. Glen Israel, Sec'y. Vaughn Stealey, Treas. Ester Lewis

Pikes Peak Cattlemen's Association

1966 Officers:
Pres: Bob Burghart, Jr., Colorado Springs
1st V.P.: Jon W. Frost, Pueblo
2nd V.P.: Charles Bradley, Colorado Spgs.
Sec'y; Everett Handle, Calhan
Treas: Joe M. Hatton, Colorado Springs
Dir.-Ralph Bennett, Ward Edwards, Henry Hammer, Ralph Janitell, Ordell Larson, Robert C. Norris, Robert M. Smith, Leonard Tarpenning, William T. Ward, III, Tom Watt
Originally two separate organizations; Pikes Peak Cattle Growers (formed spring, 1949) with Pres. Del Lichtenberg and Regional Stock Growers Assn. organized Aug. 27, 1950, at Hugh Bennett Ranch, NE of Colorado Spgs. On Apr. 12, 1952, Pikes Peak assn. merged with Regional assn. to form present association with Pres. Hugh Bennett.
Original Officers: Pres. Oscar Appelt, Sr., V.P. Hugh Bennett, Sec'y. Joe Hatton, Treas. J. D. Ackerman

Plateau Valley Stockmen's Association

1966 Officers:
Pres: Clarence J. Terrell, Collbran
V.P.: Harry Kelly, Collbran
Sec'y-Treas: Miles McDaniel, Collbran
Bd.-Wallace Currier, Ervin Lockert, Stanley Long, Dean Walch
Organized 1902 as Plateau Valley Stockgrowers Assn.; present name adopted 1955.
Original Officers; Dave Anderson, Sr., Bill Dittman, Barney Duffy, Andy Saunders, Sr., E. D. Stewart

Pueblo County Stockmen's Association

1966 Officers:
Pres: Charles Hobson, Pueblo
V.P.: Ralph Allen, Pueblo
Sec'y: Louis Guilliams, Pueblo
Treas: Johnny King, Pueblo
Dir.-Frank Cadwell, W. R. Dunn, Orval Hartman

Organized about April, 1883 (some indication to its always being member of state assn.) at Pueblo as Southern Colorado Stockgrowers Assn. Renamed Pueblo County Stockgrowers in 1914; in March, 1949 renamed Pueblo County Stockmen's Assn. with James Utt as president.

Original Officers: Pres. Robert Grant, V.P. W. J. Wilson, Sec'y. Theodore R. Jones, Treas. John McDaniel, B.d of Mgrs.-B. F. McDaniel, A. M. Pryor, John Rantschler

Ragged Mountain Stockmen's Association

1966 Officers:
Pres: George Volk, Jr., Somerset
V.P.: Warren Cockroft, Hotchkiss
Sec'y-Treas: Lee Sperry, Austin
Organized Feb. 25, 1922 at Hotchkiss.
Original Officers: Pres. George Wood, V.P. W. G. Balch, Sr., Sec'y-Treas. Sam C. Hartman

Rio Blanco Stockgrowers' Assn.

1966 Officers:
Pres: Harold Amick, Meeker
V.P.: H. R. (Ray) Nelson, Meeker
2nd V.P.: C. W. (Bill) Brennan, Rio Blanco
Sec'y-Treas: F. K. (Buss) Norell, Rio Blanco
Past Pres: Allan Rogers, Meeker
Organized 1886 at Meeker as White River Stock Growers' Association.
Original Officers: Pres. A. J. Gregory, Sec'y. L. B. Brasher, Treas. A. B. Hankey

Routt County Cattlemen's Association

1966 Officers:
Pres: Larry Whiteman, Craig
V.P.: E. J. Fox, Steamboat Springs
Sec'y: Vernon Summer, Steamboat Springs
Treas: Evelyn P. Semotan, Steamboat Springs
Organized 1895 as Brown's Park Assn. with Pres. Matt Rash; then Routt Co. also encompassed Moffat Co. In 1916, consolidation of associations (Snake River, Egeria, Park, Williams Fork, Hayden, Steamboat Spgs.) into Routt Co. Livestock Assn. Reorganized in early 1930's as Routt Co. Stockgrowers Assn. with Pres. A. A. Curtis. Present association formed from Steamboat Spgs. Stockgrowers Assn. on May 24, 1950 at Steamboat Spgs. with Pres. Si Lockhart, V. P. Ernest

Bridges, Sec'y-Treas. Howard S. Elliott, Dir.-Elmer Dorr, Raymond Gray, Marshall Nay, John Sandelin, R. E. Stee, Dr. J. A. Utterbeck.

Original Officers: Pres. J. N. "Jerry" McWilliams, Sec'y-Treas. Sam Nay, Exec. Comm.-Frank Coleman, W. F. Cross, Patrick Cullen, W. T. Laramore

San Luis Valley Cattlemen's Association

1966 Officers:
Pres: Jim Lillpop, Alamosa
V.P.: Jim Armstrong, Monte Vista
Sec'y: Melvin Coleman, Saguache
Organized before 1900 as San Luis Val-at Saguache, by Saguache Park Assn.
Original Officers: Pres. H. K. Linger, V.P. James Curtis, Sec'y. C. E. Gibson, Jr.

San Miguel Cattleman's Association

1966 Officers:
Pres: Gordon Palmer, Norwood
V.P.: Roy Davis
Sec'y-Treas. Charles Jensen, Norwood
Adv. Bd.-Steven Herndon, Tillman Reed
Organized 1885 at Norwood as Lone Cone and Plateau Basin Stock Growers Assn. Reorganized in 1934, at Nor-Wood under present name.
Original Officers: Pres. W. H. Nelson, V.P. David M. Miller, Sec'y-Treas. H. B. Adsit

Sirloin Club

1966 Officers:
Pres: Craig Anderson, Longmont
V.P.: Frank Barnes, Mead
Sec'-Treas: Everly Austin, Longmont
Past Pres: Lee Powell, Longmont
Organized about 1950 at Longmont.
Original Officers: Pres. Milton Nelson, V.P. Sidney Fredstrom, Sec'y-Treas. James Henry

Southern Colorado Livestock Association

1966 Officers:
Pres: Tony Verquer, Trinidad
V.P.: Chester Rose, Trinchera
Sec'y: Harry L. Beirne, Trinidad
Treas: Howard Melvin, Augilar
Organized 1872 at Pueblo (according to Dr. B. F. Davis; no written records to substantiate). Reorganized in 1914 at Trinidad.
Original Officers: Pres. Harry J. Capps, V.P. O. T. Clark, Sec'y-Treas. Harry West, Dir.-James Cummings, George Green, W. H. Green

Southern Mesa County Cattlemen's Assn.
1966 Officers:
Pres: Tom C. Burwell, Grand Junction
V.P.: Ray Calhoun, Delta
Sec'y-Treas. Frank W. Ward, Delta
Dir.-Steve Beach, Howard Brouse, L. L. Hubbard, Welland Smith, J. T. Wadlow
Organized Mar. 17, 1959, probably at Grand Junction. Prior to this, Western Stockgrowers Assn. formed Feb. 2, 1887 at Grand Junction headed by J. F. Brink, Allen B. Campbell, Fred S. Rockwell, F. R. Fish, W. P. Ela. Cattlemen then belonged to Delta County Assn. before formation of Kannah Creek Stockgrowers Assn. organized about 1919 or 1920, still active for 8 local members (Grand Mesa Nat'l Forest Permittees). Present association evolved from this.
Original Officers: Pres. Howard Brouse, V.P. Clyde Hollenbeck, Sec'y-Treas. Herschel Hendrickson, Dir.-Crafts Black, C. M. Hathaway, George Lockhart, James Stadleman, J. T. Wadlow

Southwestern Colorado Livestock Assn.
1966 Officers:
Pres: James Suckla, Cortez

Sec'y-Treas: Mrs. Jean Bader, Mancos
Bd. of Dir.-Russel A. Hindmarsh, John Porter, Darrel Veach, Dwight Wallace, Eldon Zwicker
Organized Feb. 1908, at Dolores, probably called Dolores Stockgrowers Assn. In Sept., 1947, at Cortez, consolidation of several local associations to form present organization with Pres. Bill McCabe, Acting Sec'y. Loraine Steves.
Original Officers: Pres. Wes Dunlap, Sec'y. Charles Hosea

Sweetwater Livestock Association
1966 Officers:
Pres: William A. Stephens, Gypsum
V.P.: Frank Haas, Gypsum
Sec'y-Treas: William F. Stevens, Gypsum
Range Bd.-James E. Stephens
Organized April, 1917, at Riland (22 miles outside of Gypsum on Sweetwater Creek).
Original Officers: Pres. John B. Green, V.P. Henry Stephens, Sec'y-Treas. Frank Maloney, Exec. Comm.-Mike E. Calvick, William D. Gannon, Arthur German, A. McGlochlin, Ward Skiff

Terror Creek Stock Association
1966 Officers:
Pres: Oran G. Houseweart, Hotchkiss
V.P.: John Morrell, Paonia
Sec'y-Treas: C. J. Lawlor, Hotchkiss
Adv. Bd.-C. B. Morgan, John Morrell
Organized Feb. 23, 1934 at Paonia.
Original Officers: Pres. Joe Leitzinger, V.P. F. C. Barnett, Sec'y-Treas. Joe Barnie, Adv. Bd.-Jess Barrow, George Campbell

Uncompahgre Cattle & Horse Growers Assn.
1966 Officers:
Pres: Alford Gray, Olathe
V.P.: Bob Hawks, Olathe
V.P.: Albert Soderquist, Cimarron
Sec'y: Sam Keeter, Montrose
Treas: Aruthur Carmichael, Montrose
Chm-Mem. Comm.-Elmo Cooper, Montrose
Organized Mar. 1, 1886 at Montrose as Montrose County Cattle and Horse Growers Assn.; present name adopted about 1900.
Original Officers: Pres. James A. Fenlon, V.P. W. T. Ryman, Sec'y. Thomas Osborne, Treas. John Deeble

Washington County Stockman's Assn.
1966 Officers:
Pres: Howard Schreiber, Woodrow
V.P.: Glen Venrick, Akron
Sec'y-Treas: Arven Vondy, Woodrow
Dir.-Dan Alt, Al Denham, Jim Durllinger, Homer Hill, Calvin McCaffery, Ed Mustain, Ed Thurer
Organized in 1937; reorganized in 1944 at Akron.
Original Officers: Pres. Pearl L. Barnhouse, Sec'y-Treas. S. B. Lewis, Dir.-Dan Alt, Fred Fassler, Sr., O. J. Grace, John C. Holtorf, E. W. Hulburd, Cleve Kennison, Henry Stuckey

Weld County Livestock Association
1966 Officers:
Pres: Ben A. Wilson, Grover
V.P.: Wilbur, Thomas, Carr
Sec'y-Treas: Michael Wright, Cornish
Bd. of Dir.-Gus Anderson, Clarence Benson, Adolph Bohlender, Andy Campbell, Arthur Carlson, Stanley Furrow, Ray Moore, Vernon McEndaffer, Homer Northup, George Owens, William Scheub, Walter Youngland
Organized May 1, 1943; reorganized Mar. 13, 1950 at Briggsdale, after four years of inactivity.

Original Officers: Pres. Stafford Painter, V.P. E. D. Stinson, Sec-Treas. R. W. Fithian, plus thirteen directors

West Divide Creek Cattle Growers' Assn.
1966 Officers:
Pres: Cecil Deardorff, Silt
Sec'y: Maurice Sweeney, Silt
Organized March 5, 1946 at Silt.
Original Officers: Pres. Dewey Williams, Sec'y. C. G. Deardorff

Yuma County Farm & Ranch Improvement Assn.
1966 Officers:
Pres: Mark M. Mulder, Yuma
Sec'y: Bernard Kerst, Wray
Organized 1948 at Yuma; reorganized Mar. 4, 1950 at Wray, as Yuma County Livestock Assn. with Pres. Frank Herman, V.P. Leo McCoy, Sec'y-Treas. Henry Bledsoe, Jr., Bd. of Dir.- Glen Ethridge, E. W. Lambert, Homer Lehman, Clarence Stults.
Original Officers; Pres. J. A. Spiers, V.P. Alva Deterding, Sec'y-Treas. David

Goeglein, Dir.-Jim Brophy, LeRoy Brueggemon, Robert Brueggemon, Sam Kramer

1966 Officers

CCA—Affiliated Associations:

Colorado Angus Association
Pres. Ward Smith, Fort Collins
Sec'y-Treas. Ira McCassland, Ault

Colorado Hereford Association
Pres. Dr. Ben Kettle, Westcliffe
Sec'y-Treas. Robert Reasoner, Denver

Colorado Scotch Highland Breeders Assn.
Pres. Jack Stroh, Fort Morgan
Sec'y. Jim Logan, Ordway

Western Shorthorn Association
Pres. Joseph Christen, Aurora
Sec'y-Treas. Joe Winkler, Castle Rock

ACKNOWLEDGEMENTS

Compiling and writing this story has, at times, seemed to take nearly as long as the actual events. Its completion is the result of a vast amount of interest, help and encouragement from a great many people.

Among the first of these are the officers and members of the Colorado Cattlemen's Association today. Probably no single president of the Association was more interested in seeing this book written than the late Tom Field, who spent an entire evening discussing it at the old Shirley-Savoy Hotel dining room, just a few weeks before his untimely death in 1958.

Another dedicated and long-time supporter of the project has been Dave Rice, a man who has probably contributed as much to the advancement of the organization as any one person in the entire 100 years. The same can also be said of Wad Hinman who ranks as one of the great presidents of the past century, and of Leavitt Booth, Chairman of the Centennial Committee.

The time-consuming and tedious research work over the past ten years was greatly helped by the interest and knowledge of the staff members of the Colorado State Historical Society, Mrs. Enid Thompson, Mrs. Louisa Arps and Mrs. Kathleen Pierson. An outstanding contributor to this project was Mrs. Laura Ekstrom, whose interest and knowledge of original source material was invaluable.

At the Denver Public Library, two members of the Western History Department, Mrs. Alys Freeze, Director, and Mrs. Opal Harber were a major help in providing information and advice.

Many special contributions were made by Association members from family records. Among these were John and Harry Benton for their loan of the Benton family scrapbook and the papers of Frank Benton, one of the most articulate cattlemen the state has ever had. Special thanks are also due Mrs. Frances B. Beal for providing the information on the sale of the Holly-Sullivan ranch, to Mrs. Jack Owen, for her material on the Big Sandy country, to Charles Lilley for material on John G. Lilley, to Mrs. Jeannette Thach for information on the Huerfano valley and its people, to Mrs. Tom (Sue) Field and to Warren Mergelman for material on the Gunnison area, and to Norman King for background on the Southwest.

Our special gratitude, also, to Mrs. Ray Bader, to Deyoe Green, to George Everett and dozens more like them who volunteered information of great value.

The historical "ramrods" who gathered a wonderful amount of material in their respective areas and associations were: Mrs. L. E. Cushman, Boulder-South Lairmer; Wendell F. Hutchinson, Chaffee county; John A. Goodier, Cheyenne county; Mrs. Harley A. Rusher, Crowley-Kiowa-Lincoln counties; Dorothy Conto, Holy Cross; LeRoy Gray, Leroux Creek; Clyde Sheek, Mancos; Mrs. Eileen Schrader, Moffat county; Mrs. Alice Donelson, North Park; H. R. Nelson, Rio Blanco; LeRoy Coleman, San Luis Valley; Clarence Stephens, Sweetwater;

353

George A. Vickerman, Custer county; Mrs. Melva Busby, Bent-Powers; and Stan Webber, Larimer county, plus a great many others.

Special help and suggestion also came from Ray McMillin, Francis P. Murphy, Leonard Horn, Stan Furrow, Steve Hart, Otto Unfug, M. O. Dunn, Tom Giacomini, Fred Betz, Jr., Eugene Hogue, Dick Jones, Vic Hansen Sr., Frank Fehling, Leavitt Booth, the late Senator Wilkie Ham, Earl Brown, Floyd Beach, and a great many more.

The help and consideration received from Dixie Savio, Dave Rice's dedicated, hard-working and attractive secretary, Margaret Maul, Joan Rewinkel and John Boyd, all members of the CCA staff made a major contribution to the volume.

And last but not least was the interest, loyalty and capable help of Doris Sterbenz, our enthusiastic and able assistant who researched, proof-read, typed and re-typed the entire manuscript.

Others like William Helming, brilliant young economist at the American National Cattlemen's Association, C. N. Guellow, USDA Statistician, Dr. Robert Maddox, Director of the Economics Department, University of Denver, who served as technical consultants on special points from time to time.

Rare books and material were loaned by Mrs. Dorothy Baker, Hugo; Oley Kohlman, Walden; Robert Schafer, Boyero; Don Clair, Denver; Conrad Schafer, Jr., Hugo; Jack Smillie, Cedaredge, Vic Hansen, Jr., Elbert Husted, Newark, N. J.; William J. Wyatt, Denver; Mrs. Harvey Rusk, Westcliffe, and Mills M. Craig, Craig.

These are only a few of the many friends we would like to thank personally for their help and interest. Time and space limitations forced us to omit a great deal of the material, pictures and help that was offered to us. One of our biggest problems was to decide what to leave out.

In the course of a hundred years many thousands of people were actively involved with this organization. Obviously only a few could be mentioned in this book. Actually, the life story of each president and a great many other figures in the Association could each be the subject for a fascinating book of their own. We sincerely hope that those who were inadvertently omitted will understand these limitations.

Far more material was gathered and actually written that could ever be included in the CCA story. Our final version is simply a brief cross-section of the cattlemen's story in order to convey some idea of the Association and the people who ran it.   R.G.

BIBLIOGRAPHY

Much of the basic material for this book was taken from the minutes book of the Colorado Stock Growers Association, donated to the organization in 1867 by Mr. Alex Atkins, and covering the period from 1867 to 1884.

The other early minutes book is a record of the meetings of the CSGA Executive Committee from January 3, 1884 to December 5, 1895. These two, plus miscellaneous files, letters, records, publications and correspondence were the backbone of the research source material. These records are now in the archives of the Colorado State Historical Society.

Throughout the century, most of the newspapers in the territory and the state have given the cattle industry excellent coverage, and the files of the older publications were invaluable. These daily and weekly newspapers, plus the livestock and farm journals were able to fill in many of the gaps that had existed in the Association files.

Another major source was the personal records of old families in the state. These were of great help in supplying details and background material in the 100-year history. Many of the local associations had excellent records, also, and the Bent-Prowers Cattle & Horse Growers Association provided us with a transcript of this organization from March, 1870 to the present. This is one of the most complete records in the state. Among the Colorado Cattlemen's Association records were the following:

Minutes and Resolutions
Minutes, Executive Committee
Minutes, Board of Control
Constitution and By-Laws (various periods)

The bibliography listed here covers only the most important sources. Much other material was used for verification, and interviews are not listed because of space.

FEDERAL DOCUMENTS

U. S. Department of Agriculture. Yearbook. Various years.
"Summary of the Report of the Federal Trade Commission on the Meat-Packing Industry." July 3, 1918.
Packers and Stockyards Act, 1921, as Amended, Livestock Division, Agricultural Marketing Service, U.S.D.A., 1955.
U.S. Department of the Interior. Rules for the Administration of Grazing Districts. June 13, 1937. Chart of Organization of Division of Grazing. September 20, 1936.
Statement of Farrington R. Carpenter at hearing before the Committee on Public Lands, House of Representatives, Seventy-third Congress, First Session on H.R. 2835 and Seventy-third Congress, Second Session on H.R. 6462.

COLORADO STATE DOCUMENTS

Colorado Agricultural Statistics. Colorado Crop and Livestock Reporting Service. Co-operating with U.S.D.A. Bul. 63-1; 65-1.
Abstract of Votes cast in Primary and General Election. 1916-1922.
House Journal of the Legislative Assembly of the Territory of Colorado.
First Session. 1861.
Sixth Session. 1867.
Ninth Session. 1870.
Session Laws of the State of Colorado. Various years.
Colorado Revised Statutes. 1963.
State Brand Book of Colorado. Pub. by authority of the Fifth General Assembly. 1886.
Colorado Year Book. Various years.
Senate Bill No. 85, 24th Session, General Assembly, 1923. Senators Callen and Warren. "A Bill for an Act to Designate the Quality of Bulls and Stallions on the Public Range."

NEWSPAPERS AND PERIODICALS

Century Magazine.
Colorado Magazine, Colorado State Historical Society.
Denver City Directory.
Denver Daily News.
Denver Daily Stockman.
Denver Field and Farm.
Denver Post.
Denver Record-Stockman.
Denver Times.
Glenwood Post (Glenwood Springs, Colorado).
Harper's Magazine.
Holyoke State Herald (Holyoke, Colorado).
Hugo Range-Ledger (Hugo, Colorado).
Logan County Advocate (Sterling, Colorado).
Montrose Press (Montrose, Colorado).
North Park Union (Walden, Colorado).
The Producer. American National Livestock Assn. (Denver, Colorado).
Rocky Mountain News (Denver, Colorado).
Sterling Democrat (Sterling, Colorado).
Sterling Evening Advocate (Sterling, Colorado).
The Trail.
Western Farm Life (Denver, Colorado).

ORGANIZATION REPORTS

American National Livestock Assn. Bulletin. July 22, 1949.
Bent-Prowers County Cattle and Horse Growers Assn. Minutes and Resolutions. 1874-
    1966.
Denver Civic and Commercial Assn. Report of Committee on Herd Law. Livestock and
    Agricultural Bureau.
Gilpin-Jefferson Livestock Assn. Minutes. 1931-1935.
Joint Cattle and Sheep Forest Advisory Board. Proceedings. January 17, 1950.
Kit Carson County Cattlemen's Assn. Kit Carson County and Its Cattlemen. 1963.
Larimer County Stockgrowers Assn. By-Laws and History. 1884-1956.
Logan County District Court. Records. 1891.
Logan County Thief Detection Assn. Minutes. 1888-1889.
Proceedings of the National Stock Growers' Convention. Denver, Colorado. January 25,
    26, 27, 1898.
Rio Blanco Stockgrowers Assn. History of Rio Blanco County Livestock Industry. 1966.
Southwestern Colorado Livestock Assn. Cattle Industry in Southwestern Colorado. 1966.

JOURNALS AND CONTEMPORARY ACCOUNTS

Bancroft, Herbert Howe. History of Nevada, Colorado and Wyoming. 1540-1888. His-
    tory Co., pub., 1890.
Benton, Frank K. Cowboy Life on the Side Track. Denver, 1903.
Brisbin, General James S. The Beef Bonanza; or How to Get Rich on the Plains. Univ.
    of Oklahoma, 1959.
Chapman Publishing Co. Portraits and Biographical Record of the State of Colorado.
    Chicago, 1899.
Clay, John. My Life on the Range. Antiquarian Press, 1961.
Cook, David J. Hands Up; or Twenty Years of Detective Life in the Mountains and on
    the Plains. Univ. of Oklahoma, 1958.
Cook, James H. Fifty Years on the Old Frontier, as Cowboy, Hunter, Guide, Scout and
    Ranchman. Yale, 1923.
Fletcher, Ernest M. The Wayward Horseman. Sage, 1958.
Hayes, A. A., Jr. New Colorado and the Santa Fe Trail, Harper, 1880.
Hough, Emerson. The Story of the Cowboy. Grosset and Dunlap, 1897.
Jones, J. M. W. Stationary and Printing Co. Brand Book of the Colorado Cattle Grow-
    ers Association. Chicago, 1884.
McCoy, Joseph. Historic Sketches of the Cattle Trade of the West and Southwest. Clark,
    1940.

Peters, Edward T. "Evils of Our Public Land Policy." Century Magazine. February, 1883.
Richthofen, Baron Walter von. Cattle Raising on the Plains of North America. Appleton, 1885.
Rowell Publishing Co. Representative Men of Colorado in the 19th Century, 1902.
Souvenir and Manual of the Fifteenth General Assembly. 1905.
Vickers, William B. History of the City of Denver, Arapahoe County and Colorado. O. L. Baskin and Co. Chicago, 1880.

MANUSCRIPTS AND UNPUBLISHED PIECES

Benton, Frank. Land Leasing. Speech to the American Cattle Growers Assn. Denver, March 5, 1902.
Carpenter, Farrington R. The Law of the Range. Address to Colorado State Bar Assn. Colorado Springs, September, 1940.
The Taylor Grazing Act.
Carr, General Eugene A. Report of Republican River Expedition. U.S. Fifth Cavalry Regiment. July, 1869.
Donelson, Mrs. Dean. Big Cattle Outfits in North Park in Early Days. Rand, Colorado. April, 1966. The North Park Stock Growers Association. Rand, Colorado, 1966.
Hamman, Mrs. Matt. My Early Recollections of Montezuma County. 1909.

SECONDARY SOURCES

Adams, Ramon F. The Old-time Cowboy. Macmillan, 1961.
Athearn, Robert G. Westward the Briton. Scribner, 1953.
Atherton, Lewis. The Cattle Kings. Univ. of Indiana, 1961.
Barnes, Will C. Western Grazing Grounds and Forest Ranges. Breeder's Gazette, 1913.
Burroughs, John Rolfe. Where the Old West Stayed Young. Bonanza Books, 1962.
Chrisman, Harry E. The Ladder of Rivers. The Story of I. P. (Print) Olive. Sage, 1962.
Clawson, Marion. The Western Range Livestock Industry. McGraw-Hill, 1950.
Collier, William Ross and Westrate, Edwin Victor. Dave Cook of the Rockies. Rufus Rockwell Wilson, 1936.
Dale, Edward Everett. The Range Cattle Industry. Univ. of Oklahoma, 1960.
Dobie, J. Frank. The Longhorns, Little, Brown, 1941.
Fowler, Bertram B. Men, Meat and Miracles. Messner, 1952.
Friggens, Paul and Anderson, Ray. "Give the Cattleman a Fair Deal." Farm Journal, October, 1948.
Frink, Maurice. Cow Country Cavalcade. Old West, 1954. When Grass Was King. By Maurice Frink, W. Turrentine Jackson and Agnes Wright Springs. Univ. of Colorado, 1965.
Garnsey, Morris E. America's New Frontier: The Mountain West. Knopf, 1950.
Gressley, Gene M. Bankers and Cattlemen. Knopf, 1966.
Haley, J. Evetts. Charles Goodnight, Cowman & Plainsman. Univ. of Oklahoma, 1949.
Hollon, W. Eugene. The Great American Desert, Then and Now. Oxford, 1966.
Johnson, Hazel E. "Out of the Past." Greeley Journal, July 5, 1959. "Story of John Klug." Greeley Journal, December 11, 1960.
Kemmerer, Donald L. and Jones, Clyde. American Economic History. McGraw-Hill, c1959.
Lavender, David. Bent's Fort. Doubleday, 1954.
Lee, Bob and Williams, Dick. Last Grass Frontier. The South Dakota Stock Grower Heritage. Black Hills Pub. Co., c1964.
Nordyke, Lewis. Great Round-up. The Story of Texas and Southwestern Cowmen. Morrow, c1955.
Ornduff, David R. The Hereford in America, Privately pub., c1960.
Osgood, Ernest Staples. The Day of the Cattleman. Univ. of Minnesota, 1954.
Parkhill, Forbes. The Law Goes West. Sage, c1956.
Peake, Ora Brooks. The Colorado Range Cattle Industry. Arthur H. Clark, 1937.
Roberts, Paul H. Hoof Prints on Forest Ranges. Naylor, 1963.
Sanders, Alvin H. Shorthorn Cattle. Sanders, c1918.
Sandoz, Mari. The Cattlemen. Hastings, c1958.
Saunderson, Morton H. Western Stock Ranching. Univ. of Minnesota, 1950.

Smiley, Jerome C. Semi-Centennial History of the State of Colorado. Lewis Pub. Co., 1913.

Spann, G. Aubrey. "Gunnison County Stockgrowers . . . Since 1894." Gunnison County Globe, May 5, 1966.

Steinel, Alvin T. and Working, D. W. History of Agriculture in Colorado. Colorado Agricultural College, Fort Collins, 1926.

Stoddart, Laurence A. and Smith, Arthur D. Range Management. McGraw-Hill, 1943.

Swearingen, Tom. "The Range Truce that Brought Prosperity." Farm Quarterly, Fall, 1966.

Swift, Louis F. The Yankee of the Yards. S. W. Shaw, 1927.

Taylor, Ralph C. Colorado South of the Border. Sage, c1963.

Thorp, N. Howard, comp. Songs of the Cowboys. Houghton, Mifflin, c1921.

Wallace, Betty. History with the Hide Off. Sage, c1965.

Wallis, George A. Cattle Kings of the Staked Plains. American Guild, 1957.

Ware, Crane and Co. The Indian War of 1864. 1911.

Weaver, J. E. and Albertson, F. W. Grasslands of the Great Plains. Lincoln, Neb., Johnsen, c1956.

Weaver, J. E. North American Prairie. Lincoln, Neb., Johnsen, c1954.

Webb, Walter Prescott. The Great Plains. Grosset & Dunlap, c1931.

Wellman, Paul. Death on the Prairie. Lippincott, 1934.

Wilhelm, Steve. Cavalcade of Hooves and Horns. Naylor, c1958.

INDEX

A

Adams, Alva (Gov.), 134, 135
Adams, George H., 98, 114
Agricultural Fair and Horse Race, 23, 28
Albertson, Orris, 290
Alexander, Morton, 218
Alford, N. C., 218
American Cattle Growers Assn., 136, 151, 220
American Land and Cattle Co., 123
American National Livestock Assn., 160, 165, 169, 173, 194, 250, 254
Ammons, E. M., 154, 155, 217, 220, 221, 223, 227, 228, 231
Amos, D. W., 218
Anderson, P., 218
Anderson, Ray, 167
Antonio Land and Cattle Company, 118
Apex Allotment, 175, 176
Arapahoe County Cattle and Horse Protective Assn., 224
Arapahoe County Claim Club, 18
Arapahoe Land and Cattle Co., 118, 123
Arapahoe National Forest, 175
Archibold, Albert W., 148
Archuleta County Stockgrowers Assn., 283
Arkansas Valley Land & Cattle Co., 112, 113, 123, 124, 146
Armour, Simeon B., 118
Arms, H. N., 148
Atchison, Mrs. Al, 293
Atkins, Alex M., 23
Axial Basin Stock Grower's Assn., 224

B

Baer, Isaac, 259
Bailey, Joseph L., 49, 50, 51, 58, 60, 66, 67, 71, 72, 73, 78, 118, 199
Baker, C. W., 137
Baker, Frank D., 217
Baker, F. R., 218
Ballantine, George W., 134
Bangs, C. W., 118
Barnes, J. W., 71

Barroll, T. D., 217
Bartels, L. F., 50, 51
Bartlett, F. G., 218
Bartlett, H. C., 218
Beach, Floyd, 162, 164, 166, 169, 173, 174, 177, 279, 280
Beals, James, 164, 165
Beaty, J. N. 218
Becker, Edmund, 218, 222
Belford, James B., 148
Bender, Edna (Mrs. John Martin), 302, 303
Benkleman, J. G., 133, 214
Bennett, H. P., 64
Bennett, I. W., 218, 223, 273
Bennett, W. L., 218
Bent, Silas, 148
Bent County Stockgrowers Assn., 64, 124, 150, 206, 217, 224, 230, 234, 238 (see below also)
Bent-Prowers Assn., 284
Benton, Frank, 151, 152, 236
Benton, John, 287
Bernard, Phil, 43, 44
Berry, D. B., 107
Berthelson, Si, 302
Beshoar, M., 148
Best, A. D., 218
Beuck, A., 214
Bishop, Edward F., 60
Blake, Charles H., 15, 29, 279
Bledsoe, Henry, 280
Block, Joseph, 34
Blunck, C., 218
Bohart, Field, 255, 256, 259, 262
Bonnifield, W., 68, 71
Booth, Leavitt, 175, 177, 291
Boulder County Stock Growers, 209, 217, 224
Bowles, C. W., 217, 223
Bowles, Joseph W., 44, 45, 133, 214, 217
Boyd, J. M. 219
Boyd, John, 283, 299

359

Breeze, Carl, 296
Brisbin, James S. (Gen.), 104, 105
Brooks, D. C., 218
Brown, Earl, 211
Brown, George W., 24, 50, 55
Brush, Jared L., 51, 58, 59, 60, 61, 66,
    67, 68, 69, 70, 71, 79, 87, 91, 98,
    107, 116, 117, 123, 129, 136, 148,
    284
Brush, William, 42
Brush Land and Cattle Co., 118
Buckley, Kenneth, 291
Burdett, William, 218
Bureau of Land Management, 168, 178,
    194, 289, 295
Burghart, Jr., Robert A., 287
Burghart, Sr., Robert A., 282, 293, 298,
    301
Burghart, Sr., Mrs. R. A., 294
Burke, Ray, 283
Burlington & Missouri Railroad, 97, 109
Bush, A. P., 136, 137
Butters, Alfred, 51, 58, 61, 71, 82
Byers, William N., 16
                        C
Cahill, Luke, 217
Callen, R. C. (Sen.), 181, 264, 266
Campbell, A. G., 260
Capps, Harry, 270
Capps, Mrs. S. J., 270
Carey, J. M., 129
Carlson, Carl, 283
Carlyle, W. L., 232
Carpenter, Delph, 259
Carpenter, Farrington R., 185, 186, 187,
    188, 189, 190, 191, 192, 193
Carpenter, J. J., 218
Case, Roy, 164, 279
Castle, Evelyn, 259, 260, 262
Cattle and Horse Growers Assn. of
    Round-Up District No. 9, 224
Cattle Guard, 298, 299
Chaffee County Stock Growers Assn.,
    217, 224, 270
Chatfield, I. W., 61, 218
Chivington, Col. John, 41, 42
Clay, John, 128, 161
Claybough, J. B., 279
Cliff, Ed, 171, 172, 173, 174, 175, 177,
    178, 290
Clough, John A., 118
Cole, L. H., 71
Collier, William Ross, 32
Collins, C. K., 168, 169, 171, 172
Colorado Agricultural Society, 16, 26

Colorado Beef Council, 293
Colorado Beef Cattle Improvement Assn.,
    285
Colorado Beef Club, 294
Colorado Beef Promotion Board, 293
Colorado Cattle and Horse Growers
    Assn., 223, 225, 227, 228, 230
Colorado Cattle Feedrs Assn., 283
Colorado Hereford Assn., 284
Colorado Junior Cattlemen's Assn., 283,
    B-6
Colorado Stockgrowers Loan Co., 258,
    260
Colton, Don, 182, 183
Columbia Land and Cattle Company,
    115, 123, 124
Consolidated Cattle Growers Assn., 129,
    131
Cook, David J., 30, 31, 32, 33, 34, 117,
    197, 198, 199, 201, 203, 204
Cooper, Job A., 34, 117, 118, 129, 214,
    280
Cowbelles, 293, B-1
Craig, Col. William, 106
Crampton, Don C., 218, 222, 223
Crane, Basil, 177
Cranmer, W. H. H., 55, 58, 68, 71
Crew, Walter, 280
Cross, Floyd, 286
Cross, Kenneth, 169
Culver, E. E., 218
Culver, Martin, 126
Currier, Mrs. Tom, 293
Curry, Clarence, 174, 175
Custer County Stockgrowers Assn., 283
Cutter, Chester G., 129
                        D
Davidson, Alex, 24, 34
Davis, Dr., B. F., 208, 267, 271, 274,
    278
Dawson, John, 25, 242
Day, Barney H. "Judd", 45
DeBerard, Fay, 290
Dedman, I., 89
Delaney, Frank, 187, 190
Denver Livestock Exchange, 266
Denver Post, 232, 244, 245, 246, 247,
    248
Denver Record Stockman, 33, 219, 224,
    245, 269
Denver Union Stock Yards, 118, 231
Dodge, David C., 118
Douglas County Stock Growers Assn.,
    217, 224
Dowling, N., 123

Drake, W. A., 218
DuBois, E. H., 217
E
Eagle Stockgrowers Assn., 217, 224
Eastern Cattle Co., 123
Eastern Colorado Stockmen's Protective Assn., 217
Edwards, Jack, 150
Edwards Stock Growers Assn., 224
Egeria Park Stockgrowers Assn., 224
Egbert, A. A., 118
Eitel, George F., 118
Elbert County Live Stock Co., 117, 217
Elk River Stock Growers Assn., 224
Ernest, Finis P., 55, 79, 98, 118, 123, 126
Eskins, Peter, 50
Euler, R. L., 217
Evans, C., 218
Evans, James C., 221, 273
Evans, J. G., 67, 69
Evans, Gov. John, 41, 118
F
Farmer, Joseph P., 61, 71, 73, 81, 82
Farmer, Thomas B., 22, 55
Fehling, Frank, 174, 175, 281
Ferguson, Ben, 286
Ferry, Watson J., 118
Field, Tom, 177
Fitzgerald, M. J., 123
Fletcher, Ernest W., 207
Ford, H. F., 34
Ford, Russell, 174
Ford, William D., 34
Foster, A. B., 218, 222, 223
Fox, M. P., 217, 219, 223
Freeman, Wiley, 164
Fremont County Cattle Growers' Protective Assn., 218, 224, 270
French, Peter, 129
Frewen, Moreton, 129
Friggins, Paul, 167, 290
G
Gage, T. A., 218
Gale, J. S., 218
Gant, John, 160
Garfield County-Grand River Stock Growers Assn., 159, 218
Gaspar, J. J., 129
Gassoway, William, 118
Gebhard, Henry, 118, 119
Gentry and Reynolds, 124
Gerry, Elbridge, 41, 42, 43
Gibson, Daniel E., 167
Giddings, Carl, 219

Giffin, Murray, 284, 302
Gillaspey, W. A., 218, 219, 222, 223, 269, 271
Gilpin-Jefferson Livestock Assn., 209
Ginkle, Thomas, 112
Gird, C. C., 71, 82
Glover, Dr. George E., 125
Godfrey, Holon, 40
Goff, Richard, 298, 299
Good, C. W., 260
Goodnight, Charles, 25, 39, 75
Gotthelf, Dr. Ike L., 255, 259, 260
Goulding, George L., 134, 135
Grand County-Middle Park Stock Growers Assn., 218
Grand Mesa Livestock Assn., 262
Grand Mesa National Forest, 168, 170, 290
Grand River Stock Growers Assn., 224
Granger Act, 173
Granger, C. M., 168
Grattan, John, 259
Gray, T. W., 218
Great Divide, 244, 245, 246, 248
Green, W. R., 128
Gresswell, Dr. Charles, 154, 216, 217, 221, 225
Grubb, Eugene, 153, 223, 231
Grubb, W. Lloyd, 153, 154, 155, 218, 222, 223, 225, 229, 232
Guilford, W. S., 231
Gunnison County Stockgrowers Assn., 170, 208, 218, 224, 268, 269, 271
Gunnison National Forest, 177
H
Haley, Oli, 98
Hall, E. S., 218
Hall, Hal, 177
Haltchuson, H., 123
Hanson, Jr., Vic, 282
Harper, T. S., 223
Harris, C. H., 137
Harris, W. C., 218, 227, 273
Hartmann, A., 218
Hartsel, Samuel, 19, 43, 154, 155, 216, 218, 219, 220, 222, 284
Hayden, Charles W., 118
Hayes, Jr., A. A., 54, 104
Haythorn, R. M., 218
Head, Richard G., 127, 128, 129, 206
Henderson, John D., 15, 16
Heney, Francis J., 253
Hereford cattle 138, 145
Herring, W. P., 129
Herrington, J. E., 218

Heyssong, John C., 218
Higginson, J., 218, 219, 222
Hinman, Wad, 305, 316
Hittson, John, 50, 55, 68, 79
Hodgson, W. E., 217
Hoggatt, Volney T., 245, 246
Hogsett, Robert, 283
Holly, Hiram S., 79, 89, 111, 112, 113, 115, 124, 126
Holly, William, 51, 55, 57, 58, 61, 64, 66, 71, 77, 78, 80, 97
Holt, John M., 137
Holtorf, John, 286, 302
Homestead Grazing Act, 148, 245
Hooper, S. K., 134
Hoover, C. J. S., 218
Horn, Leonard, 176, 290, 302
Houts, Percy, 258, 259, 260
Howard, A. A., 219
Hubbell, R. M., 218
Huerfano Cattle Company, 105
Humberg, M. C., 217
Hummel, Paul, 174, 175
Hutchinson, George, 218
Hutchinson, J., 66, 68

I

Ickes, Harold L., 184, 187, 192
Iliff, John W., 39, 54, 60, 79, 94, 107
Iliff Cattle Company, 94
International Range Assn., 127, 128, 129, 131

J

James, Fernando, 20
Johnson, Art, 269, 270
Johnson, Bruce, 148
Johnson, Ed (Sen.), 173, 300, 301
Johnson, Fred J., 32, 33
Johnson, Fred P., 155, 219, 220, 222, 223, 225, 231, 294
Johnson, Tom, 218
Johnston, Jr., Robert, 301
Jones, Dick, 176
Jones, James C., 79
Jones, Myron W., 89
Jones, W. R., 219
Jones-Connally Act, 275
Joslin, J. Jay, 118

K

Kansas Pacific Railroad, 35, 48, 93, 132
Kavanaugh, Ed, 188, 189, 190
Kayser, Lee, 217
Kebler, F., 218
Keener, F. A., 134
Kelley, David, 218
Kendall, J. M., 134

Kennedy, Fred, 175
Keon, Henry, 217
Keoper, A., 218
Kern, Lewis, 218
Kidwell, B. F., 123
Killin, B. C., 217
King, P. H., 218
Kit Carson County Live Stock Assn., 224
Klug, John P., 255, 256, 258, 260, 261, 262, 263
Kneale, Thomas, 217, 222
Knott, A. A., 218
Kountz, J. A., 70
Kramer, A. H., 248

L

Lambert, William, 266
Land Utilization Act, 275
Lankford, Garrett, 218
Larimer County Sheep Feeders Assn., 218, 224
Larimer County Stock Growers Assn., 218
Larson, C. P., 153
Latham, Dr. Henry, 56, 60, 63
Law, John E., 218, 221
Lawrie, Tom, 299
Leary, J. C., 129
Lee, M. A., 218
Lee, W. R., 218, 222
LeFevre and Powers Co., 75
Light, Fred, 159, 160, 289
Lilley, John W., 25, 50, 51, 54, 59, 60, 61, 64
Lillpop, Jim, 287
Lincoln County Cattle Growers Assn., 224, 227
Linger, Lyman, 177
Little, Sam, 170
Lockhart, J. A., 218, 223
Loftus, John W., 217
Logan County Cattle & Horse Protective Assn., 218, 238
Logan County Thief Detection Assn., 205
Londoner, Wolfe, 96, 97
Longhorns, 5, 18, 20, 26, 138, 145
Lucas, Theodore, 219
Lyons, Mrs. A. R. 295
Lyons, Jack, 89

M

McAlpine, M., 210, 211
McAtee, W. G., 218
McCaskill, William, 218
McClair, J. S., 219
McClurg, G. S., 217

McCourt, Peter, 134
McCoy, Joseph G., 78, 104, 136
McGillin's Bomb, 130
McIntire, S., 129
McIntyre, A. A., 153, 222
McMillin, M. J., 217, 230, 234, 248, 256, 262, 263, 283
McMillin, Raymond, 283
McShane, John A., 129
Magness, Peter, 23, 25
Malloy, James, 217
Manby, J. B., 218
Manitou Experimental Forest, 174
Marselus, C. H., 125
Martin, Charles F., 134, 136, 137
Martin, John W., 24
Mathews, M., 222
Maul, Otto, 282, 294
Maxwell, Charles, 217
Maynard, Joseph S., 58, 61
Meade, C., 223
Means, Ernest, 177
Meeker, N. C., 46
Memorandum of Understanding, 165, 168
Metcalf, H. H., 109, 117, 120, 123, 124, 129, 133, 134, 214
Middle Park Stock Growers Assn., 224
Mill Iron Cattle Company, 124
Miller, H. T., 218
Miller, Thomas, 217
Milliken, Eugene (Sen.), 173
Mills, William B., 118
Mitchell, Henry, 301
Monfort Packing Co., 286
Monitor Livestock Assn., 162, 164, 166
Monson, J. T., 225
Montezuma County Stock Growers Assn., 224
Montrose Cattle & Horse Growers Assn., 224
Moore, Crawford, 219, 222
Moore, R. W., 98
Morse, Charles F., 118
Mullen, J. K., 217
Mundy, H. H., 129
Munson, J. V., 218, 221
Munson, T. C., 225
Murphy, Charles P., 287
Murphy, Francis P., 287
Murray, M. H., 155, 217, 220
Musser, Kelso, 164, 171, 279

N

Nachtrieb, Charles, 217
National Live Stock Assn., 136, 137, 152, 155, 214, 215, 220, 223, 229, 230
National Stock Growers Assn., 36
National Trail, 125, 138
National Western Stock Show, 231, 284
Newman, E. S., 129
Norrell, Dewey, 177
North Park Cattle Growers Assn., 224, 237
Nuckolls, Emmett, 218, 222

O

O'Cam, Nicholas, 42
Ogden, C. S., 217, 222
Oldland, Reuben, 183
Orman, James B. (Gov.), 228
Otero Stock Assn., 217, 224
Owen, Jack, 287

P

Pabor, William E., 63
Packers and Stockyards Act, 254, 255, 266
Painter, J. E., 214, 217
Painter, Stafford C., 299
Palm, Robert E., 217, 219
Palmer, R. A., 153
Parish, A. N., 217
Park County Cattle Growers Assn., 218, 224
Parsons, Dr. John, 23, 25, 27, 28, 34, 35, 58, 59, 70, 87
Parsons, Robert, 302, 303
Patrick, G. F., 218, 221
Patton, Nate, 286
Pearson, Charles, 218
Peters, Edward T., 147
Petrie, Harry, 231
Pierce, J. H., 217, 222
Pinkerton, J. H., 50, 51, 58, 60, 61, 68, 71
Pitchforth, Ralph, 190
Planter House, 22, 23
Platt, C. E., 260
Platt, J. M., 217, 219
Platt, M. E., 217
Pope, F., 34
Porter, Henry M., 115
Potter, H. W., 218
Powell, Arnold, 223
Prairie Cattle Company, 109, 118, 127, 128, 146, 150
Preston, B., 218
Prestrud, Lars, 284, 293, 297
Prowers, John W., 39, 70, 79, 120, 284
Public Lands Commission, 148
Pugsley, C. A., 124

Pugsley, W. S., 89, 124

R

Randle, E. S., 58
Reed, A. G., 16, 22, 23, 24, 25, 28, 29, 34
Rees, Claude, 180, 183
Republican Cattle Co., 124
Reynolds, Charles A., 89, 218
Reynolds, J. E., 219
Reynolds, J. S., 217
Rhea, K. S., 218
Rhodes, L. R., 117, 201, 204, 206
Rice, Jr., David G., 170, 173, 174, 178, 278, 279, 280, 281, 284, 287, 299, 302, 303
Richardson, E. E., 118
Ricqules, A. E. de, 134
Riddell, I. C., 218
Rio Blanco County Stockgrowers Assn., 218
Rio Grande Land and Cattle Co., 118
Roaring Fork and Eagle River Stock Assn., 218, 224
Roberts, W. W., 50, 51, 58, 61, 71
Robertson, J. Scott, 217
Robinson, H. H., 154, 214, 216, 217, 219, 222, 225
Rockwell, Robert F., 266
Rocky Mountain Detective Assn., 30, 31, 32, 34, 55, 198, 203, 204
Rocky Mountain News, 22, 27, 64, 66, 69, 71, 130
Roosevelt National Forest, 170, 175
Rose, Russell, 177, 290
Rosenbaum, Mike, 217
Ross, A. R., 44
Rothschild, C. S., 61
Rourke, Eugene, 218
Routt County Range Protective Assn., 224
Routt, Eliza F., 118
Routt, John L., 34, 117, 127, 142, 204, 284
Russell, George, 129

S

Saguache Stock Growers Assn., 219
Sandvig, E. D., 169, 172, 174
San Isabel Forest, 175, 177
San Juan National Forest, 178
San Luis Valley Cattle & Horse Growers Assn., 224
Santa Fe Railroad, 109, 126
Savio, Dixie, 302, 303
Schaefer, Conrad, 214, 217, 223
Schafer, Robert, 176, 282

Scherrer, Alex, 118
Scherrer, Jacob, 57, 58, 61, 118, 204, 205
Scott, Rev. Winfield, 58, 61
Sears, George, 218
Sedgwick Thief Detection Assn., 205
Setters, J. W., 266
Severance, D. E., 219
Shaw, Donald, 170
Sheafor, Frank P., 107
Sheedy, Dennis, 134
Sherwood, Judge David W., 69, 70, 105, 106, 107
Shorthorns, 19, 20, 21, 138, 145
Slain, Andrew, 34
Slaughter, C. C., 129
Smith, H. A., 217
Snow, E. A., 165, 166, 167, 168, 174
Snow, R. P., 51
Somerville, W. K., 172
Sopris, Richard, 17, 28
Southern Colorado Stock Growers Assn., 218, 224, 227, 270
Sparks, John, 129
Spencer, John W., 169, 170, 171
Spicer, Lon, 217
Springer, F. C., 218
Springer, John W., 134, 136, 137, 227, 228
Squier, Frank, 259
Standart, Stephen H., 118, 123
Starr, Art, 164, 279, 280
Starr, W. B., 218
State Board of Brand Commissioners, 81, 82, 99, 100
State Board of Land Commissioners, 143
State Board of Stock Inspection Commissioners, 88, 99, 100, 101, 232, 234, 267
State Veterinarian, 125, 221, 227, 243
State Veterinary Sanitary Board, 37, 117, 220, 229, 243
Staylon, J. A., 218
Steamboat Springs Cattle Growers Assn., 224
Sterling, Asa, 217
Stevens, C. T., 255, 259, 260
Stone, W. F., 58
Strachan, H., 218
Stubbs, Charles E., 134
Stubbs, Donald, 163, 164, 165, 171, 174
Sullivan, Dennis, 111, 112, 113, 115
Sullivan, James J., 251
Swan, Herb, 174
Swift Bros., 127

Switzer, C. A., 262

T

Talbot, Ralph L., 36, 136
Taylor, Edward T., 184, 185
Taylor Grazing Act, 174, 183, 186, 187, 191, 192, 193
Taylor, Hugh, 217, 222
Tetsell, A. H. "Bert", 205
Thatcher, Joseph A., 112, 113, 115
Thompson, George, 35, 99
Thompson, William, 129
Thornburg, Maj. T. T., 46
Thornton, Dan, 280
Timber Culture Act, 147
Tobin, John J., 266
Tompkins, H. S., 217
Towers, I. W. A., 217
Tucker, L. R., 99
Tuttle, George, 217

U

Uncompahgre National Forest, 150, 162, 164, 165, 168, 170, 173, 290
Uncompahgre Valley Cattle & Horse Growers Assn., 164, 169, 170, 278
Underwood, Clark & Co., 109, 128
Union Pacific Railroad, 36
United Rocky Mountain Cattlemen's Assn., 208
U.S. Forest Service, Chap. VIII, 289, 290, 295
Vallery, George W., 134
Van Wormer, J. P., 50
Veterinary Sanitary Inspection Law, 220, 221, 229

W

Wadsworth, Frank, 20
Wagoner, W. A., 89
Walker, D. M., 218
Wallace, Mary, 178
Ward, J. F., 118
Watkins, Loren Edwin, 208, 217, 219
Watson, George H., 185
Watson, R. S., 218
Watts, Lyle, 173
Weare, Henry G., 129
Webster, W. W., 58

Weld County Livestock Assn., 218
Wells, Henry, 219
West, George H., 148
Western Land and Cattle Co., 118
Western Range Stock Growers Assn., 153, 154, 155, 215, 216, 220, 222, 223
Western Shorthorn Assn., 284
Western Slope Livestock Protective Assn., 167, 181, 185
Westrate, Edwin Victor, 32
Wetzel, C. Edgar, 101, 115, 117, 118, 123
Wetzel, Samuel E. (Capt.), 80, 81, 109
Wheeler, John S., 50, 51
Whinnery, Webb, 256, 258, 259, 271
White, Atwood, 58
Whitman, Dr. F., 118
Wilcox, Lute A., 222
Wilcox, P. P., 66, 67, 68
Williams, A. J., 15, 23, 34, 35, 50, 51, 55, 58, 61, 67, 71
Williams, Arthur, 134, 137
Williams, Roy, 168, 172
Williamson, A. D., 153, 155, 222
Wilmot, D. P., 218, 222
Wilson, Andrew D., 61, 70, 71
Wilson, James M., 58, 59, 61, 64, 66, 71, 74, 75, 76, 77, 118
Wilson, Robert S., 22, 25, 34, 51, 55
Wilson, Mrs. R. T., 39, 40
Wilson's Ranch, 95, 96, 97
Wilson, William J., 58, 61, 127
Winkler, Ernest, 188, 189, 190
Woodhouse, Charles, 217
Wootton, Richard L., 148
Wright, Ed, 170, 175
Wyatt, David C., 28, 44, 55, 71, 133, 134, 214

Y

Yule, George, 153, 219, 222
Yule, Joseph, 160, 218
Yuma & Eastern Arapahoe County Cattle & Horse Growers Protective Assn., 219, 224